IFIP Advances in Information and Communication Technology

498

IFIP – The International Federation for Information Processing

IFIP was founded in 1960 under the auspices of UNESCO, following the first World Computer Congress held in Paris the previous year. A federation for societies working in information processing, IFIP's aim is two-fold: to support information processing in the countries of its members and to encourage technology transfer to developing nations. As its mission statement clearly states:

IFIP is the global non-profit federation of societies of ICT professionals that aims at achieving a worldwide professional and socially responsible development and application of information and communication technologies.

IFIP is a non-profit-making organization, run almost solely by 2500 volunteers. It operates through a number of technical committees and working groups, which organize events and publications. IFIP's events range from large international open conferences to working conferences and local seminars.

The flagship event is the IFIP World Computer Congress, at which both invited and contributed papers are presented. Contributed papers are rigorously refereed and the rejection rate is high.

As with the Congress, participation in the open conferences is open to all and papers may be invited or submitted. Again, submitted papers are stringently refereed.

The working conferences are structured differently. They are usually run by a working group and attendance is generally smaller and occasionally by invitation only. Their purpose is to create an atmosphere conducive to innovation and development. Refereeing is also rigorous and papers are subjected to extensive group discussion.

Publications arising from IFIP events vary. The papers presented at the IFIP World Computer Congress and at open conferences are published as conference proceedings, while the results of the working conferences are often published as collections of selected and edited papers.

IFIP distinguishes three types of institutional membership: Country Representative Members, Members at Large, and Associate Members. The type of organization that can apply for membership is a wide variety and includes national or international societies of individual computer scientists/ICT professionals, associations or federations of such societies, government institutions/government related organizations, national or international research institutes or consortia, universities, academies of sciences, companies, national or international associations or federations of companies.

More information about this series at http://www.springer.com/series/6102

Anja Lehmann · Diane Whitehouse
Simone Fischer-Hübner · Lothar Fritsch
Charles Raab (Eds.)

Privacy and Identity Management

Facing up to Next Steps

11th IFIP WG 9.2, 9.5, 9.6/11.7, 11.4, 11.6/SIG 9.2.2
International Summer School
Karlstad, Sweden, August 21–26, 2016
Revised Selected Papers

 Springer

Editors
Anja Lehmann
IBM Research Zurich
Rüschlikon
Switzerland

Lothar Fritsch
Karlstad University
Karlstad
Sweden

Diane Whitehouse
The Castlegate Consultancy
Malton
UK

Charles Raab
University of Edinburgh
Edinburgh
UK

Simone Fischer-Hübner
Karlstad University
Karlstad
Sweden

ISSN 1868-4238   ISSN 1868-422X (electronic)
IFIP Advances in Information and Communication Technology
ISBN 978-3-319-85746-6   ISBN 978-3-319-55783-0 (eBook)
DOI 10.1007/978-3-319-55783-0

Printed on acid-free paper

This Springer imprint is published by Springer Nature
The registered company is Springer International Publishing AG
The registered company address is: Gewerbestrasse 11, 6330 Cham, Switzerland

Preface

The year 2016 saw a raft of advances in data protection regulation. Globally there were many questions raised about how to introduce and adopt data protection and data privacy legislation appropriately.

In Europe, the General Data Protection Regulation (GDPR) poses challenges to organizations and businesses that provide services based on personal data. Adopted in April 2016, the regulation will come into force in May 2018. While it retains the main principles embedded in the former Data Protection Directive 95/46/EC, it introduces new measures and strengthens others. Major changes in areas to be regulated include data subjects' rights to be forgotten and data portability, the requirement for data controllers to enable privacy by design and default, and the introduction of potentially serious fines for non-compliance with the law for global players. These elements have the potential to improve privacy and data protection, but they also pose a number of difficulties regarding scope, feasibility, and implementation. Other forms of legislation also changed the regulatory scene, with their effects on privacy and identity. The 2015 Cyber Security Directive and the "Privacy Shield," which replaces the Safe Harbour Agreement, also raise new questions.

Yet legislation is not the only driver of change in the fields of privacy and identity. Technological advances such as the use of open data, big data, and sensor development in the Internet of Things are rapidly changing who holds what data, where and how that data may be used, and the transparency of data processing. Business development is increasing in fields related to surveillance, control of mass movement, security, safety, and identity management. Cities, towns, communities, streets, house, and modes of transportation are all becoming smarter. Fields of organizational activity are merging. There are many dilemmas for communities and societies: in achieving better and safer infrastructures so that people can communicate freely without being observed either by commercial or by governmental bodies (user empowerment); in improving the relationship between individuals and institutions (especially concerning the privacy protection goals of transparency and participation); and in setting up democratic processes for effective oversight over the consequences of new technologies.

These questions, as well as many others stemming from current research on privacy and identity management in general were addressed at the 11th Annual International Federation for Information Processing (IFIP) Summer School on Privacy and Identity Management, which took place in Karlstad, Sweden, during August 21–26, 2016.

This school was the 11th in a series that continues to take a holistic approach to society and technology and support interdisciplinary exchange through keynote and plenary lectures, tutorials, workshops, and research paper presentations. Participants' contributions combined interdisciplinary approaches to bring together a host of perspectives: technical, legal, regulatory, socioeconomic, social, societal, political, ethical, anthropological, philosophical, and psychological.

The 2016 summer school was a joint effort between IFIP Working Groups 9.2, 9.5, 9.6/11.7, 11.4, 11.6, Special Interest Group 9.2.2, and several European and national projects: The EU H2020 CREDENTIAL project, the German Privacy Forum (Forum Privatheit) project, and the EU H2020 Marie Curie Innovative Training Network, Privacy&Us. Moreover, it was supported by the research center, HumanIT, at Karlstad University.

The 2016 school's keynote introduction was delivered by Roger Clarke. Invited lectures were given by Amelia Andersdotter together with Anders Jensen-Urstad, Jan Camenisch, Jolanda Girzl, Marit Hansen, Rainer Knyrim, Steven Murdoch, Charles Raab, Bernd Stahl, Angela Sasse, and Vicenc Torra. A tutorial on the state of academic research in Tor was presented by Linus Nordberg. Several other workshops were organized. In particular, reflecting the school's theme, a lively panel debate was held between Roger Clarke and Sarah Spiekermann on the ethical responsibilities of the information systems discipline when working on privacy and personal data markets. The school ended with a panel moderated by Harald Zwingelberg on future directions.

This summer school brought together more than 90 junior and senior researchers and practitioners from Europe, North and Latin America, Australia and Asia, including many young entrants to the field, who came from many disciplines. They came to share their ideas, build up a collegial relationship with others, gain experience in making presentations, and have the opportunity to publish a paper through these proceedings. Sessions were held on a wide range of topics: clearly on privacy and identity management, as the school's name suggests, but also more specifically on the GDPR and data protection in general, the law, privacy frameworks, taxonomies, transparency, and user rights. Other elements of the program focused on research methods, research ethics, privacy technology progress, privacy of personal health data, cloud privacy, and cyber security issues.

One of the school's goals is to encourage the publication of thorough research papers by students and young researchers. To this end, the school had a three-phase review process for submitted papers. In the first phase, authors were invited to submit short abstracts of their work. Abstracts in the scope of the call were selected for presentation at the school, and the authors were then encouraged to submit the full papers of their work. All papers appeared in the unreviewed online pre-proceedings on the school's website. After the school, the authors received two or three reviews from the Program Committee members, and were given time to revise and resubmit their papers for inclusion in these proceedings. In total, we received 36 short paper submissions, from which finally 20 research papers evolved and were submitted to the last review round. Out of these submissions, nine papers were accepted, including the paper by Claudia Quelle, which was judged to be the best single-authored student paper during the school.

We are particularly grateful therefore to the Program Committee, the many reviewers of abstracts and papers, and those who advised the authors on their revisions. We also acknowledge help and support at different stages of the school's preparation by Ronald Leenes and Sarah Spiekermann. Our thanks, too, to Karlstad University, and especially its Privacy and Security Group (PriSec) at the Computer Science Department and the Conference Department for their support of the school's activities.

Reflecting the school's theme of "Privacy and Identity Management – Facing up to Next Steps", it is clear that 2017 brings international challenges to many different stakeholders, not only in terms of privacy and identity management. We hope for, and are committed to, continued advocacy for the effective realization of citizens' and organizations' rights in these two highly crucial fields.

February 2017

Anja Lehmann
Diane Whitehouse
Simone Fischer-Hübner
Lothar Fritsch
Charles Raab

IFIP Summer School 2016

11th International Summer School on Privacy and Identity Management

Facing up to Next Steps

August 21–26, 2016, Karlstad, Sweden

Program Chairs

Anja Lehmann	IBM Research – Zurich, Switzerland
Diane Whitehouse	The Castlegate Consultancy, UK
Sarah Spiekermann	Vienna University of Economics and Business, Austria

General Chair

Simone Fischer-Hübner	Karlstad University, Sweden

Local Organizing Chair

Lothar Fritsch	Karlstad University, Sweden

Program Committee

Samantha Adams	Tilburg University, The Netherlands
Rose-Mharie Åhlfeldt	University of Skövde, Sweden
Stuart Anderson	University of Edinburgh, UK
Julio Angulo	Karlstad University, Sweden
David Aspinall	University of Edinburgh, UK
Lejla Batina	Radboud University Nijmegen, The Netherlands
Zinaida Benenson	University of Erlangen-Nuremberg, Germany
Michael Birnhack	Tel Aviv University, Israel
Franziska Boehm	FIZ Karlsruhe and Karlsruher Institut für Technologie, Germany
Rosamunde van Brakel	Vrije Universiteit Brussel, Belgium
Jan Camenisch	IBM Research – Zurich, Switzerland
Emiliano De Cristofaro	University College London, UK
Penny Duquenoy	Middlesex University, UK
Zekeriya Erkin	Delft University of Technology, The Netherlands
Hannes Federrath	University of Hamburg, Germany
Simone Fischer-Hübner	Karlstad University, Sweden
Pedro Freitas	University of Minho, Portugal
Michael Friedewald	Fraunhofer ISI, Germany

Lothar Fritsch   Karlstad University, Sweden
Thomas Gross   Newcastle University, UK
Bart Jacobs   Radboud University Nijmegen, The Netherlands
Kai Kimppa   University of Turku, Finland
Els Kindt   K.U. Leuven and Universiteit Leiden, The Netherlands
Sabrina Kirrane   Vienna University of Economics and Business, Austria
Eleni Kosta   Tilburg University, The Netherlands
Stephan Krenn   AIT Austrian Institute of Technology GmbH, Austria
Ronald Leenes   Tilburg University, The Netherlands
Federica Lucivero   King's College London, UK
Leonardo Martucci   Karlstad University, Sweden
Joachim Meyer   Tel Aviv University, Israel
Steven J. Murdoch   University College London, UK
Maartje Niezen   Tilburg University, The Netherlands
Siani Pearson   HP Labs, UK
Robin Pierce   Harvard Law School, USA
Jo Pierson   Vrije Universiteit Brussel, Belgium
Tobias Pulls   Karlstad University, Sweden
Charles Raab   University of Edinburgh, UK
Kai Rannenberg   Goethe University Frankfurt, Germany
Delphine Reinhardt   University of Bonn and Fraunhofer FKIE, Germany
Arnold Roosendaal   Privacy Company, The Netherlands
Joseph Savirimuthu   University of Liverpool, UK
Jetzabel Serna-Olvera   Goethe University Frankfurt, Germany
Daniel Slamanig   Graz University of Technology, Austria
Thorsten Strufe   TU Dresden, Germany
Tjerk Timan   Tilburg University, The Netherlands
Eran Toch   Tel Aviv University, Israel
Melek Önen   EURECOM, France
Melanie Volkamer   Karlstad University and TU Darmstadt, Sweden
Jozef Vyskoc   VaF, Slovakia
Erik Wästlund   Karlstad University, Sweden
Tal Zarsky   University of Haifa, Israel
Harald Zwingelberg   Unabhängiges Landeszentrum für Datenschutz,
                              Germany

Additional Reviewers

Diana Dimitrova
Marit Hansen
Agnieszka Kitkowska
Jenni Reuben
Kami Vaniea

Contents

Keynote and Invited Papers

Big Data Prophylactics

Roger Clarke[1,2,3(✉)]

[1] Xamax Consultancy Pty Ltd, Canberra, Australia
Roger.Clarke@xamax.com.au
[2] UNSW Law, Sydney, Australia
[3] ANU Research School of Computer Science, Canberra, Australia

Abstract. Data mining has been re-branded as 'big data analytics'. The techniques involved harbour a substantial set of risks, many of which will be borne by individuals. This chapter argues that safeguards are needed, to protect individuals against the potentially harmful acts that organisations will take against them. Alternative forms of such 'big data prophylactics' are outlined.

Keywords: Data quality · Decision quality · Risk assessment · Risk management · Transparency · Regulation · Activism

1 Big Data

Big data is a fashion-item. It was an invention of marketers, as a means of breathing fresh life into the flagging booms in successively data mining and mash-ups. It has been given an aura of excitement because of the vast array of sources of data. There has been massive expropriation of social media profiles and traffic, and of wellness data from individuals' self-monitoring of their physiological states. A parallel development has been the open access movement in the public sector, which government agencies in various countries are utilising as an opportunity to break down both data silos and privacy protections. Other prospects that have been heralded include flows of streams of telemetry data (fast data), and from the Internet of Things.

In order to differentiate the big data concept, it was first proposed that its key characteristics were 'volume, velocity and variety' [20]. Subsequently, commentators added 'value', while a few have recently begun to add 'veracity' [28]. Such vague formulations even find their way into the academic literature, in forms along the lines of 'data that's too big, too fast or too hard for existing tools to process'. A somewhat more useful characterisation is "the capacity to analyse a variety of mostly unstructured data sets from sources as diverse as web logs, social media, mobile communications, sensors and financial transactions" [25, p. 12]. This reflects the widespread use of the term to

Roger Clarke is Principal of Xamax Consultancy Pty Ltd, Canberra. He is also a Visiting Professor in Cyberspace Law & Policy at the University of N.S.W., and a Visiting Professor in the Research School of Computer Science at the Australian National University.

A. Lehmann et al. (Eds.): Privacy and Identity 2016, IFIP AICT 498, pp. 3–14, 2016.
DOI: 10.1007/978-3-319-55783-0_1

encompass not only data collections, but also the processes applied to those collections. To overcome this ambiguity of scope, this paper distinguishes between 'big data' and 'big data analytics'.

Some commentators consider that big data bears a stronger resemblance to an ideology than to a science. At [5, p. 663], boyd & Crawford depict 'big data' as "a cultural, technological, and scholarly phenomenon that rests on the interplay of [three elements]". Their first two elements correspond to 'big data' and 'big data analytics'. Their third element, on the other hand, emphasises the importance of "mythology: the widespread belief that large data sets offer a higher form of intelligence and knowledge that can generate insights that were previously impossible, with the aura of truth, objectivity, and accuracy".

The mythology, or as its proponents would prefer, the meme, has been spruiked in business school magazines [21], by business school academics [22], and by academics in other disciplines who might have been expected to temper their enthusiasm [23]). The high level of enthusiasm, coupled with these authors' willing suspension of disbelief, has given rise to counter-arguments, and to accusations such as "There's a mania around big data ..." (David Searls, quoted in [30, 31]).

2 Big Data Analytics

The term 'big data analytics' refers to the processes that are applied to big data collections. A substantial array of analytical tools pre-existed the big data era, and more are being developed.

One way to categorise big data analytics is according to the purpose for which the analysis is performed. In Table 1, two broad categories are first distinguished, according to whether the analysis is aiming to deliver insights into populations or about individual entities within those populations. Within each of these major categories, distinctly different kinds of problem-types can be addressed.

It would be reasonable to expect a highly-developed set of guidelines to exist, enabling analysts to recognise firstly which analytical techniques are suitable to which of those problem-categories (and, conversely, which are not); and secondly what attributes big data collections need in order to support each of those analytical techniques. However, it is very difficult to find such guidance. Despite the explosion in postgraduate degree offerings in the big data analytics area, the vague aura of art and craft has yet to be replaced by the clarity of science and engineering, the overtone of experimentation dressed up as innovation pervades, and the application of established expertise remains uncommon.

3 Risk Factors

A range of risks arise from the current spate of over-enthusiastic and uncritical adoption of the big data meme, and of its companion notions of open government data, social media exploitation, location and tracking of people and the devices that they use, and the Internet of Things.

Table 1. Purposes of Big Data Analytics [after 12]

Population Focus
Hypothesis Testing
This approach evaluates whether propositions are supported by the available data. The propositions may be predictions from theory, existing heuristics, or hunches
Population Inferencing
This approach draws inferences about the entire population of entities, or about sub-populations. In particular, correlations may be drawn among particular attributes
Construction of Profiles
This approach identifies key characteristics of some category of entities. For example, attributes and behaviours of a target group, such as 'drug mules', sufferers from particular diseases, or children with particular aptitudes, may exhibit statistical consistencies
Individual Focus
Discovery of Outliers
Statistical outliers are commonly disregarded, but this approach regards them instead as valuable needles in large haystacks, because they may herald a 'flex-point' or 'quantum shift'
Discovery of Anomalies
This approach draws inferences about individual entities within the population. For example, a person may be inferred to have provided inconsistent information to two organisations, or to exhibit behaviour in one context inconsistent with behaviour in another
Application of Profiles
A search can be conducted for individual entities that exhibit patterns associated with a particular, previously asserted or computed profile, thereby generating a set of suspect entities

3.1 Data

Tables 2 and 3 show the results of prior research, which drew on the literature – particularly [19, 7 pp. 601–605, 36, 35, 29, 26] – in order to identify and briefly define relevant quality categories. Some are 'data quality' factors (which are capable of being assessed at the time the data is collected) whereas others are 'information quality' factors (which are not assessable until the data is used).

In addition to quality, it is important that those conducting data analysis be clear about how data is to be interpreted. In syntactical terms, there must be clear answers to such questions as: Is each data-item mandatory or optional? What is the meaning of an empty (or 'null') field? What values may each field contain? At the level of semantics, the signification of each item must also be unambiguous, i.e. with which real-world attribute of which real-world entity does it correspond, and what does it say about that attribute?

During the earlier 'data mining' era, low data quality was recognised as a matter of real concern. Data was modified in a variety of ways, using a process that was referred to as 'data scrubbing' [37]. One focus of data scrubbing is on missing data – although finding an appropriate basis for interpolating appropriate values is fraught with difficulty.

Table 2. Data Quality Factors [after 11]

D1 Syntactical Validity
Conformance of the data with the domain on which the data-item is defined
D2 Appropriate Entity Association
A high level of confidence that the data is associated with the particular real-world identity or entity whose attribute(s) it is intended to represent
D3 Appropriate Attribute Association
The absence of ambiguity about which real-world attribute(s) the data is intended to represent
D4 Appropriate Attribute Signification
The absence of ambiguity about the state of the particular real-world attribute(s) that the data is intended to represent
D5 Accuracy
A high degree of correspondence of the data with the real-world phenomenon that it is intended to represent, typically measured by a confidence interval, such as '±1°C'
D6 Precision
The level of detail at which the data is captured, reflecting the domain on which valid contents for that data-item are defined, such as 'whole numbers of degrees Celsius'
D7 Temporal Applicability
The absence of ambiguity about the date and time when, or the period of time during which, the data represents or represented a real-world phenomenon. This is important in the case of volatile data-items such as total rainfall for the last 12 months, marital status, fitness for work, age, and the period during which an income-figure was earned or a licence was applicable

Modifications are mostly made on the basis of various heuristics, or after comparison with characteristics derived from the data-holdings as a whole. In only rare cases is it possible to check item-content against an external authority. There are limits to the improvements that can actually be achieved, and almost all scrubbing, by its nature, involves a proportion of false positives. Hence, while the process may achieve some improvements, there is inevitably also some worsening in quality through mistaken modifications.

By the 'big data' era, the honest term 'data scrubbing' had been replaced by 'data cleaning' and 'data cleansing' [24]. These terms imply not only that an attempt has been made to achieve 'cleanliness', but also that cleanliness has been achieved. As is apparent from the use of heuristics and the inevitability of errors, the implication is false.

Problems with data quality and data meaning are major sources of risk. Of course, this applies to all forms of administrative data processing, whether or not the data-collection in question qualifies as 'big data'. The problems are compounded, however, when data from different sources, with different and potentially incompatible meanings, and with varying levels of quality, are consolidated, and then handled as though the melange of data constitutes a single, cohesive data-collection.

Table 3. Information Quality Factors [after 11]

I1 Theoretical Relevance
Demonstrable capability of a category of data-item (a column in a table) to make a difference to the process in which the data is to be used
I2 Practical Relevance
Demonstrable capability of the content of a particular data-item (the content of a cell in a table) to make a difference to the process in which the data is to be used
I3 Currency
The absence of a material lag between a real-world occurrence and the recording of the corresponding data
I4 Completeness
The availability of sufficient contextual information that the data is not liable to be misinterpreted
I5 Controls
The application of business processes that ensure that all data quality and information quality factors have been considered prior to the data's use
I6 Auditability
The availability of metadata that evidences the data's provenance, and supports assertions relating to data semantics, data quality and information quality

3.2 Analytics

Reference has already been made to the issues arising from uncertainty about the appropriateness of analytical techniques to problem-categories, and uncertainty about the suitability of any particular data-collection for processing using any particular analytical technique.

A further inadequacy that gives rise to risks is lack of transparency. Transparency is needed in relation to the process whereby inferences are drawn, the basis on which particular data is considered to be relevant to the drawing of the inference, and the criteria that gave rise to any particular judgement.

Humans who make decisions can be called to account, and required to explain the basis on which they drew inferences, made decisions and took action. Computer systems programmed in algorithmic or procedural languages (as was the norm from the 1960s to the 1980s) embody explicit processes and criteria, and hence they are also capable of being interrogated.

Later forms of programming language, however, embody increasing layers of mystery and inscrutability [6]. With so-called 'expert systems' approaches (which most commonly involve the expression of sets of rules), both the decision processes and the decision criteria are implicit. The most that can be re-constructed is that a particular set of rules 'fired', and that particular data was what caused them to be invoked. This is seldom a clear basis for justifying an action, and in any case many rule-based applications aren't designed to support the extraction of even this inadequate form of explanation.

The current vogue in software development can be reasonably described as 'empirical'. Neural nets and machine-learning 'algorithms' do not have anything that can sensibly be described as a decision process, and it is not feasible to extract or infer decision criteria. The issues are discussed in some depth in Subsects. 2.1 and 2.2 of [10]. Use of these techniques represents blind faith, by the 'data scientists', by the organisations that apply them, by any regulator that attempts to review them, and ultimately by everyone affected by them.

3.3   Decision and Action

The challenges identified in the preceding sub-sections give rise to risk if they are not understood and managed. Where any such inadequacies carry forward into decisions made and actions taken, whether about resource allocation or about relationships between organisations and particular individuals, risks arise that the decisions may be unjustified, disproportionate, or just plain wrong.

It has been a fundamental tenet of democracy that dealings between government agencies and individuals must be subject to review and recourse. This principle has also found its way into consumer rights laws in many jurisdictions and many contexts, particularly the financial sector and health care. Purely empirical data analytic techniques are completely at odds with these public expectations. Yet these expectations are in some cases expressed as legal requirements. Hence many potential applications of AI and machine learning 'algorithms' are arguably in breach of existing laws.

3.4   Consequences

The proponents of big data analytics may rail against these restraints, and complain that conservative attitudes and slow-changing laws are stifling innovation. They may protest that human rights, anti-discrimination laws and privacy protections constrain the freedom of corporations, government agencies and 'data scientists' to act in economically efficient ways – which implies the scope to impose their will on people. They may even invoke the anti-humanitarian credo that 'logic is dead ... get over it'. Or to use their own words: "Faced with massive data, [the old] approach to science – hypothesize, model, test – is ... obsolete. Petabytes allow us to say: 'Correlation is enough'" [1] and "Society will need to shed some of its obsession for causality in exchange for simple correlations: not knowing why but only what. Knowing why might be pleasant, but it's unimportant ..." [23].

Inherent in the boisterous claims of Anderson, Mayer-Schönberger and others is the abandonment of balance between the empirical and the rational, and its replacement by empiricism dominant and systemic explanations deprecated. This 'flight from reason' has consequences. The proponents of big data analytics focus on the value that they assert society can, and that they assert society will, extract from massive, low-quality data-collections using more or less ad hoc analytical techniques. Even if their assertions turned out to be right – and such positive evidence as exists to date is merely anecdotal and unaudited – the benefits would be accompanied by massive negative impacts – for some, if not for all.

The resource-allocation and administrative decision-making errors that follow on from poor-quality inferencing will produce losers. Review will be at least hampered, and where AI and machine-learning are involved, actually not possible. The losers will be forced to 'like it or lump it', without recourse.

But social equity cannot exist in a world in which rationality has been abandoned, and decisions are made mysteriously and enforced by the powerful. This breaches the social contract. The losers' natural reaction is to stop trusting the institutions that they deal with. Some are likely to become sullen non-compliers with the diktats of powerful organisations, while others will be more aggressive in their avoidance measures. There is then an unpleasant scale up through active falsification, via electronic forms of sabotage, to violence.

The consequences of the Anderson/Mayer-Schönberger thesis are the breakdown of social cohesion, and serious challenges to the social order on which economies and polities depend. That such seers fail to look ahead to the consequences of their wild enthusiasms is quite extraordinary.

4 Big Data Prophylactics

Many of the risks identified in the previous section will be borne by individuals rather than by the organisations that make big-data-originated mistakes. So if 'big data analytics' is to be more than just a passing fad, it needs to be accompanied by 'big data prophylactics', to provide people with protections against organisations' potentially harmful acts against them.

4.1 Evaluation

One of the most important forms of protection is the conduct of evaluations of big data initiatives prior to their implementation. These should identify in advance ideas whose potential benefits do not justify the negative impacts and risks, which should then lead to their substantial re-working or their abandonment.

An examination of business case preparation gives rise to serious doubts about its effectiveness as a means of protecting organisations against bad big data. Business cases evidence many variants, some disciplined and formalised, but most pragmatic and informal. Typically, they involve spreadsheet modelling, often with primarily financial data, and perhaps cost-benefit analysis, but internal-only. The focus is on payback/ Return on Investment (RoI), or on alignment with corporate strategy. However, all such approaches are more or less explicitly designed to provide support for the proposal [18]. Business case preparation provides inadequate protection even for the organisations that conduct them; still less do such processes protect against unjustifiable negative impacts on other parties.

Previous research by this author has considered big data risks from the perspective of the organisations that conduct the analytics and/or rely on the inferences they lead to. Data quality assurance should in principle be the means whereby the risks to those organisations can be avoided, detected, investigated and managed. Further, risk assessment should be the means of tackling not only data quality issues, but also the risks arising from data semantics, non-relevance, inappropriate data analytic techniques, and lack of transparency [11, 12].

In practice, however, a large proportion of the negative outcomes of poor-quality big data and poor-quality big data analytics arise in the form of 'externalities': rather than the relevant organisation suffering them, someone else will. Most commonly the entities bearing the harm will be those that lack institutional and market power, sometimes small business enterprises, but most commonly people.

A much broader form of evaluation is needed than that provided by organisation-internal risk assessment processes. However, the incentives are such that organisations are not going to perform them, at least not of their own volition. Market failure exists, so government intervention is necessary.

4.2   Regulation

Where a proposal harbours serious threats, the protection of parties other than the proposal's sponsor depends on the conduct of a form of evaluation that takes into account the interests of all stakeholders. A consolidation of mainstream 'meta-principles' in relation to the evaluation of potentially harmful initiatives is in [2].

Beyond an obligation to conduct an appropriate form of evaluation, an effective regulatory scheme needs to be in place, to ensure that the findings from the process are carried through into actions. A variety of forms of regulatory arrangement exist, commonly referred to as organisational self-regulation, industry self-regulation, co-regulation and formal regulation. Nomatter which approach is adopted, an effective regulatory scheme needs to satisfy a range of requirements. A consolidation of criteria found in the literature is in Table 2 of [14].

Such industry and professional codes as exist in the big data analytics arena fail comprehensively when tested against criteria such as these. Examples include [34], and a flurry of recent initiatives whose intention is quite bare-facedly to hold off demands for formal regulatory measures [3, 16, 33]. For a scathing assessment of the UK 'ethical framework', see [27].

A specific regulatory mechanism that has been making considerable progress over the last two decades is Privacy Impact Assessment (PIA). A PIA is a systematic process, which identifies and evaluates from the perspectives of all stakeholders the potential effects on privacy of a project, initiative or proposed system or scheme and which includes a search for ways to avoid or mitigate negative privacy impacts [8, 38]. Unfortunately, evidence also exists that PIAs are not being effective in exercising control over inappropriate initiatives, particularly in national security contexts [13].

A recent development that has raised some people's hopes is the 'Data Protection Impact Assessment' (DPIA) requirement within the EU's General Data Protection Regulation [17], which is to come into force in 2018. The provisions are, however, very weak. The trigger is limited to "high risks" (Art. 35.1–35.6). The impacts to be assessed are only those on the protection of personal data (35.1) – which is a poor proxy even for data privacy, and which excludes other dimensions of privacy. It appears inevitable that DPIA will be interpreted as a mere Data Protection Law Compliance Assessment.

Moreover, seeking civil society's views is optional, and there is no requirement that they be reflected in the design (35.9). There is a complete exemption for authorised programs (35.10), rather than merely an exemption from the justification requirement. And it is far from clear whether any enforcement of design features will be feasible, and whether any review will ever be undertaken of the performance of schemes against the data used to justify them (35.7(d), 35.11).

A further factor that some argue to be a regulatory arrangement is the 'precautionary principle'. A strong form of this exists in some jurisdictions' environmental laws, along the lines of 'When human activities may lead to morally unacceptable harm that is scientifically plausible but uncertain, actions shall be taken to avoid or diminish that potential harm' [32]. However, no such strong form is applicable in human rights contexts. All that can be argued is that a moral responsibility exists, whereby, 'if an action or policy is suspected of causing harm, and scientific consensus that it is not harmful is lacking, the burden of proof arguably falls on those taking the action'.

These relevant and current examples all indicate that market failure is matched by regulatory failure. Neither parliaments nor regulatory agencies are providing effective restraints on organisational misbehaviour in the field of big data analytics.

4.3 Public Activism

In order to protect people's interests, public activism is needed. This could take the form of civil disobedience, in particular the obfuscation and falsification of data, traffic, location and identity. Further, pressure could be brought to bear on organisations, regulators and politicians, through coordinated actions focussed on a specific target, and the use of whatever communications channels are judged to have the greatest impact on that target at that particular point in time.

However, there are limited prospects of action by the general public, or even by the population segments most seriously affected by big data blunders. The issues are too complex and obscure for public discourse to cope with, and reduction to the simple slogans compatible with popular uprisings is very challenging. Another problem is that the regulatory failure noted in the previous section means that appropriate evaluation does not take place, and hence transparency is denied.

Rather than the general public, it appears more likely that the battle will be fought by advocacy organisations, called (originally in UN contexts) non-government organisations (NGOs), and collectively referred to as civil society. A review of privacy advocacy organisations around the world is in [4]. These associations have very little direct power, and limited resources. However, they have a wide range of techniques at their disposal [4, 15].

This author has previously proposed a further form that public activism can take. Civil society could abandon its half-hearted and ineffectual involvement in 'official' Standards processes conducted by industry and government. NGOs could develop, adopt, promulgate and promote their own series of Civil Society Standards [9]. Importantly in the big data context, these would specify principles and processes for evaluation, processes for quality assurance and audits, and checklists of mitigation measures and controls.

5   Conclusions

All uses of data involve issues with data semantics, data quality and information quality. However, the issues arising in conventional administrative systems are reasonably well-understood, and safeguards, controls, reviews, recourse and audit are factored into system designs.

Big data compounds the problems of data semantics, data quality and information quality. It merges data of uncertain and often low quality, and of often incompatible semantics, and it projects mystique rather than being founded on any real 'data science'.

Big data analytics then heaps further problems on the bonfire. One is the failure to provide a reliable way to identify appropriate techniques and to clearly specify the attributes that data must possess in order to justify processing in that manner. A second and very substantial problem is the lack of transparency inherent in contemporary analytical methods, whose rationality is not penetrable even by 'data science' specialists.

Inferences drawn by software that uses incomprehensible processes may be relied on to make decisions, and to take actions, variously affecting categories of people, particularly through resource allocation, and affecting individuals, particularly through administrative decision-making. These decisions are, quite fundamentally, unreviewable, because the rationale underlying them cannot be communicated – and a rationale, in the sense in which humans understand the notion, may not even exist.

The consequences of big data inferences, and decisions and actions based on them, will inevitably be negative for some entities, and some categories of entities. Those entities will mostly be normal human beings. They will be denied meaningful review and recourse processes, because no comprehensible information is available. Weak regulators will be cowed by the accusation of stultifying innovation. Social equity, the social contract, and ultimately social order, will be the victims.

Protections are needed, which I've referred to in this paper as 'prophylactics', to underline the fact that they are a counterpoint to 'analytics'. In the foreground are evaluation processes; but these are shown not to work, and hence market failure is evident. Various forms of regulatory mechanism should in principle come into play; but multiple examples show that market failure is matched by regulatory failure. All that remains is public activism. The conditions are not right for the general public, or even the affected segments of the public, to take decisive action. Civil society is likely to have to fill the void, if big data prophylactics are to arise, to protect the public from inappropriate applications of big data analytics.

Acknowledgements. This paper was developed from my opening keynote invited for the IFIP Summer School on Privacy and Identity Management, Karlstad, Sweden, 22 August 2016.

References

1. Anderson, C.: The end of theory: the data deluge makes the scientific method obsolete. Wired Magazine 16:07, 23 June 2008. http://archive.wired.com/science/discoveries/magazine/16-07/pb_theory

2. APF: Meta-principles for Privacy Protection. Australian Privacy Foundation, March 2013. http://www.privacy.org.au/Papers/PS-MetaP.html
3. ASA: Ethical Guidelines for Statistical Practice. American Statistical Association, April 2016. http://ww2.amstat.org/about/pdfs/EthicalGuidelines.pdf
4. Bennett, C.J.: The Privacy Advocates. The MIT Press, Cambridge (2008)
5. boyd, d., Crawford, K.: Six provocations for Big Data. In: Proceedings of Symposium on the Dynamics of the Internet and Society, September 2011. http://ssrn.com/abstract=1926431
6. Clarke, R.: A contingency approach to the software generations. Database 22(3), 23–34 (1991). http://www.rogerclarke.com/SOS/SwareGenns.html
7. Clarke, R.: A normative regulatory framework for computer matching. J. Comput. Inf. Law 13(3), June 1995. http://www.rogerclarke.com/DV/MatchFrame.html
8. Clarke, R.: Privacy impact assessment: its origins and development. Comput. Law Secur. Rev. 25(2), 123–135 (2009). http://www.rogerclarke.com/DV/PIAHist-08.html
9. Clarke, R.: Civil society must publish standards documents. In: Berleur, J., Hercheui, M.D., Hilty, L.M. (eds.) CIP/HCC -2010. IAICT, vol. 328, pp. 180–184. Springer, Heidelberg (2010). doi: 10.1007/978-3-642-15479-9_18
10. Clarke, R.: What Drones inherit from their ancestors. Comput. Law Secur. Rev. 30(3), 247–262 (2014). http://www.rogerclarke.com/SOS/Drones-I.html
11. Clarke, R.: Big Data, Big Risks. Inf. Syst. J. 26(1), 77–90 (2016). http://www.rogerclarke.com/EC/BDSA.html
12. Clarke, R.: Quality assurance for security applications of Big Data. In: Proceedings of European Intelligence and Security Informatics Conference (EISIC), Uppsala, 17–19 August 2016 (2016). http://www.rogerclarke.com/EC/BDQAS.html
13. Clarke, R.: Privacy impact assessments as a control mechanism for Australian National Security Initiatives. Comput. Law Secur. Rev. 32(3), 403–418 (2016). http://www.rogerclarke.com/DV/IANS.html
14. Clarke, R., Bennett Moses, L.: The regulation of civilian Drones' impacts on public safety. Comput. Law Secur. Rev. 30(3), 263–285 (2014). http://www.rogerclarke.com/SOS/Drones-PS.html
15. Davies, S.: Ideas for change: campaign principles that shift the world. The Privacy Surgeon, December 2014. http://www.privacysurgeon.org/resources/ideas-for-change
16. DSA: Data science code of professional conduct. Data Science Association, undated but apparently of 2016. http://www.datascienceassn.org/sites/default/files/datasciencecodeofprofessionalconduct.pdf
17. GDPR35: EU General Data Protection Regulation (EU-GDPR) Article 35 - Data protection impact assessment. http://www.privacy-regulation.eu/en/35.htm
18. Humphrey, W.S.: Justifying a process improvement proposal. SEI Interactive, March 2000. http://northhorizons.com/Reference%2520Materials/%2520Justifying%2520a%2520PIP.pdf
19. Huh, Y.U., Keller, F.R., Redman, T.C., Watkins, A.R.: Data quality. Inf. Softw. Technol. 32(8), 559–565 (1990)
20. Laney, D.: 3D data management: controlling data volume, velocity and variety. Meta-Group, February 2001. http://blogs.gartner.com/doug-laney/files/2012/01/ad949-3D-Data-Management-Controlling-Data-Volume-Velocity-and-Variety.pdf
21. LaValle, S., Lesser, E., Shockley, R., Hopkins, M.S., Kruschwitz, N.: Big Data, analytics and the path from insights to value. Sloan Manag. Rev. (Winter 2011), Research Feature. http://sloanreview.mit.edu/article/big-data-analytics-and-the-path-from-insights-to-value/. Accessed 21 Dec 2010
22. McAfee, A., Brynjolfsson, E.: Big Data: the management revolution. Harvard Bus. Rev. 90, 61–68 (2012)
23. Mayer-Schönberger, V., Cukier, K.: Big Data: A Revolution that will Transform How We Live, Work, and Think. Houghton Mifflin Harcourt, Boston (2013)

24. Müller, H., Freytag, J.-C.: Problems, methods and challenges in comprehensive data cleansing. Technical report HUB-IB-164, Humboldt-Universität zu Berlin, Institut für Informatik (2003). http://www.informatik.uni-jena.de/dbis/lehre/ss2005/sem_dwh/lit/MuFr03.pdf

25. OECD: Exploring data-driven innovation as a new source of growth: mapping the policy issues raised by "big data". OECD Digital Economy Papers, no. 222. OECD Publishing. http://dx.doi.org/10.1787/5k47zw3fcp43-en

26. Piprani, B., Ernst, D.: A model for data quality assessment. In: Meersman, R., Tari, Z., Herrero, P. (eds.) OTM 2008. LNCS, vol. 5333, pp. 750–759. Springer, Heidelberg (2008). doi: 10.1007/978-3-540-88875-8_99

27. Raab, C., Clarke, R.: Inadequacies in the UK cabinet office's data science ethical framework. Eur. Data Prot. Law 2(4), 555–560 (2016). http://www.rogerclarke.com/DV/DSEFR.html

28. Schroeck, M., Shockley, R., Smart, J., Romero-Morales, D., Tufano, P.: Analytics: the real world use of Big Data. IBM Institute for Business Value/Saïd Business School, University of Oxford, October 2012. http://www.ibm.com/smarterplanet/global/files/se__sv_se__intelligence__Analytics_-_The_real-world_use_of_big_data.pdf

29. Shanks, G., Darke, P.: Understanding data quality in a data warehouse. Aust. Comput. J. 30(1998), 122–128 (1998)

30. Stilgherrian: Big data is just a big, distracting bubble, soon to burst ZDNet (2014). http://www.zdnet.com/big-data-is-just-a-big-distracting-bubble-soon-to-burst-7000031480/. Accessed 11 July 2014

31. Stilgherrian: Why big data evangelists should be sent to re-education camps, ZDNet (2014). http://www.zdnet.com/why-big-data-evangelists-should-be-sent-to-re-education-camps-7000033862/. Accessed 19 Sept 2014

32. TvH: Telstra Corporation Limited v Hornsby Shire Council. NSWLEC 133, pp. 113–183 (2006). esp.paras. http://www.austlii.edu.au/au/cases/nsw/NSWLEC/2006/133.htm. Accessed 24 Mar 2006

33. UKCO: Data science ethical framework. UK Cabinet Office, v.1 (2016). https://www.gov.uk/government/publications/data-science-ethical-framework. Accessed 19 May 2016

34. UNSD: Declaration of professional ethics. United Nations Statistical Division (1985). http://unstats.un.org/unsd/dnss/docViewer.aspx?docID=93#start. Accessed Aug 1985

35. Wand, Y., Wang, R.Y.: Anchoring data quality dimensions in ontological foundations. Commun. ACM 39(11), 86–95 (1996)

36. Wang, R.Y., Strong, D.M.: Beyond accuracy: what data quality means to data consumers. J. Manage. Inf. Syst. 12(4), 5–33 (1996)

37. Widom, J.: Research problems in data warehousing. In: Proceedings of 4th International Conference on Information & Knowledge Management, November 1995. http://ilpubs.stanford.edu:8090/91/1/1995-24.pdf

38. Wright, D., De Hert, P. (eds.): Privacy Impact Assessments. Springer, Netherlands (2012)

Big Data Privacy and Anonymization

Vicenç Torra[1(✉)] and Guillermo Navarro-Arribas[2]

[1] School of Informatics, University of Skövde, Skövde, Sweden
vtorra@his.se
[2] Department of Information and Communication Engineering,
Universitat Autònoma de Barcelona, Catalonia, Spain
guillermo.navarro@uab.cat

Abstract. Data privacy has been studied in the area of statistics (statistical disclosure control) and computer science (privacy preserving data mining and privacy enhancing technologies) for at least 40 years. In this period models, measures, methods, and technologies have been developed to effectively protect the disclosure of sensitive information.

The coming of big data, with large volumes of data, dynamic and streaming data, poses new challenges to the field. In this paper we will review some of these challenges and propose some lines of research in the field.

1 Introduction

Data privacy studies models and methods to ensure that there is no disclosure of sensitive information. The field arose within the statistics community to ensure that sensitive data from census were not disclosed. Later, the problem appeared within the computer science community to ensure privacy in communications, and databases. Three main research communities exist today: statistical disclosure control, privacy enhancing technologies, and privacy preserving data mining. They study similar problems, although the focus is slightly different due to the types of data they consider and the type of uses of these data.

The field has now more than 40 years, starting with e.g. the seminal papers of Dalenius [5,6], Chaum [4], and Denning and Schlöder [7]. During these years, different types of privacy models have been defined, methods to protect sensitive information according to these privacy models have been proposed, and measures for evaluating disclosure risk, and information loss have also been defined. There is a large number of approaches for different types of data. This does not mean that all problems are solved, but there exists already a solid and useful set of techniques for ensuring different levels of privacy for some types of applications. See e.g. the reference books [8,11,19] for details.

The increasing amount of information available, and the coming of big data and data science poses new problems to the field. In this paper we will review some of these problems, and outline accordingly some lines for further research.

The new EU General Data Protection Regulation includes the implementation of the right to rectification and the right to be forgotten. That is, companies

A. Lehmann et al. (Eds.): Privacy and Identity 2016, IFIP AICT 498, pp. 15–26, 2016.
DOI: 10.1007/978-3-319-55783-0_2

need to modify or delete records from a database when users and citizens want
to take advantage of these rights. In order to implement these rights, data provenance plays a central role. Data provenance is not a topic specific for big data,
but it is with big data, distributed, and dynamic databases, where it can be used
in its full potentiality. We discuss in this paper some research topics related to
privacy and provenance.

The structure of the paper is as follows. In Sect. 2 we review some of the
existing approaches for privacy on standard databases. In Sect. 3 we focus on the
problem for big data. We review its definition and discuss some of the research
questions that we consider more relevant with respect to privacy for big data.
In Sect. 4 we focus on the problems related to data provenance. We discuss data
provenance and how data provenance interacts with data privacy. The paper
finishes with a summary.

2   Data Privacy for Databases

A large number of mechanisms have been developed for ensuring data privacy.
They can be classified according to different dimensions. We classify them [16]
according to our knowledge on the type of analysis a third party wants to apply
to this data.

- *Data-driven* or general purpose. In this case, we have no knowledge on the
  type of analysis to be performed by a third party. This is the usual case in
  which data is published through a server for future use. It also includes the
  case that data is transferred to a data miner or a data scientist for its analysis
  as we usually do not know which algorithm will be applied to the data. For
  this purpose, anonymization methods, also known as masking methods have
  been developed.
- *Computation-driven* or specific purpose. In this case, we know the exact analysis the third party (or third parties) wants to apply to the data. For example,
  we know that the data scientist wants to find the parameters of a regression
  model. This can be seen as the computation of a function or as solving a
  query for a database without disclosing the database. When a single database
  is considered and we formulate the problem as answering a query, differential
  privacy is a suitable privacy model. In the case that multiple databases are
  considered, the privacy model is based on secure multiparty computation and
  cryptographic protocols are used for this purpose.
- *Result-driven*. In this case, the analysis (a given data mining algorithm) is also
  known. The difference with computation-driven approaches is that here we are
  not worried on the protection of the database per se, but on the protection
  of some of the outcomes of the algorithm. For example, we know that data
  scientists will apply association rule mining, and we want to avoid that they
  infer that people buying diapers also buy beers. Similarly as in computation-
  driven analysis, prevention of disclosure for this type of analysis is specific to
  the given computation producing the specific results. In this case, however,
  the focus is on the knowledge inferred from the data instead of the actual data.

In this paper we focus on anonymization or masking methods. That is, data-driven methods. In short, anonymization algorithms (masking methods) transform a data file X into a file X' with data of less quality. This quality reduction ensures a certain privacy level according to some pre-established privacy model. This is an approach that can be applied to any type of database. It has been successfully applied to, for example, databases, documents, search logs, and social networks.

In addition, the approach is valid not only for protecting data from a syntactic point of view, but also from a semantic point of view. That is, taking into account the meaning of the terms and concepts in the data. For example, when we have words and categories in documents and search logs. For this purpose, we can use masking methods that use ontologies (as e.g. wordnet and ODP) to protect the data.

As masking methods modify the original data reducing its quality, three main research questions appear in the process. The first one is how to reduce the quality of the data. This is done by the masking methods themselves. There is a plethora of methods for this. Then, as data is modified we need to be sure that there is no information loss in the process or that this information loss is as low as possible. In other words, data utility is not reduced substantially in the masking process. Information loss measures are defined to quantify this information loss. Finally, although the quality of the data is reduced to avoid the disclosure of sensitive information, there is no guarantee that all methods satisfy this property. Disclosure risk measures have been defined to quantify the disclosure risk of anonymized data, and they are tightly related to privacy models.

As a summary, we list below the three main research issues related to masking methods.

- Masking methods. Methods that given a database X transform it into another one X' with less quality. Masking methods are usually classified into three categories: perturbative, non-perturbative and synthetic data generators. Perturbative methods reduce the quality by means of modifying the data introducing some kind of error into the data. Noise addition and multiplication, microaggregation and rank swapping are examples of perturbative methods. Non-perturbative methods reduce the quality of the data making them less detailed (but not erroneous). Generalization and suppression are examples of them. Synthetic data generators replace the original data by data generated from a model, which has been extracted from the original database. So, the data in X' is not the original data but artificial data generated from the model.
- Information loss measures. They measure in what extent the transformation of X into X' reduces the utility of the data, and the information that is lost in the process. Information loss measures are typically defined in terms of an analysis f to be performed to the data. Then, given this analysis f and the original and anonymized files X and X', we define information loss as

$$\mathrm{IL}_f(X, X') = divergence(f(X), f(X')).$$

where *divergence* is a function that evaluates how far are $f(X)$ and $f(X')$. A distance on the space of $f(X)$ can be used for this purpose. Naturally, we expect *divergence* $(Y, Y) = 0$ for all Y. Typical examples of functions f include some statistics (means, variances, covariances, regression coefficients), as well as machine learning algorithms (clustering and classification algorithms). Specific measures for some types of databases have also been considered in the literature (e.g., measures on graphs).

– Privacy models and disclosure risk measures. They focus on what extent anonymized (masked) data still contains sensitive information that can be used to compromise the privacy of the individuals of the database.

3 Data Privacy for Big Data

In this section we propose a few open research questions related to big data. To do so, we outline first a definition of big data, and the major difficulties we find with respect to disclosure risk in big data.

3.1 Big Data

There exists several definitions for big data based on the characteristics of the data. The well-known definition based on the 3Vs underlines volume, velocity, and variety as the main characteristics of big data. There are other definitions that expand this definition with additional terms. They are the definitions based on 4Vs, 5Vs, or even 7Vs.

– Volume. Databases include huge amounts of data. For example, facebook generated 4 new petabytes of data per day in October 2014 (see [21]).
– Velocity. Data is flowing to the databases in real time: real time streams of data flowing from diverse resources. Either from sensors or from internet (from e-commerce or social media).
– Variety. Data is no longer of a single type (or a few simple types). Databases include data from a vast range of systems and sensors in different formats and datatypes. This may include unstructured text, logs, and videos.

3.2 Moving Privacy to Big Data: Disclosure Risk

For big data, in principle, the same research questions mentioned in the previous section appear. We need to develop masking methods, information loss measures and disclosure risk measures. For them, we need to take into account that the amounts of data are larger, and thus we need to deal with the corresponding computational problems. Nevertheless, besides of that, a new issue appears: there is a new level for privacy risk. This new level of risk is caused by the following three problems.

- Lack of control and transparency. It is more and more difficult to know who has our data. There are different organizations that can have information about ourselves without us knowing it. Information is gathered from sensors and cameras, obtained through screening posts in social networks, and from analysis of web searches. Note also the case of tracking cookies. Finally, there are data brokers that gather as much information as possible about citizens.
- Linkability. It is usual for big data to link databases to improve the amount and quality of the information. Linking databases increase the risk of identification as there is more information for each individual. Note that the more information we have on individuals the easier to reidentify them, and the more difficult to protect them.
- Inference and data reusability. There exist effective inference algorithms that infer sensitive information (e.g., sexual orientation, political and religious affiliation [12]). One of the main goals of big data analytics is to use existing data for new purposes. This increases the inference ability. As a side effect, data is never deleted waiting for future use.

In the next section we propose a few research lines for data privacy for big data. They are proposed in relation to these three problems just mentioned.

3.3   Open Research Questions for Big Data

We propose in this section a few research questions related to big data. The first one is about the need to inform users about the risks of inference due to big data. Then, we propose some lines related to anonymization of *stand-alone* and *linked* databases. It follows another question related to the need of developing (and using) user privacy. We also discuss the need of developing efficient algorithms for data protection in data privacy. This need is both for user privacy, and respondent and holder privacy. The last one is about data provenance, an issue that is further developed in Sect. 4.

These lines of research are based on our own work (see e.g. [1,17,18]), and on the research lines discussed in [15].

- **Issue #1.** Technology should help people to know what others know and can infer about them.
  As we have stated above, effective machine learning and data mining algorithms can infer sensitive information. Some of these models use data that does not seem *a priori* sensitive. It is *insufficient* that we protect sensitive information without protecting what permits us to infer sensitive information. Technology should help people to know about this, and e.g. provide tools in social networks to make people aware of this fact.
- **Issue #2.** Databases should be anonymized/masked in origin. Machine learning algorithms for masked data are required.
  On the one hand, there exist masking methods that are effective in the sense that they achieve low information loss (with loss disclosure risk). On the other hand, there are machine learning and data mining algorithms that are resitant

to errors. In the same direction, not all data is equally important for machine learning algorithms, and some data mining algorithms for big data do not use all data but only a sample of them. Because of that, it is meaningful to consider privacy by design machine learning algorithms. That is, machine learning methods that are appropriate for data that has already been protected.

Preprocessing methods for machine learning (dimensionality reduction, sampling, etc.) should be combined with and integrated to masking methods. Masking methods can be seen as methods to introduce noise and reduce quality, but they can also be seen as methods for dimensionality reduction. See e.g. the case of microaggregation and, in general, methods to achieve k-anonymity. They reduce the number of (different) records in a database by means of generalization or clustering (i.e., building centroids). These generalized records or centroids can be seen as more consolidated (error-free) data.

– **Issue #3.** Anonymization needs to provide controlled linkability.

We have reported that linkability is one of the basic components of big data. Companies want to combine databases to increase the information about individuals (enlarging the set of variables/attributes available on them). If databases are anonymized in origin, we need ways to ensure that these databases can still be somehow linked in order to fulfill big data requirements. k-anonymity allows linkability at group level. Algorithms for controlled linkability are needed, as well as methods that can exploit e.g. linkability at group level.

– **Issue #4.** Privacy models need to be composable.

Given several data sets with a given privacy guarantee, their combination needs to satisfy also the privacy requirements. There are results on the composability of differential privacy. See e.g. [15].

– **Issue #5.** User privacy should be in place: decentralized anonymity.

User privacy [17] is when users have an active role in ensuring their own privacy. For this purpose, there are methods to protect the identity of the users as well as to protect their data. For example, there are methods for user privacy in communications and in information retrieval.

While the research questions mentioned above are to be implemented and used by data holders, user privacy provides users with tools to be used by themselves. User privacy permits that data are anonymized before their transmission to data collectors (or to the service provider). So, there is no need to trust the data collector. Local anonymization and collaborative anonymization are keywords for tools for user privacy.

– **Issue #6.** Methods for big data.

Big data have particularities (the three or more Vs discussed above) that have to be taken into account when developing methods for ensuring privacy. These particularities are for both respondent and holder privacy (i.e., methods applied by data holders) and for user privacy. We can distinguish three types of situations.

  • **Issue #6.1.** Large volumes of data. Efficient algorithms are required for data of high dimension. Algorithms are required for producing masked databases, but also for computing information loss measures and disclosure

risk. There exist already some masking methods that have been developed
with efficiency in mind for standard databases (e.g., some algorithms for
microaggregation), for graphs and social networks (e.g., based on random
noise on edges, on generalization and microaggregation), and for location
privacy. New methods are needed.

- **Issue #6.2.** Dynamic data. When data changes with respect to time, we
  may need to publish several copies of the database. In this case, specific
  data masking algorithms are required. Note that independent application
  of algorithms for k-anonymity to the same database can cause disclosure.
  So, the same applies when the database has changed between two applications of the algorithm.
- **Issue #6.3.** Streaming data. Data is received continuously and should be
  processed as soon as possible because we cannot hold them and process
  them later. In this case, difficulties arise because at any time information
  is only partial. Methods based on sliding windows have been developed
  for this purpose.

- **Issue #7.** Data provenance and data privacy.
  The new EU General Data Protection Regulation grants citizens the right
  to rectify and delete the information about themselves in companies. Data
  provenance are the data structures that permit companies to know where
  the information of customers and users is in their databases. Different open
  research questions appear in the crossroad between provenance and privacy.
  One of them is the fact that data provenance can contain sensitive information
  and, thus, privacy technologies needs to be applied to it. At the same time, the
  fact that data can be modified using data provenance according to customers'
  requirements poses new privacy problems. We discuss these issues in more
  detail in the next section. These research topics can also be considered for
  databases of small and medium size but it is with big data that the research
  becomes challenging.

4   Data Privacy and Data Provenance

Data provenance is becoming a key issue in data management, and can have a
great impact in data privacy. Despite its relevance it has not been given much
attention until recently from the data privacy community. Information provided
as provenance can be used to improve privacy data mechanisms, but it is important to note that provenance itself has to be protected from inferences [14]. In
the era of big data and online social networks, data provenance is also useful to
help users to assess the validity and trust of the information. For instance, it
can help to identify rumormongers and disinformation centers. As we show in
Sect. 4.2 data provenance can play an important role in the future of big data
privacy research.

Broadly speaking, data provenance can be seen as metadata or as an anno-
tation of the data. That is, data is expanded with information of the processes
that has led to this data. Provenance can be coarse-grained or fine-grained.

That is, we can have information on how a bunch of data (i.e., files or databases have been produced) or we can have information particularized at the record or even at the value level. Fine-grained provenance is what makes provenance useful, as it is only in this case that we have detailed information on how any data element has been produced. E.g., we can know who entered the temperature (fever) of a patient, or in which store our client claimed for a discount.

There are different ways to represent data provenance. There are two types of provenance. They are *where provenance* and *why provenance*. *Where provenance* describes the origin of the data, and *why provenance* the process that generated the data. A data element in a database typically proceeds from the combination of previous data elements by means of certain processing functions. Therefore, we need a structure to represent the transformations. The most common approaches are chains [9,10,13] and graphs [3,20].

4.1 Securing Data Provenance

Secure provenance was introduced to ensure security and privacy to provenance data. Observe that provenance data is sensitive. It may contain information on who and when data was updated. E.g., knowing that a certain doctor has modified data from a patient can lead to disclosure on who is the doctor of whom, what type of illness the patient has, and at what time the patient was at the hospital. Files and databases typically flow within departments and between companies. It is specially important to ensure that these third parties cannot access confidential information contained in the data provenance, whilst allowing them to work with the factual data and update the provenance structure itself. For example, this would allow to perform analysis on the medical data, preserving patient privacy. Hence, provenance data needs to follow these databases and this has to be done ensuring e.g., provenance integrity. Secure data provenance focuses on these type of problems. A few properties have been established as a requirement for secure data provenance [9,10,20]:

– **Distributed.** When databases flow through untrusted environments, and provenance data is associated to them, we need secure data provenance systems to be defined so that they work in a distributed environment. We cannot use a centralized approach with trusted hardware.
– **Integrity.** In distributed environments it is important that nobody can forge provenance data. Provenance data is transmitted and provenance structures are modified to add the new processes applied to the data. Nevertheless, as stated above the structure is immutable and no adversary can be granted to change any part of it. In addition, the provenance system should not allow the modification of a value without expanding the provenance structure. Finally, deletion of provenance data should not cause that a record of the database is unreadable. Additional aspects to be taken into account is to consider collusions of intruders (that coalitions of intruders should not be able to attack integrity), repudiation (that intruders should not be able to repudiate a record as it was not theirs) or creating forged structures (intruders should not be able to create new provenance structures).

- **Availability.** We are interested in providing security mechanisms to ensure provenance data availability. Auditors should be able to access provenance information in a secure, fast and reliable manner to perform any required operation, e.g. verify the integrity of an ownership sequence without knowing the individual records.
- **Privacy and confidentiality.** We need to ensure that disclosure does not take place, and this is needed for both the database and the provenance data. Only authorized users can access the information.

These properties need to be combined with the two properties that are general for any provenance system. They are, completeness and efficiency:

- **Completeness.** That is, that all actions that are relevant to computation should be detected and represented in the provenance structure. Note that this is not always easy, because some operations as e.g. cut & paste or manual copy can exclude relevant provenance information.
- **Efficiency.** Data provenance introduces an overhead to the data. Fine-grained provenance can double (or more) the size of a database. In addition, operations on the provenance structure need to be efficient because they also introduce an overhead on the computation time.

All these properties are relevant in the context of big data provenance. Big data is often distributed as different information sources can contribute in a computation or in a decision. Therefore, integrity is a basic aspect. We need that provenance structures are not modified at will, and we need to be sure that only permitted operations are applied to them. Availability is then not only a requirement for auditors but also for the subjects from which the data has been extracted. In order that individuals can access and apply the right to delete or rectify a record, they need to be able to know where their data is or if a certain record contains data that has been generated from their own data.

4.2 Considerations About Privacy and Provenance

When considering big data associated with provenance data, it is important to clearly define the possible scenarios that may arise for data privacy. An accepted classification of possible situations is given in [2] on the basis of what is protected or where do we want to ensure a given degree of privacy (see Table 1):

- *Case 1*: The data are kept private and provenance data are also private. Both need to be protected and their relation has to be preserved.
- *Case 2*: The data itself are not protected but provenance data are private.
- *Case 3*: Data are private, but the provenance data are not protected.
- *Case 4*: No privacy protection are applied to neither the data itself nor the provenance data.

Depending on the different purposes, requirements, and nature of the specific data, a given case might apply. Secure data provenance mainly focuses to the

Table 1. Cases for privacy and data provenance.

	Data	Provenance
Case 1	Private	Private
Case 2	Non-private	Private
Case 3	Private	Non-private
Case 4	Non-private	Non-private

case of private provenance when data is distributed (i.e., we need the system to satisfy the requirements discussed in Sect. 4.1). In the case of centralized private data standard anonymization techniques can be used if we want a single-shot release of this data.

Some of the problems we encounter when data provenance is used depart from standard solutions of data privacy. We discuss a few examples in the next section.

4.3 Example of Privacy Problem with Provenance Information

In this section we illustrate an example of a specific problem that can arise in big data privacy when considering provenance information. This problem might occur when individuals request the deletion of their related data from a given dataset, and thus the model obtained from the data needs to be revised. This operation will be performed by means of provenance data allowing the data operator to know exactly which specific data has to be deleted.

To describe this example, we introduce some notation. We will consider a set X (a file or a database) to which we have applied some masking method ρ to obtain a protected set χ. From χ, using a certain algorithm A we extract a piece of knowledge Γ. For example, A can be an algorithm to extract decision trees, therefore Γ is the decision tree inferred from $\rho(X)$.

The set X is modified with modifications μ to obtain a data set X', which protected with ρ will yield χ' and with algorithm A, the piece of knowledge Γ'. E.g., Γ' is a (different) decision tree inferred from $\rho(X')$.

Notation and procedures are represented in Fig. 1.

In most cases μ should not be public since it will lead to reidentification of modified records. In front of this scenario some interesting questions might arise.

- An intruder knows $S \subset X$, Γ, and Γ', can this intruder gain knowledge of μ and $S' \subseteq X \setminus S$ with certainty?
- An intruder knows χ and χ', will this intruder be able to determine μ?

In order to avoid that intruders can make the inferences outlined in the previous lines, privacy models and privacy algorithms can be defined and implemented. In [18] we introduced a privacy model related to the modifications of a database.

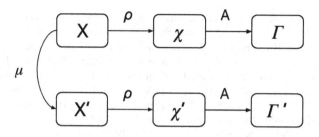

Fig. 1. Example of protected data and its modification

5   Summary

In this paper we have proposed a few open questions on the topic of data privacy for big data. On the one hand, we have discussed lines related to stand-alone and linked databases. Among them, we want to stress the need that databases are anonymized in origin, and thus technology is developed to permit controlled linkability and composability.

On the other hand, we have discussed issues related to data provenance, and its relationship with data privacy.

Acknowledgements. This work was supported by Vetenskapsrådet (VR#2016-03346), Spanish MINECO (project TIN2014-55243-P), and Catalan AGAUR (2014-SGR-691).

References

1. D'Acquisto, G., Domingo-Ferrer, J., Kikiras, P., Torra, V., de Montjoye, Y.-A., Bourka, A.: Privacy by design in big data: an overview of privacy enhancing technologies in the era of big data analytics. In: ENISA: European Union Agency for Network and Information Security (2015)
2. Bertino, E., Ghinita, G., Kantarcioglu, M., Nguyen, D., Park, J., Sandhu, R., Sultana, S., Thuraisingham, B., Xu, S.: A roadmap for privacy-enhanced secure data provenance. J. Intell. Inf. Syst. **43**, 481–501 (2014)
3. Braun, U., Shinnar, A., Seltzer, M.: Securing provenance. In: Proceedings of HOT-SEC (2008)
4. Chaum, D.L.: Untraceable electronic mail, return addresses, and digital pseudonyms. Commun. ACM **24**(2), 84–88 (1981)
5. Dalnenius, T.: The invasion of privacy problem and statistics production - an overview. Statistisk Tidskrift **12**, 213–225 (1974)
6. Dalenius, T.: Towards a methodology for statistical disclosure control. Statistisk Tidskrift **5**, 429–444 (1977)
7. Denning, D.E., Schlörer, J.: A fast procedure for finding a tracker in a statistical database. ACM Trans. Database Syst. **5**(1), 88–102 (1980)
8. Duncan, G. T., Elliot, M., Salazar, J. J.: Statistical confidentiality. Springer, New York (2011)

9. Hasan, R., Sion, R., Winslett, M.: Introducing secure provenance: problems and challenges. In: Proceedings of StorageSST. ACM, New York (2007)
10. Hasan, R., Sion, R., Winslett, M.: The case of the fake Picasso: preventing history forgery with secure provenance. In: Proceedings of FAST 2009 (2009)
11. Hundepool, A., Domingo-Ferrer, J., Franconi, L., Giessing, S., Nordholt, E.S., Spicer, K., de Wolf, P.-P.: Statistical Disclosure Control. Wiley, Chichester (2012)
12. Kosinski, M., Stillwell, D., Graepel, T.: Private traits and attributes are predictable from digital records of human behavior. In: PNAS (2013)
13. McDaniel, P., Butler, K., Sion, R., Zadok, E., Winslett, M.: Towards a secure and efficient system for end-to-end provenance. In: Proceedings of TAPP (2010)
14. Reuben, J., Martucci, L.A., Fischer-Hübner, S., Packer, H.S., Hedbom, H., Moreau, L.: Privacy Impact Assessment Template for Provenance. In: 2016 11th International Conference on Availability, Reliability and Security (ARES), pp. 653–660 (2016)
15. Soria-Comas, J., Domingo-Ferrer, J.: Big Data Privacy: Challenges to Privacy Principles and Models. Data Sci. Eng. **1**(1), 21–28 (2016)
16. Torra, V., Navarro-Arribas, G.: Data privacy. WIREs Data Min. Knowl. Dis. **4**(4), 269–280 (2014)
17. Torra, V.: Data Privacy. Springer (forthcoming, 2017)
18. Torra, V., Navarro-Arribas, G.: Integral privacy. In: Foresti, S., Persiano, G. (eds.) CANS 2016. LNCS, vol. 10052, pp. 661–669. Springer, Cham (2016). doi:10.1007/978-3-319-48965-0_44
19. Vaidya, J., Clifton, C. W., Zhu, Y.M.: Privacy Preserving Data Mining. Springer, New York (2006)
20. Zhang, J., Chapman, A., LeFevre, K.: Do you know where your data's been? – tamper-evident database provenance. In: Jonker, W., Petković, M. (eds.) SDM 2009. LNCS, vol. 5776, pp. 17–32. Springer, Heidelberg (2009). doi:10.1007/978-3-642-04219-5_2
21. https://www.brandwatch.com/2016/05/47-facebook-statistics-2016/

Data Protection by Design and by Default à la European General Data Protection Regulation

Marit Hansen[✉]

Unabhängiges Landeszentrum für Datenschutz Schleswig-Holstein, Kiel, Germany
marit.hansen@datenschutzzentrum.de

Abstract. The European data protection reform has resulted in a new regulation that will be effective from May 2018. This so-called General Data Protection Regulation contains specific provisions on data protection by design and on data protection by default. After briefly discussing related approaches such as "privacy by design", we will elaborate how these provisions can be interpreted and sketch the potential impact on data processing in Europe and possibly beyond.

Keywords: Data protection · European General Data Protection Regulation · Data protection by design · Data protection by default · Privacy · Privacy by design · Privacy by default

1 Introduction

For decades, the concept of "privacy by design" is being discussed and recommended by Data Protection and Privacy Commissioners [1]. In short, "privacy by design" means a design of systems where privacy requirements have been considered and appropriate measures to fulfil these requirements have been implemented – resulting in built-in privacy. "Privacy by design" should be applied in all phases of system development. As a rule, this method is superior to an attempt of subsequently adding some privacy features to a running system: Refraining from giving thought to privacy requirements in the design process usually yields systems that determine the data processing to a large extent with the effect that specifically data minimisation requirements won't be easy to implement in the best possible way later on. Also, tailoring an existing system to privacy needs that were ignored before may be a cumbersome and expensive task, if possible at all.

However, today's reality of system design doesn't reflect that demand. "Privacy by design" is the exception and not the rule. The monetary incentives for developers to adhere to this paradigm are few, and by now there are no perceptible sanctions for the responsible entities (data controllers or data processors) using systems without built-in privacy as long as the data processing is sufficiently legally compliant otherwise [2]. In this situation, producers of systems may regard each requirement that should be considered in addition to the bare functionality of their system as overly complex and reject any delay in the time to market. Even the often demanded "security by design" paradigm is by no means normal practice so that adversaries can frequently take advantage of vulnerabilities in IT systems.

© IFIP International Federation for Information Processing 2016
Published by Springer International Publishing AG 2016. All Rights Reserved
A. Lehmann et al. (Eds.): Privacy and Identity 2016, IFIP AICT 498, pp. 27–38, 2016.
DOI: 10.1007/978-3-319-55783-0_3

These observations were considered by the European Union lawmakers when debating the data protection reform in the recent years. One important outcome is the General Data Protection Regulation (GDPR) [3] that demands not only that appropriate security measures are implemented by controllers processing personal data, but also "data protection by design and by default" (Article 25 GDPR). The GDPR, and specifically the provisions on data protection by design and by default, may become a game changer with respect to guaranteeing the rights and freedoms of human beings, including the right to privacy. Therefore this text will provide a deeper look into the General Data Protection Regulation and its demands for designing systems according to data protection requirements.

This text is organised as follows: Sect. 2 sketches important properties of the European General Data Protection Regulation resulting from the European data protection reform initiative. The related concept of "privacy by design" is introduced in Sect. 3 which provides brief information on the history and on definitions. Sections 4 and 5 dig into the legal obligations concerning data protection by design and data protection by default, respectively. Finally, Sect. 6 summarises the findings and gives a conclusion.

2   The General Data Protection Regulation

In 1995 the European Union adopted the Data Protection Directive 95/46/EC [4] which then had to be implemented by each member state. Although the Data Protection Directive aimed at a harmonised and modern data protection regime throughout Europe, this objective was not fully achieved due to differences in the various national implementations. In 2016, more than 20 years later, the successor of the Data Protection Directive was adopted after several years of discussion and negotiation: the General Data Protection Regulation [3]. Lessons learnt from the experience of the former data protection regime were considered and, again, the goals of harmonisation and modernisation were pursued. The GDPR will become effective May 25, 2018. Its direct applicability in all member states will help unifying the data protection level. However, about 70 opening clauses – some mandatory, some optional – provide means for own national requirements and thereby deviation from a joint strategy across the member states [5].

The GDPR cannot be a panacea for data protection at its best: Not everything in the GDPR is brandnew, and the 99 Articles leave room for interpretation. The chosen level of abstraction in the legal text may at first seem to lack support for those who have to comply with the GDPR. But this is an intended feature rather than a bug: Abstract rules need to be substantiated in a way that is appropriate with respect to the ever-changing risk to rights and freedoms of natural persons and accepted among the European data protection commissioners as supervisory authorities. So the GDPR defines a process for achieving consistency in the interpretation of the legal obligations concerning cross-border cases. By this, the GDPR may be future-proof for several years or even multiple decades – unlike its predecessor. However, steady negotiation on the substantiation of abstract rules is time-consuming and may be influenced by lobbyists who don't share the goal of optimal data protection.

It has to be noted that the GDPR does not only address European data controllers, but is designed to guarantee data protection in the entire European market. The market location principle laid down in Article 3 GDPR addresses organisations that offer goods or services to people in the EU or monitor their behaviour, even if the organisations are not established in the territory of the European Union. In particular those non-EU companies dominating the digital market shall comply with the data protection requirements in the GDPR.

Whether the GDPR will provide the proper instruments for achieving data protection cannot be predicted at this early stage. However, clearly the European member states have a joint starting point to take it from there. This is true for all instruments described in the GDPR, e.g. data protection by design, data protection by default, data protection impact assessment, codes of conduct, certifications, sanctions, or the involvement of courts.

In the following, we will focus on design issues demanded by the GDPR. This is in line with the statement in Recital 4 of the GDPR: *"The processing of personal data should be designed to serve mankind."*

3 Privacy by Design

Building in privacy – or, to use the same wording as the GDPR: data protection[1] – has been proposed by various stakeholders for several decades. In addition to cryptographic functionalities to achieve confidentiality or integrity, concepts for privacy technologies were proposed for more than 30 years (e.g. [6]). Since the mid-1990ies the term "Privacy-Enhancing Technologies (PETs)" became known in the Data Protection Commissioners' community [7] and was taken up by the European Commission:

"The use of PETs can help to design information and communication systems and services in a way that minimises the collection and use of personal data and facilitate compliance with data protection rules. The use of PETs should result in making breaches of certain data protection rules more difficult and/or helping to detect them." [8]

When the former Ontario Privacy Commissioner Ann Cavoukian promoted the concept of "Privacy by Design" [9] and described seven foundational principles [10], she extended the scope by addressing IT systems, accountable business practices, and physical design and networked infrastructure. It is important to understand that system

---

[1] It has to be stressed that "privacy" and "data protection" denote different, but related concepts, and there is not one single definition each. Usually the meaning of "privacy" points to the rights of an individual and is associated with self-defence against intrusion. "Data protection", as coined in European data protection law, addresses primarily organisations that have to make sure that the rights of the individuals are not infringed. Note that Article 8 of the European Convention on Human Rights and similarly Article 7 of the Charter of Fundamental Rights of the European Union provide a right to privacy: "Right to respect for private and family life". In addition, Article 8 of the Charter focuses on data protection: "Protection of personal data". For the purpose of this text it is not necessary to precisely define the boundaries because the exact privacy and/or data protection requirements to be built in would differ for various cases and cannot be elaborated in detail at this point.

design must not be limited to adding a few PET modules, but needs a more comprehensive approach that encompasses in particular hardware and software, interfaces, organisational processes, and business models.

Engineers expect a more detailed operationalisation and specification for the task of building in privacy requirements. Different proposals have been made in the last few years to support engineering privacy (e.g., [11–15]), and there are studies such as [16] that summarise the current status of research and point out obstacles. However, today's IT development environments refrain from making developers aware of privacy requirements.

From the legal perspective, some researchers argued that the European Data Protection Directive 95/46/EC already contained the requirement for privacy by design: *"The incorporation of PETs into strategies for privacy receives some encouragement from Article 17 of the Directive, which requires data controllers to implement 'appropriate technical and organisational measures' to protect personal data, especially in network transmissions. Recital 46, which augments the meaning of Article 17, highlights the requirement that these measures should be taken 'both at the time of the design of the processing system and at the time of the processing itself', thus indicating that security cannot simply be bolted onto data systems, but must be built into them."* [17] However, this demand for "appropriate technical and organisational measures" primarily calls for "security by design" and not so much for "data protection by design", although a few member states incorporated legal provisions for anonymisation or other data minimising functionality [17, 18].

For instance, the German Federal Data Protection demands in § 3a concerning data minimisation: *"Personal data shall be collected, processed and used, and data processing systems shall be chosen and organized in accordance with the aim of collecting, processing and using as little personal data as possible. [...]"* [18] All the same, this legal provision has proven ineffective since no fines can be imposed in case the controller ignores that obligation.

This is different with Article 25 GDPR "Data protection by design and by default" where the supervisory authority has to ensure the imposition of administrative fines in case the obligations of the controller or the processor pursuant to Article 25 have been infringed (Article 83 (4) lit. a)). The administrative fine has to be effective, proportionate and dissuasive (Article 83 (1)) and may go up to 10 000 000 EUR, or in the case of an undertaking, up to 2% of the total worldwide annual turnover of the preceding financial year.

As a rule, all European language versions of the GDPR are equally valid. However, there is a noteworthy difference in the title of Article 25, as the following excerpt shows:

- [EN] Article 25: Data protection by design and by default
- [FR] Article 25: Protection des données dès la conception et protection des données par défaut
- [ES] Artículo 25: Protección de datos desde el diseño y por defecto
- [NL] Artikel 25: Gegevensbescherming door ontwerp en door standaardinstellingen
- [SV] Artikel 25: Inbyggt dataskydd och dataskydd som standard
- [DE] Artikel 25: Datenschutz durch Technikgestaltung und durch datenschutzfreundliche Voreinstellungen

Most of the languages reflect the "design" idea, the Swedish translation focuses on the "built-in" part. Only the German version adds "Technik" (technology) in the title of Article 25 which may be misleading because – as stated before – privacy by design must not be reduced to technology in a narrow sense, but has to reach out to entire systems and services. Probably this wording has been used in the German version of the GDPR in association with the long-standing concept "Datenschutz durch Technik" (literal translation: "data protection by technology") which was introduced in the mid-1990ies to denote the work on Privacy-Enhancing Technologies [7] and privacy by design. Recital 78 of the German GDPR even mentions "Datenschutz durch Technik", but adds the translation "data protection by design".

Article 25 GDPR consists of three paragraphs: The first paragraph deals with data protection by design (cf. Sect. 4), the second tackles data protection by default (cf. Sect. 5), and the third paragraph, which won't be further discussed in this text, adds a remark on the relation to certification.

4 Data Protection by Design

Article 25 (1) GDPR reads as follows:

"(1) Taking into account the state of the art, the cost of implementation and the nature, scope, context and purposes of processing as well as the risks of varying likelihood and severity for rights and freedoms of natural persons posed by the processing, the controller shall, both at the time of the determination of the means for processing and at the time of the processing itself, implement appropriate technical and organisational measures, such as pseudonymisation, which are designed to implement data-protection principles, such as data minimisation, in an effective manner and to integrate the necessary safeguards into the processing in order to meet the requirements of this Regulation and protect the rights of data subjects."

For a better understanding, this long sentence is disassembled and put into context:

Who shall take an action?
- The controller.
- There are also indirect effects on potential data processors, acting on behalf of the controller, as well as on producers of systems because the controller would have to choose products, services and applications in such a manner that the requirements of the GDPR are met and ensure the protection of the rights of the data subjects (cf. Article 28).

What is the objective?
- Meeting the requirements of the GDPR and protecting the rights of the persons concerned ("data subjects").
- This means in particular to implement the data protection principles that are laid down in Article 5 of the GDPR: lawfulness, fairness and transparency; purpose limitation; data minimisation; accuracy; storage limitation; integrity and confidentiality; accountability.

What has to be done?
- Implementing appropriate technical and organisational measures in an effective manner.

- Integrating the necessary safeguards into the processing.

How should it be done?

- Both at the time of the determination of the means for processing and at the time of the processing itself.
- In an effective manner.

Which conditions occur?

- The state of the art.
- The cost of implementation.
- The nature, scope, context and purposes of processing.
- The risks of varying likelihood and severity for rights and freedoms of natural persons posed by the processing.

The conditions are of utmost interest because they can constitute both an upper and lower bound for the actions to be taken. The data controller needs to employ these conditions to justify all decisions concerning the implementation of measures: How were the measures chosen, why were better measures omitted? In the beginning, the given conditions will probably function mainly as a limitation of what the controller has to do for data protection by design. But at least the justification has to be done and should be documented so that supervisory authorities are able to check whether the grounds for not implementing better measures are plausible.

One limiting factor will be the state of the art: In the last years the state of research in "privacy by design" has made good progress, but the transition to state-of-the-art measures is not an easy task and cannot be taken for granted. Concerning Article 25 GDPR, it will be debated in many cases whether a measure belongs to the category "state-of-the-art". However, for deciding on "state of the art" it is not sufficient to determine solely the readiness of a measure such as a Privacy-Enhancing Technologies, but also the quality for improving or ensuring data protection has to be taken into account. The metrics for such a combined maturity assessment and the evaluation procedure are by no means trivial. Instead they require expert knowledge when trust assumptions, potential side effects, or usability issues have to be considered [19].

In the realm of security, the category "state of the art" should already be known from Article 17 (1) of the European Data Protection Directive 95/46/EC:

> *"Member States shall provide that the controller must implement appropriate technical and organizational measures to protect personal data [...]. Having regard to the state of the art and the cost of their implementation, such measures shall ensure a level of security appropriate to the risks represented by the processing and the nature of the data to be protected."* [4]

Similarly, Article 32 demands the usage of appropriate state-of-the-art security measures. Judging from many discussions after the adoption of the GDPR, the exact properties of when to consider a security measure state of the art have not been fully defined, although this requirement has been laid down in European data protection law at least since 1995.

Likewise, surprisingly little information is available on state-of-the-art measures concerning privacy by design. Determining good and best practices of concepts and products as well as agreeing on their classification as state of the art will certainly become a task for the supervisory authorities. Anyhow, Article 24 on the responsibility of the controller clarifies that the controller has to implement "appropriate technical and organisational measures to ensure and to be able to demonstrate" compliance with the GDPR. The factors "state of the art" and "cost of implementation" are left out in that provision.

Article 25 (1) GDPR and the accompanying Recital 78 mention a few examples (explicitly stated: "inter alia") for measures that may be appropriate:

> "[...] minimising the processing of personal data, pseudonymising personal data as soon as possible, transparency with regard to the functions and processing of personal data, enabling the data subject to monitor the data processing, enabling the controller to create and improve security features." (Recital 78 GDPR)

Thereby not only privacy-enhancing technologies, but also transparency-enhancing technologies (TETs) are addressed. Further, this recital acknowledges that the controller may have to advance the security features, e.g. in the case of sensitive data. "One size fits all" wouldn't live up the expectations of the GDPR. The improvement of security features is also demanded when vulnerabilities in the provided functionality are becoming known. This requires an ongoing risk monitoring in a data protection management system.

What is more, Recital 78 addresses producers of products, services and applications who "should be encouraged to take into account the right to data protection when developing and designing such products, services and applications" so that controllers "are able to fulfil their data protection obligations". Recital 78 gives one example that can really encourage producers to invest in privacy by design: "The principles of data protection by design and by default should also be taken into consideration in the context of public tenders." Thus, procurement processes should from now on incorporate built-in data protection.

5 Data Protection by Default

The text of Article 25 (2) GDPR reads as follows:

> "(2) The controller shall implement appropriate technical and organisational measures for ensuring that, by default, only personal data which are necessary for each specific purpose of the processing are processed. That obligation applies to the amount of personal data collected, the extent of their processing, the period of their storage and their accessibility. In particular, such measures shall ensure that by default personal data are not made accessible without the individual's intervention to an indefinite number of natural persons."

The nature of the second paragraph of Article 25 GDPR is totally different from the first paragraph since it omits the explicit mentioning of limiting factors. Still, the word "appropriate" gives room for interpretation of which measures are suitable and right for the purpose.

Again, the controller is responsible for implementing technical and organisational measures. In the first sentence, the data minimisation principle (cf. Article 5 (1) lit. c) GDPR) and the purpose limitation principle (cf. Article 5 (1) lit. c) GDPR) are repeated. The insertion of "by default" addresses the standard configuration of a data processing system.

The second sentence specifies that not only the amount of the data collected, but also the extent of their processing, the storage duration and the accessibility of the personal data are affected. Thereby the standard configuration should prevent that personal data which are not strictly necessary for the purpose are processed at all (e.g. by limiting the personal data that is asked for), that they are processed only to the extent as necessary for the purpose (e.g. by restricting the possible processing steps or by using data minimisation measures such as anonymisation or pseudonymisation functionalities), that they are erased as early as possible regarding the purpose (e.g. by automatic erasure measures), and that their accessibility is limited as much and as soon as the purpose allows (e.g. by access control mechanisms, by carefully choosing the storage location, or by encrypting the data).

The third sentence gives an example that relates to Internet publications or social networks: that, by default, personal data must not be made accessible to an indefinite number of people.

The notion of "default" incorporates the possibility to change the default setting. The last sentence of Article 25 (2) GDPR it clarifies that "the individual's intervention" may allow changing the configuration. The default setting would be the initial configuration which can be changed by the data subject to allow that more data are processed, that other processing steps are allowed, that the data can be stored for a longer time, and that they may be accessible to other parties as well. Typical cases where this may be desired by a data subject comprise sharing information on the web or in a social network, creating accounts as returning customers so that information on their mail address or on payment methods is stored for the next visit, or providing personal data for long-term personalised consumer experiences.

The GDPR interpretation of "data protection by default" differs from previous ideas in the privacy-by-design context where Cavoukian demanded:

"Privacy as the default setting:
If an individual does nothing, their privacy still remains intact.
No action is required on the part of the individual to protect their privacy – it is built into the system, by default." [10]

This requirement sounds promising, but if "intact privacy" means that no personal data are processed at all or that there is a guarantee of no risk for the individual's privacy, many real cases with lawful and legitimate purposes would not work. As soon as the individual chooses to make use of a product or a service, this may require processing of personal data and thereby wouldn't necessarily considered as leaving the individual's privacy intact. Perhaps this notion rather addresses the individual's horizon of expectation: For users of a product or service it should be clear which personal data are needed for the purpose (e.g. basing on informed consent), and all additional data processing should be prevented unless the user intervenes and changes the setting. However, the product or service should not create the false impression that the functionality can be offered when the user sticks to a default of no-disclosure of personal data, e.g. when a governmental service will require specific attributes of the citizen for the payment of social benefits. But this will be probably meet the expectations of the user.

A more elaborate view on data protection by default was given by the European Data Protection Supervisor when commenting a previous version of Article 25 GDPR:

"The principle of data protection by default aims at protecting the data subject in situations in which there might be a lack of understanding or control on the processing of their data, especially in a technological context. The idea behind the principle is that privacy intrusive features of a certain product or service are initially limited to what is necessary for the simple use of it. The data subject should in principle be left the choice to allow use of his or her personal data in a broader way." [20]

Here the aim is not to leave privacy intact, but to – at least initially – limit privacy intrusive features. The statement stresses that the guideline for deciding what is necessary should be the simple use of a product or service. This also means that the individual should be able to use a product or service even if disclosing or storing more personal data may mean extended functionalities or a different user experience.

Today only very few guidelines on "data protection by default" exist (one example is the workflow given in [21]). So it is difficult both for data controllers and for supervisory authorities to decide on an appropriate default setting. In any case it will have to be determined in a first step which parts are hardwired without the possibility for a change (which relates back to "data protection by design" and built-in data protection) and which parts are configurable. For the configurable part it has to be figured out when and which pre-settings are reasonable for which user groups (e.g. different settings for children and adults, or different settings for EU residents and non-EU residents when it comes to storage location) and when the configuration should be better done in an interaction with the user when installing the system.

Also it has to be given thought to usable ways of changing the configuration later on in an informed manner and without giving up all protection at once. It shouldn't be the case that the solution with the data protection default setting is barely usable, but one click away is the full version that entails no protection at all (which may infringe Article 7 (4) GDPR on freely given consent). The known challenge how to prevent that people get overwhelmed or tired from the configuration possibilities may become even harder if data controllers – not being enthusiastic about data protection by default – put the blame on data protection regulators. Thus, a static "take it or leave it" default is probably not the best solution. Instead, taking the pre-configured default as a starting point, users should be supported in choosing the best fitting configuration (see e.g. [22]), or they could even profit from the approach of "on the fly" privacy management for adapting and organising their own privacy preferences [23].

Finally, data protection by default can ruffle the feathers of established Internet business models. For instance, according to Article 25 (2) GDPR user tracking on the basis of personal data (including machine identifiers) would have to be deactivated as a standard setting. This may affect the tradition of "free" services where Internet resources are paid by personal data.

6   Conclusion

The European General Data Protection Regulation contains legal provisions on data protection by design and by default. This obligation addresses data controllers who have to consider building in data protection functionality in their systems. In addition, it holds the potential of affecting the currently not well developed market in privacy and data protection systems and services. The GDPR offers the opportunity for bridging the gap between research and practice in the field of privacy and data protection.

Although not really new, both data protection by design and data protection by default are powerful mechanisms and may become a game changer if taken seriously by controllers, processors, producers, and supervisory authorities. However, employing these principles is a challenging task for all stakeholders involved and requires in-depth knowledge of research concepts and state-of-the-art implementations. So as not to negate the leverage from the GDPR, researchers, practitioners, and supervisory authorities should collaborate and propose suitable best practice approaches. It should be made difficult to ignore the laid down rules or to shirk responsibilities and obligations regarding the system design requirements. Nevertheless a broad use of data protection design methods and measures has to rely on thoroughly discussed, tested, and workable solutions. Further, infrastructures should not only realise data protection by design themselves, but also promote and support measures built on top or employing functionality offered. This will be primarily a task for the member states or the European Union.

Although the GDPR becomes effective only in May 2018, the interdisciplinary work of computer scientists, developers, lawyers, psychologists, economists etc. should begin much earlier [10]. The lack of a holistic approach for engineering and promoting privacy technologies is certainly one reason for the unsatisfactory status of their maturity and their market availability. Even good approaches can fail if the ecosystem for their usage is not sufficiently considered, business models are missing, users don't understand their value or perceive losses in comfort compared with the not-so-privacy-friendly solutions they are familiar with (see e.g. [24]). Interdisciplinary work takes time and does not happen automatically – it requires a common understanding of the problem space as well as openness for underlying incentives and values of other disciplines [25]. This includes the supervisory authorities which will have to evolve to live up the tasks they have been imposed by the GDPR and to actively seize opportunities for improving the protection of rights and freedoms of all individuals.

If recommendations and ready-to-use concepts are developed and published soon enough, this facilitates data controllers to prove their compliance with the regulation from day one and, at best, set an example of international relevance regarding data protection by design and by default. It is noteworthy that the GDPR is designed to have an influence beyond Europe because it strives to protect the personal data of EU residents even outside the European Union and obliges also non-EU controllers processing personal data in Europe. What is more, whenever successful solutions are being developed, they may be demanded by all people inside and outside Europe interested in protecting their right to privacy and may be expected especially from globally acting companies. Data protection by design and by default is of particular relevance in a world that relies increasingly on digitisation and that has to defend the rights and freedoms of individuals against attacks from powerful organisations.

Acknowledgements. Work relating to this text is partially funded by the German Ministry of Education and Research within the project "Privacy-Forum – Forum Privatheit und selbstbestimmtes Leben in der digitalen Welt (Forum Privacy and Self-determined Life in the Digital World)". For more information see: https://www.forum-privatheit.de/.

References

1. 32nd International Conference of Data Protection and Privacy Commissioners: Privacy by Design Resolution, Jerusalem, Israel, 27–29 October 2010. http://www.ipc.on.ca/site_documents/pbd-resolution.pdf
2. Roussopoulos, M., Beslay, L., Bowden, C., Finocchiaro, G., Hansen, M., Langheinrich, M., Le Grand, G., Tsakona, K.: Technology-induced challenges in privacy & data protection in Europe. Technical report. ENISA Ad Hoc Working Group on Privacy & Technology (2008). https://www.enisa.europa.eu/publications/technology-induced-challenges-in-privacy-data-protection-in-europe
3. Regulation (EU) 2016/679 of the European Parliament and of the Council of 27 April 2016 on the protection of natural persons with regard to the processing of personal data and on the free movement of such data, and repealing Directive 95/46/EC (General Data Protection Regulation). OJ L 119, 04.05.2016, pp. 1–88 (2016)
4. Directive 95/46/EC of the European Parliament and of the Council of 24 October 1995 on the protection of individuals with regard to the processing of personal data and on the free movement of such data. OJ L 281, 23.11.1995, pp. 0031–0050 (1995)
5. Roßnagel, A., Nebel, M.: Die neue Datenschutzgrundverordnung – Ist das Datenschutzrecht nun für heutige Herausforderungen gerüstet? Policy Paper, Privacy-Forum (Forum Privatheit und selbstbestimmtes Leben in der digitalen Welt) (2016). https://www.forum-privatheit.de/
6. Chaum, D.: Security without identification: transaction systems to make big brother obsolete. Commun. ACM **28**(10), 1030–1044 (1985)
7. Hes, R., Borking, J.J.: Privacy-enhancing technologies: the path to anonymity. Technical report. Registratiekamer (1995)
8. European Commission: Privacy Enhancing Technologies (PETs) – the existing legal framework. MEMO/07/159 (2007)
9. Cavoukian, A.: Privacy by Design, Take the Challenge. Information and Privacy Commissioner of Ontario, Toronto (2009)
10. Cavoukian, A.: Privacy by Design: The 7 Foundational Principles (August 2009, revised January 2011)
11. Gürses, S., Troncoso, C., Díaz, C.: Engineering privacy by design. In: Computers, Privacy & Data Protection (2011)
12. Deng, M., Wuyts, K., Scandariato, R., Preneel, B., Joosen, W.: A privacy threat analysis framework: supporting the elicitation and fulfillment of privacy requirements. Requirements Eng. J. **16**(1), 3–32 (2011)
13. Hoepman, J.-H.: Privacy design strategies (extended abstract). In: Proceedings of SEC 2014, ICT Systems Security and Privacy Protection, pp. 446–459 (2014)
14. Hansen, M., Jensen, M., Rost, M.: Protection goals for privacy engineering. In: Proceedings of the 1st International Workshop on Privacy Engineering. IEEE (2015)
15. Konferenz der unabhängigen Datenschutzbehörden des Bundes und der Länder: Das Standard-Datenschutzmodell – Eine Methode zur Datenschutzberatung und -prüfung auf der Basis einheitlicher Gewährleistungsziele (2016). https://datenschutzzentrum.de/uploads/SDM-Methode_V_1_0.pdf
16. Danezis, G., Domingo-Ferrer, J., Hansen, M., Hoepman, J.-H., Le Métayer, D., Tirtea, R., Schiffner, S.: Privacy and Data Protection by Design – from policy to engineering. Technical report. ENISA (2015). https://www.enisa.europa.eu/activities/identity-and-trust/library/deliverables/privacy-and-data-protection-by-design
17. Borking, J.J., Raab, C.D.: Laws, PETs and other technologies for privacy protection. J. Inf. Law Technol. (JILT) **1**(1), 1–14 (2001)

18. Bundesdatenschutzgesetz (BDSG). BGBl. I Nr. 3, 24.01.2003, Bonn, pp. 66–88 (2003)
19. Hansen, M., Hoepman, J.-H., Jensen, M.: Readiness analysis for the adoption and evolution of privacy enhancing technologies – methodology, pilot assessment, and continuity plan. Technical report. ENISA (2015). https://www.enisa.europa.eu/activities/identity-and-trust/ library/deliverables/pets
20. European Data Protection Supervisor: Opinion of the European Data Protection Supervisor on the data protection reform package, 7 March 2012. http://www.edps.europa.eu/ EDPSWEB/webdav/site/mySite/shared/Documents/Consultation/Opinions/ 2012/12-03-07_EDPS_Reform_package_EN.pdf
21. Hansen, M.: Data protection by default in identity-related applications. In: Fischer-Hübner, S., Leeuw, E., Mitchell, C. (eds.) IDMAN 2013. IFIP AICT, vol. 396, pp. 4–17. Springer, Heidelberg (2013). doi:10.1007/978-3-642-37282-7_2
22. Ravichandran, R., Benisch, M., Kelley, P.G., Sadeh, N.M.: Capturing social networking privacy preferences: can default policies help alleviate tradeoffs between expressiveness and user burden? In: Goldberg, I., Atallah, M.J. (eds.) PETS 2009. LNCS, vol. 5672, pp. 1–18. Springer, Heidelberg (2009). doi:10.1007/978-3-642-03168-7_1
23. Angulo, J., Fischer-Hübner, S., Wästlund, E., Pulls, T.: Towards usable privacy policy display and management. Inf. Manag. Comput. Secur. **20**(1), 4–17 (2012)
24. Harbach, M., Fahl, S., Rieger, M., Smith, M.: On the acceptance of privacy-preserving authentication technology: the curious case of national identity cards. In: Cristofaro, E., Wright, M. (eds.) PETS 2013. LNCS, vol. 7981, pp. 245–264. Springer, Heidelberg (2013). doi:10.1007/978-3-642-39077-7_13
25. Tsormpatzoudi, P., Berendt, B., Coudert, F.: Privacy by design: from research and policy to practice – the challenge of multi-disciplinarity. In: Berendt, B., Engel, T., Ikonomou, D., Le Métayer, D., Schiffner, S. (eds.) APF 2015. LNCS, vol. 9484, pp. 199–212. Springer, Heidelberg (2016). doi:10.1007/978-3-319-31456-3_12

Evaluating Websites and Their Adherence to Data Protection Principles: Tools and Experiences

Contributions to IFIP Summer School Proceedings

Amelia Andersdotter$^{(\boxtimes)}$ and Anders Jensen-Urstad$^{(\boxtimes)}$

Dataskydd.net, Alsnögatan 18, 116 41 Stockholm, Sweden
{amelia.andersdotter,anders.jensen-urstad}@dataskydd.net
https://dataskydd.net

Abstract. We present our two separate tools for data protection measurement and evaluation of websites. The first tool does a generic check on a single website and is openly available for any web user to use when evaluating data protection measures implemented on a website. The second tool was used to perform a more exhaustive evaluation of Swedish municipalities. The work focuses on leakages of personally identifiable information to third parties when a web visitor goes to a website, and in our accompanying website we have also identified measures that web developers could undertake, or that web visitors could request, to improve the data protection of their visitors.

Keywords: Privacy · Metrics · Data protection · Web tools · Guidelines · Policy procurement

1 Introduction

With the entry into effect of the new EU rules on data protection in May 2018, there is an urgent need for web developers and other actors in society to make preparations. We have developed two separate tools to identify measures which can be undertaken to improve privacy protection in public websites in Sweden. In particular, they will assist web developers and web strategists to analyse how they are currently leaking personally identifiable information (PII) to third parties, as individuals visit their websites.

Our first tool is a simple technical mechanism for private persons and web developers to evaluate the leakage of PII from websites.[1] The second tool performs more substantive measurement of PII leakage from Swedish municipal

---

A. Jensen-Urstad–Co-founders Dataskydd.net. This project was realised through the kind financial assistance provided by Internetfonden/IIS over the period January-August in 2016.

[1] *See* https://webbkoll.dataskydd.net/en/ [in English and Swedish].

A. Lehmann et al. (Eds.): Privacy and Identity 2016, IFIP AICT 498, pp. 39–51, 2016.
DOI: 10.1007/978-3-319-55783-0_4

websites.[2] In addition, we produced technical advice on how data leakage can be mitigated.[3]

We have checked the use of web analysis tools,[4] whether a referrer policy is set,[5] the usage or absence of encrypted connections as well as inclusion of third party services (fonts, forums, weather services or text-to-voice services) or the placement of cookies (both persistent tracking cookies and functional cookies).

Additionally, we provide an element of *gamification* for Swedish municipalities, in that we developed a five-step grading system. This allows for municipalities to compare their efforts to other municipalities. With current data leakage rates being generally high, we found, however, that no municipalities obtain better than mid-level results.

This study aims to achieve utility for web designers and website developers, with an emphasis on utility for public sector institutions. While there are a number of web browser plug-ins that could be installed by web visitors to mitigate harms arising from persistent online tracking,[6] this paper is guided by the belief that privacy problems can and should be solved close to the source of the problem. We believe similar methodologies and tests could also be useful in other countries, and in so far as possible we have strived to identify cost-neutral improvements.

1.1   Similar Tools in the Swedish Context

In Sweden, prior examples of web services for monitoring private and public sector compliance with applicable law include Hitta kakor[7] and extensive work in the field of accessibility [4, guideline 1].[8] More technically inspired guidelines include efforts to improve adoption rates of encrypted connections [4, guideline 7] and DNSSEC.[9]

Additionally there have been attempts in Sweden to compile guidelines for data protection on websites [4, guideline 20] and with respect to web cookies [5]. Both of these guidelines target the necessary requirements for end-user terms of service formulations given specific options implemented by the web developer.

---

[2] *See* https://dataskydd.net/kommuner/ [only in Swedish].

[3] In the right-hand column of the test-results accompanying the generic web-check on the website listed in footnote 1, or under the heading "Begrepp och tips" on the website listed in footnote 2.

[4] Google Analytics, Adobe Tealeaf, Piwik, etc.

[5] *Cf.* https://www.w3.org/TR/referrer-policy/.

[6] Some alternatives include Cookie White List, Privacy Badger, various adblocking applications (such as Adblock Plus or uBlock Origin), Ghostery, RequestPolicy, NoScript, HTTPS Everywhere, uMatrix, Disconnect, Decentraleyes, and similar. In addition to these tools web visitors may opt to use private browsing mode, which is increasingly included by default in most major browsers.

[7] PTS, http://e-tjanster.pts.se/internet/kakor/.

[8] *See also* http://www.anvandningsforum.se/om/.

[9] PTS, information webpage about ongoing work to promote DNSSEC with Swedish public authorities. https://www.pts.se/sv/Bransch/Internet/Robust-kommunikation/Atgarder/DNSSEC/.

The success rate in terms of increasing adoption rates of globally desired practises varies.

Accessibility guidelines have generally been well-received [6]. While security-oriented projects, such as the guidelines for encrypted connections and DNSSEC are ostensibly taken seriously at the national level, deployment has been slow.[10]

All of the prior guideline projects have been developed under the auspice of the Swedish national regulatory authority for telecommunications and postal services (PTS). The data protection guidelines focus on contract law, and their success rate is difficult to measure. There are no known cases where the privacy terms of a municipal website or other website have been successfully tried in court.

2   Methodology

We have constructed tests which are technically more convenient to monitor, and which assume an expansive view of the wordings of the legislation. What this means is that our technical monitoring of websites does not accomodate for flexibilities in the law to avoid certain types of data forwarding or data collection by referens to privacy terms. This is for a few reasons.

- End-users have been demonstrated not to reasonably have the time or capacity to read and understand such terms of services.[11]
- Having restricted ourselves to investigating municipalities in depth, we deemed it inappropriate to construct a set of tests which would assume the public sector should enter into extensive and difficult to understand agreements with their website visitors.
- We have assumed that it is more interesting for web developers to engage with interesting technical alternatives to monitoring and tracking over engaging with the formulation of terms of services agreements.

Instead we have focused on the ability of web developers to adhere to the data minimisation principle.[12] We have also assumed that adoption of data protection enhancing measures is more likely if website owners and managers are provided with self-measurement and top-listing tools.

---

[10] *Cf.* https://dataskydd.net/kommuner/ *and* https://www.kommunermeddnssec.se/.

[11] Aleecia M. McDonald and Lorrie Faith Cranor. The Cost of Reading Privacy Policies. I/S: A Journal of Law and Policy for the Information Society 2008 Privacy Year in Review issue *or* Lorrie F Cranor,. et al. (2014). Are they worth reading? an in-depth analysis of online advertising companies' privacy policies. Rochester, NY: Social Science Research Network *and for instance the* Terms of Service; Didn't Read (ToS;DR) project.

[12] Art 5.1 c, General Data Protection Regulation.

2.1   The Scoring System

We devised a five-step scoring system for municipalities which runs from E to A, with A being the highest and E the lowest score.[13]

A To get the highest score, a municipality should neither leak PII to third parties (Internet service providers, mobile providers, content delivery platforms, advertisers, etc.) nor collect unnecessary information for their own use. This means use of HTTPS by default, no persistent first-party cookies, no third-party requests (which implies no third-party cookies), referrer policy set to a restrictive value (i.e., *no-referrer*), setting the HTTP Strict Transport Security header (HSTS), and no insecure requests (i.e., HTTPS to HTTP).

B The second highest score relaxes the requirements for collecting PII for own, in-house use (such as a locally hosted web analysis tool). It requires HTTPS, no third-party requests, and no insecure requests.

C The middle score is obtained for those websites that either have a strong protection against PII leakage to Internet service providers (by for instance employing encrypted connections universally), or having a strong protection against PII leakage to third party web services (content delivery platforms, advertisement networks, web analysis tools, etc.): HTTPS, third-party requests (but none insecure) and third-party cookies *or* HTTP and no third-party requests. 20 municipalities out of 289 acquired this score in our latest test on August 20th 2016.[14] This can be compared with 16 municipalities obtaining this score in May of 2016.[15]

D The second lowest score is obtained from having partially encrypted connections (with insecure elements loaded in the visitor's browser) and making third-party requests and setting third-party cookies, *or* from using HTTP but not setting third-party cookies. 64 municipalities ended up with this score in our latest test on August 20th 2016. Two municipalities had shifted from a C score in our May 2016 test to a D score in the August 2016 test, after introducing non-encrypted elements on their websites.

E The lowest score, then, is when there are no data leakage protections in place: no encryption, and use of third-party cookies. In our August 2016 test, most municipalities (204 out of 289) ended up with this score.

While the scoring system is simple, we have tried not to make it biased towards any particular form of protection against PII leakage. It is, for instance, possible to get at most a C grade without using encrypted connections, but it is not possible to advance beyond a C grade without also remedying PII leakage to third parties. We chose this methodology to ensure that privacy is protected against electronic communications services as well as information society services.

Since we finalised the beta version of our in-depth tool in May 2016, we have produced scores for all Swedish municipalities on three subsequent occasions.

---

[13] *See* https://dataskydd.net/kommuner/metodologi.html.

[14] *See* https://dataskydd.net/kommuner-201608.

[15] *See* https://dataskydd.net/kommuner-201605.

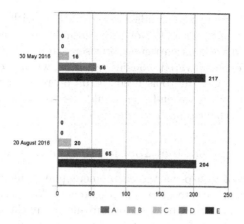

Fig. 1. Distribution of grades assigned by our tool for substantive measurement for all Swedish municipalities in two separate test runs performed on May 30th 2016 and August 20th 2016.

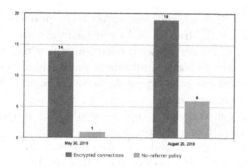

Fig. 2. Number of municipalities which have adopted encrypted connections and protection against referrer-leaks in May 30th 2016 and August 20th 2016 respectively. The total number of municipalities tested amounted to 290.

The last scores, produced in November 2016, are not accounted for in this text but are available online.[16] In Figs. 1 and 2 you will find comparisons of scores between May and August of 2016.

3   Technical Design

We made two tools: a generic tool for privacy checks for individuals (a web service), "Webbkoll",[17] and a more sophisticated tool for checking municipality websites (not a publicly available service).[18]

---

[16] *See* https://dataskydd.net/kommuner.
[17] *Supra*, footnote 1.
[18] *Supra*, footnote 2.

In both cases we attempt to simulate a typical user with a typical browser with default settings – e.g., with Do Not Track disabled, as that is normally the browser default – and with no particular browser extensions installed, and see what happens (requests generated, cookies set, etc.) when a certain web page is visited. This means that the tools need to run a "real", normal browser, or something as close to what an end-user would use as possible, ruling out for example web scrapers that do not execute JavaScript.

3.1   Generic Check: Choice of Tool for Backend/Frontend

There are a number of web privacy measurement platforms available, but the ones we found were all targeted towards researchers. We wanted to provide a simple web service that could be used by anyone to quickly check any given website, without having to install anything. There are numerous online services for checking various other aspects of websites – e.g., SSL/TLS configuration,[19] HTTP headers,[20] performance[21] – but we found none for generic privacy checks.

Technical Choices. Since our tool was meant to be publicly available (as well as completely open source)[22] free to use by anyone at any time, and operated by ourselves on a typical Linux server, we needed something that (1) could process requests quickly, (2) could process multiple requests simultaneously, (3) could easily scale, (4) could be run on a typical low-cost VPS, and (5) would be built purely on open source components.

This called for a typical design where we would have a user-facing frontend server communicating with one or more separate backend servers (which in turn perform the actual visiting and rendering of webpages) through a REST API.

The most resource-intensive part of the infrastructure is the backend. We considered running a "real" consumer browser such as Firefox through the Selenium framework (as in [1]), but found that the overhead was too great. It should be noted that while Selenium offers more possibilities and a more stable environment, this was less of a concern here than in our later municipality test. Our online tool is not meant to be used for studies or rigorous analysis, but rather as a starting point for web developers and web visitors. Therefore we opted for "good enough" with our choice falling on PhantomJS,[23] a lightweight headless browser based on WebKit (also used by Safari; and a fork of WebKit is used by Chrome).

Deployment. The frontend is written in Elixir, a functional language running on the Erlang VM, and uses the Phoenix web framework. When visiting the

---

[19] Qualys SSL Labs SSL Server Test. https://www.ssllabs.com/ssltest/.

[20] Securityheaders.io. https://securityheaders.io/.

[21] Sitespeed.io (https://www.sitespeed.io/), Google's PageSpeed Tools (https://developers.google.com/speed/pagespeed/).

[22] By grant condition. Code (MIT license): https://github.com/andersju/webbkoll.

[23] *See* http://phantomjs.org/.

website of the tool the user is presented with a single text form field for entering the domain name or URL of any web page. When the "Check" button is clicked, the frontend does a number of things:

(1) It checks whether the user is possibly a bot, and if so, rejects the request.
(2) It makes sure the input is transformed into a proper URL – e.g., example.com becomes `http://example.com`. Since we check whether a site uses HTTPS by default, we always check the `http://` version of a site first to see whether it redirects automatically; so `https://example.com` is transformed into `http://example.com`. It is possible to visit specific pages on a domain (e.g., `http://example.com/subpage.html`); we keep the path (`/subpage.html`) but, for security reasons, no query parameters nor anything else. An input of `http://user:password@example.com/subpage.html?foo=bar` would be transformed into `http://example.com/subpage.html` before being passed on.
(3) If the URL resulting from (2) has already been checked and is in the database, the old data is fetched and rendered. If the URL is not in the database, or if it is in the database but the user has clicked "Check again", we force a new check, and the frontend proceeds to (4).
(4) To prevent abuse, it does some basic rate limiting: per IP (a user can only make a certain number of requests during a certain span of time) and per host (a certain host can only be queried a certain number of times during a certain span of time – this is not user-specific). If either criteria is violated, an error is returned.

Finally, if steps 1–5 completed successfully, the user's request is sent to a queue in the job handler – also on the frontend – for background processing (this handles concurrency, retries, queueing, etc.). To allow for multiple backend servers, multiple queues, each having a certain backend URL tied to it, can be specified.

The job handler runs a worker to handle the user's request. The worker sends a HTTP GET request to the backend server. This request contains the URL of the webpage to visit.

The backend server runs PhearJS,[24] a server written with Node.js, handling a number of PhantomJS workers. When PhearJS receives a request from the frontend, it's passed on to one of the workers. The PhantomJS workers visits the URL and renders it, waiting a specified period of time – in our case, ten seconds – before returning the results. This is to make sure scripts have time to run. When finished, the resulting data is sent back as JSON to the frontend. This JSON contains all the request and response headers, cookies, HTML content, etc.

The JSON is decoded by the worker process and checked for errors. The worker then proceeds with processing of the data:

---

[24] *See* https://github.com/Tomtomgo/phearjs.

(1) The final URL is noted. This is the actual page rendered, after any redirects.

(2) From the final URL the registerable domain is extracted and noted with the help of a library that uses Mozilla's Public Suffix List.[25] This list is used by browsers to determine where cookies can be set (or not), and we use it to distinguish between first-party and third-party sites.

(3) Cookies are split into first-party and third-party. We also count the number of unique third-party cookie domains.

(4) From requests, third-party requests and insecure first-party requests are extracted. Request types (secure vs. insecure) are counted.

(5) Using a HTML parser we check whether a referrer policy is set using meta referrer (a referrer policy can also be set in a Content-Security-Policy header; this is checked at a later point).

All the above is saved to the database and the status of the user's request is updated.

Meanwhile, the user is redirected to a status page where the ID of the request is in the URL. The page is reloaded automatically every five seconds using meta refresh. On every request the frontend checks the status of the page in the database—if state has changed, the user is redirected to a results or error page, otherwise the status page is shown again. While there are smoother ways to present status and do transitions, this way we avoid having to use cookies.

Finally, the user is presented with a results page. It shows the following (Fig. 3):

- Whether HTTPS is used by default; and, if so, whether the site uses HTTP Strict Transport Security, and whether there are any insecure requests.
- Whether referrers are leaked.
- First-party cookies.
- Third-party cookies.
- Third-party requests, categorized using Disconnect's public tracker list.
- Certain HTTP headers that can be beneficial for privacy and security: Content-Security-Policy, Strict-Transport-Security, Public-Key-Pins, X-Content-Type-Options, X-Frame-Options, X-Xss-Protection.

We also explain what these things are and what one can do and why. Additionally, we check for certain third-party services (such as Google Analytics and Disqus) and suggest alternatives.

Limitations. The tool is limited to what can be checked non-interactively, i.e., things that can be observed by merely loading the page – it does not perform any actions such as clicking on links.

Except for rejecting sites with invalid certificates (and checking the headers for HSTS and Public Key Pinning), it does not do any deep analysis of a site's SSL/TLS configuration – e.g., vulnerability to various attacks, forward secrecy,

---

[25] *See* https://publicsuffix.org/.

Fig. 3. Screenshot of part of results page for regeringen.se, the website of the Government Offices of Sweden.

support for insecure protocols, etc. Currently we provide a link to Qualys SSL Labs free online service.

At first some of the tools used did not have all the necessary functionality for our purposes. We contributed some code to PhearJS to add support for returning cookies and requests,[26] and to the Elixir library PublicSuffix to add support for checking whether a domain matches a specific rule in Mozilla's Public Suffix List.[27]

3.2 Municipalities: Choice of Tool for Backend/Frontend

Technical Choices. Although we had already created our online tool "Webbkoll", we opted for the web privacy measurement framework OpenWPM [1] for our municipality study. Our online tool was meant to be used by web developers and others to quickly check a website and gain ideas about possible improvements, while OpenWPM was built specifically for collecting data for privacy studies and supported more features, such as the ability to visit internal links.

Deployment. We fed a list of the websites of Sweden's 290 municipalities into OpenWPM. OpenWPM – which uses Firefox, Selenium and a HTTP proxy – then visited each site and tried to visit up to five internal links. Firefox was configured to run without any particular extensions installed, and with Do Not Track disabled. All data (all HTTP requests and responses, cookies, etc.) was saved to a SQLite database.

We then wrote a program to enrich the database, mainly using information already contained therein, but made more easily accessible to make it easier to produce statistics and (at a later stage with the same program) generate the reports pages.[28] For example, the http_requests table was extended with

---

[26] https://github.com/Tomtomgo/phearjs/pull/5.
[27] https://github.com/seomoz/publicsuffix-elixir/pull/17.
[28] Code (MIT license): https://github.com/andersju/municipality-privacy.

columns for base_domain (shortest domain assigned to a registrant; used to determine first-party vs. third-party cookies/requests) and scheme (HTTP or HTTPS); site_visits was extended was extended with e.g. HSTS value, referrer policy, third-party requests, insecure requests and multiple columns for cookies (first-party and third-party profile and session cookies). Each municipality was also scored using the criteria mentioned in Sect. 2.1.

It should be noted that the results for a municipality are based not on a single page, but on the collected data from the initial page plus up to five internal pages.

In our setup OpenWPM did not save the HTML content of pages. As referrer policy can be set in both a HTTP header and in a HTML meta element, we let our post-processing tool visit the initial URL of each municipality website, get and parse the HTML and look for meta referrer.

Finally, our tool generated a static website with (1) an overview with a table containing all municipalities, sortable by score/scheme/referrer leakage/number of cookies/etc., and (2) a detailed results page for each municipality, much like the results pages produced by our web service Webbkoll.

Limitations. While we did visit a number of internal links in this test, we are limited by what can be done in an automated fashion when we have no prior knowledge of the sites being visited. The internal links are chosen at random, and at the moment we cannot check whether it is, for example, possible to contact one's municipality in a secure way.

The browse command in OpenWPM 0.6.2 loads a specified URL and then tries to visit a specified number of internal links (from the same hostname as the URL) on the initial page. However, we found that no internal links were visited if the initial URL was a redirect; we thus had to use curl and a few command-line tools to process the list of municipality websites, figure out the final URL of each website, and then write those URLs to a new file that we then used as input to OpenWPM.

We found a bug that in rare instances would make OpenWPM treat external links as internal. This was reported and fixed.

4   Discussion

The following chapter is based on structured interviews with employees from the Swedish public sector as well as interactions with such employees that we have had since the beginning of our project. These interviews and interactions were, however, conditioned on anonymity of the individual civil servants concerned.

4.1   The Municipality of Enköping

We were in touch with civil servants working in the Swedish medium-sized municipality Enköping [7] since before we started our project. The municipality was, and still is, in the process of refurbishing their public-facing web environment.

The municipality lacked prior guidelines for web development beyond graphical profiles at the start of the project. The changes in the website could therefore be planned freely by responsible staff. While responsible staff had support for a data protection friendly shift from their immediate superiors in the hierarchy (the communications department), interest was more shallow in the municipal IT department. The data protection focus did, however, receive attention from the highest publicly elected official in the municipality when the new website was launched.

The focus on data protection in the development of the new website emerged only after the initial steps to change the website had already been taken [2]. Because of this, specifications which would have been useful to integrate at an earlier stage had to be appended to the specification afterwards (such as removing referrer leaks and using local analytics tools). This caused additional costs for the municipality (a one-time fee of approximately EUR 2000 for the Piwik server). While this is not a large sum, a continuing problem is the lack of qualified Piwik administrators available from subcontractors. Access to third party analytics specialists is simply higher, making it more time- and cost-efficient to use third party analytics tools.

In November 2016, the municipality has still not crossed the TLS hurdle in spite of having a pre-existing cryptographic certificate which was valid across all the municipality's domains when we first got in touch with them. The provision of municipal maps stopped working when TLS was turned on, but there is ongoing work to fix this problem. Changes in staff in summer of 2016 means that many of the planned changed are stuck, while new staff get accustomed to the work environment. The municipality is still not able to obtain a higher grade than D in the Dataskydd.net privacy web check tool.

4.2 Other Municipalities

After launching our municipal top list, we have noticed that more municipalities are adopting the use of referrer policy. We have also had questions from municipalities about the use of encryption.

For instance, it is still the case that some web developers fear that encryption may reduce the availability of the site (for instance, making it slower to load and requiring more server resources). While this is not supported in practical knowledge,[29] and in fact HTTP/2—which brings superior performance—in practice *requires* the use of encryption as no major browser supports unencrypted HTTP/2, it's a legacy concern that is likely to remain for some time.

Additionally, and as with many things that may require alterations in current work flows or technical tools, we have noticed that municipalities that are refurbishing their public web environments with data protection enhancements are likely to be concerned that the data protection enhancements are the cause of problems. For instance, use of referrer policy may get the blame for broken

---

[29] https://www.maxcdn.com/blog/ssl-performance-myth/.

links even if, upon careful analysis, it turns out not to have been the problem. Other questions that have emerged are covered above in Sects. 3.1 and 3.2.

4.3 Analysis

The experiences of Enköping indicates that a data protection focus becomes both cheaper and quicker if integrated from the beginning. This provides support for the utility of data protection by design.

One municipal employee indicated that it would be helpful if some form of procedural standard was developed, equivalent to the standards for web site accessibility which have just been adopted in European law [3].

It may be assumed that the prevalence of non-third party analytics tool specialists increases if the demand for such services increase. The municipality staff also experienced that the most frequent questions they would face from other municipalities related to their experiences of Piwik. A detailed analysis of municipality websites indicates that Enköping is not alone in trying out self-hosted alternatives to Google Analytics.[30]

The environment for making changes will differ between municipalities. While Enköping experienced significant delays in ordering and installing Piwik servers and a low degree of interest in data protection from their IT department,[31] in other municipalities it is the IT department which is responsible for the design and features of the website.[32]

We have not received any feedback from private persons who've tried to use our tool to inspire changes in websites that they themselves did not manage.

5 Conclusions

Many of the tools under development for privacy measurement are primarily used to investigate large numbers of the most popular websites. Our work has focused on a minor subset of websites, those of Swedish municipalities, which were unlikely to be the most visited.

While our goal was to make cost-neutral suggestions for improvements in so far as possible, we found out that even nominally free ("gratuite") products or simple changes in the specifications for a municipal website may imply significant enough costs to the municipality that many parts of the municipal administration must be involved in enacting change. The experience of Enköping is that it is doable, but requires considerable effort from responsible civil servants.

The observations from the municipal civil servants are straight-forward, for instance requesting a guideline for data protection friendly developments. But such guidelines are unlikely to be adopted without significant effort. The tools we developed are not designed to make use of flexibilities in the data protection

---

[30] Alingsås, Arvika, Örnsköldsvik, as per Dataskydd.net:s municipal mapping 20th August 2016 (cf. footnote 16).

[31] Informal dialogue with municipal civil servant in Enköping.

[32] Informal dialogues with municipal civil servants in other cities.

laws, but to provide simple and cheap means to maximise adherence to the principles enshrined in the General Data Protection Regulation Art. 5.

Some of our suggestions are more likely to be adopted than others: the number of Swedish municipalities using encrypted connections is increasing, as is the number of Swedish municipalities that introduce a referrer policy. We also believe that adoption of alternative analytics tools will increase, but this will depend on a few front-runners creating a demand for alternative analytics expertise.

We hope that our effort provide a humble starting point for future projects seeking to make data protection by default a feasible option for web developers.

References

1. Englehardt, S., Narayanan, A.: Online tracking: a 1-million-site measurement and analysis. In: Proceedings of ACM CCS (2016). doi:http://dx.doi.org/10.1145/2976749.2978313
2. Enköpings kommun, Förstudie ny webbnärvaro för Enköpings kommun, 10 April 2014. http://blogg.enkoping.se/webbutveckling/wp-content/uploads/sites/3/2014/04/enkoping-forstudie-nywebb.pdf
3. EU Commission, Statement by Vice-President Ansip and Commissioner Oettinger welcoming the adoption of the first EU-wide rules to make public sector websites and apps more accessible. http://europa.eu/rapid/press-release_STATEMENT-16-3549_en.htm
4. PTS, Vägledning för webbutveckling. https://webbriktlinjer.se
5. PTS, Faktablad - Cookies och lagen om elektronisk kommunikation - PTS-F-2005:2. http://www.pts.se/upload/Documents/SE/Faktablad_Cookies_PTS_F_2005_2.pdf
6. PTS, På väg mot användbar IKT PTS slutredovisning av myndighetens delmål inom ramen för regeringens strategi för genomförande av funktionshinderspolitiken 2011–2016, PTS-ER-2016:19. https://www.pts.se/upload/Documents/SE/Dokument%20funk/160311_PTS%20slutrapport%20uppf%C3%B6ljning%20delm%C3%A5l.pdf
7. Sveriges kommuner och landsting, Kommungruppsindelning (2011). http://skl.se/download/18.5e95253d14642b207ee86e1f/1402935660165/SKL-rapport-kommungruppsindelning+2011_101020.pdf

Privacy in the Human Brain Project:
The Perspective of Ethics Management

Bernd Carsten Stahl[✉]

De Montfort University, Leicester, UK
bstahl@dmu.ac.uk

Abstract. The paper describes the ethics management function of the human brain project. It highlights some of the specific privacy-related issues of the project and the strategies that ethics management uses to address these.

Keywords: Human brain project · Neuroinformatics · Data protection · Privacy · Ethics management

The Human Brain Project (HBP; www.humanbrainproject.eu) is a European, Flagship initiative that facilitates and supports a global, united effort to understand the brain by providing platforms and tools along with neuroscientific and medical data, to study the brain, its diseases and to catalyze new brain-inspired technologies [1].

The HBP aims to create and operate a European scientific research infrastructure for brain research, cognitive neuroscience and other brain-inspired sciences. It gathers, organizes and disseminates data describing the brain and its diseases. Of particular importance for us is the stated aim that the **HBP is dedicated to responsible and ethical research.** In addition, the HBP is an extensive collaboration between scientists, researchers and institutions around the world. This includes is nature as an open-science initiative. The HBP is developing Information Communication (ICT) Tools that have applications in neuroscience, medicine and computing.

It is important to underline that the focus on responsible research and innovation (RRI) figures prominently among the aims of the project. This is explained by the fact that the project's funder, the European Commission, is keen to promote RRI in research [2–4]. At the same time, the HBP raises a number of potential ethical and issues, ranging from the immediate and practical, like the approval of research protocols, to the more general and philosophical, like the possibility of machine consciousness or novel approaches to artificial intelligence (AI).

In order to address these issues, the HBP has a sub-project dedicated to ethics and society. The overall HBP is split in 12 sub-projects which are the organizational home to scientific, technical and administrative activities. The society and ethics sub-project, the home of RRI in the project, is divided into four sections which look at foresight research, conceptual and philosophical analysis, public engagement and ethics management [5]. This abstract highlights the role of privacy and data protection in ethics management.

A. Lehmann et al. (Eds.): Privacy and Identity 2016, IFIP AICT 498, pp. 52–55, 2016.
DOI: 10.1007/978-3-319-55783-0_5

Ethics management is broken down into several tasks. It covers principles and implementation of ethics management, which includes the development and maintenance of an overview of ethical issues called the HBP Ethics Map (https://www.human-brainproject.eu/ethics-management). Working with other sections of the society and ethics sub-project as well as the scientists of the scientific and technical sub-projects, the ethics management team develops bespoke ethics issue action plans. It develops Standard Operating Procedures (SOPs) and undertakes the identification and management triage of ethical issues. In order to ensure that all work in the HBP happens in accordance with laws and regulations, the ethics compliance task maintains an HBP Ethics Registry which contains an overview of the ethical issues of all other tasks and a collection of ethics approvals of those tasks that require them. Ethics management communicates with the European Commission and its ethics reviewers in the context of regular ethics reviews. In order to have an understanding of specific issues, the ethics management group manages a so-called Rapporteur Programme which includes representatives of all other 11 sub-projects. These rapporteurs are scientists from all areas of the HBP who spend a portion of their time working on issues of RRI. This includes physical meetings, teleconferences and interaction with members of the Ethics Advisory Board, which made up of independent experts who provide advice to the HBP.

Privacy is a key issue that the HBP has to address. There are different types of human data that are potentially affected by data protection regulation and therefore subject to scrutiny during ethics review. This refers to research data that was collected from human volunteers as well as patient data. For volunteer data the processes of collecting informed consent are fairly well established which links to the possibility of using the data for research purposes. The use of patient data raises bigger obstacles. The medical informatics platform, one of the HBP sub-projects which aims to gain neuroscientific insights by mining patient data has therefore developed a complex process to allow querying patient data which is held by partner hospitals. This includes several steps of de-identification, anonymisation and aggregation of the data in order to ensure that no personally identifiable information is used. While these aspects are concerned with complying with data protection legislation, including the incoming European data protection regulation, privacy concerns in the HBP go beyond such reactive measures. The HBP strives to establish good practice in the data governance of big neuroscience and aims to put in place ideas of broader data stewardship. The ethics management function plays a central role in this.

Ethics management operates according to the principle of subsidiarity, which means that the responsibility for appropriately dealing with ethical issues remains with the local Principal Investigator. Ethics management supports these PIs and collects approvals. Most importantly, ethics management works with all stakeholders involved (researchers, ethics reviewers, EC, Ethics Advisory Board) to find ways of appropriate dealing with ethical issues. In this way ethics management seeks to develop good practice for managing ethics in large data-drive biomedical research.

Compliance management follows categorisation of ethical issues as described the Horizon 2020 ethics self-assessment manual. During the ramp-up phase, the first phase of the project which lasted from October 2013 to March 2016 the following approvals were collected: 19 "animals" 25 "Humans", 1 "Human Cells/tissues", 1 "None" (retained because of general relevance). It was interesting that no issue was collected under the heading of "privacy". This is not because of a lack of privacy-related issues, but because they generally fell under human research with privacy being only one aspect of the complex ethical issues.

In fact, privacy was recognised as a key issue in the HBP and, as a consequence, the ethics and society sub-project, together with the Ethics Advisory Board wrote an Opinion on Data Protection[1]. This was based on work undertaken in all sections of ethics and society as well as prior work of several EAB members. This Opinion made the following recommendations.

- Create coherent data governance
  - Nominate individual responsible for data
  - Set up data governance committee
  - Include stakeholders and general public
  - Establish PIA and data audit
  - Ensure data stewardship
- Adopt privacy model

The ethics management team is in the process of turning these recommendations into practice. Due to the size and complexity of the project this is not a trivial exercise. The chosen approach is therefore to develop what we call an ethics issue action plan. This is a document that lists all the requirements and suggest possible ways of addressing them. It is developed by the ethics management team and then discussed with the various stakeholders. At the time of writing (January 2017) an internal meeting is being planned to discuss the different measures which include technical measures, implementation of privacy impact assessments, the appointment of a data protection officer and stakeholder engagement with a view to ensuring that the measures are consistent, realistic and fit for purpose.

Ethics management is well placed for such a task, given its prior engagement with all HBP stakeholders. One key insight arising from this work is that privacy and data protection is an important issue, but it is by no means the only one. Different ethical and social issues intersect and privacy issues tend to overlap with other issues in a complex mixture of interests. It is important to create structures that can deal with these issues and that have the potential to react to external developments and learn from mistakes. Ethics management is one such structure that will help the HBP successfully deal with privacy and data protection.

Acknowledgements. This project has received funding from the European Union's Horizon 2020 research and innovation programme under grant agreement No. 720270 (HBP SGA1).

---

[1] Available at: https://www.humanbrainproject.eu/documents/10180/1384155/EthicsandSocie-tyOpinionDataProtectionandPrivacy.pdf/3612d948-fc33-4e57-baf3-a9cfe2cd673c, accessed 10.01.2017.

References

1. Amunts, K., Ebell, C., Muller, J., Telefont, M., Knoll, A., Lippert, T.: The human brain project: creating a european research infrastructure to decode the human brain. Neuron **92**, 574–581 (2016)
2. European Commission: Responsible Research and Innovation - Europe's ability to respond to societal challenges. European Commission, Publications Office, Brussels (2012)
3. Owen, R., Heintz, M., Bessant, J. (eds.): Responsible Innovation. Wiley, Hoboken (2013)
4. Stilgoe, J., Owen, R., Macnaghten, P.: Developing a framework for responsible innovation. Res. Policy **42**, 1568–1580 (2013)
5. Evers, K.: The contribution of neuroethics to international brain research initiatives. Nat. Rev. Neurosci. **18**, 1–2 (2016)

Workshop Papers

Smart Cars Cruising on the Road Paved with Good Intentions? – Workshop on Big Data Applications and Individual Rights Under the New European General Data Protection Regulation

Felix Bieker[1], Barbara Büttner[2], and Murat Karaboga[3(✉)]

[1] Unabhängiges Landeszentrum für Datenschutz (ULD, Independent Centre for Privacy Protection) Schleswig-Holstein, Kiel, Germany
fbieker@datenschutzzentrum.de
[2] Department of Sociology, University of Kassel, Kassel, Germany
barbara.buettner@uni-kassel.de
[3] Fraunhofer Institute for Systems and Innovation Research ISI, Karlsruhe, Germany
murat.karaboga@isi.fraunhofer.de

Abstract. In this workshop we addressed the protection of individuals in the EU General Data Protection Regulation with regard to threats posed by big data applications. Using smart cars as an example, the workshop focused on the individuals' rights under the new Regulation. After an introduction to these topics, participants were invited to discuss these issues in groups and draw general conclusions on the effectiveness of the rights for individuals under the General Data Protection Regulation.

Keywords: Smart cars · Individual rights · Big data · General Data Protection Regulation · EU law

1 Introduction

After years of political struggle, the General Data Protection Regulation (GDPR) has finally been adopted. Ever since the reform process was announced, questions arose on whether and to what extent the regulation would address the requirements of emerging technologies and applications. Among these, the topic of big data and its implications for data protection were particularly contentious.

The purpose of this workshop was to analyse the effectiveness of the protection of individuals under the new European General Data Protection Regulation, which implements the fundamental rights to private life and the protection of personal data, with regard to big data applications. In order to introduce participants to this complex issue

This work is partially founded by the German Ministry of Education and Research within the project 'Forum Privacy and Self-determined Life in the Digital World'.

A. Lehmann et al. (Eds.): Privacy and Identity 2016, IFIP AICT 498, pp. 59–75, 2016.
DOI: 10.1007/978-3-319-55783-0_6

and to provide a basis for the discussion, we focused on one specific case of big data applications, namely smart cars. The ultimate goal of the workshop was a contribution to the question how personal data protection should be regulated in order to address the privacy challenges of big data applications while still preserving its benefits.

In the following we will give a short introduction to smart cars in the context of Big Data applications and their potential threats (Sect. 2). We will then show how the EU data protection law protects individual rights (Sect. 3). The next section presents the five smart car scenarios of the workshop and the discussion of the participants (Sect. 4). We will discuss the results of the workshop (Sect. 5), ending with a final conclusion (Sect. 6).

2   Smart Cars and Big Data

The use of computerized systems in cars is not new. Features for safety or driver assistance began appearing in the 1970s with the anti-lock braking system (ABS) followed by the electronic stability program (ESP) and the standardization of on-board diagnostics (OBD) in the 1990s. These systems were already able to collect data and process this information to check the performance of various car systems (e.g. emission control; early warning of malfunctions by way of the dashboard "Check Engine" light). Since then, numerous additional in-car technologies like event data recorders (EDRs) or OBD-II standards were developed and are fitted almost as standard nowadays. Connectivity often complements these existing in-car technologies and also maximizes the data collection capabilities of a car [1, 2].

2.1   What Is Connectivity of Smart Cars?

The connectivity of smart cars refers to their ability to exchange information between the car and its surroundings. It can be differentiated between the data collected and stored inside the car which is only accessible through a physical connection and data that are transmitted. The interactions range from car to car, car to infrastructure, car to devices up to car to service providers and manufactures, usually referred to as car2x connectivity. Thus, connectivity describes the digital exchange between cars. The idea behind the concept is to send relevant traffic or road information to other cars around. The car can also communicate with the infrastructure and receive information about road conditions (e.g. construction sites) or other external objects (e.g. traffic lights or traffic signs). Furthermore, cars can set up a wireless connection to other devices, for instance helping the driver to navigate. Moreover, the car can connect with service providers and manufactures and send errors reports or get a reminder for the next check-up [2–4]. Consequently, car2x connectivity produces a vast amount of data and exacerbates the issue of data collection.

2.2   Which Data Are Collected?

Typically, three groups of collected data can be differentiated: data of the car, data of the car occupants and data about the environment of the car.

Car. Every car has several identifiers which are transferred with every communication of the respective device. This can include the vehicle identification number (VIN), mobile device identifiers, SIM-cards, media access control (MAC) addresses, Bluetooth identifiers and radio frequency identification (RFID). The so called telematics data of a car include information on the location and changes of the location (e.g. geo tracking data, route, speed). Telematics can be compared to a black box that records information about the driving behaviour on how, when and where a person drives. Cars are also equipped with many sensors which collect the operational state and functionality of the single components during the drive (inter alia the engine, gear, brakes, tire pressure, fumes). In addition cars can be equipped with event data recorders (EDRs). They collect data shortly before, during and after a car accident and, for instance, store the direction of movement, longitudinal acceleration or the status of the brakes [1, 5, 6].

Occupants. The car also collects a multitude of information referring directly to the occupants of a car. Using the connected components of the car for example requires registration with the provider (car manufacturer) and the creation of a user account. For registration, data such as name, address or date of purchase can be required. Additionally internal sensors might obtain information about the physical or biological characteristics using biometric detection systems to identify the driver. The car can keep personalized information about the voice or data communication from text messages and remember habits of the driver, for instance music choice or seat and mirror position. The car might even be able to test the physical fitness of the driver by analysing the heartbeat, breathing or head- and eye-movement [1, 6].

Environment. The car also collects information about its environment, be it the physical surrounding or the human environment. This includes information about upcoming obstacles, blind spots, traffic sign analysis or even the social network of the driver. Including, for example, if drivers connect their phone with the car, it might gain access to their address book. Smart cars can also function as Wi-Fi-Hotpots and through this, collect the identification and use data of other devices and their users and owners [1, 2].

Although many of the collected data are not directly linked to a person, in many cases personal details can be revealed through other information (e.g. workplace information through geo tracking data). From a legal point of view, personal data are any information that relate to an identified or identifiable natural person according to Article 4(1) GDPR. Under this legal definition, a person is identifiable when he or she can be identified by reference to an identifier such as name, an identification number, location data or one or more factors specific to inter alia the physical, genetic, economic or cultural identity of the natural person in question. As smart cars use several identifiers for communications, these, in consequence, constitute personal data [1, 7]. Furthermore, the combined analysis of several attributes, which by themselves do not make a person identifiable, can turn the information in question into personal data [1]. This is especially true where location data, as explicitly referenced in Article 4(1) GDPR, are used.

These types of data collected and the purposes of use receive new dynamism in the context of modern technologies of data collection and processing that can be subsumed under the term of big data which will be the topic of the next section.

2.3 What Is Big Data?

Big data is a controversial buzzword which is used by a variety of stakeholders (e.g. private sector, public sector, science, and press and media) to characterize modern tendencies of data collection and processing in the networked, digitized, information-driven world. It is not a precise scientific concept, but rather a highly contested idea that differs depending on the context [8].

Although there is no uniform definition of big data, many definitions revolve around an understanding which involves three major aspects of the phenomenon: *volume*, *variety*, and *velocity*, with *volume* referring to the vast amounts of data that are being generated and accumulated, *variety* referring to the different types of data and data sources that are brought together, and *velocity* referring to the ability of real time analyses based on elaborate algorithms, machine learning and statistic correlations. Over the time, the three V's were expanded to cover other important aspects, including particularly: *veracity* and *value*. The former refers to the correctness and accuracy of information, the latter to the assessment of the societal *value*, big data analyses may or may not offer [9–11].

The types of data included in big data analyses might comprise any type of structured or unstructured (text, image, audio, or video) data. These data might be collected from public datasets (e.g. administrative data and statistics about populations, geography, economic indicators, education etc.), from businesses, web pages, newspapers, emails, online search indexes, and social media, or from any kind of sensors (mobile, such as sensors carried on the body or drones as well as stationary sensors such as CCTVs or Wi-Fi/Bluetooth beacons) [12].

Big data analyses are used for several purposes that can be grouped under the terms of descriptive statistics and inductive statistics. The former relates to big data analyses that are based on the elaborate analysis of data sets with high information density to measure things, or to detect trends. The latter relates to the analysis of large data sets with low information density in order to reveal relationships and dependencies, and to predict outcomes and behaviour. However, one important characteristic of big data that spans all areas of application is that its analyses are not limited to specific purposes. Instead, the continuous analysis of data is supposed to generate new purposes for which the existing data can be used [13].

As a result, many observers agree that big data is a disruptive technology with possible implications for all economic and policy areas (transport, energy, education, security, health, research, taxation, etc.) and that it represents a particularly weighty shift that will affect society as a whole [12, 14, 15].

2.4   Who Profits from These Data?

Regarding smart cars, many promises are made to the public about the potential benefits of big data.

Users. New technologies in cars promise drivers advances in safety and convenience. Through intense car2x communication and background analyses of the collected data, the prevention of accidents and better traffic management (better traffic light control, avoidance of traffic jams, and so on), indications of discounts (special deals at a nearby petrol station, or restaurant, etc.) and many more potential benefits are promised not only to allow more secure travelling, but also to return monetary benefits to the car owners, allow more comfort and at the same time being less damaging to the environment [16, 17].

The State. Big data opens new prospects of control for the state. Courts, financial authorities and law enforcement agencies could use the generated data for purposes of criminal prosecution, hazard prevention or the collection of public revenue. Very similar to how many other big data applications are framed, smart mobility concepts focus on emphasizing the societal surplus promised. Such promises include that traffic controls enhanced by big data analytics will be more economic, ecological, efficient, cost-effective, comfortable and secure. This may be achieved by an array of sensors that are spread all over a city and which allow the continuous collection of various data [16, 17]. In the meantime, many cities around the world have already introduced smart city concepts to innovate and enhance city life through lower costs and less environmental pollution. These concepts, however, vary in scope and depth and range from pioneering cities such as Stockholm and Amsterdam which rely on individual agencies or research bodies to comprehensively networked and highly centralized smart cities such as Singapore [18, 19]. For many years, the rise in the numbers of cars caused problems regarding the maintenance and expansion of city infrastructures, especially regarding automobile traffic. In times of strict budgets, municipalities and government agencies welcome these new opportunities as means of a more cost-effective and ecologically sound urban infrastructure and land use planning.

Industry. The interrelation of big data applications and smart cars needs to be understood in the broader context of digitized, networked, sensor-laden environments. Therefore, the development of smart car services should not only be understood in the isolated context of catchwords such as smart mobility and smart traffic controls. Rather, the whole environment, including all its artefacts such as infrastructures, buildings and inhabitants, should be regarded as both the provider of data and user of data-driven analyses [17]. The main interest of the industry lies in the monetarization of the data that is generated in such environments either to improve their current business or to develop new business models. Manufacturers and garages can use the car's diagnostic and performance information to improve their products or develop new business models (e.g. customer relations management, marketing and after-sales services). The use of data surfaces also offers new business fields like traffic information, fuel price data banks, driver-apps, or hotel booking systems. Service providers might offer real time navigation or maintenance services based on telematics. Also, the advertising industry can profit from the vast amounts of data and initiate personalized advertising. Insurance companies may offer their customers personalized insurance rates based on their tracked individual driving behaviour [2, 20–22].

2.5 Potential Risks

The generated data offer a variety of information about the users and therefore are open for misuse. These data are collected inter alia in the interest of car manufacturers, suppliers, garages, insurances, courts, financial authorities, law enforcement agencies, and municipalities. Interfaces unnoticeably transfer the data outside the connected car. The user cannot avoid this and/or is not aware of this fact. Every car will leave a digital trace which allows the deduction of detailed profiles of every movement, behaviour and the personality of the driver, passengers and any other person within range of the sensors. It offers potential for surveillance activities and unauthorized persons might be able to gain access to the car by exploiting security vulnerabilities. Furthermore, companies might use this data for their insurance or credit decisions or use it to reject warranty or guarantee claims of customers [6, 22, 23].

However, these characteristics apply not only to smart cars; rather they can be seen as an illustration of the potential risks of big data in the age of the internet of things. The ability of smart devices to connect and the resulting system of systems (thinking for example of smart homes or smart cities) offers many opportunities to collect personal data and to use it for further purposes. And while data protection is still predominantly considered as an individual right, proponents of big data analyses often frame their initiatives by means of the societal benefits that big data promises in a variety of sectors (aside from traffic management, a special focus is on the health care sector) [15, 24].

Regardless of whether personal data are included in the underlying datasets [which may or may not be the case, cf. 25], the results of any big data analysis might very well impact certain individuals[1] as well as groups or even society at large. The Article 29 Working Party draws particular attention to the issues of insufficient data security, loss

---

[1] Recital 75 GDPR lists some risks that may result from data processing and may "lead to physical, material or non-material damage, in particular: where the processing may give rise to discrimination, identity theft or fraud, financial loss, damage to the reputation, loss of confidentiality of personal data protected by professional secrecy, unauthorised reversal of pseudonymisation, or any other significant economic or social disadvantage; where data subjects might be deprived of their rights and freedoms or prevented from exercising control over their personal data; where personal data are processed which reveal racial or ethnic origin, political opinions, religion or philosophical beliefs, trade union membership, and the processing of genetic data, data concerning health or data concerning sex life or criminal convictions and offences or related security measures; where personal aspects are evaluated, in particular analysing or predicting aspects concerning performance at work, economic situation, health, personal preferences or interests, reliability or behaviour, location or movements, in order to create or use personal profiles; where personal data of vulnerable natural persons, in particular of children, are processed; or where processing involves a large amount of personal data and affects a large number of data subjects".

of transparency for users, inaccurate, discriminatory or otherwise illegitimate analysis results as well as increased possibilities of government surveillance [26]. Group discrimination along racial lines, for example, as opposed to obvious and nowadays illegal racial profiling practices of past decades, might simply result from (for example, credit scoring or risk assessment) decisions based on algorithms that evaluate the data in a biased and inaccurate way [27, 28].

When the legislative procedure for the GDPR officially started in January 2012, critics of big data hoped it would provide a legal solution. The following section will provide some insights if the GDPR achieved this and how it tries to protect individual rights in the digital age.

3 EU Data Protection Law and Individual Rights

The GDPR will become applicable in May 2018. It aims to further harmonize the EU data protection law. At its core, data protection addresses the imbalance in power between the data subject and the controller who offers services that require personal data. Thus, the raison d'être of data protection law is to protect the rights of the individual, as is stipulated by Article 1 para. 2 GDPR. In order to achieve this, the processing of personal data is not allowed, unless there is an explicit legal basis according to Article 6(1) GDPR and Article 8 CFR. Special categories of personal data, such as inter alia on ethnicity, sexual orientation, political opinions, as well as genetic or health data demand special safeguards under Article 9 GDPR. Generally, the data may only be processed for the purposes for which they were collected, as prescribed by Article 5(1)(b) GDPR.

3.1 Fundamental Rights to Private Life and the Protection of Personal Data

The protection of personal data on the EU level is also enshrined in the Union's primary law: the EU Charter of Fundamental Rights protects the right to private life in its Article 7. It also explicitly provides for a right to the protection of personal data in Article 8 CFR. According to the settled case-law of the Court of Justice of the EU (ECJ), any processing of personal data is an interference with these fundamental rights of the individual [29–32]. While such an interference may be justified under the conditions of Article 52(1) CFR, this provision requires that any processing has to be permitted by law and proportionate.

Further, Article 8 CFR imposes requirements as to the storing of the data and access rights: the purpose of the data collection must be sufficiently clear, access to and use of the data have to be limited on a technical and procedural level and the relevant provisions have to provide sufficient safeguards against abuse and unlawful access or use [32].

3.2 Individual Rights in the General Data Protection Regulation

These abstract principles are implemented in the rules of the GDPR. Chapter III of the GDPR includes various specific rights of data subjects vis-à-vis the controller.

As all personal data has to be processed lawfully, fairly and in a transparent manner, as stipulated by Article 5(1)(a) GDPR, Article 12 GDPR generally requires that all information and the modalities for the exercise of these rights have to be transparent for data subjects and presented to them in a concise, transparent and comprehensible way. When data are collected, the data subjects must be informed of the controllers, the purposes and legal basis for the processing, the recipients of the data and the transfer to third countries. Access to this information is also enshrined as a right of the data subject in Article 15 GDPR. While these rights are applicable for any data collection, this information is particularly important in cases where the legal basis of the processing is the consent of the data subject. According to Article 4(11) GDPR consent is any freely given, specific and unambiguous indication by the data subject. Thus, without the appropriate information, consent is not possible. The data subject may withdraw his or her consent with regard to future processing according to Article 7(3) GDPR at any time. If there is no other legal basis for the processing, it has to be ceased. However, this does not affect the lawfulness of the processing prior to the withdrawal of consent.

When there no longer is a legal basis for the processing, the purpose of the processing has been achieved, the data subject objected to the processing or data have been processed unlawfully, the data subject has the right to demand the erasure of the data from the controller under Article 17 GDPR.

In addition to erasure of data and restriction of the processing, the data subject under Article 20(1) GDPR now has a right to data portability. The right applies whenever automated processing of data is based on consent or a contract with the controller and concerns data provided by the data subject him- or herself. It entitles the data subject to receive his or her personal data in a structured, commonly used and machine-readable format. Data subjects may also demand that the controller transmits the personal data directly to another controller.

4   Can the Data Subject's Rights Resolve the Concerns for Individuals with Regard to Smart Cars?

The third part of the workshop was aimed at identifying and analysing the rights of individuals relevant in the legislative process for the GDPR with regard to smart car scenarios.

4.1   Application of Individual Rights to Smart Car Scenarios

Participants were divided in small working groups in order to assess different scenarios with regard to the effectiveness of data subject's rights in a smart car and big data context. The scenarios touch upon issues which arise in smart cars with regard to data processing and the rights of data subjects (e.g. collection of data, acquisition of the data subject's informed consent in the car, managing various drivers, right to data portability, right to deletion, exercise of right to withdraw consent, objection to direct marketing, notification of breaches, transfer of data, categories of data stored and who has access to which data). The scenarios furthermore strove to test the limits of data protection law with regard to the protection of individuals by raising issues such as societal disadvantages that might be the result of big data processing in a smart car context and demonstrate its limitation with regard to the practical implementation in everyday situations.

After the group work session, participants discussed whether the new EU data protection legislation adequately addresses and effectively resolves the identified issues and if these could be resolved in a more appropriate manner.

Scenario 1: Owning a Smart Car. After six months of driving her new smart car without any incident, A suddenly receives a call from the dealership's garage, asking her to bring her car in for repairs. When A inquires as to the nature of these repairs, the garage replies that her car has been sending error messages and therefore needs to be taken in for a check-up. Please consider the following alternate scenarios:

– A does not want to receive further calls. She tells the garage to delete her personal data, as she wants an independent garage to take care of necessary repairs. The garage refuses, as
  - the error messages relate to an issue with the airbag deployment, which may occur at random. Due to this potentially life-threatening situation, the garage states it had a responsibility to inform A.
  - the error messages relate to an issue with the infotainment system, but a repair at the dealership was necessary if A wanted to keep the manufacturer's warranty.
– A does not take the car for repair at the garage. However, three weeks later she has an accident due to a failure of the electronic stabilization programme. The garage links the failure to the error messages and, stating that A had been informed of the need for a repair, the manufacturer whose erroneous programming caused the failure refuses to pay for the necessary repairs, which resulted from the accident.

After these experiences, A considers buying a smart car by another manufacturer. However, as she has personalized many of her current cars features, she is reluctant to switch brands, until she reads about the right to data portability in a tech blog. After ordering the new car, she requests that all of her data stored in her old car is transferred to the manufacturer of her new car. Please consider the following alternate scenarios:

– The old car's manufacturer refuses to submit the data to the other manufacturer, arguing that the systems are not compatible. When A insists she is provided with a text file including the code containing her data
– The old car's manufacturer states that it can only transfer certain types of data, relating to the infotainment system, but not all personal data. For instance it is not possible to transfer the data concerning the seat adjustments, as another manufacturer has different specifications and the data can thus not be converted.

Discussion Among the Participants. Regarding the first part of the scenario, the participants pointed out that A can generally request the deletion of her data in case she turns to an independent garage for the necessary repairs. However, if the contract included a valid service contract with the dealership's garage, her right to consult another garage could be limited. In the case at hand it was only a warranty offered by the manufacturer, which A is free to waive and choose another garage. If the processing of A's data is dependent on her consent, she can freely revoke it and the garage must not contact her anymore. When the data are processed for the purpose of direct marketing, as is the case here, the data subject may object at any time and the controller has to cease the processing immediately (Article 21(2) GDPR). However, in the case of a life-threating situation, the manufacturer may continue to use her data under Article 6(1)(d) GDPR, independent of her consent. Another danger for data subjects highlighted in the second indent of the first part is that the manufacturer might use data of the car against the owner in order to limit its own responsibility. This illustrates the importance of transparent data processing and informed consent of the data subject.

Regarding the data portability part of scenario 1, the participants indicated that the Article 20 GDPR only specifies that personal data have to be provided in a structured, commonly used and machine-readable format. The question of compatibility, however, is not solved in the Regulation as Article 20(2) states that the transmission of personal data directly from one controller to another should only occur where technically feasible, which leaves much room for interpretation.

Scenario 2: Renting a Smart Car. B rents a car with his local car rental company. Arriving at the company, he is pleasantly surprised to find a brand new car. The rental company agent informs him that the car is fitted with a telematics device, which electronically transmits data on the car's location, the speed and acceleration. The agent assures B that the device does not store any personal data. B signs the contract, including a separate section where he consents to the use of the telematics device.

As B gets in the car, he connects his smartphone via Bluetooth to listen to his music. On the way he receives a phone call from his friend. B is surprised to find that the call is relayed through the car's infotainment system using the built-in microphone and speakers. When B returns the car after two days, he is in a hurry to get to his appointment and just grabs his phone as he leaves the car. After two days, he remembers the phone call and wonders whether the contact information is still stored in the car. He calls the rental company and asks them whether his data was deleted from the car, however, the rental company does not answer his question and instead refers B to the manufacturer of the car. In turn, the manufacturer claims that this is the rental company's responsibility.

Two months after the return of the rental car, B receives a letter from the police relating to a hit-and-run accident, where a witness saw a black car of the same model as the one rented by B swerve on the road and hit a parked car's side-view mirror, before speeding away. The police then requested the data from the telematics device of the rental company's car as well as their costumer database and found that B had been at the site of the incident. B is surprised that his data was handed to the police so easily, especially as the agent had specifically told him that the telematics device collected no personal data. He thinks the car rental company had no legal basis to submit his data.

Discussion Among the Participants. The participants argued that the collection of personal data is only lawful in case that the consent of the user was obtained on the basis of the principles of fairness and transparency which includes the provision of specific and unambiguous information about the processing operation and its purposes (Article

4(11); Article 5(1)(a) and Article 13 GDPR). It was stressed, that in the scenario at hand, the specific contents of the contract are crucial in order to assess whether the controller met his obligations under the relevant provisions. However, the misleading information by the agent suggests that this was not the case. Participants also stated that the contract would have to specify the purpose of collection in order to be lawful. If the data were lawfully collected they would have to be deleted after a certain time. In case the data were collected unlawfully they would have to be deleted right away. However, as the scenario suggested, it may be difficult in practice for the data subject to find the controller and have his or her data deleted. Especially in the context of smart cars it can be a challenge even for lawyers to determine who is responsible for the data processing.

Regarding the request of information by authorities, it was stated that such provisions are specified in the context of national laws, but that the collection of data, and especially telematics data, could induce the national legislator to pass provisions for access of public authorities, which intensified the risks for the individuals.

Scenario 3: Lending a Smart Car – Without the Ability to Distinguish Between Individual Drivers – To a Friend. A, the owner of a smart car, lends his car to his good friend B who wants to use the car to visit her mother at a retirement home several times a week. Since her mother suffers from various illnesses, B sometimes has to rush to help her and assist the nurses at the retirement home or at the nearest hospital. A chose an insurance company which analyses his driving habits. While this may serve to offer special conditions and financial benefits, the opposite may also be the case under the contract's conditions: as a result of the dangerous driving style of B (driving fast, approaching other cars too fast, and driving too close to others cars), and as there is no method to assess whether A or B was the one driving dangerously, the insurance company increases the annual fee of A.

Further, B, a tech-enthusiast with an information science background, – as opposed to A, who never does that – regularly uses the integrated infotainment system (with Internet functionality) of the car (for example, sometimes when her mother undergoes special medical treatment that she is not allowed to attend or when she has to wait for her children when picking them up from school, etc.). She researches information on hotshot technologies such as virtual reality glasses and high-speed computers to use the glasses and on specialized computer-issues. As the car's search history relates to A and not B, and with the help of cookies and third-party cookies, the customer profile of A changes considerably due to the search input which indicates that A is quite wealthy. Subsequently A is regarded as a tech-affine person, not only resulting in a change of the advertising displayed to A, but also in higher prices for flight tickets and for several kinds of devices, he buys online. The price-conscious A is irritated by the increasing prices and contacts one of the shops, why he has to pay more for a flight than other customers have stated on online-comparison websites. The shop's customer service assures that there is no discrimination, as prices may change from minute to minute.

Discussion Among the Participants. Regarding the inability to distinguish between different drivers it was stated that this scenario poses a serious issue as only more surveillance would help to solve the problem, but which would also raise new privacy issues. The insurance company would have to collect even more data to differentiate between the two persons.

Regarding the issue of profiling, Article 15(h) GDPR was mentioned which requires the data controller to provide meaningful information about the logic involved, as well as the significance and the envisaged consequences of such processing for the data subject in cases of automated decision-making, including profiling. However, the definition of meaningful information remains unclear: it has not been decided on a European level what kind of information this involves (i.e. the whole algorithm list or only parts). Concerning this question, it was stated that trade secrets, as mentioned in recital 63 GDRP, are protected right of others and may restrict the right of access to personal data.

Further, the question arose whether A had been discriminated against. In the Regulation discrimination is not an independent category. It has to be related to other characteristics which is not the case in scenario 3. Article 9(1) only prohibits the processing of personal data revealing racial or ethnic origin, political opinions, religious or philosophical beliefs, or trade union membership, and the processing of genetic data, biometric data for the purpose of uniquely identifying a natural person, data concerning health or data concerning a natural person's sex life or sexual orientation.

Additionally, the lawfulness of processing personal data depends on the content of the insurance contract. The insurance company can prescribe that only A can use the car and that B would need an extra insurance package. The insurance contract could also include a lifelong tracking consent, which, however, would have to be transparent for the user. Nevertheless, in case that personal data of another person was erroneously used for profiling of the user, he or she has the right to either demand rectification of the data or even to object such processing according to Article 15(e). However, although there is the same difficulty to distinguish between different persons, as in the first part of the scenario, detailed information on which products were bought and which websites were visited might help to distinguish between different users. Yet, this would also raise the potential threat of revealing personal data of B to A.

Scenario 4: Lending a Smart Car – With the Ability to Distinguish Between Individual Drivers – To a Friend. A, the owner of a smart car, lends his car to his friend B. B, the proud upholder of public transportation, tells him that he needs the car to buy larger quantities of goods from the wholesaler. The smart car is a pretty new model and has – among several other high-tech features – facial, voice and haptic recognition technology on board in order to distinguish different drivers. The majority of these features, however, are only accessible when the system recognizes the car owner, A. Although details like photographs and voices of other drivers are not stored, A is able to access the routes driven by any other driver.

After shopping, B calls his friend A and asks him whether the car stores any information on routes and destinations. A thinks that his friend sounds particularly nervous and finds his behaviour suspicious. A assures B that no such data is stored by the car. Out of curiosity, A opens the route of his happily married friend B. This is when he realizes that his friend was not driving to the wholesaler, but to a remote brothel with poor public transportation connections. Following the shock of the unveiling and as he is also friends with B's wife, he decides to inform her about her husband's infidelity.

Discussion Among the Participants. The participants especially discussed whether A might be regarded as a data controller in the context of this scenario. Article 4(7) defines the controller as the natural or legal person, public authority, agency or other body which, alone or jointly with others, determines the purposes and means of the processing of personal data. Opinions, however, were divided: some participants regarded A as responsible for providing all the information that needs to be provided by a data controller and that it is unlawful to link information of A (marriage status) with the information that is unlawfully obtained by accessing the route of B and using the conclusion for the purpose of telling another person about it. Other participants stated that the responsibility also lies with the car/service manufacturer that has to shape its products in a way that such an abuse is not possible. From a legal perspective it depends on whether A is actually the person determining the purposes and means of the processing. It is thus a crucial factor whether B could potentially also turn it off. Certainly, his influence on the means of collection is rather limited. These two factors point to the car's manufacturer as the actual controller. However, it was pointed out that this is one of the yet unresolved legal issues of smart cars.

Scenario 5: Car Manufacturers and Service Providers as Part of Road Traffic Management. A lives in a small town that suffers under a chronic budget deficit. After an intense public debate on the economic opportunities and privacy risks, which traffic monitoring would impose on citizens, the municipalities eventually decide to introduce the new smart city concept. However, due to limited financial resources, the responsible members of the city's smart mobility working group decide not to distribute expensive sensors around the city. Instead, a traffic management system is introduced which is based on low-priced sensors that use Bluetooth technology. By connecting with car drivers' smartphones or directly with smart cars via Bluetooth, this new system promises to collect anonymized data on which routes are preferred most amongst the city dwellers. By this, municipalities strive to provide a better and evidence-based traffic management and lower the costs of building new roads or maintaining existing ones. In the meantime, the municipalities reduced staff numbers in the traffic office to compensate the smart city concept's costs. As a result of staff shortages and following the idea of "smart regulation", the maintenance and construction of roads is increasingly based on the data generated from the Bluetooth sensor network.

However, A and most of his neighbours are privacy-aware citizens who opposed the smart city concept in this form and would have preferred either none or at least a more ecologically oriented concept that could have provided alternatives to driving by car but which, due to budget problems, were rejected by their municipality. Thus, many people in his district turn off the Bluetooth functionality of their smart cars and smartphones so that they are not detected by the city's Bluetooth sensor arrays. Thereby, the district inhabitants' driving habits are no longer registered by the municipality as they are not recorded by the Bluetooth sensors. Thus, in contrast to other districts, where a lot more inhabitants agreed to the data policy and allowed the automated Bluetooth connections of their phones and cars, the district's roads are not maintained in a proper way and the much needed construction of new roads is currently not in sight. From the newspaper,

A learns that similar problems also occur in other districts of the city. Accordingly, the situation is even worse in poor districts.

Discussion Among the Participants. In the discussion it was pointed out that it is not possible to anonymize route data in a small town and that the Bluetooth solution has fundamental problems, as it raises several privacy issues. According to the participants, it is basically an engineering problem which could be solved by using appropriate technology. A less privacy-invasive low-tech solution minimizing the collected data would thus be preferable.

In contrast, some participants stressed that, apart from the concrete technology used, the action of the municipality does not really meet the requirements of good democratic governance, while other participants indicated that municipalities do not have to initiate referenda on such matters as the introduction of traffic surveillance and CCTV prove. It was furthermore stressed that data protection rights of the mentioned groups (privacy-aware citizens and citizens of poor districts) might have been violated even in case of a referendum if the vote was in favour of the municipalities' proposal.

5   Results of the Workshop

The discussion showed that the upcoming GDPR still leaves several issues relating to big data applications in a smart car context unresolved. From the discussions of the participants, the following general themes could be identified:

The discussion of the importance of specific contents of contracts (see discussion of scenario 1 and scenario 2) shows that some issues are difficult to solve with rather general data protection laws. At the same time, it highlights the lack of transparency in current contract clauses, especially with regard to obtaining the consent of the data subject. Consumers are confronted with opaque consent forms on a regular basis. In many instances, the clauses cannot be the basis of a valid consent. However, the requirements for valid consent had already been addressed in the Data Protection Regulation. While this is therefore an issue that has been solved legally, it is not properly implemented in practice. With regard to smart cars, manufacturers have to be sure to properly inform customers of the capabilities of their cars and obtain valid consent for processing operations which cannot be based on another legal basis. The data subject must be aware of processing that takes place in a smart car. However, this legal requirement is not easily implemented in such an environment. While ideas like a privacy dashboard [33] have been put forward, it has to be borne in mind that the driver also has to be able to focus on the driving itself.

Similar to the issue of valid consent, the problem of identifying the controller of data processing operations is also inherited from the former legislation. However, it can be seen that concepts such as the question of who controls a data processing operation may be difficult to answer in practice, especially in complex environments with many data flows, such as in the context of smart cars. Especially with regard to such new technology, a definition of data flows, as it is required by a data protection impact assessment under Article 35 GDPR, is essential. Furthermore, while the GDPR follows a technology neutral approach based on the risks for the individual [34], specific complex technologies such as smart cars may also require more detailed risk adequate provisions, either in the form of codes of conduct or sector specific regulation.

The discussion on the new right to data portability (see scenario 1), the difficulty of distinguishing two persons that use the same car (see scenario 3) and the question of responsibility in case of multiple controllers (see scenario 4) point to the necessity of specific decisions of the supervisory authorities, which will coordinate their efforts in the upcoming European Data Protection Board (EDPB), as well as judgments of the European Court of Justice on the interpretation of specific legal terms and concepts.

In scenario 3 the issue of discrimination based on data processing was discussed. The discussion showed how difficult it is to prevent or prove discrimination through scoring activities and to supervise the use of such technologies while respecting the interests of businesses, such as trade secrets. The GDPR does not answer this question, but instead resorts to the abstract legal definition of 'meaningful information', which will have to be interpreted by those applying the law in practice. For the individual, in most instances, the only possibility may be to provide additional personal information in order to rectify the data. However, this creates a privacy conundrum, as the data subject has to reveal even more information.

The discussion concerning scenario 5 indicated that the balance of the needs of individuals (data protection rights) and of the needs of society (more efficient and cost-effective road infrastructure management) might regularly be decided in favour of the greater societal benefits. However, rather than choosing one option over another, an actual balancing of positions has to reconcile both positions as far as possible. Furthermore, it should be emphasised that data protection in itself is a value for society as a whole: to determine what others know about a person is part of their autonomy in a free society. Data protection thus is at the heart of democratic processes [24, 35].

6   Conclusions

As has been shown, the GDPR does not exhaustively solve all issues relating to the protection of individuals with regard to big data analyses in the context of smart cars. While the Regulation offers some new solutions, such as the right to data portability, these will have to be interpreted and implemented in a meaningful way in practice. Further, the new legislation inherited some of the problems of the old legislation, such as the proper implementation of a valid consent or the question of responsibility for data processing operations. Especially the latter becomes relevant with regard to the specifics of smart cars. Moreover, it remains to be seen whether some member states will make use of opening clauses (including in particular Art. 6(2) but also Art. 9(4) and Art. 22(2) GDPR) to establish more accurate sector-specific rules and if other member states will harmonize their legislation accordingly (maybe in tandem with the EDPB and CoJ rulings) or if this, in contrary, will lead to a patchwork of different rules [36]. In conjunction with legal regulation, and especially in complex data processing structures, as is the case with smart cars and big data, the development and application of Privacy by Design (PbD) and Privacy Enhancing Technologies (PETs) remains an important but not yet effectively implemented cornerstone.

All in all, the workshop has served both to raise awareness of individual rights under data protection law in general and also to show some of the deficits in practice. However, in order to address the challenges of big data to society in a more democratic way, we need societal debates and further development of institutional structures addressing the power imbalances of different voices and interests. The debates on the GDPR and the ongoing discussions on the review of the e-Privacy-Directive can be regarded as a good starting point, but an expansion of these discussions both within the member states and within non data protection-affine communities is essential.

References

1. Hansen, M.: Das Netz im Auto & das Auto im Netz. Datenschutz und Datensicherheit **39**(6), 367–371 (2015)
2. Future of Privacy Forum: The connected car and privacy. Navigating new data issues. White paper (2014)
3. Cohen, A., Arce-Plevnik, L., Shor, T.: IoT in automotive industry: Connecting cars. Unpublished paper (2016). http://works.bepress.com/luis-arce-plevnik/2/
4. European Commission: Business Innovation Observatory. Internet of things. Connected cars. Case Study 43 (2015). http://ec.europa.eu/DocsRoom/documents/13394/attachments/2/translations/en/renditions/pdf
5. Hornung, G.: Verfügungsrecht an fahrzeugbezogenen Daten. Das vernetzte Automobil zwischen innovativer Wertschöpfung und Persönlichkeitsschutz. Datenschutz und Datensicherheit **39**(6), 359–366 (2015)
6. Lüdemann, V.: Connected Cars. Das vernetzte Auto nimmt Fahrt auf, der Datenschutz bleibt zurück. ZD **6**(2015), 247–254 (2015)
7. Kremer, S.: Connected Car – intelligente Kfz, intelligente Verkehrssysteme, intelligenter Datenschutz? Recht der Datenverarbeitung **5**(2014), 240–252 (2014)
8. Bennett, C.J., Bayley. R.M.: Privacy protection in the era of 'big data': regulatory challenges and social assessments. In: Van der Sloot, B., Broeders, D., Schrijvers, E. (eds.) Exploring the Boundaries of Big Data, pp. 205–227. Amsterdam University Press, Amsterdam (2016)
9. Klous, S.: Sustainable harvesting of the big data potential. In: Van der Sloot, B., Broeders, D., Schrijvers, E. (eds.) Exploring the Boundaries of Big Data, pp. 27–47. Amsterdam University Press, Amsterdam (2016)
10. Ward, J.S., Barker, A.: Undefined by Data: A Survey of Big Data Definitions (2013). arXiv Preprint: arXiv:1309.5821
11. Gartner, Inc.: IT Glossary: Big Data. http://www.gartner.com/it-glossary/big-data/
12. Poel, M., Schroeder, R., Treperman, J., Rubinstein, M., et al.: Data for Policy: A Study of Big Data and Other Innovative Data-Driven Approaches for Evidence-Informed Policymaking (Report about the State-of-the-Art). Oxford Internet Institute, Center for European Policy Studies, Amsterdam: technopolis (2015). http://www.data4policy.eu/#!state-of-the-art-report/cjg9
13. Gandomi, A., Haider, M.: Beyond the hype: big data concepts, methods, and analytics. Int. J. Inf. Manag. **35**(2), 137–144 (2015)
14. Executive Office of the President: Big Data: Seizing Opportunities, Preserving Values. The White House, Washington, DC, May 2014
15. Mayer-Schönberger, V., Cukier, K.: Big Data: A Revolution That Will Transform How We Live, Work and Think. John Murray, London (2013)
16. DIVSI, and iRights.Lab. "Big Data." Hamburg, January 2016

17. Xu, F.: Smart data for mobility (SD4M): eine big-data-analytik-plattform für multimodale smart mobility services. Presented at the Bitkom Big Data Summit 2015, Congress Park Hanau, 25 February 2015

18. Watts, J.M., Purnell, N.: Singapore Is Taking the 'Smart City' to a Whole New Level. Wall Street J., 25 April 2016. http://www.wsj.com/articles/singapore-is-taking-the-smart-city-to-a-whole-new-level-1461550026

19. Albino, V., Berardi, U., Dangelico, R.M.: Smart cities: definitions, dimensions, performance, and initiatives. J. Urban Technol. **22**(1), 3–21 (2015)

20. DeBord, M.: World Economic Forum: Who owns connected car data? (2015). https://www.weforum.org/agenda/2015/09/who-owns-connected-car-data/

21. Derikx, S., de Reuver, M., Kroesen, M.: Can privacy concerns for insurance of connected cars be compensated? Electron Markets **26**(1), 73–81 (2016)

22. Stöhring, M.: Mein Auto, meine Daten? Fahrzeuggeneriertes Datenmaterial: Nutzung und Rechtsansprüche. c't Magazin für Computer und Technik **11**(2016), 128–133 (2016)

23. Federal Trade Commission: The Internet of Things: Privacy and Security in a Connected World. FTC Staff Report (2015). https://www.ftc.gov/system/files/documents/reports/federal-trade-commission-staff-report-november-2013-workshop-entitled-internet-things-privacy/150127iotrpt.pdf

24. Van der Sloot, B.: The individuals in the big data era: moving towards an agent-based privacy paradigm. In: Van der Sloot, B., Broeders, D., Schrijvers, E. (eds.) Exploring the Boundaries of Big Data, pp. 177–203. Amsterdam University Press, Amsterdam (2016)

25. Clavell, G.G.: Policing, big data and the commodification of security. In: Van der Sloot, B., Broeders, D., Schrijvers, E. (eds.) Exploring the Boundaries of Big Data, pp. 89–115. Amsterdam University Press, Amsterdam (2016)

26. Article 29 Data Protection Working Party: Opinion 03/2013 on purpose limitation. Brussels, 00569/13/EN, WP 2013, 2 April 2013

27. Angwin, J., Larson, J., Mattu, S., Kirchner, L.: ProPublica. Machine Bias: There's software used across the country to predict future criminals. And it's biased against blacks. ProPublica, 23 Mai 2016. https://www.propublica.org/article/machine-bias-risk-assessments-in-criminal-sentencing

28. Yu, P., McLaughlin, J., Levy, M.: Big Data: A Big Disappointment for Scoring Consumer Credit Risk. NCLC, National Consumer Law Center, Boston, MA, 14 März 2014

29. ECJ, Joined Cases C-465/00, C-138/01 and C-139/01 Österreichischer Rundfunk and Others, ECLI:EU:C:2003:294

30. ECJ, Joined Cases C-92/09 and 93/09 Schecke and Eifert, ECLI:EU:C:2010:662

31. ECJ, Joined Cases C-293/12 and C-594/12 Digital Rights Ireland and Seitlinger, ECLI:EU:C:2014:238

32. ECJ, Case C-362/14 Schrems, ECLI:EU:C:2015:650

33. Security and Privacy in your Car Act by the Senators Markey und Blumenthal from 21 July 2015. https://www.congress.gov/bill/114th-congress/senate-bill/1806/text

34. Boehme-Neßler, V.: Big Data und Demokratie – Warum Demokratie ohne Datenschutz nicht funktioniert. Das Deutsche Verwaltungsblatt, pp. 1282–1287 (2015)

35. Roßnagel, A.: Schriftliche Stellungnahme zum öffentlichen Fachgespräch zur Daten-schutz-Grundverordnung am 24. Februar 2016 im Ausschuss Digitale Agenda des Deutschen Bundestags (2016). https://www.bundestag.de/blob/409512/4afc3a566097171a7902374da77cc7ad/a-drs-18-24-94-data.pdf

36. Roßnagel, A., Geminn, C., Jandt, S., Richter, P.: Datenschutzrecht 2016 "Smart" genug für die Zukunft?: Ubiquitous Computing und Big Data als Herausforderungen des Datenschutzrechts. Bd. 4. Kassel University Press GmbH, Kassel (2016)

Opportunities and Challenges of CREDENTIAL

Towards a Metadata-Privacy Respecting Identity Provider

Farzaneh Karegar[1], Christoph Striecks[2], Stephan Krenn[2(✉)], Felix Hörandner[3], Thomas Lorünser[2], and Simone Fischer-Hübner[1]

[1] Karlstad University, Karlstad, Sweden
{farzaneh.karegar,simone.fischer-huebner}@kau.se
[2] AIT Austrian Institute of Technology GmbH, Vienna, Austria
{christoph.striecks,stephan.krenn,thomas.loruenser}@ait.ac.at
[3] Graz University of Technology, Graz, Austria
felix.hoerandner@iaik.tugraz.at

Abstract. This paper summarizes the results of a workshop at the IFIP Summer School 2016 introducing the EU Horizon 2020 project CREDENTIAL, i.e., Secure Cloud Identity Wallet. The contribution of this document is three-fold. First, it gives an overview of the CREDENTIAL project, its use-cases, and core technologies. Second, it explains the challenges of the project's approach and summarizes the results of the parallel focus groups that were held during the workshop. Third, it focuses on a specific challenge—the protection of metadata in centralized identity providers—and suggests a potential architecture addressing this problem.

Keywords: Metadata privacy · Identity provisioning · Data sharing

1 Introduction

With increasing mobility and Internet use, the demand for digital services has increased and already reached critical and high assurance domains like eGovernment, eHealth, and eBusiness. Those domains have particularly high security and privacy requirements, and services are harnessed with various novel mechanisms for securing access. Handling all the different authentication and authorization mechanisms requires user friendly support, which can efficiently be provided by digital identity management (IdM). Due to business mergers and acquisitions as well as the increasing number of cloud applications, IdM is currently experiencing a paradigm shift, moving away from company-internal custom-tailored IdM system towards non-standard fragmented authentication situations. However, under the given change, many current solutions fall short with respect to

This project has received funding from the European Union's Horizon 2020 research and innovation programme under grant agreement No 653454. The ordering of the authors was determined using a fair dice.

A. Lehmann et al. (Eds.): Privacy and Identity 2016, IFIP AICT 498, pp. 76–91, 2016.
DOI: 10.1007/978-3-319-55783-0_7

security, privacy, or usability. Therefore there exists a strong demand to delegate the management of multiple credentials, as well as traditional corporate identity and access management (IAM) functions, like single sign-on (SSO), to a cloud-based service.

The transformation in the IdM world goes hand in hand with the tremendous shift to cloud computing that has shaped the information and communications technology (ICT) world during the last years. IdM has not remained unaffected in this respect. By now, numerous IdM systems and solutions are available as cloud services, providing identity services to applications operated both in closed domains and in the public cloud. This service model is referred to as Identity (and Access) Management as a Service (IDMaaS). Popular examples for cloud IDMaaS providers are big companies from the sectors of social networks, search engines, business solutions, or online retailers. They offer their user identity base for authentication and identification at various services. However, for increased usability, identity services should cover more than login and authentication. For instance, they could also serve as online password vaults, replacing local password managers for providing better portability and anytime-anywhere access to protected resources. Finally, more general online vaults retaining entire identity documents or personal files and records (e.g., OneDrive, Dropbox, tresorit) can also be considered as identity services. However, currently no satisfactory approaches allowing for the privacy-preserving storage and advanced sharing of identity data by cloud service providers exist.

The vision of CREDENTIAL is to fill this gap, and to develop a privacy-preserving solution for data sharing and identity provisioning. Users will be able to store identity data and other sensitive data such as health records in a cloud-based CREDENTIAL wallet such that confidentiality and privacy are upheld. In particular, the wallet provider will not be able to access the users' personal data, and can build its business strategy around this advantageous security property. If a user wants to share specific data with other users, or share identity information with a service provider in order to log on to a system, she will be guaranteed that after transmission the intended receiver of the data will be the only party capable of accessing the data items in plain text.

At the IFIP Summer School 2016 in Karlstad, Sweden, the CREDENTIAL project organized a workshop to present the project, raise awareness of the existing technologies and solutions, and to receive feedback and input from experts from different domains. To do so, the project's ambition, the used core technologies, and a representative use case from the eHealth pilot were presented to the audience. This was then followed by three focus groups to discuss different aspects and challenges of the CREDENTIAL approach. This paper summarizes the content and results of this workshop as well as subsequent findings that were inspired by those discussions.

1.1   Outline

This document is structured as follows. In Sect. 2 we give a short overview of the CREDENTIAL project and introduce the pilots and underlying core technologies.

Section 3 then describes the challenges discussed during the workshop, as well as the inputs and recommendations received from the participants. In Sect. 4, a special focus is put on privacy-related challenges introduced by a central identity wallet. We recap existing countermeasures to those issues in Sect. 5 and explain their shortcomings, before we describe a potential high-level architecture solving those problems in Sect. 6. Finally, we briefly conclude in Sect. 7.

2   The CREDENTIAL Project

The overall vision of CREDENTIAL is to develop a user-centric cloud-based data storage and sharing platform, which enhances the user's privacy compared to current approaches and keeps the user in control, while retaining the benefits of cloud-based solutions. In order to achieve this, CREDENTIAL will employ advanced cryptographic mechanisms, such as proxy re-encryption [1] and redactable signatures [2]. The developed solution will follow state-of-the-art security and privacy by design principles. By using and extending well-established standards and protocols, we aim to not only apply the CREDENTIAL approach to a comprehensive cloud system but to also facilitate integration into existing solutions. In the following, we will first explain CREDENTIAL's basic technologies and architecture, and then highlight its application to three different domains, namely eGovernment, eHealth, and eBusiness.

2.1   Basic Technologies

CREDENTIAL uses the following two cryptographic mechanisms as a foundation to enable confidentiality, integrity, and authenticity from end-to-end during the sharing process of whole messages or subsets.

Proxy re-encryption, introduced by Blaze et al. [1], extends asymmetric encryption with the ability to transform a ciphertext c_A encrypted for party A into another ciphertext c_B of party B without revealing the underlying plaintext in an intermediate step. To enable this transformation, party A generates a re-encryption key $rk_{A \to B}$ from her private key sk_A and the public key pk_B of party B. As neither plain text nor decryption keys are exposed during re-encryption, this operation can be outsourced to a semi-trusted proxy. The technology is therefore well suited for end-to-end encrypted data sharing.

Redactable signatures, introduced by Johnson et al. [2], make it possible to black-out parts of a signed message and still verify the signature on the remaining parts; this is in contrast to plain digital signatures, where every bit flip in the message invalidates the signature. This redaction can be performed without access to the signer's private key. The technology is therefore well suited for realizing selective disclosure.

2.2   Architecture

CREDENTIAL's basic architecture integrates the above presented cryptographic mechanisms into three key actors: user, CREDENTIAL wallet, and data receiver. After outlining these actors, their interactions are described.

The *user* owns data that should be securely stored or shared with other participants. A client application is deployed in the user's domain to handle operations involving user's private key material, such as signing or generating a re-encryption key. This application should not be accessible or online when the intended receiver wants to access the data.

The *wallet* represents the central component of CREDENTIAL. This wallet is a data storage and sharing service deployed in the cloud yielding among others benefits such as constant availability, scalability, and cost effectiveness. A powerful identity and access management system performs multi-factor authentication and authorizes access to the stored data. With proxy re-encryption, the confidentiality of the stored and shared data is ensured even when deploying the wallet at an honest-but-curious cloud provider, as no plain data is exposed. Furthermore, once a re-encryption key is provided, the data can be shared with other participants even when the user or her client application are not available.

The *data receiver* might be a service provider or another CREDENTIAL user. It relies on data stored in or authentication assertions issued by the wallet. With this information, the data receiver reaches authorization decisions and performs arbitrary data processing.

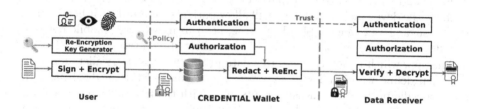

Fig. 1. CREDENTIAL's basic architecture

A simple *data sharing process* highlighting the interaction among the individual components is shown in Fig. 1. First, the user authenticates to the wallet to get permission to upload signed and encrypted data c_U. This data c_U is encrypted for the user herself to retain maximum control. To share encrypted data, the user generates a re-encryption key $rk_{U \to DR}$ towards a selected data receiver DR. This generation operation has to be performed in the user's domain, as the user's private key is involved. Along with this re-encryption key, a policy defining which data may be disclosed is transmitted to the wallet. Upon request of a data receiver, not-required data is redacted based on the policy. Then, using the re-encryption key $rk_{U \to DR}$, the user's redacted ciphertext c'_U is transformed into data encrypted for the data receiver c'_{DR}. Finally, the data receiver is able to decrypt the data c'_{DR} and verify the signature on the disclosed parts.

2.3 Pilot Scenarios

The CREDENTIAL technologies and architecture are showcased by pilot scenarios from three different domains. A more detailed description of the scenarios can be found in Hörandner et al. [3].

eGovernment. In the eGovernment pilot, the focus lies on identity management to authenticate citizens and assess their eligibility for a service, based on – often sensitive – identity attributes. This identity management is considered an instance of CREDENTIAL's data sharing process via standardized identity protocols such as SAML [4] or OpenID Connect [5]. In such a protocol, the service provider (i.e., the data receiver) triggers the process by requesting user authentication and identity attributes from the identity provider (i.e., the CREDENTIAL wallet). Concerning authentication, we will not only integrate national eID solutions, but also look at a broader context and enable cross-border authentication according to the eIDAS regulation [6]. The wallet prompts the user for consent as well as a re-encryption key, and then selectively discloses re-encrypted attributes to the service provider.

eHealth. The eHealth pilot is concerned with a data sharing between patients, doctors, and further parties, in particular in the context of Type 2 Diabetes. Namely, the developed components will allow patients to record their health data (blood sugar level, weight, blood pressure, etc.) using external mobile devices. The data measured on these devices will be collected by a CREDENTIAL eHealth mobile app, which remotely stores this data in the CREDENTIAL wallet. The user can then define who is allowed to access which parts of this medical data, to share specific parts of the measurements, e.g., with the family doctor, diabetologist, nutritionist, or personal trainer. Based on the data they see, they can then provide recommendations back to the patient. This remote data sharing functionality between patients and doctors is of key importance also in other telemedicine applications, as the patients' privacy is respected while the doctor still obtains high authenticity guarantees for the received data.

eBusiness. The eBusiness pilot showcases how easy the privacy offered by existing solutions can be enhanced through the integration of modular libraries implementing CREDENTIAL's technologies. Encrypted mails are a requirement for many companies to protect their data and inventions, but they also represent a significant challenge when employees are temporary unavailable, e.g., because of vacation. Currently, employees have to expose their private key material so that a substitute member of staff can still read and answer incoming mail. In contrast, with proxy re-encryption, an employee generates a re-encryption key for his or her deputy before leaving, with which the mail server is able to translate incoming mail during the absence. Advanced re-encryption schemes even allow one to program expiration dates into the re-encryption keys, thereby further reducing the required trust assumptions.

3   Summary of Focus Groups

In this section, we summarize the outcome of three parallel focus groups that were held at the end of our workshop with CREDENTIAL project members and participants of the IFIP Summer School. In these groups, we discussed open research challenges in regard to the tradeoff between privacy, efficiency, and usability, end user trust, and adoption factors that we identified for the CREDEN-TIAL project. Possible approaches and solutions in regard to how these challenges could be addressed were discussed.

3.1   Focus Group 1: Privacy Challenges in CREDENTIAL

In the first focus group, we discussed privacy issues and the technologies to solve them, as well as the effects they may have on usability and efficiency. In particular the discussion was about the need of metadata privacy, i.e., whether information like access patterns, file sizes, or access rights need to be considered as sensitive or not. The following lines summarize the questions and discussions:

Which metadata needs to be protected, which may be leaked? It was discussed that it is not possible to generally say what kind of metadata is sensitive because it depends on the use cases, to what extent we want to trust the central identity wallet, and possible leakages from other sources the wallet might be able to access. If your file includes health data and the wallet already knows it, the frequency of accessing the file may divulge the severity of your disease. Knowing about the access rights of the files also reveals a lot about the type of the document. It was also suggested that we shall apply anonymization techniques on the receiver side and we should review the regulations related to the health domain to ascertain what kind of metadata is sensitive due to regulations. Furthermore, we should define some performance and privacy goals to see the added-value that we may gain by utilization of cryptographic techniques to hide the metadata.

May the wallet be allowed to see access patterns? In general, participants discussed that we should define objective decision criteria to decide on the assumptions we want to or we can make. Those criteria should not only be security-related, but also cover acceptable running times on well-defined devices or required costs to realize the solution. This is because exerting enhanced cryptographic tools like oblivious transfer (OT) or private information retrieval (PIR) would massively increase the requirements on the computational capabilities of the server. Depending on the available resources, this might render the entire system impracticable or too expensive.

How could access and behavior patterns be hidden from the wallet? Specifically, this question aimed at receiving feedback on whether splitting the identity providers into two components and making a non-collusion assumption would be a viable alternative to cryptographic "sledgehammers" like PIR. Alternatively, one could think about routing all data through the user's device so as not to enable the identity provider (IdP) learn which service provider is currently contacted.

It was discussed that the information about access patterns are definitely sensitive and should be hidden from the IdP or disguised. It is therefore valuable for users' privacy to avoid the IdP from learning access patterns in a usable way. The participants discussed that—depending on the concrete context—they tend to prefer to trust their own mobile phones rather than identity providers, meaning that information should be routed through the user's device. However, this approach would typically require key management and/or heavy computations on the user's side, which might not always be possible. Furthermore, this approach would contradict the idea of a fully cloudified solution, and therefore might work for identity provisioning but not for data sharing in general, as the data owner might not be online when the receiver wants to access the data.

3.2   Focus Group 2: Establishing Trust in CREDENTIAL

In the second focus group, we discussed how to build the user's trust into the solution developed within CREDENTIAL, as this represents a key factor for adoption. The following lines summarize the questions and discussions:

Which aspects could be used to build trust? It was suggested that both the ability as well as motivation of the entity deploying and maintaining the CREDENTIAL solution has to be clearly stated. The competence assessment can be delegated to another trusted party, for example a consumer agency, which issues certificates or simplified results as icons. Also, the motivation of the deploying party is an important factor, which is influenced by this party's business plan but also legal consequences of not complying, for example, to the General Data Protection Regulation (GDPR) [7]. Furthermore, a gradual approach of first experiencing the system with non-sensitive data and later expanding to further use cases might help users to gain familiarity and overcome trust obstacles.

How should users be informed about potential risks, which still remain even after applying the CREDENTIAL approach? It was discussed that potential risks should be explained honestly and concisely, as users are then able to make informed decisions and are more willing to accept consequences if they occur. This information could be provided in a layered approach, where non-technical scenarios are first presented, for example as cartoons, but further details are also available. However, a balance has to be found where users are sufficiently informed but are not scared away so that they use less secure alternatives which do not explain their potential weaknesses with the same level of detail.

Should users be offered detailed access records for their data? Providing access logs to users would be very beneficial, as these records can not only be used to detect abuse, but they also inform the user about progress and involved people, for example when sharing data for a hospital visit. Having a detailed log might also be helpful in law suits or for quality assurance reasons.

3.3   Focus Group 3: Technology Adoption and Applications

The third focus group discussed challenges and strategies for promoting the adoption of CREDENTIAL technology by individuals and organizations and formulated hypotheses for questions which the project could investigate in its future research on adoption factors:

How can users be convinced to change to CREDENTIAL technology? It was suggested that adoption of a CREDENTIAL application could be promoted by framing and marketing it as a "Secure App", similarly to the Swedish BankID solution [8] that is basically perceived as a secure and trustworthy authentication solution by Swedish citizens. Moreover, additional functionalities should be provided and marketed, which CREDENTIAL could in contrast with other solution providers offer in a secure and privacy-friendly way. For instance, additional data sharing applications could be offered enforcing data minimization, e.g., for social sharing of pictures and posts, or sharing of confidential documents by companies. If CREDENTIAL can promise compliance with the GDPR for its applications, this can be another important adoption factor for industry and government.

Who should pay for the adoption of CREDENTIAL technology? The reason for this question was that protecting the privacy of end-users might harm the business model of currently free data sharing or identity provisioning services, as other sources of income (e.g., personalized advertisements) would not be possible any more. It was discussed that in Sweden and other countries, there are efforts spent by the government to offer patients more treatments at home and to keep them away from hospitals as long as possible, as this has been proven to be also a more cost-efficient solution. The CREDENTIAL eHealth solution should therefore not only provide benefits for the patients, but should also enable cost savings for Health insurances and the public Health Care system, which should therefore also have incentives to pay for it. Other options could be non-monetary payment solutions such as novel "tagging-based payment systems", where users could use the service basically for free, in return for getting every X minutes a picture in which they should tag people or objects.

4   Why Metadata-Privacy Matters

As already briefly discussed in Sect. 3.1, hiding metadata is an essential requirement for a privacy-preserving identity provisioning and data sharing platform. This section is dedicated to defining metadata in more detail and to explaining some of the potential privacy risks related to metadata.

Metadata defines and describes the data and is often referred to as "data about data". It is the information about a particular data set which may describe how, when, and by whom it was received, created, accessed, and/or modified and how it is formatted. Metadata is not limited to the files. It also encompasses the records of interactions (e.g., a history of login times) or simple facts about individuals (e.g., an account number or mailing address) [9]. Metadata comes from a variety of sources; it can be created automatically by a computer, supplied by a user, or inferred through a relationship with another document to serve various purposes and functions, including enhancing the editing, viewing, filing, and retrieval of documents [9]. It opens the possibility for search engines to index the information. It promotes clearer understanding, better data management, and efficient use and reuse of information.

However, despite the benefits of collecting and analyzing metadata, all too often metadata lacks the privacy protections afforded to the content [10] and limited privacy protection may expose sensitive information to the wrong people and present significant risks. Possible inferences from metadata can invade a user's privacy in the same way as sensitive personal information obtained from the content [11]. Literally, the emergence of new technologies manifests how sensitive metadata can be: how friend lists can reveal a person's sexual orientation or political views, purchase histories can identify a pregnancy before any visible signs appear, and location information can expose individuals to harassment for unpopular political views, theft, or even physical harm [10]. Thus to protect the privacy of personal data we should consider the necessity of minimizing the amount of accessible metadata.

As mentioned previously, all the contents stored in the CREDENTIAL wallet are encrypted and the wallet does not have access to the plain-text. Ostensibly, the idea of the encrypted content implies the elimination of privacy issues. Nonetheless, metadata of encrypted content can still leak lots of personal and sensitive information not originating from the content itself but from its properties or generated information during content management to the CREDENTIAL wallet. Ergo, we want to illustrate which threats to the users' privacy still remain when metadata is available in plain-text. We only consider a simple design of the cloud-based IDMaaS system in order to give a comprehensive overview of the possible problems with honest-but-curious adversary model for the CREDENTIAL wallet.

In the following sections, we analyze the consequences of metadata privacy leakage and access to metadata by the wallet as an IdP and file hosting service.

4.1   Metadata for Identity Providers

When users select CREDENTIAL to be authenticated for different services, CREDENTIAL wallet as an identity provider can infer lots of information from the communication flow as explained in the following.

Behavioral pattern. Albeit by design the wallet cannot see the plain attributes which service providers request to authenticate the users, it is aware of when, from where, and how frequent the users connect to service providers and what kind of attributes are required. As an IdP, CREDENTIAL can glean the information about the IP address and the devices from which users connect to different services and it can guess the location. Knowing the IP address, the wallet could further infer general usage patterns, such as the user's online times or working habits (when the user connects from which device). Furthermore, even in the case that the IP address is disguised (e.g., using Tor) the accessed services might reveal some information about the user's physical location, as one often uses regional or at least national services, e.g., for online banking or governmental tasks.

Moreover, the type of the service provider could leak information about the user's gender (some services are mainly used by a specific sex) or income situation (prices of services). Based on the attributes they require to authenticate users (e.g., if the user is over 18), CREDENTIAL can learn about the user's age range withal. The user's age range can also be derived from kind of service providers they use (e.g., pension-related services). The broader the range of authentication and usage of service providers, the more CREDENTIAL can learn about the users' attitudes and personal lives (e.g., websites related to special political parties or communities in society). Also very sensitive information might be leaked through access frequencies (e.g., addictions).

Behavioral pattern combined with background information. While CRE-DENTIAL can learn a lot directly from analyzing when, from where, how frequently and to whom the users communicate, it can also combine this kind of information with some background information it has extracted about the user and learn more. For example, if the wallet already knows that a user shares health data frequently with another user (probably a doctor), a request from an online pharmacy website to authenticate the user, reveals that the illness is in a new stage or user's health has not improved because the patient has to buy new medicine or repeat the previous ones.

4.2   Metadata for Data-Sharing

Similarly to the case of identity provisioning the CREDENTIAL wallet infers lots of information about stored content when acting as a file hosting service. The size, structure, modification time and access rights of a file may reveal information that the user originally intended to hide. In the following we give examples for each of these properties.

Size, name and type. Even if the type of an object was not known to the wallet, the size of the cipher-text would act as an indicator of the content type of the stored object (e.g., text, image, and video). Type or size of an object when combined with the object's name (especially if it is assigned by the users and not the system) divulge more information about the content. Additionally, consider a scenario in which some users (patients) should upload and share their blood pressure collected over three months with another user (doctor). Users benefit from the same kind of health devices (sphygmomanometers introduced by doctors using CREDENTIAL) and health applications (applications for health devices) to collect the necessary information and send it to the wallet. Blood pressure is collected over a specific period so the number of records in each file is probably the same and due to the fact that they are collected from the same kind of health devices and apps, they have some common metadata like size, type and access rights defined by the data owner. Correspondingly, the wallet can guess that the users have the same disease and the type of illness may also be derived from the identity of the one with whom the files are shared. Doctor's identity or field of expertise might be revealed previously from some background data.

Access rights and patterns. Metadata describing access rights granted to different objects reveals not only some extra information to the wallet but also some information to the people who have been granted access to a same file. For example, all users who have the read access to a file can see between whom the file is shared which may not be desirable for the owner. In addition, being aware of the fact that some users have shared medical or identity documents with the same user or the request to access some files initiated by a specific user is always accepted helps CREDENTIAL to infer the identity or occupation of the user with whom the files have been shared. Because that user seems to be trusted by the others and the characteristics of the files shared with her support the inferences that she may be a doctor or from government sector. Gradually learning about users' occupations, the fact that a file is shared between different people can reveal lots of sensitive information. A high amount of medical documents related to a user indicates frequent consultations of medical practitioners. A document shared among several medical practitioners may indicate an uncommon disease. On the other hand, certain access patterns by a gynecologist may leak more positive news than regular accesses by an oncologist.

More interestingly, the user's behaviors not only progressively contribute to the information CREDENTIAL collects in the user's profile but also add to what CREDENTIAL knows about the people who have some common characteristics with the user (e.g., they all share some documents with a doctor). As a consequence, requesting to authenticate to a service provider like a psychiatric hospital by one of the users can reveal the type of common disease they share together.

Date of modification. Monitoring the cipher-text for changes reveals possibly sensitive information considering the fact that type and location are also among visible metadata. The modification history can for example tell something about the frequency of a user's illness updates, the intensity of her illness or monitoring her illness activity, or other general usage patterns.

Structure. The structure of an encrypted object may be needed to selectively download or insert some parts to an object or to enable redacting some parts. But it can also result in leaking extra information. For example, a folder is shared between different users but not all of them have the same access rights for all objects in the folder. Inferring from the data structure that there are more objects in the folder than what a user has access to, the user learns the exact numbers of objects that the owner of the folder has made hidden for her.

5   Hiding Metadata

In this section, we briefly recap some important solutions from the cryptographic literature that address the metadata problem and offer partial solutions by hiding certain types of metadata. Unfortunately, for many of the proposed solutions, only inefficient instantiations are known and therefore the given techniques are not entirely suitable for real-world usage. Nevertheless, solving the hiding-metadata problem with efficient instantiations is an active and vibrant area of research.

Private information retrieval. In a private information retrieval (PIR) protocol, a user is able to query database records such that the database server is unable to tell which of the records the user accessed during that query and which not. The cryptographic literature offers a variety of proposed instantiations which can be categorized at least in single-server and multi-server variants in the information-theoretic or computational setting with different communication and computation complexity overhead, see, e.g., [12,13]. Unfortunately, in such systems, each database record has to be accessed by the database server for each user query, since otherwise the server would trivially gain at least some information about the query which renders the schemes inherently inefficient (if the server does not need to touch a record, it can not have been queried by the user). Additionally, within the PIR setting, a user might be able to obtain any record of the user's choice; hence, the PIR paradigm lacks some hidden access control mechanisms which, however, can be overcome with the following Hidden Access Control Policies (HACOT) technique.

Oblivious transfer with hidden access control policies. In the work of Camenisch et al. [14], the term Oblivious Transfer with HACOT was coined and the most efficient instantiation by now (and also a real-world implementation thereof) was given by Camenisch et al. [15]. Within their setting, each database record is associated with some hidden access control policy while any user is able to query the database in an anonymous fashion. The proposed solution uses attribute-based encryption and the user can obtain a database record if and only if the attribute(s) associated with the user's secret key matches the policy of the database record. In particular, the HACOT technique does not reveal to the database provider what database record was being accessed, what the policy of that record is, who accessed the record, and whether the access was denied or granted. (This holds even in a strong adversarial model, where a malicious database server is allowed to collude with the key issuer.) Nevertheless, the database server can monitor the amount of total accesses. Unfortunately, the given HACOT real-world implementation from [15] is quite inefficient in a large-scale setting.

Oblivious random-access memory. All described techniques above only consider reading of database records. If however one wants to deal with oblivious write operations, one has to consider oblivious random-access memory (ORAM). The technique and a scheme was proposed by Goldreich and Ostrovsky [16]. A more efficient ORAM instantiation (based on the Goldreich-Ostrovsky system) was given by Pinkas and Reinman [17]. Unfortunately, as with the other described techniques above, ORAM is still considered to be quite impractical for real-world large-scale usage.

Anonymous credentials. Specifically in the case of identity provisioning, anonymous credentials can be used to authenticate a user while only revealing the absolutely minimum necessary information. Such schemes have been envisioned by Chaum [18,19], and several practically efficient instantiations exist, with the most prominent ones being IBM's identity mixer [20,21] and Microsoft's UProve [22]. In such a system, the user receives a credential on its attributes, and can dynamically choose which attributes to reveal to a service provider, while not leaking any information about undisclosed attributes. In those schemes, the authentication process is done fully locally, and thus there is no need for a central IdP and also the related metadata-privacy problems disappear. However, these constructions are inherently non-cloudified, as the attributes are required in the plain for performing authentication, contradicting the ambition of a solution not requiring any key material, dedicated software, or heavy computations on the user's side, cf. Sect. 3.1.

Recently, Krenn et al. [23] suggested the first anonymous credential system based on proxy re-encryption, where the authentication can be outsourced to a semi-trusted IdP, having the advantage that neither specific software nor heavy computations are required on the users' side. However, re-inventing the central IdP also re-introduces all the metadata problems, which are not further addressed in their work.

6   Metadata-Hiding Identity Provisioning

As discussed in the previous section, existing cryptographic mechanisms are either not suited or too inefficient for usage in a large-scale central identity provider. In the following we will therefore present a potential high-level architecture of a metadata-privacy respecting IdP. The main idea is to split the identity provider into two components. A first component communicates with the user, whereas a second component communicates with the service providers. Assuming that those two entities do not collaborate, we can circumvent many of the discussed metadata problems while not negatively impacting the usability of the overall system.

In the following we assume that a user U received an authentication credential in form of a signature on encrypted attributes from an issuer, and stored it to the first part of the identity provider, i.e., IdP_1, together with a re-encryption key from its personal public key to the public key of the second part of the identity provider, i.e., IdP_2 (note here that this computation requires access to the user's secret key). The used encryption scheme needs to support at least two subsequent proxy re-encryption operations. Furthermore, we assume that the user wants to log in to a service provider SP, which has already been accessed by some user previously. If this was not the case, the SP and the two identity providers jointly perform in a multi-party computation protocol, at the end of which IdP_2 learns the required re-encryption key from its own public key to that of SP. This protocol is necessary because for obvious reasons neither IdP_1 nor IdP_2 must learn the secret key corresponding to IdP_2's public key, but rather the key needs to be appropriately shared between them.

The following protocol shows the message flow for a login process, assuming that every sent message is supplemented by a zero-knowledge proof of knowledge showing the correctness of the performed computations [24].

- In a first step, U contacts SP (via some anonymized network layer, e.g., using Tor as an anonymization service). The two parties agree on a random session identifier *sid* and the set of attributes to be disclosed.
- Next, the user encrypts the indices of the required attributes, *sid*, and the identity of SP under the public key of the second part of the identity provider, IdP_2, yielding a ciphertext c.
- The user then contacts (and potentially authenticates itself towards) the first part of the identity provider, IdP_1. It hands c to IdP_1.
- In a fourth step, IdP_1 re-encrypts a re-randomized version of U's encrypted credential to the public key of IdP_2, and forwards the result together with c to IdP_2.
- Next, IdP_2 decrypts c and computes a presentation token for SP. It therefore re-encrypts the requested attributes for SP, thereby redacting the remaining attributes in order to show the validity of the underlying credential. This can, e.g., be done similar to Krenn et al. [23].
- The service provider contacts IdP_2 and hands over *sid*.
- If the received *sid*'s are equal, IdP_2 forwards the presentation token to SP, which grants the user access in case that the presentation token is valid.

The above approach requires that the two parts of the identity provider do not collude. In this case, the following privacy requirements can be given. On the one hand, IdP_1 only learns that U is authenticating to some service provider, but it neither learns which attributes will be disclosed nor the identity of the service provider. Therefore, no sensitive information is leaked to IdP_1. On the other hand, IdP_2 only learns that some user is authenticating itself towards a specific service provider, but it neither learns the user nor the plain values of the revealed attributes. Again, IdP_2 therefore does not learn critical information about a specific user if the number of users is sufficiently large.

From a computational point of view, the costs of our conceptual architecture should be comparable to previous single IdP solutions such as, e.g., Krenn et al. [23], while giving far higher privacy guarantees. Security-wise the above protocol achieves similar guarantees as [23] by assuming essentially passive adversaries in the sense that the identity providers try to learn as much information about the user, but do not actively behave maliciously.

7   Conclusion

The workshop took advantage of the different expertise present in the focus groups. Experts from different domains discussed the opportunities and challenges of the CREDENTIAL approach towards a privacy-preserving IDMaaS and data sharing solution. The discussions covered various aspects such as challenges related to user trust, or potential business models and applications of the resulting systems. Special attention was paid to the necessity of metadata-privacy and the related technical obstacles. This report summarizes the results of the focus groups. Furthermore, it presents a potential high-level architecture of a metadata-privacy respecting identity provider which arose based on the inputs from the focus groups.

A first step for future work will include the formal modeling, specification, and security and privacy analysis of this proposed concept architecture.

Acknowledgement. The authors would like to thank the workshop participants for their valuable comments and inputs during the focus groups. In particular, we want to thank Anna Klughammar for her introductory presentation on the eHealth pilot, Charlotte Bäccman and John Sören Pettersson for moderating the second focus group, and Karl Koch for providing us with his extra notes for the third focus group.

References

1. Blaze, M., Bleumer, G., Strauss, M.: Divertible protocols and atomic proxy cryptography. In: Nyberg, K. (ed.) EUROCRYPT 1998. LNCS, vol. 1403, pp. 127–144. Springer, Heidelberg (1998). doi:10.1007/BFb0054122
2. Johnson, R., Molnar, D., Song, D., Wagner, D.: Homomorphic signature schemes. In: Preneel, B. (ed.) CT-RSA 2002. LNCS, vol. 2271, pp. 244–262. Springer, Heidelberg (2002). doi:10.1007/3-540-45760-7_17
3. Hörandner, F., Krenn, S., Migliavacca, A., Thiemer, F., Zwattendorfer, B.: CREDENTIAL: a framework for privacy-preserving cloud-based data sharing. In: Availability, Reliability and Trust - SECPID@ARES 2016, pp. 742–749 (2016)
4. Cantor, S., Kemp, J., Philpott, R., Maler, E.: Assertions and protocols for the OASIS Security Assertion Markup Language (SAML) V2.0 - Errata Composite. Technical report, OASIS (2009)
5. Sakimura, N., Bradley, J., Jones, M., de Medeiros, B., Mortimore, C.: OpenID Connect Core 1.0. Technical report, OpenID (2014)
6. European Commission: Regulation (EU) No 910/2014 of the European Parliament and the Council of 23 July 2014 on electronic identification and trust services for electronic transactions in the internal market. Official Journal of the European Union **L257/73** (2014)
7. European Commission: Regulation (EU) No 679/2016 of the European Parliament and of the Council of 27 April 2016 on the protection of natural persons with regard to the processing of personal data and on the free movement of such data, and repealing Directive 95/46/EC (General Data Protection Regulation). Official Journal of the European Union **L119/59** (2016)
8. BankID: Swedish BankID. https://www.bankid.com/en/. Accessed 27 Oct 2016
9. Breen, M.: Nothing to hide: why metadata should be presumed relevant. Kans. Law Rev. **56**(2), 439 (2008). Kansas Law Review Inc
10. Conley, C.: Metadata: piecing together a privacy solution **56**(2) (2014). https://ssrn.com/abstract=2573962 or doi:10.2139/ssrn.2573962
11. Greschbach, B., Kreitz, G., Buchegger, S.: The devil is in the metadata - new privacy challenges in decentralised online social networks. In: PerCom 2012, 333–339. IEEE Computer Society (2012)

12. Chor, B., Kushilevitz, E., Goldreich, O., Sudan, M.: Private information retrieval. J. ACM **45**, 965–981 (1998)
13. Kushilevitz, E., Ostrovsky, R.: Replication is NOT needed: SINGLE database, computationally-private information retrieval. In: FOCS 1997, pp. 364–373. IEEE Computer Society (1997)
14. Camenisch, J., Dubovitskaya, M., Neven, G., Zaverucha, G.M.: Oblivious transfer with hidden access control policies. In: Catalano, D., Fazio, N., Gennaro, R., Nicolosi, A. (eds.) PKC 2011. LNCS, vol. 6571, pp. 192–209. Springer, Heidelberg (2011). doi:10.1007/978-3-642-19379-8_12
15. Camenisch, J., Dubovitskaya, M., Enderlein, R.R., Neven, G.: Oblivious transfer with hidden access control from attribute-based encryption. In: Visconti, I., Prisco, R. (eds.) SCN 2012. LNCS, vol. 7485, pp. 559–579. Springer, Heidelberg (2012). doi:10.1007/978-3-642-32928-9_31
16. Goldreich, O., Ostrovsky, R.: Software protection and simulation on oblivious RAMs. J. ACM **43**, 431–473 (1996)
17. Pinkas, B., Reinman, T.: Oblivious RAM revisited. In: Rabin, T. (ed.) CRYPTO 2010. LNCS, vol. 6223, pp. 502–519. Springer, Heidelberg (2010). doi:10.1007/978-3-642-14623-7_27
18. Chaum, D.: Untraceable electronic mail, return addresses, and digital pseudonyms. Commun. ACM **24**, 84–88 (1981)
19. Chaum, D.: Security without identification: transaction systems to make big brother obsolete. Commun. ACM **28**, 1030–1044 (1985)
20. Camenisch, J., Herreweghen, E.V.: Design and implementation of the idemix anonymous credential system. In: Atluri, V. (ed.) CCS 2002, pp. 21–30. ACM (2002)
21. Camenisch, J., Lysyanskaya, A.: An efficient system for non-transferable anonymous credentials with optional anonymity revocation. In: Pfitzmann, B. (ed.) EUROCRYPT 2001. LNCS, vol. 2045, pp. 93–118. Springer, Heidelberg (2001). doi:10.1007/3-540-44987-6_7
22. Paquin, C., Zaverucha, G.: U-prove Cryptographic Specification v1.1 (Revision 2). Technical report, Microsoft Corporation (2013)
23. Krenn, S., Salzer, A., Striecks, C.: Attribute-based credentials on encrypted attributes (2016, unpublished manuscript)
24. Bellare, M., Goldreich, O.: On defining proofs of knowledge. In: Brickell, E.F. (ed.) CRYPTO 1992. LNCS, vol. 740, pp. 390–420. Springer, Heidelberg (1993). doi:10.1007/3-540-48071-4_28

The Role of Privacy in the Framework for Responsible Research and Innovation in ICT for Health, Demographic Change and Ageing

Bernd Carsten Stahl[1(✉)] and Emad Yaghmaei[2]

[1] De Montfort University, Leicester, UK
bstahl@dmu.ac.uk
[2] University of Southern Denmark, Sonderburg, Denmark
emad@mci.sdu.dk

Abstract. Responsible Research and Innovation (RRI) is an approach to research governance that promotes the sustainability, acceptability and desirability of research and innovation processes and outputs. Given the importance of private sector companies in funding and executing research and in particular innovation, it is important to understand how their practices map onto RRI. This paper describes the role of RRI in industry and then focuses on the way in which privacy can be considered. It draws on a workshop undertaken in the context of the IFIP Summer School on Privacy and Identity Management to develop some suggestions on future integration of privacy in RRI for industry.

Keywords: Responsible innovation · Privacy · Data protection · RRI framework · RRI in industry

1 Introduction

Responsible Research and Innovation (RRI) is now a well-known approach in the field of research governance. The RRI concept has been progressing and received support from of previous European research programmes, as well as European and national policies. It is now widely acknowledged that the future of new technologies requires consideration of the social and ethical aspects and a genuine engagement of all stakeholders. Stakeholder engagement approaches have been widely accepted among research and innovation actors as the new normative foundation (e.g. Greenwood 2007; DEECD 2011). These approaches are especially fruitful for the development of emerging technologies, quantum computing, nanotechnologies, internet of things or synthetic biology, to name but a few, where multiple innovative initiatives are in place to address advanced innovation issues, and stakeholder dialogue are organized at different levels (i.e. local, regional, national, and international levels).

The European Commission report "Options for Strengthening Responsible Research and Innovation" (European Commission 2013) outlines the fact that a large number of innovation fields still lack RRI approaches. In fact, the focus of RRI is currently mainly

© IFIP International Federation for Information Processing 2016
Published by Springer International Publishing AG 2016. All Rights Reserved
A. Lehmann et al. (Eds.): Privacy and Identity 2016, IFIP AICT 498, pp. 92–104, 2016.
DOI: 10.1007/978-3-319-55783-0_8

on the project and policy level of publicly funded research, and little attention has been given to industry contexts. Research and innovation in industry need to embed consideration of values, such as privacy, security, sustainability, among others, into the innovation process for industrial stakeholder and citizens.

For example, when big data and internet of things (IoT) are combined with stakeholder engagement, and comply with privacy regulation and data protection principles, they enable a better understanding of users' expectations and behaviors. These could ultimately support the creation of innovative products and services, anticipate the right designs for them, and help discover appropriate ways to use them.

The paper starts by discussing the concept of RRI and explaining how it relates to industry. This is followed by a description of the framework for RRI in Industry that was used as a basis for the workshop. This workshop, and the way it was framed around the question of privacy in RRI for Industry, is discussed in the subsequent section. The discussion section highlights key insights which inform recommendations spelled out in the conclusion.

2   RRI in Industry

In defining RRI, Von Schomberg (2011) argues that "a transparent, interactive process by which societal actors and innovators become mutually responsive to each other with a view on the (ethical) acceptability, sustainability and societal desirability of the innovation process and its marketable products".

The European Commission's reading of RRI comprises six key areas: Governance; Public engagement; Gender equality; Science education; Open access/open science; Ethics (European Commission 2012). More recent work on RRI focuses on expanding the notion in relation to societal challenges. The Rome Declaration in 2014 emphasizes that "the benefits of Responsible Research and Innovation go beyond alignment with society: it ensures that research and innovation deliver on the promise of smart, inclusive and sustainable solutions to our societal challenges." (Rome Declaration 2014). In line with this approach, the recent report from the Expert Group on Policy Indicators for Responsible Research and Innovation (Strand et al. 2015) has considered two additional areas: "sustainability" and "social justice/inclusion", in reference to the Europe 2020 strategy.

An alternative reading of RRI that is based on the work undertaken by Owen, Stilgoe and their collaborators (Owen et al. 2013; Stilgoe et al. 2013), and that was subsequently adopted by the UK Engineering and Physical Sciences Research Council, which proposed the AREA framework as key to RRI (Owen 2014). AREA stands for anticipation, reflection, engagement and action. It suggests that research and innovation, in order to be responsible, need to anticipate possible outcomes and impacts, to reflect on the research and innovation activities themselves as well as the way they are implemented, to engage with relevant stakeholders and to take action according to the outcomes of the first three steps. This reading of RRI is arguably broader than the one proposed by the European Commission based on its policy agendas, but they both aim in the same direction of rendering research and innovation more open to societal influences with a view to ensuring they meet societal needs.

One shortcoming of the RRI discourse is that it is mostly focused on publicly funded research. This is understandable, as it is driven by public research funders who have an interest in ensuring that their work contributes to the wellbeing of the taxpayers who provide the funding for the research. At the same time, it is a shortcoming, as much research and most of the innovation activities that are closer to the market are undertaken by companies. The question of whether and how RRI principles and ideas are already implemented in industry and how current practices can improve industrial research and innovation activities is therefore at the heart of this paper.

To give a number of examples, the benefits of mitigating risks associated with the innovative actions, the enhancement of company brand value, greater competitive advantage in the market, and attracting the best talent by engaging citizens and public authorities are perfectly understood as advantages by industrial stakeholders that can be encouraged to develop a genuine interest in RRI. In so far as responsible innovation leads, for a company, to developing added value, making its business more sustainable and enabling its customers to have more privacy, tapping into new markets, launching new business models, and increasing customers and stakeholders' confidence, industrial stakeholders can be expected to commit to an RRI approach.

However in practice, industrial stakeholder engagement in responsible innovation as it stands is facing significant obstacles. These limitations most often come from the fact that these benefits are long-term objectives, and responsible innovation can be viewed in the first place as a constraint, or an additional norm – in both cases, an external element, far away from the core business and immediate value of the company. While the ambition to move towards RRI is supported, the practical route to responsible innovation for industry remains difficult. In markets where awareness of social and environmental impacts can deliver economic value, can companies continue to avoid Responsible Innovation? Is RRI a prerogative of those public research organizations and large companies that have either a duty or the resources to address these aspects?

A lack of awareness of ethical, legal, environmental and social issues often leads companies to either overestimate or underestimate the associated risks (Carroll and Shabana 2010). Fundamentally, costs and time to overcome the environmental, social or ethical challenges of an innovation are considered too high, and the business will opt for the development of other – more standardized – products and services that do not raise 'unmanageable' concerns. In another case, companies equally consider that they have insufficient time and resources to take these challenges on board and would then prefer to ignore them, and push their service or product forward, overlooking stakeholders' concerns or legal and social regulations, irrespective of the fact that these may eventually jeopardize their business model (Carroll and Shabana 2010). In both cases, the "environment" is seen as a threat, not as an opportunity. Furthermore, the detriment to innovation is obvious: new products and services are not launched, or they are developed with a weak consideration of their environment and ultimately have a greater chance of failing.

However for companies, ignoring responsible innovation challenges is no longer an option either. The acceptability of their business is at stake and opportunities of advanced positions in markets can be lost.

More regulation may not be the answer to engage companies in RRI because few new issues have arisen that were not anticipated. Many aspects of RRI are subject to regulation, but exclusively relying on public regulation is unlikely to achieve the aim of ensuring RRI acceptability and desirability.

This leads to key questions such as: How can the route to responsible innovation be made easier? Is this a matter of leading companies to responsible innovation, or of growing responsible innovation in the business innovation?

The range of innovation support methods (e.g. Dahlander and Gann 2010) becomes richer every year with new approaches and concepts developed: eco-design, cradle to cradle, the circular economy, open innovation etc. These methods have proven to be efficient in many respects. Nonetheless, they often face limits as they only consider one aspect of the business. Whilst a particular value can be gained e.g. making privacy for research and innovation, the whole business model depends on a larger series of aspects that are all equally important. Often the gap to applying responsible innovation lies in the fact that these innovation support methods are used in isolation.

Collectively, social, environmental and ethical issues should be addressed in particular industries. Specific issues such as privacy need to be taken into account, and specific knowledge needs to be taken on board, for example with regards to established ways of dealing with such issues. This requires support tools and roadmaps to be adapted to the particular features of the industry and calls for a collaborative approach, where companies and support organizations draw external resources of knowledge and advice, whilst engaging with stakeholders. The questions remain, however, how this can happen, who should be in charge and how success can be measured. In order to respond to these questions we have developed what we called a framework for RRI in industry that we outline in the next section.

3   Framework of RRI in Industry

In order to better understand how RRI is currently undertaken in industry and which gaps remain, the Responsible-Industry project (www.responsible-industry.eu) undertook a number of activities to map current practice, compare it with the RRI discourse, and develop ideas about how RRI can be integrated into industrial practice. The activities undertaken by the project include a review of the literature on RRI and industry, five illustrative case studies, a set of 30 expert interviews with stakeholders from the information and communication technology (ICT) industry and a Delphi Study comprising more than 170 respondents. On this basis we developed a framework for RRI in industry.[1]

This framework starts with a vision of RRI industry that shows its roots as well as the link with existing activities. It provides options and recommendations for

---

[1] The full text of this framework is available on the project website. The full URL is: http://www.responsible-industry.eu/activities/framework-for-implementing-rri (accessed 11.11.2016).

implementing RRI in companies. These are grouped around key questions such as who is responsible for what? How can RRI be integrated along the value chain? How can ethical and social impact analysis be performed? What tools can be used for RRI?

The ensuing recommendations can be summarized as follows:

- Reflect on a vision for RRI within the organization, promoting capacity building and instilling RRI in the culture of the organization.
- Integrate RRI into existing structures and processes, including research and innovation (R&I), corporate social responsibility, quality and other company functions.
- Promote reflection and awareness of ethical and societal issues related to specific R&I products in ICT for an ageing society.
- Perform in depth ethical analysis of ICT products/services from early stages of the R&I value chain.
- Support early identification of appropriate preventive and precautionary measures.
- Foster stakeholder engagement, and in particular end users, from early stages of product development.
- Pursue open and transparent communication with stakeholders about risk and impact.
- Perform ongoing assessment and management of the impacts of ICT products and services, both in the short/medium term and longterm.
- Ensure training and professional development opportunities to enable staff to fully participate and take responsibility.
- Foster multidisciplinarity between engineering, natural sciences, ethics and social sciences.
- Apply equality principles in recruitment and career progression.

The framework also provides examples of policy and communication actions that can support and foster RRI in industry and links to resources that enable these to be realized.

This framework is currently being tested and scrutinized through a number of in-depth case studies and industry-led focus groups. It will be finalized in early 2017. The workshop during the IFIP summer school served as one way of assessing the quality and value of the framework. Its specific question was whether privacy is well represented in the framework and how this might be improved.

4 RRI, Privacy and Economic Concerns

Privacy is the most widely discussed ethical and social concern linked to ICT (Stahl et al. 2016). Concerns around privacy are not novel and contemporary discussion is often led back to Warren and Brandeis' seminal paper on the topic (Warren and Brandeis 1890). It is therefore not surprising that privacy has been highlighted as a key concern that RRI in ICT needs to deal with (Stahl 2013). Achieving data safety and security in ICT is not what companies might expect by applying RRI in the first place but it is certainly something that is highly discussed in responsibility in ICT in long run. The threat is obvious. Breaches of privacy occur not just from a theft of customer data and passwords or credit cards. In fact, if companies have too many breaches of data privacy that undermines consumer trust, which is absolutely counter productive to the use of technologies that could otherwise have a beneficial effect on environmental and social questions. Thus, it is absolutely essential that ICT must comply with basic privacy principles as laid down by the General Data Protection Regulations (GDPR)[2].

Before we discuss how privacy concerns have been integrated into the framework for RRI in industry, however, we think it is important to highlight that privacy is far from the only ethical issue that companies need to consider. This implies that ways of addressing privacy need to be sensitive to other ethical and social issues. Similarly, privacy as a social value can conflict with other values. Ways need to be found to balance competing values. Data ownership, quality of data, intellectual property and traceability are some of the most important issues of debate from a legal and technical point of view (Baysinger et al. 1991; Granstrand 1999; Batini et al. 2009). Based on an open innovation model, these technologies challenge traditional business models: where does the value stem from: the data or the service? What is the most effective way to redistribute dividends to different links in the value chain?

Emerging technologies and big data imply a significant pervasiveness of technology in every place and a new set of relations between individuals and objects, with a stronger dependence on ICT, despite and because of its original ambition to increase its relevance and adherence to users' needs. Big can include the collection of large amounts of personal information, the protection of which is regularly challenged. Regardless of the definition of privacy, one can realize a significant role for it in solving research and innovation challenges in emerging technologies and big data. The GDPR and its requirements for privacy impact assessment (Clarke 2009; Information Commissioner's Office 2009) or an ethics impact assessment (Wright 2011) are very high on the companies' agenda these days because of either the necessity of assessment activities towards privacy issues or the increased fines that the GDPR (see Section 148) will introduce and which therefore may scare industry. As such, industrial stakeholders dealing with ICT must consider privacy in order to address RRI issues, and ICT designers must highlight privacy by design in their design process (Guerses et al. 2011; Hoven et al. 2012; Information Commissioner's Office 2008).

From an economic viewpoint, being aware of these challenges and developing a capacity to address them will enable any company to become more competitive and sustainable. While emerging technologies and big data are more than ever at a crossroad between ethical issues and economic opportunities, what role can a company play in this area? How can a company seize and create value from big data whilst still operating in an ethical and safe environment? Some initiatives have been taken to draw entrepreneurs' attention to the ethical and legal issues raised by emerging technologies and big data. However, companies support services often remain segmented: business development, legal and ICT aspects and social issues (such as stakeholder engagement) are not addressed systematically, and are usually separated from one another for the simple reason that they relate to different expertise and organizational units.

---

[2] See: http://eur-lex.europa.eu/legal-content/EN/TXT/?uri=uriserv:OJ.L_.2016.119.01.0001. 01.ENG&toc=OJ:L:2016:119:TOC, accessed 27.01.2017.

The responsible innovation framework will take the ambition to address all related challenges in a comprehensive approach by bringing together stakeholders and experts, and eventually help companies, in particular ICT companies to benefit from the big data revolution whilst securing their own development.

4.1 Privacy in the RRI Framework

In light of the importance of privacy in ICT in general, as well as the possible conflict between privacy and other values, it is important to spell out which role privacy plays in version of the framework for RRI in industry that was used in the workshop.

Privacy first appears in the framework document in the context of open questions that should motivate companies to consider RRI. These are a list of likely upcoming developments that can raise concern and of which companies should be aware. This list was compiled on the basis of the AALIANCE2 roadmap[3], a document stemming from the AALIANCE 2 project for the purpose of planning the future of assistive technologies. Privacy is recognized in this list as one of the likely concerns that can motivate companies to take RRI seriously. It forms part of a set of concerns that were summarized as individual rights and liberties that may be vulnerable to challenge from new ICTs.

One way of dealing with open questions in RRI is through the introduction and use of standards. The framework therefore highlights issues that may be subject to standardization: this includes privacy and data protection. The idea of privacy by design is strongly promoted by privacy advocates and can be seen as an attempt to create standards to safeguard this particular value. The framework therefore references these ideas as one option that companies can pursue in the governance of their research and innovation activities.

Privacy is furthermore already a well-established right enshrined in legislation and regulation. Companies wanting to be responsible need to comply with such legislation. The framework therefore makes reference to legislation such as the Privacy Directive (EC) 95/46/EC on processing and free movement of data, regulation (EC) 45/2001 on processing and free movement of data by EU institutions and bodies, Directive 2002/58/EC (e-Privacy) processing of personal data and the protection of privacy.

One can thus argue that there is significant attention paid to privacy in the framework. However, in order to ascertain whether this way of including privacy is sufficient and convincing, we undertook the workshop around privacy in the IFIP summer school that is described in the next section.

4.2 Workshop on Privacy in RRI in Industry

The idea behind the workshop was thus to collect feedback on privacy as a particular component of the framework from an audience which is either expert in privacy issues or has a high level of interest in privacy and identity management. We wanted to find out whether the way in which privacy was included in the framework resonated with

---

[3] http://www.aaliance2.eu/newaalroadmap, accessed 12.11.2016.

this audience and whether audience members could provide further insights into how to improve the framework.

It was decided to assess the framework with five groups of participants (each group consist of 2–3 members). Each group was asked whether the framework would have helped them to gain an insight into RRI, how they could develop the current responsible business model, and whether it could help the RRI community promote responsibility within research and innovation initiatives. The workshop was also used to gain further insights into whether questions of privacy and data protection are currently covered well enough, which aspects could be strengthened and how they could be communicated to intended audiences.

The aims of the workshop included:

- to reflect on the effectiveness of the RRI framework:
- to discuss the way in which privacy is represented in the framework; to explore opportunities to refine the RRI framework;
- to explore facilitation methods to best use the RRI framework.

The workshop developers introduced the responsible industry project framework, elaborated on the main aspects of RRI in industry, and presented responsible industry case studies in the domain of ICT for healthy ageing. The intention of RRI to ensure acceptability and desirability of research and innovation is often translated as a focus on grand social challenges. One of the key ones in Europe, due to its demographic development is that of healthy ageing. ICT is often portrayed as a technology that can help address this challenge, which renders ICT for healthy ageing a primary candidate for RRI.

During the second half of the workshop, participants were asked to comment directly on the framework. The aim was to gather a structured form of feedback from participants at the end of the workshop using the RRI framework to identify which methods or techniques should be applied to fulfill key responsibilities for RRI within the organization.

Relevant feedback was expected to arise from the following questions:

- How can the framework be improved?
- How should the framework be communicated and disseminated?
- Is privacy adequately covered?
- Which aspects are missing?
- How should they be included?

Documentary evidence from the workshop supported assessment of the quality and value of the framework. The collected data were used in the discussion section of this work to address the above questions.

5 Discussion

During the workshop there was a general recognition by the participants of the necessity to embed privacy in the framework for RRI in industry. This discussion section covers two different sets of concerns, both of which are important for RRI in industry. On the one hand there are issues of organizational structure and governance, which are not related to privacy per se but which are relevant in order to instill the very idea of RRI into an organization. On the other hand there are privacy issues in a narrow that immediately pertain to personal data.

The organizational issues of privacy were recognized as crucial. There was a discussion about engaging companies' owner(s) and investor(s) into RRI actions. One participant argued that "whilst probably individual investors will be more willing to implement ethical procedures, institutional investors will likely respond only to financial considerations." In principle, consultation with owner(s) in addition to chief executive officers was highly valued by the participants.

There was also discussion about the usefulness of the framework for different sizes of companies. From the responses, it is understood that the framework seems to assume a large rigid organization. It is less clear how small and medium sized enterprises (SMEs) can implement it, which has to be taken into account for further development of the framework.

The discussion and further recommendations from participants for improving the framework can be summarized as follows:

- Acknowledge the need for engaging companies' owners and stress the distinction between individual investors and institutional counterparts;
- Consider SMEs for the framework;
- Refine the actual information flows in the framework;
- Highlight the process of embedding responsibility in industry which will likely be an iterative, rather than a one-off, exercise;
- Develop some practical tools to assist thinking about RRI principles.

First, there is a common recognition by participants to involve owners of the company as well as the chief executive officer (CEO). Since the CEO executes the plan set by the owners, there is a need for the framework to stress the role of companies' owners and investors. Second, workshop participants stressed that the RRI framework targets mainly multinational corporations, and misses somewhat to consider specific approaches of applying RRI in SMEs. Third, understanding actual information flows in the framework between different sections needs to be revisited: e.g. innovation can come from any group; marketing may provide customer requests as well as disseminate information. Fourth, industrial stakeholders must consider RRI as an iterative process rather than a one-off exercise. Finally, there are still a limited number of practical RRI tools that can be used by industrial stakeholders, and this generally needs to be drawn attention to in any improved version of the RRI framework.

The RRI framework and workshop results identified the need to embed privacy into Responsible-Industry framework. Figure 1 demonstrates the interaction between privacy and various organizational functions. This figure was used to stimulate the discussion among workshop participants.

Fig. 1. Embedding privacy into the Responsible-Industry framework

Accordingly, privacy should be at the core of Responsible-Industry framework. In fact, the workshop represents the benefits delivered to industry by embedding privacy in the RRI framework. Individual stakeholders and different departments collectively may apply privacy in company' governance, innovation, compliance, and communication initiatives. Put differently, privacy helps to improve executive management, research and innovation, corporate social responsibility, legal, human resources, and marketing; steers company activities to new level of ethical behaviour"; and introduces new RRI-oriented products and services.

Whereas there was broad acceptance of the fact that a RRI framework requires privacy, one participant made an observation with regard to the relatively abstract nature of the concept of privacy used in the framework:

"Privacy is perhaps too abstract a concept in the example given of the healthcare user. Privacy as an abstract concept may not be important but personal autonomy or freedom from discrimination may be important despite requiring privacy".

The results of the discussion and the recommendations made by the workshop participants highlighted the relevance of privacy in RRI. This did not come as a surprise, given that privacy and data protection have long been recognized as a key aspect that raises concerns across a vast range of ICTs. The discussion showed furthermore that privacy is interlinked with other ethical and social concerns. It is furthermore distributed across the organization, and it is difficult to pinpoint one particular area that has exclusive or dominant responsibility for it.

From the point of view of the framework, we learned that the level of attention paid to privacy in the framework itself seems to be appropriate. There was very little discussion of the concept of privacy in the workshop. This may reflect the backgrounds of the workshop participants who had a significant amount of expertise in privacy, and who may not therefore have felt the need to delve into the conceptual side of privacy in any more detail. It may also reflect the fact that there is a finite amount of space in a document like the framework and therefore there must be a limit to the level of conceptual discussion that can be included.

An interesting finding from the workshop, from the perspective of the Responsible-Industry project and framework, was that there was also relatively little discussion of the technical detail concerning specific privacy measures. When presenting the framework to an expert audience with a particular interest in privacy and identity management, we had expected requests for more detail of the way in which privacy in ICT for health, demographic change and wellbeing is addressed. There was little discussion of such detailed questions, which we interpret as a sign that the treatment of privacy in the framework is at an appropriate level.

6   Conclusion

From the perspective of the Responsible-Industry project, the workshop described in this paper constituted an opportunity to reflect on and further refine the framework. For the participants it gave an opportunity to see the way privacy is addressed in a slightly different context where privacy is one of many different issues.

In substantive terms, the outcomes of the workshop constitutes a confirmation of the principles and content of the way in which privacy is treated by the Framework for RRI in ICT as developed by the Responsible-industry project. It did not lead to any significant changes or point to major omissions in the framework. Interestingly, it also did not point to particular technical developments that might need to be included.

The value of the workshop was in improving the presentation of the framework and raising awareness of its existence in the community of privacy scholars. It should thereby contribute to a better uptake of RRI by industrial actors, with specific reference to privacy and data protection. Privacy is a key to delivering future responsibility. The RRI framework is intended as a primary step in RRI literature for embedding privacy into the core of industrial stakeholder activities. The workshop's participants helped in raising awareness of privacy within subsequent versions of RRI frameworks, to support industrial stakeholders on the journey towards responsibility.

The workshop contributed to:

- Raising awareness of RRI principles among privacy scholars;
- Improving privacy and social inclusiveness within RRI principles and actions.

In addition to helping reflect on and improve the Responsible-Industry framework, we believe that the workshop will have developed participants' understanding of the way in which social and ethical issues in ICT more broadly can be addressed in an industrial setting.

Much research in the area of data protection and privacy is technical, focusing on questions of encryption, storage, data transmission etc. Such work is of vital importance for privacy preservation. However, we believe that the framework shows clearly that many of the key privacy concerns are not technical. A company developing a new technology needs to have the organizational resources and processes in place, in order to safeguard privacy. Without these pre-requisites, the technical capability to protect privacy is unlikely to suffice.

Working with the RRI in industry framework showed the participants the complexity and number of linkages between different organizational functions, environments and processes that need to be considered when addressing privacy issues. Finally, at the risk of stating the obvious, we believe that the workshop made it clear that privacy and data protection are one important issue but, at the same time, they are one issue among many. Privacy must not be seen in isolation, rather it should be understood as an important and valid social concern that interacts with and links to numerous others.

In this spirit, we hope that the insights gained by the Responsible-Industry consortium that will help us further refine the RRI in industry framework have been matched by the learning of workshop participants. Both of these aspects will hopefully have contributed to the overall shared goal of ensuring that new and emerging technologies contribute to the greater good of society.

Acknowledgements. The research leading to these results has received funding from the European Community's Seventh Framework Programme (FP7/2007-2013) under grant agreement n° 609817 (Responsible-Industry; www.responsible-industry.eu). The authors acknowledge the contribution of all consortium partners to the development of the framework which is the basis of this paper.

The authors would also like to thank the participants in the IFIP summer school for their input that informed the discussion section of this paper.

References

Batini, C., Cappiello, C., Francalanci, C., Maurino, A.: Methodologies for data quality assessment and improvement. ACM Comput. Surv. (CSUR) **41**(3), 16 (2009)

Baysinger, B.D., Kosnik, R.D., Turk, T.A.: Effects of board and ownership structure on corporate R&D strategy. Acad. Manag. J. **34**(1), 205–214 (1991)

Carroll, A.B., Shabana, K.M.: The business case for corporate social responsibility: a review of concepts, research and practice. Int. J. Manag. Rev. **12**(1), 85–105 (2010)

Clarke, R.: Privacy impact assessment: its origins and development. Comput. Law Secur. Rev. **25**, 123–135 (2009). doi:10.1016/j.clsr.2009.02.002

Dahlander, L., Gann, D.M.: How open is innovation? Res. Policy **39**(6), 699–709 (2010)

Department of Education and Early Childhood Development (DEECD) (2011). http://www.education.vic.gov.au/

European Commission, Investing in Research and Innovation for Grand Challenges. European Commission, DG Research. Brussels (2012). http://ec.europa.eu/research/erab/pdf/erab-study-grand-challanages-2012_en.pdf

van den Hoven, J.: European Commission, Options for Strengthening Responsible Research and Innovation. Report of the Expert Group on the State of Art in Europe on Responsible Research and Innovation. Publications Office of the European Union, Luxembourg, EUR25766 EN (2013)

Granstrand, O.: The Economics and Management of Intellectual Property. Books (1999)

Greenwood, M.: Stakeholder engagement: beyond the myth of corporate responsibility. J. Bus. Ethics **74**(4), 315–327 (2007). doi:10.1007/s10551-007-9509-y

Guerses, S., Troncoso, C. Diaz, C.: Engineering privacy by design. Paper presented at the Fourth Conference on Computers, Privacy and Data Protection, Brussels, 25–7 January 2011 (2011)

Hoven, J. van den, Helbing, D., Pedreschi, D., Domingo-Ferrer, J. et al.: FuturICT - The Road towards Ethical ICT. (2012). arXiv:1210.8181. Accessed 14 Nov 2012

Information Commissioner's Office. Privacy by design, (2008). http://www.ico.gov.uk/upload/documents/pdb_report_html/privacy_by_design_report_v2.pdf. Accessed 24 Aug 2009

Information Commissioner's Office. Privacy Impact Assessment Handbook, v. 2.0 (2009). <http://www.ico.gov.uk/upload/documents/pia_handbook_html_v2/files/PIAhandbookV2.pdf>. Accessed 24 Aug 2009

Rome Declaration on Responsible Research and Innovation in Europe. Under the Italian presidency of the European Council, November 2014

Stahl, B.C., Timmermans, J., Mittelstadt, B.D.: The Ethics of Computing: A Survey of the Computing-Oriented Literature. ACM Comput. Surv. **48**(4), 55:1–55:38 (2016). doi:10.1145/2871196

Stahl, B.C.: Responsible research and innovation: the role of privacy in an emerging framework. Sci. Public Policy **40**(6), 708–716 (2013). doi:10.1093/scipol/sct067

Stilgoe, J., Owen, R., Macnaghten, P.: Developing a framework for responsible innovation. Res. Policy, **42**(9), 1568–1580 (2013). doi:10.1016/j.respol.2013.05.008

Strand, R et al.: Indicators for promoting and monitoring responsible research and innovation. DG Research and Innovation, SWAFS June 2015

Von Schomberg, R.: Prospects for technology assessment in a framework of responsible research and innovation. In: Technikfolgen abschätzen lehren, Bildungspotenziale transdisziplinärer Methode. Springer VS, Wiesbaden (2011)

Warren, S.D., Brandeis, L.D.: Right to Privacy. Harvard Law Rev. **4**, 193 (1890)

Wright, D.: A framework for the ethical impact assessment of information technology. Ethics Inf. Technol. **13**(3), 199–226 (2011). doi:10.1007/s10676-010-9242-6

Owen, R., Heintz, M., Bessant, J. (eds.): Responsible Innovation. Wiley (2013)

Evidence-Based Methods for Privacy and Identity Management

Kovila P.L. Coopamootoo[1] and Thomas Groß[2(✉)]

[1] University of Derby, Derby, UK
[2] Newcastle University, Newcastle upon Tyne, UK
thomas.gross@newcastle.ac.uk

Abstract. In the advent of authoritative experiments and evidence-based methods in security research [2,4,21,29], we are convinced that privacy and identity research will benefit from the scientific method, as well. This workshop offers an introduction to selected tools of experiment design and systematic analysis. It includes key ingredients of evidence-based methods: hallmarks of sound experimentation, templates for the design of true experiments, and inferential statistics with sound power analysis. To gauge the state of play, we include a systematic literature review of the pre-proceedings of the 2016 IFIP Summer school on Privacy and Identity Management as well as the participants' feedback on their perception on evidence-based methods. Finally, we make our case for the endorsement of evidence-based methods in privacy and identity management.

1 Introduction

The Encyclopaedia Britannica defined *science* as a "system of knowledge that is concerned with the physical world and its phenomena and that entails unbiased observations and systematic experimentation." In general, it is a purpose of science to advance human knowledge. The scientific method is evidence-based, includes principles such as falsification or reproducibility as well as statistical tools to decide between hypotheses.

To what extent is security/privacy research a science? How does research in this field advance human knowledge? In the recent years, funding bodies have sought to strengthen evidence-based research in security and privacy and, arguably, those methods have seen adoption in the field, especially under the flag of "science of security" [2,4,21,29].

Challenges. Whereas the tenets of the scientific method are often demanded, they are easily subverted by methodological mistakes or insufficient power under the all too polished surface. Ioannidis [19] gave a harsh account of the situation, arguing "why most published research findings are false."

K.P.L. Coopamootoo—Major contributions were made while the author was at Newcastle University.

Published by Springer International Publishing AG 2016. All Rights Reserved
A. Lehmann et al. (Eds.): Privacy and Identity 2016, IFIP AICT 498, pp. 105–121, 2016.
DOI: 10.1007/978-3-319-55783-0_9

To make matters worse, there is a replication crisis in science. For example, 270 researchers of the Open Science Collaboration [27] have reported on a dire situation after having sought to reproduce 100 well-known results published in three major psychology journals [28]. They could only reproduce 39% of the results. It is deemed likely that the replication crisis also pertains to other fields, including security or privacy and identity management.

Even down to the nitty-gritty of statistical inference, many misconceptions and controversies have been observed, including, for instance, a comprehensive account of null hypothesis testing by Nickerson [26].

All that glitters is not gold. While evidence-based methods hold a promise to support the pursuit of knowledge in security and privacy, they ask of us great diligence to live up to their tenets. This IFIP workshop sought to sensitize participants to the hallmarks and inference methods of evidence-based research in privacy and identity management. It includes examples for true experiments as well as systematic literature reviews as two classes of evidence that are considered as most reliable.

Scope. Research methodology for evidence-based methods is a vast topic, filling tomes in the sciences. Consequently, this workshop summary will only offer a primer—an introduction to hallmarks, experiment design and statistical inference. Given that the workshop aimed at sensitizing for evidence-based methods and its requirements, we make a number of simplifications. We only focus on (a) true experiments (inducing an experiment condition), (b) hypothesis testing (rejecting a null hypothesis), (c) two conditions (control and experiment), (d) simple statistics (difference between means, *t*-test). Explicitly out of scope are: qualitative methods, observational studies and complex statistical models.

Outline. This workshop summary contains two theory sections on hallmarks of empirical research and statistical inference, where each of the theory section concludes with a concise checklist of quality criteria. Section 2 contains the hallmarks discussion, leading up to hypothesis testing. Then, we interleave a section on practical experiment design in Sect. 3 which reflects a round-table discussion of the workshop. From this intermezzo, we continue our theoretical inquiry with Sect. 4 on statistical inference and power. Section 5 reports on participants responses to the workshop questionnaire. We detail areas of privacy research with interest in experimental methodology, methodological issues encountered and their personal learning objective from the workshop.

2   Hallmarks of Empirical Research

Definition 1 (True Experiment [10]). *An investigation in which the investigators have sufficient control of the system under study, in particular to be able to determine the assignment of different units of study to different conditions.*

A true experiment follows requirements contributing towards rigorous science. The requirements include (a) definition of a falsifiable hypothesis, (b) defining and controlling variables, (c) assessing internal and external validity, (d) repeatability and reproducibility of the method and analysis [4, 21].

2.1   Falsifiable Hypotheses

Definition 2 (Hypothesis [12]). *Specific testable predictions made generally about the response and explanatory variables in a study.*

Testing hypotheses is one of the tenets behind scientific discovery.

Popper [30] coined the theory of falsification, whereby the researcher formulates a hypothesis such that the experiment can show it to be false. According to Popper, hypotheses cannot be inductively verified, but only empirically falsified. Falsifiable hypotheses are formulated such that they can be measured and observed.

Example 1 (Falsifiable Hypotheses).

- All swans are white. [30] (Falsifying observation: a black swan)
- Higher cognitive workload implies more click-throughs on phishing links. (Falsifying observation: experiment showing equal phishing click-troughs across workloads)

2.2   Controlled Variables

In experiments, we distinguish between three types of variables: manipulated, controlled or measured. A variable that is manipulated, the independent variable, is to predict or explain the dependent or response variable.

Definition 3 (Variable). *A* variable *is some characteristic that differs from subject to subject or from time to time [12].*

(a) The independent variable *IV is a variable that is induced/manipulated [23].*
(b) The dependent variable *DV is a variable that is observed/measured [23]. A systematic change in the IV causes a change in the DV.*
(c) A confounding variable *(short:* confounder*) is an extraneous variable whose presence affects the variables being studied, so that the results do not reflect the actual relationship between the IV and DV.*

Methods to actively control confounding variables include random assignment of subjects to conditions, restricting variation in confounders (e.g., selecting subjects of the same age eliminates confounding by age) and matching potential confounders across conditions. Statistical models can also be used to adjust for the bias introduced by a confounder during analysis.

2.3 Validity

Validity refers to the extent to which a measuring instrument is measuring what was intended [12], where a change in the IV entails a change in the DV.

Definition 4 (Validity [9]). *The best available approximation to the truth and falsity of propositions.*

What we seek to validate are the statements, inferences and conclusions that we draw from results of empirical research [3]. We differentiate between internal and external validity.

Internal Validity. In most experiments, researchers are aiming to find out if IV A has an effect on DV B. If the experiment does not offer any alternative causes nor explanations on the outcome on B, then the experiment is internally valid.

Definition 5 (Internal Validity [3]). *The truth that can be assigned to the conclusion that a cause-effect relationship between an IV and a DV has been established within the context of the particular research setting.*

External Validity refers to the extent to which the study findings are generalizable from a laboratory setting to other settings.

Definition 6 (External Validity [3]). *The question of whether an effect (and its underlying processes) that has been demonstrated in one research setting would be obtained in other settings, with different research participants and different research procedures.*

Not all experiments can be both internally and externally valid. Depending on the purpose of the experiment, researchers need to make a trade-off.

2.4 Repeatability and Reproducibility

Replication is the attempt to recreate the conditions sufficient to obtaining a previous observed finding [28]. Scientific claims gain credence when their supporting evidence can be replicated [28].

Replication has been highlighted as a problem in scientific research. For example, the Open Science Collaboration [28] conducted a large-scale replication study ($N = 100$) of psychological journals and found that replication effects were on average half the magnitude of original effects.

We distinguish between repeatability and reproducibility as two conceptual frames for replication.

Definition 7 (Repeatability [12]). *The closeness of the results obtained in the same test material by the same observer or technician using the same equipment, apparatus and/or reagents over reasonably short intervals of time.*

Definition 8 (Reproducibility [12]). *The closeness of results obtained on the same test material under changes of reagents, conditions, technicians, apparatus, laboratories and so on.*

Remark 1 (Repeatability vs. Reproducibility). While repeatability refers to replicating the experiment by keeping everything same (including the experimenter), reproducibility refers to altering specific components while keeping the design consistent, especially when the experiment is reproduced by an independent experimenter.

2.5 Hypothesis Testing

In this workshop summary, we limit the scope of our inquiry to *hypothesis testing* [15,20,25], a particular method of statistical inference that seeks to distinguish between hypotheses. We focus on making a decision between a null hypothesis and an alternative hypothesis.

Definition 9 (Hypothesis Testing)

(a) A statistical hypothesis test is a method of statistical inference in which a hypothesis of a proposed statistical relationship is compared to an idealized null hypothesis that claims there is no relationship.

(b) The null hypothesis H_0 is the statistical hypothesis that there is no effect, no difference between conditions.

(c) The alternative hypothesis H_1 is the statistical hypothesis that there is an effect, a difference between conditions.

Hypotheses are expressed on the population statistics, not the sample statistics.

> *Example 2 (Difference of Means).* When considering the means across two conditions, the two hypotheses are:
> – Null hypothesis H_0: $\mu_1 = \mu_2$,
> – Alternative hypothesis H_1: $\mu_1 \neq \mu_2$.

A sound procedure for hypothesis testing will proceed as illustrated in Fig. 1.

1. State null hypothesis H_0 and alternative hypothesis H_1 explicitly, first.
2. Evaluate the statistical assumptions made, select a relevant test statistic, and select a significance level α, a probability threshold below which the null hypothesis will be rejected (cf. Sect. 4.1).
3. Evaluate the statistical inference by calculating the test statistic. Reject the null hypothesis if and only if the p-value is less than the specified significance level α.

We will discuss statistical inference and p-values in Sect. 4.1.

Remark 2 (Controversy and Criticism) There has been much controversy about hypothesis testing. Among its most vocal critics is Jacob Cohen [7]. First, we need to note that a statistically significant result only means that the effect is deemed not *nil*, nothing more. Slavishly following the "sanctification by significance" has been considered as one of great ailments in scientific reasoning. Nickerson [26] offers a comprehensive overview of the controversies around *Null*

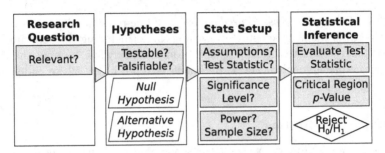

Fig. 1. Simplified process of hypothesis testing.

Hypothesis Significance Testing (NHST), of which we highlight misconceptions on p-values in Remark 3 (Sect. 4.1).

Multiple proponents have argued to deprioritize hypothesis testing in favor of robust estimation with confidence intervals, e.g., as expressed by Gardner and Altman [17]. The American Psychology Association (APA) [1] has consequently made the reporting of confidence intervals a minimum standard.

While this workshop summary adheres to hypothesis testing, we advocate a cautious and diligent interpretation: Consider the size of effects investigated, the required power and sample size to detect those effects (cf. Sect. 4.2).

2.6 Checklist: Hallmarks

☐ Make hypotheses falsifiable, i.e., construct them such that experiments or observations can show them to be false.

☐ Specify independent variables (IVs) and their manipulation. Operationalise dependent variables (DVs) and specify validated measurements.

☐ Explicitly declare null hypothesis and alternative hypothesis *a priori*.

☐ If feasible, prepare a randomized controlled testing the hypotheses.

☐ Control for confounders, e.g., by restricting variation or matching subjects.

☐ Establish to what extent a change in IV entails a change in DV. Report biases and assumptions that impact this entailment.

☐ Make it clear whether the study is repeating or reproducing existing research. Document recruitment, sampling, procedure, experiment design, manipulations, measurements, analyses clearly for forward reproducibility.

3   An Exercise in Experiment Design

We have prepared the ground by introducing hypothesis testing. Before we proceed with statistical inference in Sect. 4, we discuss an exercise in experiment design based on a hypothetical scenario.

> *Example 3 (Scenario "When the cat's away, the mice do play").*
> A security company observes that in the evenings—when the boss—is away more dangerous sites are accessed than during day times.

3.1 Developing Research Questions

The participants are asked to answer the following questions:

1. What is an interesting research question (RQ) for the scenario of clicks to dangerous sites?
2. Independent Variable (IV): What factor influences the number of clicks on dangerous sites?
3. Dependent Variable (DV): How can we measure the outcome reliably?
4. What is a testable null hypothesis (H_0)?
5. What is the alternative hypothesis (H_1)?

We advocate for the simple example research questions to create a core experiment design to nail down how the IV is manipulated, how he success of this manipulation is checked, and how the DV is reliably measured. We offer a template in Fig. 2. Cf. Field and Hole [14] or Montgomery [24] for experiment designs.

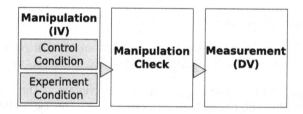

Fig. 2. A core template for a two-condition experiment with manipulation check.

The following examples were designed by workshop participants in round-table discussions in response to the questions above.

> *Example 4 (Design Group 1).*
> **RQ.** How does the presence of the boss impact clicking dangerous links? **IV.** Presence of the boss. **DV.** #mistakes clicking dangerous links. **H_0.** The mean number of mistakes is equal between the conditions "boss present" and "boss absent." **H_1.** The mean number of mistakes is greater when the boss is absent.

Example 5 (Design Group 2).
RQ. How does cognitive workload impact clicking phishing links? **IV.** Cognitive workload. **DV.** #mistakes clicking phishing links. H_0. The mean number of phishing mistakes is equal between the depleted experiment condition and the non-depleted control condition. H_1. The mean number of phishing mistakes is greater in the depleted condition than in the control condition.

Example 6 (Design Group 3).
RQ. How does down-time impact clicking of dangerous sites? **IV.** Down-time without customer. **DV.** #mistakes accessing dangerous sites. H_0. The mean number of accesses to dangerous sites is independent from the measured down-time. H_1. An increased down-time implies an increased mean number of accesses to dangerous sites.

We see from this example that for a given scenario a variety of relevant research questions and operationalizations in statistical hypotheses is possible. Consequently, it is crucial to write down precisely what is being investigated before the experiment is designed. The key points here are to commit to the independent and dependent variables, to settle the manipulation and measurement methods used, and to express the null and alternative hypotheses in the exact terms of these variables.

3.2 Structured Abstract

We recommend a *structured abstract* as a concise tool of stating the intention of an experiment (in less than one page). The structured abstract covers

1. **Background.** The motivation and theoretical context of the experiment.
2. **Aim.** The goal of the experiment expressed in one concise sentence.
3. **Method.** The concise method of the experiment, including sample size, group design, what is manipulated (IV) and what is measured (DV).
4. **Expected Results.** The factual outcomes expected from the experiment.
5. **Expected Impact.** So what? What does the experiment mean?

A structured abstract is a superb tool in reporting findings soundly and endorsed by specialist venues, such as Learning from Authoritative Security Experiment Results (LASER)[1]. Example 7 reports the outcome of the scenario study.

---

[1] http://www.laser-workshop.org.

Example 7 (Structured Abstract).
Background. Psychology research predicts an impact of tiredness on decision making.
Aim. We investigate the impact of tiredness on mistakes on phishing click-throughs.
Method. Two groups of 20 participants each were asked to evaluate 50 mixed e-mails (25 phishing), one group was tired, the other was not. We compared the number of mistakes across groups.
Results. The mean number of mistakes of the tired group ($M_E = 13.9, SD_E = 5.77$) was significantly greater than that of the control group ($M_C = 10.75, SD_C = 3.75$), two-tailed $t(38) = -2.047, p = .049$, 95% CI[0.18, 6.28]. We observed a medium effect size ($d = 0.68$).[a] The experiment achieved a power of 55%.
Impact. Tired users succumb to phishing.

---

[a] Reporting confidence intervals (CI) and the effect size as mandated by the APA guidelines [1].

4 Statistical Inference and Power

4.1 Statistical Inference

As we have seen in Sect. 2.5, we seek to decide between the null hypothesis H_0 and the alternative hypothesis H_1. We do not know what the situation in reality is: whether H_0 is true or false. All we can do is making an observation (in an experiment) and base a decision to reject or accept H_0 on the likelihood of that observation. Because H_0 and H_1 are meant to be complements, we end up with four decision outcomes summarized in Table 1.

Let us consider the left-hand column of Table 1 first: In reality, the null hypothesis H_0 is true. We specify in advance a significance criterion α, which quantifies the likelihood of mistakenly rejecting the null hypothesis H_0. As Cohen formulates it [8], "α represents a policy: the maximum risk of attending such a rejection." If we reject H_0 even though H_0 is true, we commit a *Type I Error*.

If we correctly reject the alternative hypothesis H_1 and hence accept the null hypothesis H_0, we do so at a confidence level $1 - \alpha$ Fig. 3.

Table 1. Statistical inference decision matrix.

Reality / Decision	H_0 is TRUE. H_1 is FALSE.	H_0 is FALSE. H_1 is TRUE.
We reject H_1.	**Confidence Level** $1 - \alpha$	**TYPE II ERROR** β
We reject H_0.	**TYPE I ERROR** α	**POWER** $1 - \beta$

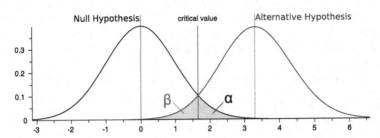

Fig. 3. Hypothesis testing with null hypothesis $\mathsf{H_0}$ test distribution on the left and alternative hypothesis $\mathsf{H_1}$ test distribution on the right. The null hypothesis is rejected if the a critical value is passed. The graph marks the critical areas for α and β, that is, the likelihoods to make Type I and Type II errors.

Test Statistics and p-Value. We conduct statistical tests to evaluate how likely the observation is, *assuming the null hypothesis to be true.*

Definition 10 (p-Value [22]). *A p-Value is the probability of data as extreme or more extreme as that obtained, computed under the presumption of the truth of the null hypothesis $\mathsf{H_0}$. In symbols, if we let D stand for data as or more extreme as that obtained, then a p-value is the conditional probability*

$$p = Pr(D|\mathsf{H_0}).$$

Hypothesis testing with significant p-values (Fig. 3) attempts a statistical *proof by contradiction* indirectly.

Remark 3 (p-Value Misconceptions). Unfortunately, p-values are often misinterpreted, even in text books. Maxwell and Delaney [22, p.48] as well as Nickerson [26] offer some pointers for typical misinterpretations.

(a) We emphasize that in almost all cases, it holds that

$$p = Pr(D|\mathsf{H_0}) \neq Pr(\mathsf{H_0}|D).$$

Considering these two conditional probabilities equivalent is a fallacy, called "the confusion of the inverse."

(b) It is also a grave mistake to believe that p is the probability of the null hypothesis being true.

(c) The likelihood of the alternative hypothesis $\mathsf{H_1}$ is only indirectly related to the p-value [19,31].[2] Cohen [7] is vocal that the p-value "cannot tell us anything about the probability that the [alternative] hypothesis is true."

(d) Note especially that $p = Pr(D|\mathsf{H_0})$ is not a complement of $Pr(D|\mathsf{H_1})$ [26].

---

[2] Conditional probabilities follow Bayes' Theorem,

$$Pr(\mathsf{H_1}|D) = \frac{Pr(D|\mathsf{H_1})Pr(\mathsf{H_1})}{Pr(D|\mathsf{H_1})Pr(\mathsf{H_1}) + Pr(D|\mathsf{H_0})Pr(\mathsf{H_0})}.$$

Nickerson [26] discusses the links and caveats in depth.

4.2   Effect Size and Power

Cohen [8] exhorts that an effect that is statistically significant is not necessarily *scientifically significant* or important. The importance of an effect is largely linked to the magnitude of the effect. For the example of the difference between two means, we are interested how large the difference between the two populations is, and whether it constitutes a non-trivial difference.

Effect Size. We seek to quantify of the magnitude of an effect.

Definition 11 (Effect Size [8]). *The effect size (ES) is the degree to which* H_0 *is false. It is indexed by the discrepancy between* H_1 *and* H_0. *Each statistical test has its own ES index. All the indexes are scale free and continuous, ranging upward from zero, and for all, the* H_0 *is that ES = 0.*

The importance of a significant effect with effect sizes is considered that crucial in the science, that the American Psychology Association (APA) [1] states that "estimates of appropriate effect sizes [. . .] are the minimum expectations."

There are two main families of effect sizes [11]: (a) the d family, assessing the differences between groups, and (b) the r family, measuring the strength of a relationship. Effect sizes can be further specified by, for instance, regression coefficients or odds ratios. In this workshop summary, we focus on the d-family of effect sizes, especially on the difference between two means, measured with Cohen's d. We refer to Cohen [6,8], Ellis [11] and Fritz et al. [16] for overviews of different effect size types and their calculations.

Power. Now we are prepared to consider the right-hand side of Table 1: How do we fare in a situation in which the null hypothesis H_0 is actually false?

If we accept the null hypothesis H_0 mistakenly even though the alternative hypothesis H_1 is true, then we have committed a *Type II Error*. The likelihood of committing such an error is called β (cf. Fig. 3).

Consequently, if we are in the case that the alternative hypothesis H_1 is actually true, and we make a correct decision to reject the null hypothesis H_0 we do so at the likelihood of the power of our test.

Definition 12 (Power [8]). *The statistical power of a significance test is the long-term probability, given the population ES,* α, *and* N *of rejecting* H_0. *Power is* $1 - \beta$, *the probability of rejecting a false* H_0.

The four quantities sample size N, effect size (ES), significance level α and power $1 - \beta$ are mathematically connected; given three of them, the fourth quantity can be computed. We recommend G*Power [13] for this computation.

In authoritative experimentation, we seek to create experiments with sufficient power (as a commonly used rule-of-thumb, $1 - \beta > .8$) to have a sufficient likelihood of correctly rejecting the null hypothesis H_0. Cohen [5] and others have observed time and again an abysmal lack of power in scientific experiments.

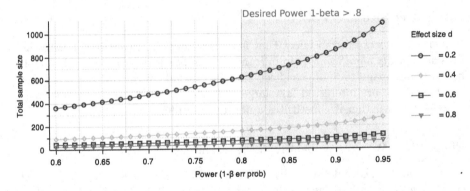

Fig. 4. Power achieved for different effect sizes and sample sizes. It is apparent that a desired power of more than $1 - \beta = .8$ needs large sample sizes N for smaller effect sizes d. (Here for an one-tailed independent samples t-test, $\alpha = .05$)

Underpowered Experiments. For research in privacy and identity management, we anticipate that the power of experiments is often too low, below $1 - \beta = .5$, and the likelihood of correctly rejecting the null hypothesis basically a coin toss. We believe the experimenters underestimate the sample size, because of a missing understanding of effect sizes and *a priori* power analysis. Figure 4 illustrates the sample sizes needed for different levels of power.

Remark 4 (N = 30 debunked). There was a myth of a "rule-of-thumb" to run experiments with a per-group sample size of $N = 30$. This was debunked by Jacob Cohen [7], *Some Things You Learn Aren't So.* The sensitivity of two-tailed independent samples t-test for significance level $\alpha = .05$ and power $1 - \beta = .95$ implies required effect size: $d = 0.94$ (large). Smaller effect sizes d will not be detected at this power. At a medium effect size $(d = .5)$, such an experiment will only achieve a power $(1 - \beta) = .48$, a coin toss.

High-Powered Experiments. As Cohen argues [7], the null hypothesis—that there is no effect whatsoever—is never actually true in reality. With a large enough sample—and thereby large enough power—even infinitesimal effects can still be detected with statistical significance (cf. Fig. 5). Consequently, it is crucial to put the hypothesis testing and the rejection of the null hypothesis with statistical significance into context of the sample size and achieved power.

4.3   Checklist: Statistical Inference

Table 2 contains further reading.

☐ Specify the exact contents of the statistical inference precisely, e.g., in a structured abstract naming IVs, DVs and hypotheses.

☐ Choose relevant test statistics and evaluate their assumptions carefully.

☐ Conduct an *a priori* power analysis to determine the required sample size for a committed significance level α and an appropriate power $1 - \beta > 80\%$.

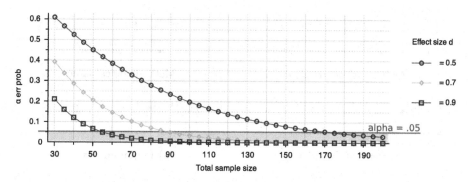

Fig. 5. α-probability for different sample sizes N and effect sizes d (one-tailed independent-samples t-test at $1 - \beta = .95$), illustrating that—with a large enough sample size—even smallest effects can be detected with statistical significance.

Table 2. Further reading on statistical inference and power.

Reference	Title	Comment
Montgomery 2012 [24]	Design and Analysis of Experiments	Detailed treatment of design and analysis of experiments.
Howell 2012 [18]	Statistical Methods for Psychology	Statistics for experiments with human factors.
Cohen 1992 [8]	A Power Primer	The quintessential concise introduction to effect size and power.
Fritz et al. 2012 [16]	Effect size estimates	Survey of the use of effect size types incl. best practices for their computation and transformation

☐ Exercise diligence in interpreting p-values and significance, putting them into context with effect sizes and the post-hoc power the experiment achieved.

☐ Report the results following the APA Guidelines [1], especially by reporting appropriate effect sizes and confidence intervals. Include all data needed to recompute the results and their effect sizes (test statistics, standard deviations, coefficients, etc.).

5 Participant Feedback

We asked participants to fill in a questionnaire just before starting the workshop. We summarize the outcomes of the 12 respondents in Fig. 6.

5.1 Area of Privacy Research

Second we asked participants *"What area(s) of privacy do you research/interests you?"* Of the 12 participants, six reported the human dimension of privacy, three

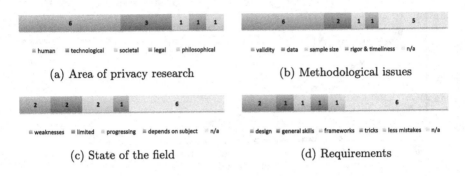

(a) Area of privacy research

(b) Methodological issues

(c) State of the field

(d) Requirements

Fig. 6. Feedback of 12 participants

reported technological aspects (geolocation and transparency), one reported the societal dimension and personal data (P3: "personal data, social exclusion, effect on the use of personal data"), one reported legal dimension in the context of health-care (P12: "Privacy for health-care systems, compliance with legal frameworks of privacy and data protection"), one philosophical dimension.

The human dimension responses covered aspects of P1: "attitude, behaviour, decision-making;" P2: "HCI, usability;" P8: "views of privacy among 'normal' people;" P9: "perceptions of privacy, how to make people more aware;" P10: "genomic privacy;" P11: "corruption and human behaviour."

5.2   Methodological Issues

Third, we asked participants *"What methodological issues have you encountered?"* From the 12 response sheets, five were excluded as they did not answer the question. Validity was the most recurring response (six), with three participants pointing towards internal validity: P11 "measuring what is intended;" P4 "software can have errors and it is unclear if experimental results can be caused by error programs." One participant stated on validity and confounders, P9 "not understanding behavioural issues [...] may ruin months of data gathering." Three responses were about external validity. P4 and P9: "generalisability;" P4 and P5: "representativeness." Two responses were about data: P1: "difficulty investigating categorical data" or large-scale data gathering (P3) The other responses included P1: "sample size;" P8 mentions running timely rigorous experiments: "experiments that can be done rigorously yet in a timely manner."

5.3   Opinion on Experimental Research in Privacy

Fourth, we asked *"What is the state of experimental research in privacy?"* From the 12 participants, five were new to privacy or reported they did not know. Two participants pointed to weaknesses, with P9 suggesting the state to be "dubious" and P11: "fairly poor." Two participants suggested an early state, P10, suggested experimental research in privacy is in "early development;" P5 stated it is "limited." Two participants suggested the state is progressing, with

P1: "there are many longitudinal studies on privacy behaviour" and P6: "in progress." One participant, P4, suggested that it depends on the subject.

5.4 Requirements on Workshop

Fifth, we asked *"What would you like to learn in this workshop today?"* Of the 12 participants, six either did not provide a response or understand the question; six other thought the workshop would improve their skills in one way or another. Two participants were concerned with experiment design; P8 thought of "Good ways of running experiments;" P9 expected "better ideas to design experiments." P11 sought to learn about: "frameworks." P2 mentioned "tips and trades (*sic*) in ways forward;" and P1 expected help on "how to perform research with less mistakes."

6 Conclusion

From the participants' feedback in Sect. 5 we see that, on the one hand, participants are interested in research that lend themselves to evidence-based methods, such as human dimensions of privacy and identity. On the other hand, they report a dire situation of the state of play in the field and a need to learn more on research methodology.

> *"[Perhaps], we should simply study our Mr. Pritchard and learn our rhyme and meter and go quietly about the business of achieving other ambitions."*
> — John Keating, Dead Poets Society

Should we simply run studies that receive "pass" marks in our community— ignoring the depths of evidence-based methods—and go quietly about the business of achieving other ambitions? Mastering evidence-based methods is a challenging prospect, daunting at times. However, what is at stake here is our capacity as a community to truly learn from our research and advance our field's body of knowledge. Consequently, we certainly advocate going deep in research methodology.

How? From the workshop experience, we believe there are three key ingredients that are reinforcing each other. (a) First, we would focus on the tenets of reaching clarity on research questions, hypotheses and variables, ideally specified in concise structured abstracts. (b) Second, we advocate the specification of sound experiment designs that not only replicate validated methods but also specify their components in such detail that they propagate forward reproducibility by other investigators. (c) Finally, we stress the importance of the quantitative tools from correct statistical inference, over effect sizes and power, to interval estimation, all strengthening the reliability of the reported results. We are convinced that these three ingredients are essential to advance the body of knowledge of our field.

Acknowledgments. We are grateful for the contributions and feedback from participants of the workshop. We are grateful for the discussions with Roy Maxion on evidence-based methods for cyber security. The preparation of the evidence-based methods workshop was in parts funded by the EPSRC Research Institute in Science of Cyber Security (RISCS), grant *EP/K006568/1*. This work was supported by a Newcastle-sponsored International Research Collaboration Award (IRCA) for work with Carnegie-Mellon University (CMU). We have been asked by a number of people, whether this paper could be used as primer for lectures or student projects. We certainly approve of that. We ask that the paper be cited and the corresponding author sent a brief notification, such that we can track interest in evidence-based methods in the community.

References

1. American Psychological Association (APA): Publication Manual of the American Psychological Association. American Psychological Association (APA), 6th revised edn., July 2009
2. Balenson, D., Tinnel, L., Benzel, T.: Cybersecurity Experimentation of the Future (CEF): Catalyzing a New Generation of Experimental Cybersecurity Research - Final Report. Technical report, SRI International and USC Information Sciences Institute, July 2015
3. Brewer, M.B.: Research design and issues of validity. In: Handbook of Research Methods in Social and Personality Psychology, pp. 3–16 (2000)
4. Carroll, T.E., Manz, D., Edgar, T., Greitzer, F.L.: Realizing scientific methods for cyber security. In: Proceedings of the 2012 Workshop on Learning from Authoritative Security Experiment Results, pp. 19–24. ACM (2012)
5. Cohen, J.: The statistical power of abnormal-social psychological research: a review. J. Abnorm. Soc. Psychol. **65**(3), 145–153 (1962)
6. Cohen, J.: Statistical Power Analysis for the Behavioral Sciences, 2nd edn. Psychology Press, Taylor & Francis Group, LCC, New York (1988)
7. Cohen, J.: Things I have learned (so far). Am. Psychol. **45**(12), 1304–1312 (1990)
8. Cohen, J.: A power primer. Psychol. Bull. **112**(1), 155–159 (1992)
9. Cook, T.D., Campbell, D.T.: Quasi-Experimentation: Design and Analysis for Field Settings. Rand McNally, Chicago (1979)
10. Dodge, Y. (ed.): Oxford Dictionary of Statistical Terms. Oxford University Press, Oxford (2006)
11. Ellis, P.D.: The Essential Guide to Effect Sizes: Statistical Power, Meta-Analysis, and the Interpretation of Research Results. Cambridge University Press, Cambridge (2010)
12. Everitt, B.: Cambridge Dictionary of Statistics. Cambridge University Press, Cambridge (1998)
13. Faul, F., Erdfelder, E., Lang, A.G., Buchner, A.: G*Power 3: a flexible statistical power analysis program for the social, behavioral, and biomedical sciences. Behav. Res. Methods **39**(2), 175–191 (2007)
14. Field, A., Hole, G.: How to Design and Report Experiments. Sage, London (2003)
15. Fisher, R.A.: Statistical Methods for Research Workers. Genesis Publishing Pvt Ltd, Edinburgh (1925)
16. Fritz, C.O., Morris, P.E., Richler, J.J.: Effect size estimates: current use, calculations, and interpretation. J. Exp. Psychol. Gen. **141**(1), 2–18 (2012)

17. Gardner, M.J., Altman, D.G.: Confidence intervals rather than p values: estimation rather than hypothesis testing. Br. Med. J. (Clin. Res. Ed.) **292**(6522), 746–750 (1986)
18. Howell, D.C.: Statistical Methods for Psychology, 8th edn. Cengage Learning, Wadsworth (2012)
19. Ioannidis, J.P.: Why most published research findings are false. PLoS Med. **2**(8), e124 (2005)
20. Lehmann, E.L.: The fisher, neyman-pearson theories of testing hypotheses: one theory or two? In: Selected Works of EL Lehmann, pp. 201–208. Springer (2012)
21. Maxion, R.: Making Experiments Dependable. Springer, Heidelberg (2011)
22. Maxwell, S.E., Delaney, H.D.: Designing Experiments and Analyzing Data: A Model Comparison Perspective, vol. 1, 2nd edn. Psychology Press, New York (2004)
23. Miller, S.: Experimental Design and Statistics. Routledge, London (2005)
24. Montgomery, D.C.: Design and Analysis of Experiments, 8th edn. Wiley, New York (2012)
25. Neyman, J., Pearson, E.S.: On the use and interpretation of certain test criteria for purposes of statistical inference: Part I. Biometrika, 175–240 (1928)
26. Nickerson, R.S.: Null hypothesis significance testing: a review of an old and continuing controversy. Psychol. Methods **5**(2), 241–301 (2000)
27. Open Science Collaboration: an open, large-scale, collaborative effort to estimate the reproducibility of psychological science. Perspect. Psychol. Sci. **7**(6), 657–660 (2012)
28. Open Science Collaboration: estimating the reproducibility of psychological science. Science **349**(6251), aac4716 (2015)
29. Peisert, S., Bishop, M.: How to design computer security experiments. In: Futcher, L., Dodge, R. (eds.) WISE 2007. IIFIP, vol. 237, pp. 141–148. Springer, Boston, MA (2007). doi:10.1007/978-0-387-73269-5_19
30. Popper, K.: The Logic of Scientific Discovery. Routledge, London (2005)
31. Wacholder, S., Chanock, S., Garcia-Closas, M., Rothman, N., et al.: Assessing the probability that a positive report is false: an approach for molecular epidemiology studies. J. Natl. Cancer Inst. **96**(6), 434–442 (2004)

Selected Papers (Part I) - Legal Aspects and User Rights

Enforcing Data Protection Law – The Role of the Supervisory Authorities in Theory and Practice

Felix Bieker[✉]

Unabhängiges Landeszentrum für Datenschutz Schleswig-Holstein
(ULD, Independent Centre for Privacy Protection), Kiel, Germany
fbieker@datenschutzzentrum.de

Abstract. This paper examines the role of the supervisory authorities for the enforcement of the EU data protection regulation. It therefore examines the case law of the Court of Justice of the European Union and the upcoming legislative changes under the General Data Protection Regulation, which includes detailed provisions for the cooperation of all European supervisory authorities.

Keywords: Data protection · Privacy · General Data Protection Regulation · Enforcement · Supervisory authorities · Data protection authorities · Court of Justice of the European Union

1   Introduction

The raison d'être of data protection law in general is to protect the rights of individuals. Specifically, this is laid down in Article 1(1) of the current Data Protection Directive 95/46/EC (DPD) [1] as well as Article 1(2) of the upcoming General Data Protection Regulation (EU) 2016/679 (GDPR) [2]. The law thereby aims to compensate for the asymmetry in power between organisations (as controllers) and individuals (the data subjects) created by modern means of data processing [3]. However, this does not only affect the secondary law, but is also enshrined on the level of EU primary law: Article 8 of the EU Charter of Fundamental Rights (CFR) [4] guarantees the right to the protection of personal data. Furthermore, Article 7 CFR protects the right to private life, which also includes the protection of personal data relating to the private life of an individual [5]. The enforcement of these rights is entrusted to supervisory authorities in each Member State. According to the Court of Justice of the European Union, which interprets Union law authoritatively, the supervisory authorities protect the rights of the individuals with regard to the protection of personal data and "are therefore the guardians of those fundamental rights" [6].

This paper has received funding by the Bundesministerium für Bildung und Forschung (German Federal Ministry of Education and Research) for the project Forum Privatheit – Selbstbestimmtes Leben in der Digitalen Welt (Privacy Forum), www.forum-privatheit.de.

A. Lehmann et al. (Eds.): Privacy and Identity 2016, IFIP AICT 498, pp. 125–139, 2016.
DOI: 10.1007/978-3-319-55783-0_10

In order to fulfil this advocacy role, Article 28 DPD requires that the authorities act in complete independence and have effective investigative powers (including access to all necessary information), powers of intervention (such as ordering the erasure of data or imposing bans on processing) and the power to engage in legal proceedings when the national provisions implementing the DPD have been violated. Additionally, the data subjects themselves have the right to lodge complaints directly with a supervisory authority, in order to enforce their rights.

Since the coming into force of the DPD, there have been several judgments of the EU's Court of Justice (ECJ or the Court) concerning the interpretation of the supervisory authorities' role. The notion of independence was scrutinized with regard to the implementation in Germany [6], Austria [7], and Hungary [8, 9]. Additionally, the Court ruled on questions concerning the scope of application of the national rules implementing the DPD in the Member States [9, 10] and the competence of the authorities to hear complaints of individuals under Article 28(4) DPD [10, 11]. Furthermore, the supervisory authorities have been [9, 10] and continue to be [12] involved in proceedings before the ECJ in order to obtain an authoritative interpretation of the EU data protection legislation.

The upcoming secondary data protection law, the GDPR – which has already entered into force and will become applicable in the first quarter of 2018 – considerably extends the EU provisions on the supervisory authorities. As the legislator chose the form of a regulation, EU law will prescribe the role of the supervisory authorities in much greater detail.

This paper therefore analyses the jurisprudence of the ECJ to define the status quo of the law on supervisory authorities and examines in how far the forthcoming GDPR advances that status and thereby enables the supervisory authorities to fulfil their role as guardians of the rights to the protection of personal data. The requirements for the organization of the supervisory authorities will be examined (2) as well as the question of which supervisory authority is competent to enforce data protection law in a given case (3). Lastly, the power to hear individual claims (4) is assessed. It is concluded (5) that in order to honour their role as prescribed by EU law, the supervisory authorities have to be allocated the means and resources to fulfil their role as advocates of fundamental rights.

2   Organization of Supervisory Authorities

Article 28 DPD requires that the supervisory authorities "act with complete independence." As the Court held in its very first judgment concerning the role of supervisory authorities, this notion includes multiple dimensions: being without influence not just by those who are supervised – private sector companies or public authorities, as the case may be – but generally without taking any instructions or being pressured, including direct as well as indirect influence [6].

Due to their advocacy role, as public enforcers of individual rights, the supervisory authorities have a unique position within their Member States. As they oversee both private companies and (other) public authorities, they must be independent from the public sector, i.e. the State they form part of themselves. In practice, this is achieved in different ways, for instance the members of the French Commission Nationale de l'Informatique et des Libertes are appointed from various institutions, such as the parliament and the courts [13, Article 13]. In Germany, the heads of the supervisory authorities are elected by the respective federal or regional parlament [Cf. inter alia 14, § 35; 15, § 22].

However, as the ECJ found, the State itself may not only be interested in influencing a supervisory authority where its own actions are concerned, but also protect the interests of the private sector. Thus, there is no room for state scrutiny, which might allow the government to cancel or even replace decisions in the interests of public contractors in the private sector or adopt a lenient approach towards economically important companies [6].

The members of the supervisory authorities have to be functionally independent from the government. While Member States are not obliged to grant them a separate budget, there can be no overlap in personnel between the government and the authority, which could lead to direct influence of the former. However, even indirect influence such as an unconditional right to be informed about the work of the supervisory authority is seen by the ECJ as not permissible [7].

Another form of undesirable influence is any act of the government that might coerce the authority into a certain course of action in order to avoid disadvantages in the future. This issue was contentious in a case against Hungary, where the government decided to discharge the head of the supervisory authority before the end of his regular term [8]. The ECJ held that these measures, which in the case at hand did not even conform to the national rules and safeguards, were liable to induce such acts of prior compliance, which contravene the authority's independence.

The forthcoming EU data protection regime incorporates the ECJ's rulings into secondary law. Under Article 52(1) GDPR the supervisory authorities remain completely independent in their work and it is now expressly stated in Article 52(2) GDPR that they may not be subject to direct or indirect influence. The functional independence from the government is explicitly laid down in Article 52(6) GDPR.

There will be specific rules for the expiry of the term of office or a resignation of members of the supervisory authorities and the requirement that they may be dismissed solely in cases of serious misconduct or if they no longer fulfil the conditions required for their position, which are to be provided by the Member States according to Article 54(1) GDPR. While the ECJ found that under Article 28 DPD the Member States did not have to provide the authorities with a separate budget, that same obligation is now laid down in Article 52(7) GDPR.

3   Enforcement of Data Protection Law and Cooperation of Supervisory Authorities

3.1   Enforcement of Data Protection Law

As each of the Member States has its own supervisory authority, their jurisdiction is linked to the applicability of the national law implementing the DPD. Therefore, the determination whether the national law is applicable in a given case is crucial. According to Article 4 DPD this is the case when the controller carries out the processing "in the context of the activities of an establishment". In the *Google Spain* case, this was an issue, as Google argued that its data processing did not take place in its Spanish establishment, but at its corporate headquarters in the USA [10]. However, the ECJ pointed out that the DPD explicitly stated that the processing only had to occur in the context of the establishment's activities. It then ruled that when an establishment promotes and sells advertising space to make the operation profitable, this is sufficient to link the activities of the establishment and the processing of data. The Article 29 Working Party has generalized this requirement as meaning that the "activities and the data processing are 'inextricably linked'" [16, at p. 6].

Further, Recital 19 DPD refers to the effective and real exercise of an activity under a stable arrangement, while the legal form of that establishment is not decisive. Accordingly, in the *Weltimmo* case, the Court held that even the operation of a website in a Member State, using exclusively that State's language, fulfils the criteria of an establishment, if the processor has a representative in that country [9]. However, the nationality of the users of the website is of no relevance for determining the applicable law. Thus, different national implementations of the DPD may apply to the establishment and the main establishment, depending on their location, even though they all concern the same data processing carried out by the main establishment. This interpretation is explicitly regulated in Article 4(1)(a) clause 2 DPD, which states that where a controller is established on the territory of several Member States, it must ensure that each establishment complies with the respective national law.

As each supervisory authority is competent to enforce the national implementation of the DPD on its territory, a supervisory authority may choose to enforce the national law against any processor who is established on its territory. The Court found, however, that where the main establishment of the controller is in another Member State, the supervisory authority may not enforce its national law against that main establishment. Rather this rests within the jurisdiction of the supervisory authority of that Member State and would infringe the principles of territorial sovereignty and legality, as well as the rule of law [11]. Nonetheless, it follows from this and Article 4(1)(a) clause 2 DPD that the supervisory authority of a Member State may enforce the national data protection rules against the establishment even when the data processing is carried out by the main establishment located in another Member State.

The provisions on the enforcement of the data protection regime by the supervisory authorities have been left largely untouched by the current reforms. Especially the link to the enforcement in the territory of the supervisory authority's Member State under Articles 55(1) and 57(1)(a) GDPR remains unchanged. Article 3(1) GDPR on territorial scope, which replaces Article 4(1)(a) DPD, contains the same notion of processing personal data "in the context of an establishment" as interpreted by the ECJ. Furthermore, the Courts' conclusions have been partially incorporated in the Recitals. Just as Recital 19 DPD, Recital 22 GDPR states that the concept of establishment implies the real and effective exercise of activity through stable arrangements, while the legal form of these arrangements does not prejudice a finding of an establishment. The question of whether a website is aimed at persons in a particular Member State is dealt with in Recital 23 GDPR, which also proposes to consider factors such as the language or currency used on the website. However, this is not done in the context of whether there is an establishment, but rather under the category of offering goods and services while the controller is not established in the EU according to Article 3(2)(a) GDPR. Although the wide scope of the DPD in the interpretation of the ECJ has been seen critically by some [17, 18], the EU legislator has thus explicitly reiterated the Court's reasoning in the GDPR. This is not necessarily surprising, as the case law is closely linked to the wording of the DPD, which the ECJ interprets in the light of the individual rights of the primary law, in order to ensure effective and complete protection of individual rights.

3.2 Cooperation of Supervisory Authorities

As the 28 Member States set up one or multiple supervisory authorities[1] in accordance with their national law, there is currently a multitude of authorities in the EU which interpret the EU data protection regime, which poses the threat of fragmentation of the application of the law in practice.

Status Quo. Article 28(6) DPD thus lays down a duty to cooperate. This includes inter alia the exchange of information. In its eponymous Article 29 the DPD set up a Working Party consisting of representatives of the supervisory authorities of each Member State as well as a representative of EU institutions and bodies and one of the Commission. While the latter have no voting rights, the Working Party adopts its decisions by a simple majority under Article 29(3) DPD.

The Article 29 Working Party is charged with examining questions such as the application of national implementation measures or issuing opinions to the Commission on the level of protection in the EU and third countries. It may further put forward recommendations on any matter related to the protection of personal data in the EU.

Upcoming Changes. The system of cooperation between the respective national supervisory authorities is overhauled completely in the forthcoming legislation [on the genesis of these provisions, cf. 19]:

Lead Supervisory Authority. In an effort to streamline the jurisdiction of supervisory authorities in cases where the controller or processor is in another Member State than the data subject, the supervisory authority of the (main) establishment acts as lead

---

[1] In the Federal Republic of Germany, for instance, there are 18 different supervisory authorities: one on the federal level and seventeen regional authorities of the *Länder*.

supervisory authority.[2] Under this one-stop-shop scheme it is the sole interlocutor of the controller or processor according to Article 56(6) GDPR.[3]

While the lead authority is in charge of operations, under Article 60(1) GDPR it ultimately has to reach a consensus and therefore cooperate with the other supervisory authorities concerned. To this end, the lead authority may request assistance from other authorities under Article 61 GDPR, and – especially for purposes of carrying out investigations or monitoring the implementation of measures taken – may conduct joint operations in accordance with Article 62 GDPR.

Concerning a decision, it is for the lead supervisory authority to submit a draft to the other concerned supervisory authorities. According to Article 60(3) GDPR, their views have to be taken duly into account. Further, the other concerned supervisory authorities may express relevant and reasoned objections as provided by Article 60(4) GDPR.[4] The coordination then proceeds as follows:

- If the lead supervisory authority does not follow the objection or regards it as not relevant and reasoned, it has to apply the consistency mechanism (explained below) and the Board has to adopt a binding decision according to Article 65(1)(a) GDPR.
- If the lead supervisory authority agrees with the objection, it has to submit a revised draft to the other concerned supervisory authorities according to Article 60(5) GDPR.
- If no objections are submitted within the prescribed period, a consensus is deemed to exist by Article 60(6) GDPR and all supervisory authorities concerned are bound by the decision.

---

[2] The term main establishment is defined in Article 4(16)(a) GDPR with regard to a controller as the place of central administration within the EU, except where another establishment within the EU is tasked with deciding the purposes and means of data processing and has the power to implement such decisions, which then in turn is regarded as main establishment. Recital 36 GDPR requires the effective and real exercise of activities determining the main decisions regarding the means and purposes of processing through stable arrangements. A processor's main establishment is defined in Article 4(16)(b) as the place of central administration or, in lieu of such a place, the establishment where the main processing activities take place to the extent that the processor is subject to specific obligations under the GDPR. In cases involving both, a controller and processor, the main establishment of the controller should be decisive to determine the lead supervisory authority according to Recital 36 GDPR.

[3] Where the processing takes place within the EU in the context of a controller's or processor's establishments in multiple Member States or where the processing takes place in the sole establishment of a controller or processor in the EU, but which substantially affects or is likely to substantially affect data subjects in more than one Member State, this is defined as cross-border data processing by Article 4(23) GDPR. If there are conflicting views on which of the concerned supervisory authorities is competent for the main establishment of a controller or processor, the Board has to adopt a binding decision under the consistency mechanism of Article 65(1)(b) GDPR.

[4] This term is defined in Article 4(24) GDPR as stating whether there is an infringement of the GDPR, whether the envisaged action is in accordance with the GDPR and clearly demonstrate the significance of risks incurred by the draft decision with data subjects' fundamental rights and freedoms or the free flow of personal data.

When the decision is adopted, it is for the lead supervisory authority to take action with regard to the controller or processor, while the supervisory authority to which a complaint was lodged has to inform the complainant according to Article 60(7) GDPR.

However, there are exceptions from the one-stop-shop scheme:

- It only applies to private companies; if public authorities or private bodies acting with public authority process data, the supervisory authority of the Member State concerned has the competence to act according to Article 55(2) GDPR.
- Where a complaint concerns a matter which relates only to one specific establishment in one Member State or only substantially affects data subjects in one specific Member State, the supervisory authority of the Member State concerned[5] has to inform the lead supervisory authority. The latter then decides whether it invokes the cooperation procedure of Article 60 GDPR.
  - If it does, the concerned supervisory authority prepares a draft for decision, which has to be taken "into account to the utmost" by the lead authority for its own decision under Article 60(3) GDPR.
  - If the lead supervisory authority decides not to deal with the case, the supervisory authority which informed it handles the case either with the assistance of other supervisory authorities according to Article 61 GDPR or as a joint operation under Article 62 GDPR.

The new rules for the cooperation of the supervisory authorities set up a formal system of procedures and strict deadlines of only two to four weeks. This can be attributed to the complexity of a one-stop-shop approach for the enforcement of common rules across 28 Member States. While this is intended to allow effective cooperation, the deadlines also put a burden on the supervisory authorities. They will have to be able to follow proceedings in other Member States and respond to requests within the deadlines. Aside from the substantive and often very specific questions of EU data protection law, this also requires a timely and appropriate translation of documents. Thus, considerable resources will be required to enable the authorities to actively participate in investigations, supply information to other authorities and process information received within the short prescribed time periods.

Mutual assistance. The mutual assistance procedure of Article 61 GDPR especially concerns information requests and supervisory measures, for instance requests to carry out prior authorizations and consultations, inspections and investigations. Article 61(3) GDPR introduces the idea of purpose limitation for supervisory authorities: the use of information exchanged is expressly limited to the purpose for which it was requested. The requested supervisory authority has to submit the information no later than a month after the request and may refuse requests only when it is not competent ratione materiae

---

[5] Article 4(22) GDPR defines the supervisory authority concerned as the one which is concerned by the processing, due to the controller's or processor's establishment on the territory of its Member State, the data subjects residing in its Member State are substantially affected or likely to be affected, or a complaint according to Article 77 GDPR has been lodged with that supervisory authority.

or the measures requested violate provisions of Union or national law. Any refusal to submit information has to be substantiated with reasons.[6]

Joint operations. The joint operations mechanism under Article 62 GDPR extends to investigations and enforcement measures and gives the supervisory authorities of all Member States concerned a right to participate in such operations. They are either invited by the competent supervisory authority or can request to participate. If such a request is not granted within one month, Article 62(7) GDPR provides that the other supervisory authorities may take provisional measures.[7]

In a joint operation a supervisory authority may, in accordance with national law, grant investigative powers on a seconding supervisory authority or, if allowed by national law, confer its powers on the seconding supervisory authority as provided by Article 62(3) GDPR. Both modi are subject to the guidance and presence of members or staff of the host supervisory authority and subjects the supervisory authorities own members or staff to the national law of the host Member State. In turn, the host supervisory authority assumes responsibility for the actions of the supervisory authority acting in its Member State under Article 62(4) GDPR.

This is an interesting possibility, which has the potential to further European integration. Even though EU law is not a subset of international law, but rather its own, independent and sui generis legal order [20], the principle of the sovereignty of Member States is still paramount. In its *Schrems* judgment, the ECJ heavily emphasized that supervisory authorities could only exercise their jurisdiction within their own Member State and invoked this general principle [11]. In this regard, the GDPR goes beyond the status quo in allowing for joint operations and exercise of jurisdiction in another Member State, albeit subject to consent and supervision of the Member State concerned. However, as the Member States are reluctant to give up sovereignty with regard to other Member States, it will have to be determined in the future, whether these provisions found any practical application.

European Data Protection Board. The Article 29 Working Party will be succeeded by the European Data Protection Board, which consists of the heads of each supervisory authority of the Member States and the European Data Protection Supervisor.[8]

The Board generally takes all decisions by a simple majority. Its tasks are similar to those of the Article 29 Working Party: according to Article 70 GDPR, it advises the Commission, for instance by providing it with an opinion on the adequacy assessment

---

[6] If the requested supervisory authority fails to act within the prescribed period, Article 60(8) GDPR authorizes the requesting supervisory authority to take provisional measures in its Member State. However, the urgency procedure of Article 66 GDPR is triggered: While the urgent need to act is presumed, an urgent binding decision by the Board prescribed by Article 66(2) GDPR is required.

[7] In that case, as under Article 60(8) GDPR for the mutual assistance procedure, the urgency mechanism of Article 66 GDPR is then triggered.

[8] In Member States where there is more than one supervisory authority a joint representative is to be appointed under the national law as a single point of contact for other members of the Board (Recital 119 GDPR), which facilitates coordination.

for the transfer of data to third countries or examines any matter of general application or affecting more than one Member State, at the request of a Board member. This particularly concerns cases where a supervisory authority does not comply with its obligation to provide mutual assistance under Article 61 GDPR or engage in joint operations as prescribed in Article 62 GDPR (as described above). The opinions of the Board have to be issued within eight weeks and are non-binding.[9]

Consistency Mechanism. A major change in the working of the supervisory authorities on the EU level is the consistency mechanism. It allows the Board to issue binding decisions according to Article 65(1) GDPR. This particularly concerns instances when the lead supervisory authority does not follow the objections of a supervisory authorities concerned or when the competent supervisory authority decides not to follow an opinion of the Board under Article 64 GDPR.

All binding decisions are adopted with a two-thirds majority and generally within one month.[10] During the time of deliberation, the competent supervisory authority is barred from adopting its draft decision. As pointed out in Recital 142 GDPR decisions of the Board can be brought before the ECJ in an annulment action under Article 263 TFEU by supervisory authorities, as they are addressees of these decisions. As the binding decisions of the Board can be seen as an interference with the independence of the individual authorities, the possibility to bring a decision before the Court is a mitigating factor.

For cases with an urgent need to protect the rights and freedoms of data subjects there is also an urgency procedure provided by Article 66(1) GDPR, which allows the supervisory authority concerned to circumvent the consistency mechanism under exceptional circumstances and adopt immediate provisional measures in its Member State. However, these measures have to specify a period of validity, which may not exceed three months. In order to adopt final measures, the supervisory authority concerned may request an urgent opinion or decision of the Board.[11]

In the opposite case, where a supervisory authority concerned does not take measures although there is an urgent need to act in order to protect the rights and freedoms of data subject, any supervisory authority may request an urgent opinion or decision of the Board according to Article 66(3) GDPR.

Even though the Board is mainly based on cooperative action, certain elements such as the possibility to take a supervisory authority refusing to grant mutual assistance or

---

[9] However, when a supervisory authority requests an opinion, for adoption of one of the measures listed in Article 64(1) GDPR it has to "take utmost account" of the opinion. If it deviates from the opinion, another supervisory authority or the Commission may request the adoption of a binding decision. Article 64(1) GDPR includes the list defining when a Data Protection Impact Assessments has to be carried out under Article 35(4) GDPR, standard protection clauses under Articles 46(2)(d) and 28(8) GDPR, and the approval of binding corporate rules according to Article 47 GDPR.

[10] If the Board fails to adopt a decision by that time the quorum is lowered to a simple majority for an additional two weeks. In the case of a split vote, the chair decides.

[11] According to Article 66(4) GDPR urgent opinions and decisions have to be adopted within two weeks by a simple majority.

refusing to let another supervisory authority join investigations before the Board or to invoke the urgency procedure where a supervisory authority fails to take action introduce an adversarial mode to the Board. In practice, these instruments will have to be handled carefully in order to allow productive cooperation between all of the supervisory authorities. However, these concerns may in practice well be outweighed by a coherent enforcement strategy of 28 Member States.

4   Power to Hear Individual Complaints

Individuals have the right to file a complaint with the supervisory authority, which is enshrined in EU primary law as a fundamental right in Article 8(1) and (3) CFR [cf. 11]. Correspondingly, the supervisory authorities under Article 28(4) DPD/Articles 77 and 52(1)(b) and (4) GDPR have the power to hear these complaints. These powers therefore are not merely an end in themselves, but rather serve to implement these individual rights.

4.1   Complaints Concerning Processing Within the EU

Status Quo. According to the ECJ, individuals may bring a claim to the supervisory authority when they are not successful in the exercise of their rights as data subjects, for instance under Articles 12 or 14 DPD [9]. If the competent supervisory authority finds a violation of fundamental rights, it may order the controller to take certain action. In the infamous case of *Google Spain*, this included the order to remove certain links from the search results of an internet search engine, when the interest of the data subject outweighs the interest of the public to this information [10].

Further, the Court has ruled that when a claim is lodged with an authority and it is unclear which national legislation applies, this does not change that authority's competence to hear that claim under Article 28(4) DPD [9]. However, the territorial restriction of the rules it enforces according to Article 28(1) and (3) DPD still applies. Thus, a supervisory authority which is confronted with such a claim may exercise its investigative powers even if the law applicable is that of another Member State. This means that, generally, any supervisory authority may investigate the practice of controllers in another Member State. Yet, its powers may be limited, especially regarding the imposition of penalties, as that would violate the territorial sovereignty of the other Member State and raise issues regarding the principle of legality and the rule of law [9]. In such cases, the supervisory authority can only rely on the duty of cooperation under Article 28(6) DPD for the enforcement of its actions on the territory of another Member State. If, however, there is an establishment on the territory of the supervisory authority's own Member State, it may take action against that establishment, where the required nexus to the processing as detailed above Sect. 3.1 exists, i.e. the establishment's activities are inextricably linked to the activities of the main establishment.

Upcoming Changes. Under Article 77 GDPR, individuals may now choose the supervisory authority where they want to lodge their complaints: they may select the authority of their habitual residence, place of work or the place of the alleged violation. Just like the lead supervisory authority provides a one-stop-shop for controllers and processors, the supervisory authority where the complaint is lodged is responsible to inform the individual on the progress and outcome of the complaint.[12]

Individuals may also challenge any legally binding decision of a supervisory authority addressing them, as they have the right to an effective judicial remedy according to Article 47 CFR. Recital 142 GDPR states that the proceedings following national law should give the courts full jurisdiction including the examination of all questions of fact and law. This clarifies that the notion of independence of the supervisory authorities, as introduced above (2), only extends to the organisations it supervises. However, as the executive has thus only limited influence and control, this must be compensated by adequate judicial supervision.

If the supervisory authority competent under Articles 55 et seq GDPR does not deal with a complaint or even when it fails to inform the individual of the progress or outcome of a complaint lodged under Article 77 GDPR within three months, individuals must have a judicial remedy against the supervisory authority. Additionally, Article 79 GDPR introduces a right for individuals to an effective judicial remedy against a controller or processor, including public authorities, before the courts of the Member State.

In order to pursue these rights, data subjects under Article 80(1) GDPR have the right to mandate a non-profit organization active in the field of data protection to exercise them on their behalf. Taking this point even further, Article 80(2) GDPR contains an opening clause allowing Member States to introduce a right of non-profit organizations to initiate proceedings under Articles 77-79 GDPR independent of a mandate by a data subject.

4.2 Complaints and the Transfer to Third Countries

The competence of the supervisory authority is not limited to actions concerning controllers within the EU. In the *Schrems* case, the ECJ dealt with the powers of the supervisory authorities with regard to the processing of personal data in third countries. The Court argued that while the supervisory authorities could carry out their powers within the territory of their own Member State under Article 28(1) and (6) DPD, the transfer of data from a Member State to a third country under Articles 25 and 26 DPD was a processing of data within the meaning of Article 2(b) DPD, which was carried out in a certain Member State [11]. Consequently, the national supervisory authorities under Article 28 DPD read in conjunction with Article 8(3) CFR were also responsible to monitor compliance with the DPD in the case of data transfers to a third country.

The ECJ explicitly held that adequacy decisions of the Commission under Article 25(1) and (6) DPD do not curtail the power of the supervisory authorities to examine

---

[12] As laid down by Article 56(2) GDPR with regard to actions taken by the lead supervisory authorities, Article 60(7)-(9) GDPR concerning cooperation between supervisory authorities and Article 65(6) GDPR for decisions of the Board.

the actual level of protection in that third country.[13] The Commission decision does not prejudice the examination of an individual complaint put before the supervisory authority, which must assess these with due diligence [11]. However, the supervisory authority itself cannot declare the Commission decision invalid. In EU law, it is within the exclusive jurisdiction of the Court to declare any acts of EU organs or institutions invalid. For the complaints before the supervisory authority there are thus two possibilities:

- If the authority rejects the claim, the individual must have the possibility of judicial remedies according to Article 28(3) subparagraph 2 DPD.
- If the supervisory authority upholds the claim, it must, in turn, be able to instigate legal proceedings in compliance with Article 28(3) third indent DPD.

In either case, the competent national court seized of the matter has to submit questions concerning the validity of the decision to the ECJ by way of a preliminary reference under Article 267 TFEU.

While the GDPR brings some changes to the system of transfer of personal data to third countries in Articles 44 et seq. GDPR – mostly in the form of more detailed provisions – the general concept remains the same. Thus, the finding of the ECJ that any transfer of personal data begins with a processing within the EU still stands. The supervisory authorities further retain the power to suspend data flows to recipients in third countries according to Article 58(2)(j) GDPR and must thus be able to investigate complaints concerning an alleged violation of provisions set out in the GDPR.

The process for the adoption of adequacy decision is now set out in more detail in Article 45 GDPR: the Commission has to take into account factors such as whether the country in question respects the rule of law, human rights and fundamental freedoms, the relevant national legislation concerning public and national security and access rights of public authorities. Further, it must assess whether there are effective and enforceable data subject rights as well as effective administrative and judicial remedies for data subjects. The existence of an effective, independent supervisory authority is also required. With these provisions the legislator anticipated the requirements laid down by the Court in the *Schrems* judgment.

If the Commission concludes that the level of protection is adequate in a third country or a specific sector in that country, the implementing act has to provide a mechanism for periodic review, as required by the ECJ in the *Schrems* case, which has to be carried out at least every four years. When information reveals that the relevant country no longer meets the adequacy threshold, Article 45(5) GDPR demands that the Commission repeals, amends or even suspends its decision.

It thus becomes clear, that in the view of the EU legislator as well as the judiciary, the entire EU data protection regime must be read in the light of the fundamental rights of the individuals it aims to protect. Therefore, the protection standard established within the EU may not be undermined by a transfer to a third country which does not provide

---

[13] The fact that the Commission's Safe Harbor Decision curtailed the supervisory authorities' powers with regard to self-certified organizations under Article 28 DPD was, as the ECJ held in *Schrems*, actually one of the reasons for its invalidity.

at least a level of protection that is 'essentially equivalent' to these safeguards, as the Court put it in *Schrems* [11]. Furthermore, the ECJ has emphasised the crucial role of the supervisory authorities, which must act not only independently of their Member States, but also the Commission where it acts within the framework of the data protection law. The authorities may not defer to an assessment provided by Brussels, but must examine the merits of each complaint, especially where it concerns a violation of individual rights on a massive scale. Furthermore, the Court empowers individuals to use the instrument of complaints in order to enforce their rights in a meaningful way.

5   Outlook

While the ECJ's judgments in the cases of inter alia *Google Spain* or *Schrems* attracted praise [10, 11], but also considerable criticism [12], it has been demonstrated that the GDPR incorporates many of the principles laid out by the Court. It is thus not to be expected that the ECJ will change its approach to enforce data protection law from a fundamental rights perspective under the new legislation.

The Court itself as well as the upcoming legislation emphasize the importance of lodging proceedings before the ECJ in order to ensure coherent interpretation. Yet, the supervisory authorities already find themselves in a position where they have to engage in proceedings before the ECJ, a development which is likely to continue and even expand in frequency with the GDPR, as it will be more obvious that EU law is at issue in a case – a fact that may currently be overlooked in practice, as the parties before national courts focus on the national implementation legislation.

The Court, in the few cases that reached it, has definitely played an important role in advancing the level of data protection in the EU. However, it has to be borne in mind that in most instances, i.e. the preliminary reference procedure, it takes considerable time before a case comes before the Court. Under Article 267 TFEU only national courts of last instance are obliged to refer their questions on EU law to the ECJ. So far, national courts of lower instance have been reluctant to forward questions on EU law and there might be a considerable amount of proceedings which ended before they reached the court of last resort. Remarkably, the Court, twenty years after the coming into force of the DPD, has been concerned with fundamental questions such as the application of the DPD or the concept of the controller only in recent years.

As the proceedings before the Court differ from those before national courts, they require representation of the supervisory authorities by lawyers familiar with the intricacies of EU procedural law, which incurs substantial costs for the supervisory authorities in order to resolve contentious cases. And even though in the preliminary reference procedure, which is of concern here, the language of the case is that of the referring national court according to Article 37 of the Rules of Procedure of the Court of Justice, translations of the questions submitted by the national court and its own written submissions are required in order to allow meaningful cooperation of the national supervisory authorities among each other and with the European Data Protection Supervisor, who may also submit observations to the ECJ according to Article 47(1)(i) Data Protection Regulation (EC) No 45/2001 [22]. Furthermore, the supervisory authorities in these proceedings are dependent on the questions submitted by national courts, which enjoy discretion as to how to phrase them and which questions to put forward.

If binding decisions of the Board would, in practice, be brought before the Court this would allow the supervisory authorities to have a greater influence in the proceedings. However, such proceedings would also be adversarial in nature and thus might lead to conflicts between the supervisory authorities, which also depend on each other in order to properly enforce data protection law across the EU.

6 Conclusions

From the case-law and the new legislation, the picture of the supervisory authorities as agents of individuals and their rights emerges. With this conception, based on the provisions of EU law, there is an agency capable of engaging in the protection of the individual's rights and effectively counter interests and ambitions of multi-national companies processing personal data. Ideally, due to their complete independence, the supervisory authorities are also capable of discursive interaction with other State actors, especially in the executive. This is the justification for awarding a public authority far-reaching independence from the executive. Where the authorities do not live up to this vision, individuals can request them to engage on their behalf by submitting complaints and, if an authority is unwilling, take them to court. A strong judicial oversight in the conception of the Court is the key to ensuring that the supervisory authorities do not take their independence as a purpose of itself – they must use it in order to fulfil their advocacy role (cf. Sect. 2).

Taking this concept of supervisory authorities as envisioned in the current and future EU law seriously in practice, will require awarding them the appropriate means and funds to exercise these powers. This has two dimensions: the supervisory authorities must be outfitted with personnel competent to assess specific substantive issues of EU law and also to be able to engage in the actual communication with 27 other Member States, which requires considerable translation efforts (cf. Sect. 3.2).

While the new means of cooperation offer great opportunities, it will have to be seen whether the Member States, for instance, will opt for an extra-territorial enforcement of data protection among the Member States in practice. Among the supervisory authorities at least, there will be much more interaction and dependence with the introduction of the Board, which provides a powerful tool in the form of the consistency mechanism that will have to be used carefully. The Board's modus operandi has to keep a balance between cooperative and adversarial action (cf. Sect. 3.2).

The Court on the other hand has made it clear that it will not allow for a lowering of standards with regard of transfer to third countries in particular and the enforcement of EU data protection law in general (cf. Sect. 4). It has consistently strengthened the role of the authorities in its jurisprudence and in turn expects them to use their independence to fulfil their role as guardians of individual rights with regard to privacy and data protection. Furthermore, the ECJ has empowered individuals to ensure that their rights are properly enforced and thus added an additional measure of control.

References

1. Directive 95/46/EC of the European Parliament and of the Council of 24 October 1995 on the protection of individuals with regard to the processing of personal data and on the free movement of such data, OJ L 281 of 23 November 1995, pp. 31–50. http://eur-lex.europa.eu/LexUriServ/LexUriServ.do?uri=CELEX%3A31995L0046%3AEN%3AHTML

2. Regulation (EU) 2016/679 of the European Parliament and of the Council of 27 April 2016 on the protection of natural persons with regard to the processing of personal data and on the free movement of such data, and repealing Directive 95/46/EC (General Data Protection Regulation), OJ L 119 of 4 May 2016, pp. 1–88. http://eur-lex.europa.eu/legal-content/EN/TXT/PDF/?uri=CELEX:32016R0679&rid=1

3. Rost, M.: Was meint eigentlich "Datenschutz"? Der Landkreis, 445–448 (2014)

4. Charter of Fundamental Rights of the European Union, OJ C 326 of 26 October 2012, 391–407. http://eur-lex.europa.eu/legal-content/EN/TXT/PDF/?uri=CELEX:12012P/TXT&from=EN

5. ECJ, Joined Cases C-465/00, C-138/01 and C-139/01 *Österreichischer Rundfunk and Others*, ECLI:EU:C:2003:294

6. ECJ, Case C-518/07 *Commission v Germany*, EU:C:2010:125

7. ECJ, Case C-614/10 *Commission v Austria*, EU:C:2012:631

8. ECJ, Case C-288/12 *Commission v Hungary*, EU:C:2014:237

9. ECJ, Case C-230/14 *Weltimmo*, EU:C:2015:639

10. ECJ, Case C-131/12 *Google and Google Spain*, EU:C:2014:317

11. ECJ, Case C-362/14 *Schrems*, EU:C:2015:650

12. ECJ, Case C-210/16 *Wirtschaftsakademie Schleswig-Holstein*, pending

13. Act No. 78-17 of January 1978 on Information Technology, Data Files and Civil Liberties. https://www.cnil.fr/sites/default/files/typo/document/Act78-17VA.pdf

14. Schleswig-Holsteinisches Gesetz zum Schutz personenbezogener Informationen (Landesdatenschutzgesetz - LDSG -) vom 9. Februar 2000. https://datenschutzzentrum.de/gesetze/ldsg/

15. Federal Data Protection Act in the version promulgated on 14 January 2003 (Federal Law Gazette I p. 66). http://www.gesetze-im-internet.de/englisch_bdsg/englisch_bdsg.html

16. Article 29 Working Party, Update of Opinion 8/2010 on applicable law in light of the CJEU judgement in Google Spain, adopted on 16 December 2015. http://ec.europa.eu/justice/data-protection/article-29/documentation/opinion-recommendation/files/2015/wp179_en_update.pdf

17. Revolidis, I.: The Long Arm of the European Data Protection Law. Zeitschrift für Datenschutz-aktuell, 04756 (2015)

18. Nwankwo, I.S.: Weltimmo s. r. o. v. Nemzeti Adatvédelmi és Információszabadság Hatóság and the Concept of "Establishment" under Art. 4 (1)(a) Directive 95/46/EC, Zeitschrift für Datenschutz-aktuell, 04879 (2015)

19. Nguyen, A.M.: Die zukünftige Datenschutzaufsicht in Europa. Zeitschrift für Datenschutz, 265–270 (2015)

20. ECJ, Case 26-62 *van Gend en Loos*, ECLI:EU:C:1963:1

21. Kühling, J., Heberlein, J.: EuGH "reloaded": "unsafe harbor" USA vs. "Datenfestung" EU. Neue Zeitschrift für Verwaltungsrecht, 7–12 (2016)

22. Schwartmann, R.: Datentransfer in die Vereinigten Staaten ohne Rechtsgrundlage, Konsequenzen der Safe-Harbor-Entscheidung des EuGH. Europäische Zeitschrift für Wirtschaftsrecht, 864–868 (2015)

Not just User Control in the General Data Protection Regulation

On the Problems with Choice and Paternalism, and on the Point of Data Protection

Claudia Quelle[✉]

Tilburg Institute for Law, Technology and Society, Tilburg University,
Tilburg, The Netherlands
c.quelle@tilburguniversity.edu

Abstract. User control is increasingly prominent in the discourse surrounding the General Data Protection Regulation (GDPR). However, alongside user control, the GDPR also tries to achieve what will be called controller responsibility. Is this unjust paternalism or does it correctly place the responsibility for data protection with the controller and its supervisory authority? This paper argues that the question of responsibility should be evaluated in light of the overarching objective of the GDPR to protect the fundamental rights of natural persons. It describes the problems of a focus on the "choice" of data subjects, but also takes seriously the charge of paternalism which more protective data protection laws are faced with, tying the resulting dilemma to the objectives of data protection and ultimately to the debate on the nature of rights. Does data protection law seek to protect certain interests, such as secrecy and seclusion, or does it seek to give data subjects control over their data, and thereby political power regarding the substance of their fundamental rights? The paper concludes that a further exploration of will theories and interest theories of rights would shed light on the appropriate roles for user control and controller responsibility.

Keywords: Data protection · Controller responsibility · Informational self-determination · Consent · Paternalism · Fundamental rights

1 Introduction

Should the General Data Protection Regulation (GDPR) serve to give data subjects control over the information pertaining to them, or should it require controllers to protect data subjects? This paper argues that the GDPR emphasizes and strengthens the rights to control of data subjects, but also seeks to reinforce the fairness and due care exercised by the controller. Throughout the paper, controller responsibility is contrasted with user control [cf. 1]. Controller responsibility covers the notion that it is up to the primary norm-addressees of the GDPR — the controllers — to ensure, through fair data processing practices, that the objective of data protection law is met. Controllers have

A. Lehmann et al. (Eds.): Privacy and Identity 2016, IFIP AICT 498, pp. 140–163, 2016.
DOI: 10.1007/978-3-319-55783-0_11

to ensure that the fundamental rights of natural persons are protected in the context of personal data processing, irrespective of whether data subjects put forward any claims or demands. The tenet of user control seeks to give data subjects a measure of influence over the way in which their fundamental rights are protected, typically by granting them the power to demand certain protections or to shield themselves from certain intrusions.

According to van der Sloot [2], data protection law originally posed principles of good governance. Recently, however, there is an increased focus on the individual and her rights of control. Scholars like Purtova [3] would consider it radical to reject informational self-determination as 'a foundation of the European approach to data processing'. At the same time, the tenet of user control has been subject to scrutiny lately, as it is increasingly recognized that current notice-and-consent practices do not empower the average data subject in a meaningful way. This has lead Matzner et al. [4] to speak of *responsibilization*, defined as 'the process whereby subjects are rendered individually responsible for a task which previously would have been the duty of another — usually a state agency — or would not have been recognized as a responsibility at all' [5]. Matzner et al. argue that the state should be responsible for granting citizens data protection. Indeed, on the one hand, data subjects should not be burdened with the task of safeguarding the protection of their personal data, preventing that the processing operations of controllers bring about unwanted consequences. On the other hand, there might be something about data protection which requires the involvement of data subjects — e.g. to prevent abuses of power and to define the boundaries between the permissible and the impermissible in the first place.

This paper deepens the debate by tying it to the nature of rights in general. Is the protection of the fundamental rights of individuals something which controllers, under the supervision of supervisory authorities, could take on for the benefit of the rights-holders? The paper does so in three parts. The following section will examine the presence of the two tenets of user control and controller responsibility in the GDPR. Next, section three explores the virtues and drawbacks of a user control approach, taking seriously Solove's worry regarding paternalism. Section four looks into the objectives of data protection law and proposes that the question of responsibility should be evaluated in light of the overarching objective of the GDPR to protect the fundamental rights of natural persons. A dilemma is found: fundamental rights protection by others than the data subjects themselves is (at best) based on the way in which their interests are perceived. However, the alternative is to require them to express their interests and their opinions on what counts as an appropriate or an inappropriate collection or use of personal data, which might impose too high a burden. The debate between interest-based and will-based theorists is identified as a possible area of research to investigate the legitimate roles of user control and controller responsibility.

2   The General Data Protection Regulation

The GDPR has been increasingly presented as an instrument which seeks to strengthen user control, although another major drive of the reform was to strengthen the responsibility and accountability of controllers. At the start of the reform process in 2009 and

2010, the Commission [6] and the Article 29 Working Party [7] sought to strengthen the rights of data subjects, but also explored 'ways of ensuring that data controllers put in place effective policies and mechanisms to ensure compliance with data protection rules' [6]. Controllers should show how responsibility is exercised and make this verifiable; '[r]esponsibility and accountability are two sides of the same coin and both essential elements of good governance' [8]. This is how the obligations to conduct a data protection impact assessment, implement data protection by design, and appoint a data protection officer came to be. While the Impact Assessment of 2012 [9] does discuss these accountability mechanisms, the problems it identifies with regard to the Data Protection Directive are only (1) 'barriers to business and public authorities due to fragmentation, legal uncertainty and inconsistent enforcement' and (2) 'difficulties for individuals to stay in control of their data'. The Impact Assessment laments that 'individuals are often neither aware nor in control of what happens to their personal data and therefore fail to exercise their rights effectively'. At this point in time, also the Commission [10] talks about putting individuals in control of the data pertaining to them. Anno 2016, recital 7 of the GDPR states unequivocally that '[n]atural persons should have control of their own personal data'. In the press release on the adoption of the GDPR, rapporteur Jan Philipp Albrecht [11] even emphasised that '[c]itizens will be able to decide for themselves which personal information they want to share'. Behind the scenes, however, his amendment stating that 'the right to the protection of personal data is based on the right of the data subject to exert control over the data that are being processed', was removed from the text agreed upon by the European Parliament [12, 13]. Meanwhile, Article 5(2) provides that the controller shall be responsible for compliance with the data protection principles.

Despite the rhetoric of user control, it will become clear that many provisions in the GDPR serve both the tenet of user control and the tenet of controller responsibility. I will first discuss consent and data subject rights, after which I proceed to the data protection principles, emphasizing their link to the responsibility of the controller.

2.1   Consent and Data Subject Rights

The tenet of user control is guaranteed primarily by the role of consent and the presence of data subject rights in the GDPR and in the ePrivacy Directive. The consent of individuals is a frequently relied upon ground to legitimize the processing of personal data. In many cases, it is the only available legal ground (GDPR, art 9; ePrivacy Directive, arts 6, 9 and 13). The GDPR tightens the definition of consent and strengthens its role. The Data Protection Directive already contained a number of conditions which had to obtain for consent to be valid: consent has to be a 'freely given specific and informed indication of [the data subject's] wishes' (art 2(h)). The GDPR clarifies that consent must always be unambiguous, given either through a statement or a clearly affirmative action (art 4(11), recital 32). The special categories of data, for which consent must be explicit, are expanded (art 8). Further, when assessing whether consent is freely given, 'utmost account shall be taken of whether, inter alia, the performance of a contract, including the provision of a service, is conditional on consent to the processing of personal data that is not necessary for the performance of that contract' (art 7(4)). Recital

43 clarifies that consent is presumed not to be freely given if the deal is "take it or leave it": if appropriate, consent must be obtained separately for separate processing activities. The provision of a good or service must, in addition, not be made conditional on consent if the consent is not necessary for the performance of the contract. Moreover, the request for consent must be clear. If consent is obtained through a contract or general terms and conditions, the request for consent must stand out, for example by presenting it in a separate text box, and it must be requested in an intelligible and easily accessible form, using clear and plain language (art 7(2)). The information requirements are accompanied by similar demands regarding the form in which they are presented, as necessitated by the principle of transparency (art 12) [14]. In addition to the other information requirements, the data subject must also be informed whether she 'is obliged to provide the personal data' and further 'of the possible consequences of failure to provide such data' (art 13(2)(e)). Finally, if the provision of information society services to children is based on consent, it must have been given or authorized by the holder of parental responsibility over the child (art 9). Purtova [17] argues that developments such as the tightening of the definition of consent have reduced the informational self-determination of the data subject. As a result of these changes, consent will indeed play a smaller role, but it will be more meaningful. Because the conditions under which consent is valid are more stringent, situations under which the data subject did not really make an informed choice will be less readily regarded as an expression of her will.

Individuals are further granted a number of rights, including the right to be informed of a number of categories of information about the processing operation (GDPR, arts 12-14), to access, rectify or erase their personal data (including the "right to be forgotten", arts 15-17), the newfound right to data portability (art 20), and the rights to object and to not be subject to decisions based solely on automated processing (art 21-22). They should be informed of these rights, with the exception, for some reason, of the latter (arts 13(2)(b) and 14(2)(c)). The burden of proof regarding the right to object now unequivocally lies with the controller. If the data subject objects, it is up to the controller to demonstrate 'compelling legitimate grounds for the processing which override the interests, rights and freedoms of the data subject or for the establishment, exercise or defence of legal claims' (art 21(1)). As befits the level of specificity of an EU regulation, which has direct effect in the legal orders of the Member States, the GDPR now also provides for access to justice and redress, specifying the right to lodge a complaint, the right to an effective remedy, the right to mandate a representative body to lodge a complaint on behalf of the data subject, and the right to compensation (arts 77-80 and 82). These additions serve to provide what Lynskey [13] calls 'an architecture which bolsters individual control', to be distinguished from the control rights themselves. Such an architecture must go beyond the mere provision of information to also include, inter alia, the possibility to take collective action and the availability of actual alternatives in the market. It must be noted, however, that the rights of data subjects do not only serve to grant individuals a certain measure of control. The right to erasure also enables data subjects to ensure that controllers take their responsibility seriously and comply with their obligations, as they can have their data erased if storage is no longer necessary or if it has become unlawful to keep the data (art 17(1)). The rights to lodge a complaint and to obtain redress can similarly be understood as mechanisms of private enforcement. Further, as discussed in the next section, the rights to be informed and to gain access to the data can also serve to inspire responsible behaviour by shedding "sunlight" on the conduct of controllers.

2.2   The Data Protection Principles and Controller Responsibility

The tenet of controller responsibility can be found in the data protection principles. It is also strengthened in the GDPR through the addition of a number of novel provisions. The data protection principles of Article 5[1] traditionally sought to establish good governance or due care; requiring that the processing of data is fair and reasonable [3]. Indeed, data protection law can be seen as a substantiation of the overarching principle to process data fairly and lawfully [18, 19], which itself is a reflection of the requirements of good governance or fair administration in the public sector and due care in the private sector under the Dutch tradition [20].

The data protection principles make informational self-determination possible, but they should also spark concern for the interests of data subjects. The principle of lawfulness requires the processing to be based on a legal ground. While consent is one of the legal grounds, a number of other grounds require the controller to gauge the interests of the data subject or of the public at large (GDPR, arts 6(1)(d), 6(1)(e) and 6(1)(f)). The principle of fair processing should also cause the controller to take the interests of data subjects into account. It is frequently understood as requiring that controllers are transparent and do not unduly pressure data subjects into consent, thereby protecting the tenet of user control. However, Bygrave [19] explains that in addition, fairness 'undoubtedly means that data controllers must take account of the interests and reasonable expectations of data subjects', which 'has direct consequences for the purposes for which data may be processed'. This is a form of proportionality, as the interests of data subjects and controllers are balanced [19].

One of the functions of the principle of purpose limitation is to ensure that there are clearly defined processing conditions which can be consented to [21, 22, cf. 23]. Data minimization, storage limitation and integrity and confidentiality all require the controller to ensure that these conditions are kept to: that data are not kept longer than necessary or used unnecessarily, and that they are not accidentally processed in unauthorized or unlawful ways. These restrictions should ensure that the processing and its results are legitimate and align with the reasonable expectations of the data subject [19]. This is beneficial for informational self-determination. However, the limitations also serve (or are supposed to serve)[2] as a limit on data processing, preventing the risks posed by aimless collection, unlimited dissemination, and misuse or arbitrary use of personal

---

[1] The principles include lawfulness, fairness and transparency; purpose limitation, data minimization and storage limitation; and accuracy, integrity and confidentiality. Purpose limitation entails that the personal data may only be processed insofar as this is necessary for a legitimate and specified purpose.

[2] Moerel and Prins [24] convincingly argue that purpose limitation does not serve as a useful constraint on the processing of personal data when the purpose of controllers is, and is permitted to be, to collect and analyse data.

data [25]. Controllers have the responsibility to ensure that the purpose of the processing is legitimate, meaning that they may not process data in ways which do not accord to legal principles, fundamental rights, or other sources of law and that they must take into account the 'reasonable expectations' of the data subject. The Article 29 Working Party [26] mentions by way of example that controllers are prohibited from processing the data 'for purposes that may result in discriminatory practices'. To be clear, this obligation applies irrespective of whether the controller obtained consent from the data subject.

The required transparency towards the data subject clearly makes possible informed consent and the exercise of her rights [14], but also serves to inspire fair and reasonable processing operations: 'sunlight is the best of disinfectants' [15, 16]. It is therefore noteworthy with regard to both tenets of the GDPR that the information requirements are made more specific, requiring controllers to be open about, *inter alia*, their legitimate interest; the storage period; the presence and logic of automated decision-making and the significance and envisaged consequences thereof; and the source of the data, if it had not been provided by the data subject (arts 13(1)(d), 13(2)(a) and (f), and 14(2)(f)). Whereas the Directive only provided a short, non-exhaustive list of the information which should be provided in order for the processing to be fair, the GDPR specifies extensive requirements relating to both the form and the substance of the notices (arts 12-14). These requirements are still to be supplemented under the principles of fairness and transparency, if necessary.

In short, the data protection principles imply that controller responsibility has been, and still is, an important aim of the principles of data protection. A great share of the novelties of the GDPR serve to strengthen the data protection principles. This includes the accountability mechanisms introduced in Chap. 4. Controllers are required to take technical and organisational measures to implement the data protection principles and to protect the rights of data subjects, whereby they have to, by default, limit the processing to what is necessary in accordance with the data protection principles (art 25). Data protection by design should improve compliance with principles such as data minimisation, data quality and confidentiality, as well as ensure that the system is transparent and provides data subjects with effective means of control [7]. Controllers are further obliged under the GDPR to be transparent about data breaches towards both data subjects and supervisory authorities, incentivizing controllers to avoid them in the first place (arts 33 and 34). Moreover, controllers are required to assess and find ways to mitigate high risks to the rights and freedoms of individuals posed by their processing activities (art 35). Recital 75 clarifies that controllers should keep an eye on whether data subjects are able to exercise control over their personal data, but also mentions a large number of other threats and risks, including discrimination, identity theft or fraud, loss of confidentiality of personal data protected by professional secrecy, and unauthorized reversal of encryption. The responsibility to assess and address risks protects data subjects and can function to create a trust relationship between the data subjects and the controller. The two tenets come together here as the controller's responsibility can be indispensable for the data subject's trust and thus her consent, while this trust relationship also makes the controller responsible to the data subject [27, 28].

Controller responsibility takes place under the supervision of regulatory agencies. The principle of accountability requires controllers to be able to demonstrate compliance (art 24) and to employ and involve a data protection officer (arts 37-39). The GDPR also stimulates the proper translation of data protection law to practice through codes of conduct which can be certified by supervisory authorities (arts 40-43). Although the duty to notify supervisory authorities has been abolished, it has been replaced by the data protection impact assessment and the prior consultation. This should shift the attention of the authorities to potentially harmful cases and enable them to readily gauge the situation at hand (arts 35-36). Article 83 introduces fines up to 20 000 000 EUR or 4% of the total worldwide annual turnover of an undertaking, whichever is higher.

The second tenet of data protection law should get controllers to provide proper ex ante protection, preventing the occurrence of possible harm to the data subject irrespective of whether she withheld consent or otherwise exercised her control rights. As observed by González Fuster [29], '[r]esponsibility for such compliance had always fallen on their shoulders, irrespective of whether somebody was looking, or whether somebody complains'. In other words, it is the responsibility of the controller to engage in fair practices, although the data subject can have a say in or 'a measure of influence over' what that entails, if she wants to [19].

3   The "Choice" to Consent and the "Paternalism" of Protective Legislation

The GDPR attempts to strike a balance between the two tenets of user control and controller responsibility. It affords a number of protections irrespective of whether the data subject has consented to the processing. At the same time, consent is an important legal ground for those processing operations which are not easily justifiable on the basis of another ground, e.g. those processing operations which are not necessary to protect the vital interests of the data subject, to perform a task of public interest, or to serve a legitimate interest of the controller which is not outweighed by the rights and interests of the data subjects. Otherwise illegitimate processing operations can only be legitimized through consent. Unsurprisingly, in practice, consent is a weak spot of the GDPR. But what of more protective approaches? The appropriateness of the two tenets depends, firstly, on the significance of the constraints on the free and autonomous choice of data subjects and, secondly, on the permissibility of state intervention for the perceived benefit of the data subject. If data subjects are severely constrained in their choice to consent or not to consent, or are too weak-willed to do what they think is right, there are three options, each of which features in data protection law: their "choice" is still respected; they are protected by default but with the option to opt-out, which may influence their decisions but still allows them, in theory, to "consent away" their rights; or their freedom is curtailed for their protection. I will first discuss the constraints on choice, after which I will discuss whether the alternative of protection through controller responsibility is paternalist.

3.1 The "Choice" to Consent

There is extensive literature on the problems with user control, notice-and-consent, privacy self-management, or DIY-data-protection. The majority of the concerns are about constraints on the ability of individuals to freely and autonomously make an informed choice about the data processing operations pertaining to them. Choice always occurs under a set of conditions or parameters [30]. In the words of Cohen [23]: '[s]ome of these parameters, such as the fact that we need gravity to walk and oxygen to breathe, are relatively fixed. Others, such as the design of legal institutions and technological tools, are slightly more malleable'. Benn [31] clarifies that the conditions of choice also relate to states of the agent, distinguishing between the resources which are available to her, the opportunity costs involved in pursuing X, the goals of the agent in light of which the choice is made, and the beliefs which the agent holds about these conditions. Restrictions of the freedom of choice can result from restrictions with regard to all four conditions. This means, for example, that the social or economic consequences of refusing to consent and the influence of marketing and online personalization affect the extent to which choice is free. The way in which data protection law regulates consent is bound to legitimize some of these conditions, and change others [32]. It remains to be seen to what extent the changes to the consent regime in the GDPR will make a difference, ameliorating the constraints on the data subject's choice or qualifying consent as invalid because of these constraints. Some data protection scholars think that, in the context of digital services, the restrictions are such that we often can no longer speak of a real choice. If this is so, consent should not be considered informed and freely given.

In the following, the relevant constraints to choice are presented as pertaining to three related categories. Firstly, data subjects do not have enough time to consider each type of processing operation because they engage with services which collect data so very frequently. Or, put differently, they lack the will to make time for this burden — and understandably so, considering how uneconomical it would be [33, 34]. In a well-known study from 2008, McDonald and Cranor 'estimate that reading privacy policies carries costs in time of approximately 201 h a year, worth about \$3,534 annually per American Internet user. Nationally, if Americans were to read online privacy policies word-for-word, we estimate the value of time lost as about \$781 billion annually' [35]. While this problem can be addressed by grouping together different types of processing operations, this solution also lumps together different situations in which different values and interests may play a role. It thereby reduces the choice available to data subjects.

Secondly, in the world of "big data", data subjects will often not fully comprehend what it means to consent to a data processing operation. It is difficult, if not impossible, to make data processing operations transparent to the data subjects. Data can be inferred from other available data, so that data which was shared by or inferred about others can be used to infer things about you [33, 36, 37]. If complex or self-learning algorithms are used, the way in which this occurs may not even be explainable in human language [33, 38]. As discussed above, the updated information requirements in the GDPR attempt to increase transparency by requiring controllers to give information on the logic employed by self-learning algorithms, the significance and envisaged consequences thereof, and the other data sources which will be accessed. This information could be presented in accessible and less time-consuming ways, for example through logos or seals. Doing so, however, 'conflicts with fully informing people about the consequences of giving up data, which are quite complex if explained in sufficient detail to be meaningful' [33]. Or, in the words of Koops [39], 'the simpler you make the consent procedure, the less will users understand what they actually consent to; and the more meaningful you make the consent procedure (providing sufficient information about what will happen with the data), the less convenient the consent will become'.

These first two types of constraints exist irrespective of the actual practices of notice and consent, which oftentimes only make matters worse. Many notices are long and couched in inaccessible language [40], yet fail to shed light on the data flows; they are subject to frequent change; and the privacy policies of those who collect the data are often different from the policies of the entities to which they sell the data [41].

The third type of constraint concerns more or less imposed limitations to the freedom and autonomy of choice. In many situations, data subjects are faced with non-negotiable and excessive "terms", under which personal data can be collected, used and shared almost without limit, while they are unable to get the desired goods or services elsewhere under more reasonable conditions. Underlying this is 'the fact that there are practically no alternative business models that generate revenue from other sources than user-data-based profiling and advertising', given that users are unwilling to pay for services, 'conditioned as they are in thinking that the Internet offers free lunches' (in the words of Koops) [39]. Further, there may well be all kinds of pressures which lead data subjects to desire the product or service. Matzner et al. [4] remind us of the costs which are, for many, involved in not owning a smart phone: 'less contacts with friends, missing career opportunities, more complicated dating, being considered inefficient as a colleague, being considered suspicious at border controls'. At the same time, the reasons for using products and services like smart phones and social media 'are promoted by the best advertising agencies in the world'. The situation is grave enough for Hull [32] to imply that the focus on notice and consent in data protection law, rather than decreasing the power dissymmetry, is actually a means to hide and legitimise it. By acting as though the individual has the possibility to exercise real choice, while she in actuality is moulded by the possibilities offered by her (digital) environment, the social struggle is obscured and the individual is disempowered. Cohen [42] also does not mince words, pointing to the power exercised by 'public and private regimes of surveillance and modulation' to turn us into 'citizen-consumers' with diminished capacities of democratic self-government. Cohen [23] suspects that under these conditions of choice, 'individuals may simply concede, and convince themselves that the loss of privacy associated with this particular transaction is not too great'.

Cohen, Solove, Schwartz, Acquisti, and a number of other scholars treat bounded rationality and bias as though they pose cracks through which government and corporate actors manipulate our choices [30, 33, 34, 43, 44]. Schwartz [29] argues that 'consumers' general inertia toward default terms is a strong and pervasive limitation on free choice' which permits industry to set the terms. Hull [32], on the other hand, sees the notion of *homo economicus* and the resulting reliance on notice and consent in data protection law as the real problem. But if we do not assume that individuals can make autonomous, rational decisions, what is the alternative?

3.2   The "Paternalism" of Protective Legislation

The previous section describes a number of constraints on the ability of data subjects to freely and autonomously form an opinion regarding the appropriateness of certain (aspects of) processing activities, as a result of which they agree to operations which might cause them harm. What conclusion should be drawn from the fact that these constraints exist? Solove [33] believes that 'the most apparent solution — paternalist measures — even more directly denies people the freedom to make consensual choices about their data'. He emphasises that some people want their data shared and want to be profiled, as for them the benefits outweigh the costs. Indeed, proponents of privacy self-management argue that, through a system of user control, 'everyone may attain his own desired level of data protection' [3]. While this is too simple a picture, as there are interdependencies and inequalities — e.g. the data shared by one person can be used to profile another, and some people may be more pressured to share their data than others — [4],[3] control rights do allow an expression of what the data subjects involved consider appropriate in a given situation. Solove sees the EU data protection regime as paternalist because of the many rules which restrict processing even in the absence of any wish or demand on the side of the data subject [33].

To appreciate this point, it is crucial to see that the appropriate limits on data flows and uses of data are not self-evident. Whether a data processing operation is legitimate, entails a normative appraisal of the circumstances at hand. This entails, by way of example, that it is necessary to be sceptical of Cavoukian's attempts to distance her approach to Privacy by Design from paternalism. Cavoukian [45] argues that if controllers implement the fair information practice principles by design, then 'individuals are not placed in the position of having to be concerned about safeguarding personal information — they can be confident that privacy is assured, right from the outset'. She assumes that if controllers simply stick to the principles of purpose limitation and data minimization, the expectations of individuals are respected. The default should be 'the most privacy-protective', and anything extra requires consent [45]. But what is the most privacy-protective default setting? Unlike secrecy, the multi-faceted and contested notion of privacy is not something which can easily be maximized, as it contains conflicting and incommensurable facets which cannot be subsumed under one overarching value without discussion (see Sect. 4.1) [cf. 46]. It is difficult to imagine a situation in which secrecy, confidentiality, or even privacy is the only possible consideration,

---

[3] Matzner et al. [4] show that there are inequalities which cannot be addressed on an individual level. Technological means to effectuate control rights are often not free of charge, while, following research of Gilliom, data protection needs are unequally distributed and are likely to hit the poorest. As a result, 'this additional cost is especially put on those who already face discrimination or social inequalities'. Further, there are differences in privacy norms, requiring some individuals to be more revealing than others.

as sometimes data should be shared (see Sect. 4.2).[4] It is therefore problematic to maintain that the implementation of the data protection principles "by design" will protect individuals upfront without the danger of paternalism. The controller will need to consider, for example, whether the purpose is legitimate and whether the impact on data subjects will necessitate extra precautions. Cavoukian's arguments are tempting because we think that it is *right* that certain protections are afforded. The implication is that if we consider something to be of enough moral importance, it should be protected, at least by default, irrespective of what the people concerned actually think about it. This happens to be exactly what paternalism is about.

To start, paternalism can be understood as 'the usurpation of one person's choice of their own good by another person' [47]. While paternalism has a negative connotation, many paternalist measures are accepted on both sides of the Atlantic. To call something paternalist, is only the start of the debate [see e.g. 48]. That said, is the GDPR indeed paternalist, as Solove makes it out to be?

Some provisions in data protection law are not only there to protect the data subject, but mainly to empower her or to protect others. Many of the EU rules are necessary preconditions to meaningful consent. Further, some provisions of the GDPR were enacted for the main reason to protect third parties and society as a whole against the harmful or selfish choices which individual data subjects could make in a market-based system of privacy self-management. The legal grounds next to consent and contract all, directly or indirectly, pertain to the interests of others or to the public interest. They allow one's data to be used for the benefit of others. Other provisions limit the use of data, possibly to address societal problems posed by function creep. It has been argued that the problems which should be addressed by data protection law, pertain to the interests of society as a whole; because everyone is or might be a data subject, it is no longer about protecting specific individuals [3]. Privacy is seen as a 'common good' [43]. Insofar as the provisions of the GDPR were not included to protect the individual whose choice is usurped, they do not qualify as paternalist [49]. At the same time, however, a concern for the interests of the specific data subject and the risks or possible consequences for this data subject is present throughout the GDPR. The data subject cannot "consent away" the protection offered to her by the principles of fairness, purpose limitation, data minimization, data quality and data security, and this is in part for the protection of her own rights and freedoms. The GDPR thus includes paternalist provisions.

---

[4] It is possible to hold that secrecy or confidentiality *should be* the only mandatory consideration when technology is designed, as appears to be the case under the Privacy by Design requirement in the proposed ePrivacy Regulation. Article 10 of the leaked Proposal for a Regulation of the European Parliament and of the Council concerning the respect for private life and personal data in electronic communications and repealing Directive 2002/58/EC requires that the default setting of terminal equipment and of software should be that third parties can neither store information on the equipment, nor process information which is stored thereon. Internet browsers, for example, should automatically reject all third-party cookies. The end-user can consent to these processing activities of third parties by changing the browser settings per Article 9(2) — assuming that this option is provided by the developers of the browser.

Sometimes, the data subject can opt out of the protection which is offered, as when she can opt in to more extensive processing as per data protection by default. Under some definitions of paternalism, such as that of Thaler and Sunstein [50] and of Dworkin in his later work [51], the fact that a user can, at least in theory, opt out of the paternalist measure, does not mean that the intervention is not in fact paternalist. Any nudge, including a change in the default setting, is considered paternalist if it is for the agent's own good. This is because the choice or decision-making of the agent is influenced [50–52]. Her choice is not necessarily usurped, but it is certainly affected. Since the nudge only seeks to prevent actions that stem from irrational tendencies, which assumedly should be kept in check by one's rational, 'Econ' side [53], it bears resemblance to Feinberg's [54] 'soft paternalism'. However, paternalism can also be understood as entailing that the agent's freedom is curtailed. The paternalism of a nudge then depends on whether or not the agent truly has the option to opt out. Because the default setting is often followed, it could be argued that a change in the default affects the options available to the agent. It thus limits her freedom, albeit the freedom to be irrational, as well as her autonomy [cf. 55].

The GDPR thus seeks to protect data subjects, although they can sometimes opt out of this protection. What if this is what they want? In theory, the protections which are afforded could be in accordance with what the data subject would want and possibly even with what she would choose, if she had the time, the knowledge and the capacity to fully reflect on it [cf. 'anticipated consent', 56]. This appears to be Cavoukian's answer to the charge of paternalism. However, it is unlikely that a general set of rules will meet the anticipated wishes of every data subject, as they are bound to differ. Moreover, even if people value their privacy, many do find themselves giving away their data. This is the so-called "privacy paradox". Following Shiffrin [57], protecting people from the privacy paradox would count as paternalism. Shiffrin discusses the case in which the friend of a smoker hides her cigarettes because, even though she wants to stop smoking, she might be weak-willed and light another cigarette. Such an intervention should be considered to be paternalist because 'efforts to supplant or maneuver around an agent's agency when motivated by distrust of that person's agency, can deliver the same sort of insult to her autonomy as distrust of her judgment'. Archard [47] takes a different approach. According to Archard, it is necessary that the paternalist discounts the agent's belief that his intervention does not promote her own good, and so there must be disagreement about the benefit of the intervention.

Would the protection afforded by the GDPR be paternalist if the data subject has not formed a conscious choice? Users are bound to accept cookies and download apps without fully considering the data protection consequences (see Sect. 3.1). In that case, protective legislation would restrict the freedom of the data subject, but it would not necessarily impinge her autonomy, as the data subject is not giving expression to a full-fledged decision. Her choice is not necessarily usurped, as she did not really make a choice, but the option to act differently has been taken from her. Clarke [58] considers cases in which a choice is made for someone who was unable to make the choice herself, to be paternalist. In his example, an unconscious patient is given a blood transfusion. The incapacity to reflect on each exchange of personal data in today's information society could be considered to similarly affect whether a data subject has the ability to choose, albeit to a lesser extent. It is important to note that while a choice can be formed more or less reflectively or deliberately, meaning that factual autonomy is gradual, a person is often morally and legally granted the freedom of 'a valid decision-making body' if she meets a certain threshold of rationality, self-reflection and self-control [31, 59]. Consumer law, for example, sees consumers as reasonably well-informed, observant and circumspect, which strikes a particular 'balance between the need to protect consumers and promoting free trade' [14]. While it is now popular in data protection scholarship to 'question the very possibility of [user] control by deconstructing the conventional figure of the "rational and autonomous agent" that is at the core of "privacy as control" theories' [43], only a limited "amount" of rationality and autonomy is needed to sustain the tenet of user control in data protection law. The legal question is whether the average data subject, who could not take the time to find and read an incomprehensible privacy policy and who was nudged by her digital environment and socio-economic context to click on 'OK' in favour of short-term gain, should qualify as autonomously and freely making an informed choice. And if the answer is no — if we assume that data subjects cannot make autonomous, rational decisions in the online context — the follow-up question is whether this means that her freedom can be restricted, or whether her "choice" should be respected nonetheless.

4   How to Evaluate the Tenets of User Control and Controller Responsibility

It follows from the analysis in Sect. 2 that the GDPR places heavy reliance on enforcement by both private and supervisory authorities so as to ensure that controllers process data fairly — both to enable data subjects to exercise their control rights and to prevent controllers from bringing about unjustifiable harm. The GDPR seeks to *empower* and to *protect*. But how to interpret and apply these tenets? On the basis of which benchmarks do we decide whether to foster choice and accept indications of consent, despite the constraints discussed, or to opt for more protective, even paternalist, approaches instead? Evaluations of user control are fraught with conceptual difficulty. As remarked by Lazaro and Le Métayer [43], it is important to distinguish between user control as part of the foundation of data protection and user control as nothing but private enforcement. Private enforcement options may have been introduced to overcome the failing of a purely administrative set of rules, but they also restore, in the words of Purtova [3], 'the balance of power between individuals and data processing actors'. In the evaluation of Bygrave and Schartum [60], data protection law is about protecting privacy and data protection interests, whereby consent should 'strengthen the bargaining position of individuals'. In the next sections, I will argue that the aim of data protection can be to protect specific interests but also to empower, depending on how the objective of the GDPR to protect fundamental rights is conceptualized. Under a will theory of rights, user control is indispensable, despite the constraining conditions of choice, while an interest theory of rights supports a large role for controller responsibility, despite the paternalism of this tenet.

4.1 User Control or Controller Responsibility — to What End?

Whether private enforcement is a welcome addition or whether it is essential to the goal of data protection, depends on how the foundation and objective of data protection is conceptualized (and in particular, as will be argued in Sect. 4.3, on how rights are conceptualized). I will discuss the protection of interests of the data subjects, including the interest in being granted 'a zone of relative insulation from outside scrutiny and interference' [23], and informational self-determination: an empowering objective which is frequently seen as the justification for the tenet of user control.

If the focus is on a protective goal of the GDPR, it is easy to conclude that data protection law is the responsibility of controllers, meaning that protective rules are an appropriate response to the constraints on the ability of data subjects to exercise choice. When Matzner et al. [4] argued that it is not normatively desirable 'to choose the individual user as the main responsible actor to improve the state of data protection', they saw data protection as is something which citizens 'need'. They asked whether it should be up to data subjects to ensure that their data is protected in the sense that 'particular pieces of data should not be accessible to particular actors'. Since they have identified an interest which deserves protection, they can see data protection as something which needs to be protected by controllers and by the state for the benefit of data subjects. The GDPR protects a wide range of interests of individuals or society in general in relation to the processing of personal data. It protects not only confidentiality and data security, but also the right not to be discriminated and the right not to be unduly subjected to a profile. The GDPR takes on board all these different harms, seeking to ensure that the controller takes the interests of data subjects into account and abstains from taking unjustifiable risks. Interestingly, it also asks for particular attention 'where personal data of vulnerable natural persons, in particular of children, are processed' (recital 75).

One privacy interest which can be protected by controllers, is the interest in having a space to develop one's identity without undue outside interference. Multiple theories of privacy view this right as granting individuals a private zone within which they can consciously and with relative autonomy engage in self-formation [42, 61]. For Cohen, privacy in this sense is severely affected by profiling. The practice of profiling can make data flows less transparent and predictable [22], and it can lead to harmful and unjust decisions. However, privacy scholars like Cohen [23] are particularly concerned about the impact of the use of profiles for online personalisation on an individual's ability to autonomously construct her identity. The nudging effect of digital environments complicates autonomous user control and creates an interest which can be protected. To ask data subjects to ensure that they are not subject to undue modulation and interdiction, defeats the purpose. If it is done well, they will not be aware of the effect; they will perceive their preferences and actions as authentic. They may even offer their consent in the future [23, 32]. Thus, if certain interferences with an individual's process of self-formation simply should not be undertaken, then it is primarily the responsibility of controllers to refrain from adopting such illegitimate purposes. In the typology of Koops et al. [62], seclusion, secrecy, and control lie on a continuum of accessibility from private to public. While this may be so, the former two require protection, and the latter requires empowerment.

User control necessarily plays a prominent role in data protection if the focus is on the right to informational self-determination and on the power available to individuals to push back and to engage in 'boundary management' [42]. It was of great influence to the EU data protection tradition that the German *Bundesverfassungsgericht* brought to life the right to informational self-determination in 1983 [63]. This right is defined as follows: 'the authority of the individual to decide himself, on the basis of the idea of self-determination, when and within what limits information about his private life should be communicated to others' [21, 22, 64]. Underlying this right is a concern about chilling effects. If you cannot predict which information is known about you in certain 'social milieus', then your decisions will be subject to 'pressure influence' [21]. For example, the *Bundesverfassungsgericht* [21] argued that '[i]f he [the individual] reckons that participation in an assembly or a citizens' initiative will be registered officially and that personal risks might result from it, he may possibly renounce the exercise of his respective rights'. More generally, as noted by Hornung and Schnabel [22],' [i]f citizens cannot oversee and control which or even what kind of information about them is openly accessible in their social environment, and if they cannot even appraise the knowledge of possible communication partners, they may be inhibited in making use of their freedom'. The court [21] ties this to the German constitutional right to personality, arguing that chilling effects impair an individual in her chances of self-development and thereby stand in the way of a free democratic society.

Taking a cue from Purtova's [3] view of data protection law as restoring the power balance between data subjects and controllers, and from the focus of the *Bundesverfassungsgericht* [21] on chilling effects to fundamental rights, I propose that informational self-determination protects political power. It protects the influence which an individual or group of individuals can have over what it means to hold fundamental rights in a given polity. This is because it limits the extent to which other actors in society, be they governmental or private, can preclude certain activities. For example, if the state is aware of the meetings of a controversial political group, it is in the position to prohibit the assembly, thereby determining that it is not worthy of protection under the relevant rights and freedoms. Similarly, an individual may wish to hide sensitive information about herself in specific contexts so as to prevent others from discriminating her on the basis of that information — thereby protecting her right to equal treatment, as she perceives it. Her ability to control whether the sensitive information is known, allows her to act on her belief that the information should be irrelevant to others: that it is private in the sense that it is *just* for her to hide it. Informational self-determination therefore indirectly safeguards the ability of individuals to define, for themselves, what their interests and needs are and how they should be protected in a just society. For example, the right to object allows data subjects to object to processing which takes place on the basis of the public interest or a legitimate interest of the controller or of a third party (GDPR, art 21(1)). This means that, if a data subject does not agree with the balance between this other interest and her own rights, the right to object provides an avenue through which she can make herself heard.

The *Bundesverfassungsgericht* considered it crucial that individuals have control over information flows for the protection of other rights and freedoms, to the extent that control was deemed to be a right of its own. Informational self-determination protects an interest or need, but it is different from other interests as it is now essential that the data subject takes an active role. The state may need to require controllers to amend their conduct in order to establish a situation in which effective control is possible. If control rights are unenforceable because of the complexity of the Big Data landscape [39], the right to informational self-determination would demand state intervention to remedy the situation.

It is important to note that the right to informational self-determination is not absolute. Thus it is possible that certain information flows should or should not occur, irrespective of the wishes of the data subject. Depending on the political theory of choice, it could be desirable to limit the use of profiles so as to protect the relatively autonomous self-formation of individuals, or perhaps profiles should be used to create a public space where political deliberation occurs, or, alternatively, to offer the safety promised by the Hobbesian state [cf. 65]. In the German tradition, informational self-determination is only the 'intermediate value' adopted by the *Bundesverfassungsgericht* to protect the higher rights to dignity and personality [63]. Rouvroy and Poullet [63] argue, in this vein, that the two facets of privacy tied to seclusion and control ultimately do not pursue different goals, as they together sustain self-determination and collective decision-making. Both the right to be let alone so as to engage in relatively autonomous self-formation, and the right to informational self-determination, advance 'the capacity of the human subject to keep and develop his personality in a manner that allows him to fully participate in society without however being induced to conform his thoughts, beliefs, behaviours and preferences to those thoughts, beliefs, behaviours and preferences held by the majority'. Undeniably, however, the two tenets do come into tension. When an individual is or is not granted privacy against her wishes, she has little say over what the right to privacy means or should mean. Her capacity to develop thoughts, beliefs, behaviours and preferences may be protected, but her power to affect what the right to privacy should entail is diminished for the sake of developing this capacity, limiting the control she has over the boundary between her and others.

4.2 Fundamental Rights Protection as the Overarching Objective of the General Data Protection Regulation

To evaluate the roles for user control and controller responsibility, given the issues these tenets face with choice and paternalism, it is necessary to look beyond either informational self-determination or another interest or need which can be protected. How do we get past stand-offs in which scholars emphasize one side or the other? While the *Bundesverfassungsgericht* can appeal to the higher right to personality, the EU legal order lacks an equivalent. In the absence of a similar over-arching right, this paper proposes to ask the question of responsibility with an eye to fundamental rights in general.

From a doctrinal perspective, the objective of the GDPR to protect fundamental rights overarches the different tenets of data protection. The question of responsibility thus becomes an inquiry into what it means to protect or enjoy fundamental rights. In accordance with Article 1, the GDPR protects the fundamental rights and freedoms of natural persons and *in particular* their right to the protection of personal data with regard to the processing of personal data. The GDPR no longer protects, in particular, the right to privacy, as did the Data Protection Directive. The right to the protection of personal data, laid down in Article 8 of the Charter, has taken this place. Article 8(2) elevates the status of a number of data protection principles, which were designed to regulate the processing of personal data in a manner which achieves an appropriate balance between the different rights and interests involved. The processing of personal data has a bearing on many different fundamental rights. When the EU legislature decided to further substantiate the meaning of the right to the protection of personal data by adopting the GDPR, it remained fully aware that no single right could take priority in the resulting legal framework [e.g. 66]. This is made evident by the frequent reference to "the rights and freedoms of individuals" throughout the GDPR, which must, according to the Article 29 Working Party [67], be understood as referring to not only privacy, but also to 'other fundamental rights such as freedom of speech, freedom of thought, freedom of movement, prohibition of discrimination, right to liberty, conscience and religion'. Importantly, recital 4 reminds us that the right to the protection of personal data is not an absolute right, and that it must accordingly be balanced against other fundamental rights so as to respect them, too. It thus states that the GDPR respects all fundamental rights, mentioning explicitly 'the respect for private and family life, home and communications, the protection of personal data, freedom of thought, conscience and religion, freedom of expression and information, freedom to conduct a business, the right to an effective remedy and to a fair trial, and cultural, religious and linguistic diversity.' The Commission's draft General Data Protection Regulation [10] similarly enumerated a number of relevant rights, including further the right to property, the prohibition of discrimination, the rights of the child, the right to health care, and the right to access documents.

The free flow of personal data is a particularly important consideration in EU data protection law. Article 1 GDPR refers to the fundamental freedoms of the internal market and provides that the free flow of personal data shall neither be restricted nor prohibited to protect fundamental rights. This is a remnant of the focus of the EU on the establishment of an internal market. In the area of data protection law, fundamental rights protection is articulated and offered by the EU partly because differences in the level of protection would affect the free flow of information (recital 9) [10]. This rationale must, however, not be overestimated. The CJEU pays less and less attention to the internal market dimension [13, 68]. Although the EU can still be characterized as a separate legal order by virtue of its pursuit of 'the market-driven integration of nation states into a supra-national entity', it also 'increasingly commits itself to the political project of protecting fundamental rights' [69]. Lynskey [13] points to Article 16 TFEU as freeing data protection law from its internal market constraints. She also highlights the contentious nature of this second, economic, ambition of the GDPR. The free flow of information is no longer the main aim of EU data protection law, but it can be one of the considerations which needs to be taken on board when the balance between the relevant rights and other considerations is struck.

The turn of data protection law away from the internal market and away from privacy alone, towards fundamental rights in general, ties in well with modern privacy and data protection scholarship. The recognition of other rights and freedoms is present in Nissenbaum's [70] theory of privacy, as some data flows are appropriate and others are not. The appropriateness of data flows is not at all dependent solely on the amount of secrecy or control which is provided. The processing of certain types of information can be deemed inappropriate because, amongst other reasons, it may lead to restrictions of other fundamental rights. Rouvroy and Poullet [63] observe that 'data protection is also a tool for protecting other rights than the right to privacy', as data protection law also prevents potential discrimination given the regime for special categories of data. Some data protection scholars [71–74] consider data protection a purely procedural body of law which serves other rights and freedoms. It 'does not directly represent any value or interest per se, it prescribes the procedures and methods for pursuing the respect of values embodied in other rights' [71]. In the words of De Hert and Gutwirth [74], data protection law provides channels for the coordination of different rights and competing consider-ations, through which controllers should 'reconcile fundamental but conflicting values such as privacy, free flow of information, the need for government surveillance, applying taxes, etc'.[5]

4.3   The Nature of (Fundamental) Rights

It is not only doctrinally appropriate, it is also illuminating to assess the appropriate roles of user control and controller responsibility with reference to the nature of fundamental rights. This perspective opens up the discussion on whether or when it is appropriate for the GDPR to empower or to protect. At first sight, it makes sense to encumber the controller and state institutions with the protection of fundamental rights. The state is under both negative and positive obligations to respect and protect fundamental rights. Respect for fundamental rights makes a legal order legitimate. The required action or abstention does not need to be claimed by the rights-holder. However, the matter of rights becomes more complicated if one recognizes that the substance of fundamental rights is not a given. It is determined by the polity in which they apply, and it is subject to intense contestation. As noted by Waldron [75], '[a]ny theory of rights will face disagreements about the interests it identifies as rights, and the terms in which it identifies them. Those disagreements will in turn be vehicles for controversies about the proper balance to be struck between some individual interest and some countervailing social considerations' [69]. This gives the concern over paternalism in data protection law a particular sting, as it affects not only the forms of freedom and autonomy which an individual can legitimately enjoy, but also, in particular, her say regarding the substance of fundamental rights protection in her polity. In other words, it affects her say on what justice entails and on when authority is legitimate.

The answer to the question of responsibility depends on whether a will-based theory or an interest-based theory of rights is adopted. Interest theories see it as the function of rights to promote the interest or well-being of the rights-holder by giving her the benefit

---

[5] A difficulty is that the protection of personal data is conceptualised differently in the different Member States. Gellert, De Hert and Gutwirth have developed their view on EU data protection from a Belgian background, and according to González Fuster [64], Belgium is one of the Member States 'where the protection of personal data is conceived as primarily serving other existing rights'.

of another's duty. The idea is that some interests merit special attention. A right exists because there is an interest which requires protection [76]. One's right is a legal, possibly a fundamental, right 'if it is recognized by law, that is, if the law holds his interest to be sufficient ground to hold another to be subject to a duty' [77]. The rights-holder is protected for her benefit, as under many of the provisions of the GDPR. The fact that rights are respected "by default" and cannot be waived, entails that individuals who lack the freedom, autonomy or agency to adequately claim and defend their rights, are protected. However, this raises the question whether the interest-based approach should be taken on, particularly in the legal context, as rights are granted or withheld on the basis of another's perception of the rights-holder's interests (at best) [77]. If someone is perceived as having an interest, and accordingly is granted a right which the duty-holder respects, while the person concerned would not agree to this state of affairs, her choice is usurped for her own good. Thus, interest-based rights promise us the same double-edged sword as controller responsibility. Data subjects are afforded the protection of the principles of fairness, purpose limitation, data minimization, etcetera, even if they cannot adequately make use of their legal powers to choose what to consent to and to object to a processing operation. However, they are afforded this protection whether they want it or not. As under an interest theory of rights, data subjects are denied the political power to fully determine what the protection of their rights should look like. It is therefore interesting for the evaluation of controller responsibility to see how interest theories tackle the charge of paternalism.

If the tenet of controller responsibility shares the problems of an interest theory of rights, the correlate of the tenet of user control is a will theory of rights. Will theories see the function of rights not as the protection of one's interests (unless perhaps the interest is that of autonomy [78]), but as granting the rights-holder control over the duty of another [79]. The purpose and value of rights is precisely that it grants authority and permits the exercise of choice. The rights-holder can waive, annul or transfer the duties of the duty-bearer; the right is at her disposition. 'To have a right is to have the ability to determine what others may and may not do, and so to exercise authority over a certain domain of affairs' [80]. This is akin to how the right to privacy is often used in common parlance: as a shield which allows an individual to exclude others from a certain sphere within which she should have full sovereignty. It is also akin to the notion of informational self-determination, which grants the rights-holder control over whether others may access her information and over what they may do with this information. The options to withhold or withdraw consent, to opt-in to more extensive processing operations, to correct your data, and to object, grant a measure of control over the conduct of others. Again, though, this theory offers a double-edged sword. A challenge for will theory is that it 'could (…) be used, at least in principle, to justify slavery or absolute subjugation, since people could be thought of as having sold or abdicated their liberty, for the price of subsistence or security, to a master or a king' [81]. Will theory leaves those who are not able to demand their rights in line with their interests, without protection. The role of consent in data protection law similarly exposes data subjects who do not act in accordance with their interests when they agree to a data processing operation. Without additional protection, data subjects would be able to "consent away" their privacy, irrespective of the conditions under which this choice occurs. In the extreme, will theory leaves incompetent or non-autonomous individuals without any protection, as they do not even qualify as a rights-holder. This forces the will theorist to resort to proxies that can exercise power for them, such as parents or legal guardians [78]. One of the challenges for will theorists is whether rights apply to all those who can express a preference (in the worst case, like a mollusc "chooses" to close its shell to avoid intruders and to open it to admit nourishment [78]), or only to those who have made a conscious, autonomous choice — and where to draw the line. In the GDPR the line is drawn at the age of 16, as children are unable to give consent without the authorisation of the holder of parental responsibility (art 8(1)). It is relevant for the role of user control to assess how and why will theorists justify the alienability of rights and the reliance on proxies. Should data protection law follow their cue, if it is to take its aim to protect fundamental rights seriously, and if not, why not?

5 Conclusion

Asking whether data protection is the responsibility of the state, this paper has explored the presence of user control and controller responsibility in the GDPR and paved the way for an in-depth evaluation of these two tenets in light of the overarching objective of the GDPR to protect fundamental rights. The paper brings to the fore a dilemma which is present in the debate on "notice-and-consent" and which ties in well with the debate between will-based and interest-based theories of rights. If one has in mind a set of pre-defined interests, such as the interest in seclusion or the interest in secrecy, it is not problematic to conclude that the GDPR should require controllers to protect data subjects. In practice, however, the appropriateness of data flows is not clear-cut. When data processing operations are restricted for the benefit of data subjects, certain rights, interests or other considerations are accorded greater weight than others even though data subjects themselves may disagree. User control is important because it gives data subjects the political power to assert whether they think specific data flows are appropriate. Control rights allow them to decide on the appropriateness of the data processing operations which affect them in light of the balance between the applicable rights and interests which they think should be struck. Thus, there is something to be said for placing the responsibility for data protection primarily with data subjects. This enlarges their power to partake in the formulation of the meaning of fundamental rights in specific situations. Then again, the constraints on the ability of a data subject to freely and autonomously exercise her control rights might lead her to inadequately defend her interests. We need to consider the conditions under which choice is or is not respected: the information which is presented, and how it is conveyed; the availability and popularity of other options in the market; the digital environment within which data is collected and used; and the overall socio-economic context, influencing not only what is possible for the data subject in the given architecture or code, but also her goals and desires, and how her options, goals and desires are perceived [3, 13, 63]. The more constraining the conditions of choice, the more attractive the protective track of controller responsibility. If we truly do not regard the data subject's choice as free and autonomous, this may entail that her freedom should be restricted so as to offer protection. Perhaps, then, it is better for the GDPR to offer protection with the perceived interests of data subjects and society as a whole in mind.

How to assess which edge of the double-edged sword to sway; user control, or controller responsibility? Under the GDPR, the benchmark is that of the protection of the fundamental rights and freedoms of individuals. The question of responsibility thus becomes whether the protection of the fundamental rights of data subjects is something which controllers, under the supervision of supervisory authorities, should take on for the benefit of the individuals concerned. This perspective allows the dilemma to be further analysed and evaluated in light of will-based and interest-based theories of rights. How do these theories justify the shortcomings of an approach which protects the perceived interests of individuals, and those of an approach which vests authority in the individual? Presumably, if, on the one hand, the rights of data subjects serve to protect their interests, the bullet of paternalism has to be bit; on the other hand, if their rights assume a great deal of moral and political capacity and thereby require them to engage in an active expression of their preferences or choices, any further protection cannot occur in the name of fundamental rights.

References

1. Zuiderveen Borgesius, F.J.: Improving privacy protection in the area of behavioural targeting. Ph. D thesis, University of Amsterdam, Amsterdam (2014)
2. van der Sloot, B.: Do data protection rules protect the individual and should they? an assessment of the proposed general data protection regulation. Int. Data Priv. Law **4**, 307–324 (2014)
3. Purtova, N.N.: Property Rights in Personal Data: A European Perspective. BOXPress BV, Oisterwijk (2011)
4. Matzner, T., Masur, P.K., Ochs, C., von Pape, T.: Do-it-yourself data protection – empowerment or burden? In: Gutwirth, S., Leenes, R., De Hert, P. (eds.) Data Protection on the Move. Law, Governance and Technology, vol. 24, pp. 277–305. Springer, Heidelberg (2016)
5. O'Mailey, P.: Responsibilization. In: Wakefield, A., Fleming, J. (eds.) The SAGE Dictionary of Policing. SAGE, London (2009)
6. European Commission: Communication on personal data protection in the European Union. COM(2010) 609 final
7. Article 29 Data Protection Working Party, Working Party on Police and Justice: The Future of Privacy. Joint contribution to the Consultation of the European Commission on the legal framework for the fundamental right to protection of personal data. WP 168 (2009)
8. Article 29 Data Protection Working Party: Opinion 3/2010 on the principle of accountability. WP 173 (2010)
9. European Commission: Impact Assessment accompanying the General Data Protection Regulation. SEC(2012) 72 final
10. European Commission: Proposal for a Regulation of the European Parliament and of the Council on the protection of individuals with regard to the processing of personal data and on the free movement of such data (General Data Protection Regulation). COM (2012) 11 final
11. European Parliament. http://www.europarl.europa.eu/news/en/news-room/20160407IPR21776/Data-protection-reform-Parliament-approves-new-rules-fit-for-the-digital-era

12. Parltrack Jan Philipp Albrecht, 2012/0011 (COD) Personal data protection: processing and free movement of data (General Data Protection Regulation), 2013/01/16 LIBE, Amendment 29. http://parltrack.euwiki.org/mep/ALBRECHT%20Jan%20Philipp

13. Lynskey, O.: The Foundations of EU Data Protection Law. Oxford University Press, Oxford (2015)

14. Fuster, G.G.: How uninformed is the average data subject? a quest for benchmarks in EU personal data protection. Revista de Internet Derecho y Politica 19, 92–104 (2014)

15. Koops, B.J.: On decision transparency, or how to enhance data protection after the computational turn. In: Hildebrandt, M., De Vries, K. (eds.) Privacy, Due Process and the Computational Turn, pp. 196–220. Routledge, Abingdon (2013)

16. Moerel, E.M.L.: Big data protection: How to make the draft EU Regulation on Data Protection Future Proof. Inaugural lecture, Tilburg University, Tilburg (2014)

17. Purtova, N.N.: Default entitlements in personal data in the proposed regulation: informational self-determination off the table … and back on again? Comput. Law Secur. Rev. 30(1), 6–24 (2013)

18. Bainbridge, D.: Introduction to Computer Law. Pearson Longman, Harlow (2004)

19. Bygrave, L.A.: Data Privacy Law. Oxford University Press, Oxford (2014)

20. Kamerstukken II 1997/98, 25892, 3

21. BVerfGE 65, 1 – Volkszählung

22. Hornung, G., Schnabel, C.: Data protection in Germany I: the population census decision ad the right to informational self-determination. Comput. Law Secur. Rep. 25(1), 84–88 (2009)

23. Cohen, J.E.: Examined lives: informational privacy and the subject as object. Stanford Law Rev. 52(5), 1373–1438 (2000). Symposium: Cyberspace and Privacy: A New Legal Paradigm?

24. Moerel, L., Corien, P.: Privacy voor de homo digitalis: Proeve van een nieuw toetsingskader voor gegevensbescherming in het licht van Big Data en Internet of Things. In: Homo Digitalis. Preadviezen 2016 Nederlandse Juristen-Vereniging, pp 9–124. Kluwer Juridisch, Deventer (2016)

25. Brouwer, E.: Legality and data protection law: the forgotten purpose of purpose limitation. In: Besselink, L., Pennings, F., Prechal, S. (eds.) The Eclipse of the Legality Principle in the European Union, pp. 273–294. Kluwer Law International, Alphen aan den Rijn (2011)

26. Article 29 Data Protection Working Party: Opinion 03/2013 on purpose limitation. WP 203 (2013)

27. Nickel, P.: Consent and uncertainty in biobanking and biomedical data (forthcoming)

28. Pellizzoni, L.: Responsibility and environmental governance. Environ. Politics 13(3), 541–565 (2004)

29. Fuster, G.G: Beyond the GDPR, above the GDPR. In: Internet Policy Review, 30 November 2015. http://policyreview.info/articles/news/beyond-gdpr-above-gdpr/385

30. Schwartz, P.M.: Internet privacy and the state. Conn. Law Rev. 32, 815–859 (1999)

31. Benn, S.I.: Freedom, autonomy and the concept of a person. In: Proceedings of the Aristotelian Society, New Series, vol. 76, pp. 109–130 (1975-1976)

32. Hull, G.: Successful failure: what Foucault can teach us about privacy self-management in a world of Facebook and big data. Ethics Inf. Technol. 17(2), 89–101 (2015)

33. Solove, D.: Introduction privacy self-management and the consent dilemma. Harvard Law Rev. 126, 1880–1903 (2013)

34. Van Alsenoy, B., Kosta, E., Dumortier, J.: Privacy notices versus informational self-determination: minding the gap. Int. Rev. Law Comput. Technol. 28, 185–203 (2014)

35. McDonald, A.M., Cranor, L.F.: The cost of reading privacy policies. J. Law Policy Inf. Soc. I/S 4(3), 540–565 (2008)

36. Hildebrandt, M.: Who is profiling who? invisible visibility. In: Gutwirth, S., Poullet, Y., De Hert, P., de Terwangne, C., Nouwt, S. (eds.) Reinventing Data Protection?, pp. 239–253. Springer, Heidelberg (2009)

37. Le Métayer, D., Le Clainche, J.: From the protection of data to the protection of individuals: extending the application of non-discrimination principles. In: Gutwirth, S., Leenes, R., De Hert, P., Poullet, S. (eds.) European Data Protection: In Good Health?, pp. 315–331. Springer, Heidelberg (2012)

38. Zarsky, T.: Transparent predictions. Univ. Ill. Law Rev. **4**, 1503–1570 (2013)

39. Koops, B.J.: The trouble with European data protection law. Int. Data Priv. Law **4**, 250–261 (2014)

40. Article 29 Data Protection Working Party: Opinion 10/2004 on More Harmonised Information Provisions. WP 100 (2004)

41. Barocas, S., Nissenbaum, H.: On notice: the trouble with notice and consent. In: Proceedings of the Engaging Data Forum: The First International Forum on the Application and Management of Personal Electronic Information, Cambridge (2009)

42. Cohen, J.E.: What privacy is for. Harvard Law Rev. **126**, 1904–1933 (2013)

43. Lazaro, C., Le Métayer, D.: Control over personal data: true remedy or fairytale? SCRIPT-ed **12**(1), 3–34 (2015)

44. Cohen, J.E.: Between truth and power. In: Hildebrandt, M., van den Berg, B. (eds): Freedom and Property of Information: The Philosophy of Law Meets the Philosophy of Technology, Routledge (forthcoming). http://papers.ssrn.com/sol3/papers.cfm?abstract_id=2346459

45. Cavoukian, A., Dix, A., El Emam, K.: The Unintended Consequences of Privacy Paternalism. Information and Privacy Commissioner, Ontario, 5 March 2014

46. van de Poel, I.: Translating values into design requirements. In: Michelfelder, D.P., McCarthy, N., Goldberg, D.E. (eds.) Philosophy and Engineering: Reflections on Practice, Principles and Process. Philosophy of Engineering and Technology, vol. 15, pp. 253–266. Springer, Heidelberg (2013)

47. Archard, D.: Paternalism defined. Analysis **50**(1), 36–42 (1990)

48. Conly, S.: Against Autonomy. Justifying Coercive Paternalism. Cambridge University Press, Cambridge (2013)

49. Bullock, E.: A normatively neutral definition of paternalism. Philos. Q. **65**, 1–21 (2015)

50. Thaler, R.H., Sunstein, C.R.: Libertarian paternalism. Am. Econ. Rev. **93**(2), 175–179 (2003)

51. Dworkin, G.: The Theory and Practice of Autonomy. Cambridge University Press, Cambridge (1988)

52. Dworkin, G.: Defining paternalism. In: Schramme, T. (ed.) New Perspectives on Paternalism and Health Care. Library ofEthics and Applied Philosophy, vol. 35, pp. 17–29. Springer, Heidelberg (2015)

53. Hansen, P.G.: The definition of nudge and libertarian paternalism: does the hand fit the glove? EJRR **1**, 155–174 (2016)

54. Feinberg, J.: Harm to Self. The Moral Limits of the Criminal Law. Oxford University Press, Oxford (1986)

55. Bernal, P.: Internet Privacy Rights. Rights to Protect Autonomy. Cambridge University Press, Cambridge (2014)

56. Kleinig, J.: Paternalism. Manchester University Press, Manchester (1983)

57. Shiffrin, S.V.: Paternalism, unconscionability doctrine, and accomodation. Philos. Public Aff. **29**(3), 205–250 (2000)

58. Clarke, S.: A definition of paternalism. Crit. Rev. Int. Soc. Polit. Philos. **5**(1), 81–91 (2002)

59. Fateh-Moghadam, B., Gutmann, T.: Governing [through] autonomy. the moral and legal limits of "soft paternalism". Ethical Theor. Moral Pract. **17**, 383–397 (2014)

60. Bygrave, L.A., Schartum, D.W.: Consent, proportionality and collective power. In: Gutwirth, S., Poullet, Y., De Hert, P., de Terwangne, C., Nouwt, S. (eds.) Reinventing Data Protection?, pp. 157–173. Springer, Heidelberg (2009)

61. Richards, N.M.: Intellectual privacy. Tex. Law Rev. **87**, 387–445 (2008)

62. Koops, B-J et al: A typology of privacy. Univ. Pennsylvania J. Int. Law 38(2) (2016)

63. Rouvroy, A., Poullet, Y.: The right to informational self-determination and the value of self-development: reassessing the importance of privacy for democracy. In: Gutwirth, S., Poullet, Y., De Hert, P., de Terwangne, C., Nouwt, S. (eds.) Reinventing Data Protection?, pp. 45–76. Springer, Heidelberg (2009)

64. González Fuster, G.G.: The Emergence of Personal Data Protection as a Fundamental Right of the EU. Springer, Cham (2014)

65. van der Sloot, B.: Privacy as a tactic of norm evasion, or why the question as to the value of privacy is fruitless. In: Janssens, L. (ed.) The Art of Ethics in the Information Society. Amsterdam University Press, Amsterdam (2016)

66. Joined cases C-92/09 and C-93/09 Volker und Markus Schecke [2010] ECR I-11063

67. Article 29 Data Protection Working Party: Statement on the role of a risk-based approach in data protection legal frameworks. WP218 (2014)

68. Irion, K.: A special regard: the court of justice and the fundamental rights to privacy and data protection. In: Faber et al. (eds): Festschrift für Wolfhard Kohte. Nomos, Baden-Baden (forthcoming)

69. Augenstein, D.H.: Disagreement – commonality – autonomy: EU fundamental rights in the internal market. Camb. Yearb. Eur. Legal Stud. **15**, 1–26 (2013)

70. Nissenbaum, H.: Privacy as contextual integrity. Wash. Law Rev. **79**, 119–158 (2004)

71. de Andrade, N.: Oblivion: the right to be different. from oneself. Reproposing the right to be forgotten. Revista de los Estudios de Derecho y Ciencia Política de la UOC **13**, 122–137 (2012)

72. Zanfir, G.: Forgetting about consent. why the focus should be on "suitable safeguards" in data protection law. In: Gutwirth, S., Leenes, R., De Hert, P. (eds.) Reloading Data Protection: Multidisciplinary Insights and Contemporary Challenges, pp. 237–257. Springer, Heidelberg (2014)

73. Gellert, R., Gutwirth, S.: The legal construction of privacy and data protection. Comput. Law Secur. Rev. **29**, 522–530 (2013)

74. De Hert, P., Gutwirth, S.: Data protection in the case law of Strasbourg and Luxemburg: constitutionalisation in action. In: Gutwirth, S., Poullet, Y., De Hert, P., de Terwangne, C., Nouwt, S. (eds.) Reinventing Data Protection?, pp. 3–44. Springer, Heidelberg (2009)

75. Waldron, J.: A rights-based critique of constitutional rights. Oxf. J. Legal Stud. **13**(1), 18–51 (1993)

76. Nickel, J.: Making Sense of Human Rights. Blackwell, Malden (2007)

77. Eleftheriadis, P.: Legal Rights. Oxford University Press, Oxford (2008)

78. Edmundson, W.A.: An Introduction to Rights. Cambridge University Press, Cambridge (2012)

79. Hart, H.L.A.: Essays on Bentham: Studies in Jurisprudence and Political Theory. Clarendon Press, Oxford (1982)

80. Wenar, L.: Rights. The Stanford Encyclopedia of Philosophy (Fall 2015). http://plato.stanford.edu/archives/fall2015/entries/rights/

81. Waldron, J.: Dignity, Rights and Responsibilities. New York University School of Law. Public Law & Legal Theory Research Paper Series. Working Paper No. 10–83 (2010)

Visualizing Exports of Personal Data
by Exercising the Right of Data Portability
in the Data Track - Are People Ready for This?

Farzaneh Karegar[✉], Tobias Pulls, and Simone Fischer-Hübner

Department of Mathematics and Computer Science,
Karlstad University (KaU), Karlstad, Sweden
{farzaneh.karegar,tobias.pulls,simone.fischer-huebner}@kau.se

Abstract. A transparency enhancing tool called Data Track has been developed at Karlstad University. The latest stand-alone version of the tool allows users to visualize their data exports. For analyzing the users' perceptions of the Data Track in regard to transparency features and the concepts of data export and data portability, we have conducted a qualitative user study. We observed that although users had rather little interest in the visualization of derived data activities revealed in the Google location file, they were interested in other kinds of derived data like usage patterns for different service providers. Also, as earlier user studies revealed, we again confirmed that it is confusing for users to differentiate between locally and remotely stored and controlled data. Finally, in spite of being concerned about the security of the data exported to their machines, for exercising data portability rights pursuant to the General Data Protection Regulation, most participants would prefer to first export and edit the data before uploading it to another service provider and would appreciate using a tool such as the Data Track for helping them in this context.

Keywords: Transparency Enhancing Tools · Data portability · visualization · Data Track

1 Introduction

Transparency of personal data processing is an important principle for the privacy of individuals as well as for a democratic society [9]. People rarely have a clear understanding about how their personal data are collected, used, shared or accessed [1]. Consequently, transparency of personal data processing is enforced by most Western privacy laws, including the EU Data Protection Directive (DPD) 95/46/EC [6] and new General Data Protection Regulation (GDPR) [7] which will replace the DPD in 2018. The GDPR grants enhanced data subject rights for transparency and intervenability, such as the right of access by the data subject including the right to receive a data copy of her personal data

© IFIP International Federation for Information Processing 2016
Published by Springer International Publishing AG 2016. All Rights Reserved
A. Lehmann et al. (Eds.): Privacy and Identity 2016, IFIP AICT 498, pp. 164–181, 2016.
DOI: 10.1007/978-3-319-55783-0_12

undergoing processing in a commonly used electronic format (Art. 15), the right to rectification and erasure (Art. 16, 17), and the right to data portability (Art. 20). The right to data portability is aiming at increasing user choices of online services and allows users to request all their data from a data controller that in turn has to provide the users with the data in a structured, commonly-used machine readable format which can then be transmitted to any other controllers. Alternatively, the users can also request to transmit their data directly from a service provider to another one, if technically feasible. One way to exert these rights pursuant to GDPR is using technologies which enhance transparency and provide user control. These kinds of technologies are commonly referred to as Transparency Enhancing Tools (TETs) [12].

The Data Track (DT) developed at Karlstad University (KaU) is an example of a TET that shows users what data they have disclosed to which service providers under what agreed-upon policies and how their data have been processed. The Data Track development started as a part of the European PRIME[1] and PrimeLife[2] projects and continued as part of the A4Cloud project[3]. This paper reports about a user study on the perception of a new function for visualizing exports of personal big data to the data subjects, which we added recently to the Data Track tool. Already today, many service providers, such as Google and Facebook, provide users with data export functions for downloading their personal data. The newly added functionality to the Data Track for visualizing personal data exports from a service provider, which is also available in the form of a stand-alone open source Data Track version[4], can for instance provide users with an overview of the location data they (or more precisely their devices) have disclosed to Google by first exporting their data from myaccount.google.com as a file and then importing the data to the Data Track for visualization. At least when the GDPR will apply in May 2018, users could export their personal data from all types of service providers (beyond those providing export functions already today) by exercising their right to receive an electronic copy (Art. 15) or their data portability right (Art. 20) and could import them to the Data Track for visualizing their disclosed data to different services providers.

In this paper, we present a qualitative user study which has the objective to analyze the users' perceptions of the stand-alone Data Track in regard to the transparency features that it is providing and in regard to the concept of data export from a service provider to the Data Track running at the user's machine by exercising the rights to access and of data portability.

More precisely, we have been addressing the following two research questions and related sub-questions:

1. **What are the users' perceptions of transparency with the stand-alone Data Track?** Does the interface convey that Google has more information about the users other than what they have sent explicitly or implicitly?

---

[1] EU FP6 project PRIME, http://www.prime-project.eu/

[2] EU FP7 project PrimeLife, http://primelife.ercim.eu/.

[3] EU FP7 project A4Cloud, http://www.a4cloud.eu.

[4] https://github.com/pylls/datatrack.

What kind of transparency options are the users interested in and would they like the Data Track to provide more transparency information related to their data? Do users have any concerns in regard to using the Data Track?

2. **What are users' perceptions of data export and portability with the stand-alone Data Tack?** Do users understand and value the idea and the concept of exporting data from a service provider (Google in this case) and importing it to a tool running on their own machines or to another service provider? Consequently, do users understand the differences between locally stored (and thus user controlled) and remotely stored data? (i.e., data stored on their computers in the Data Track under their control after being exported from a service provider vs. data stored at the service's side)?

In the remainder of this paper, Sect. 2 briefly presents background and related work in regard to TETs and related user studies, Sect. 3 explains the methods used in our work and the test plan. Section 4 is devoted to analyzing the results. Finally, Sect. 5 discusses our conclusion and future work.

2 Background and Related Work

In this section, we first explain the different kinds of TETs. Then we elaborate more on Data Track versions and finally we describe the related user studies.

2.1 Transparency Enhancing Tools

There is a variety of TETs that have been developed and evaluated with different types of user tests in the past. TETs can in general be divided into ex-ante TETs—which enable the anticipation of consequences before data are actually disclosed (e.g., with the help of privacy policy statements)—and ex-post TETs which inform about consequences if data already have been revealed (cf. [12]).

TETs can be further categorized, in dependence on where the transparency information is stored and controlled, into services side TETs, user side TETs and Third Party TETs. Services side TETs run at the service provider's side and allow authenticated users to receive information about collected, processed or forwarded data at those sides. Examples of services side TETs are the Google Dashboard[5] or PrivacyInsight [4]. A Third Party TET requires the user to entrust a third party with the user's personal data for providing transparency services. An example for a Third Party TET is the DataBait tool by the EU project USEMP [20], which derives guesses and predictions about the user's personality by analyzing the user's social media and browser data with machine learning software. User side (or user controlled) TETs store the user's personal information to be made transparent locally on the user's device under the user's control. While user side TETs require the user's device to keep the data safe and may be more demanding to set up and get running from a usability perspective, they are in principle the more privacy-friendly solution, as the users retain control over

---

[5] Google dashboard. https://www.google.com/settings/dashboard.

their data. Examples of user side TETs are Mozilla's Lightbeam [15] or personal data vaults, such as Mun's et al. work [16], and the different versions of the Data Track that are briefly presented in the next section.

2.2 Data Track Versions

The first version of the Data Track was developed within the PRIME project [18] and included a "history function" for each transaction, in which the user's disclosed personal data to a service, a record describing to whom the personal data was disclosed (i.e., the identity of the controller), for which purposes and, more precisely, under which agreed-upon privacy policy, as well as a unique transaction pseudonym are stored in a secure manner. It was later complemented in the PrimeLife project with online access functions, which allow users (authenticated as data subjects of data held by a service provider via those transaction pseudonyms) exercising data subject rights to access, correct, rectify or erase those data at the service provider's side [10].

For the next Data Track versions developed in the A4Cloud project [1,9], we have mainly improved the user interfaces (UIs) and interaction concepts, replacing the tabular presentations of the PrimeLife Data Track with the graphical UI illustrations, as previous research studies suggest that network-like visualizations provide a simple way to understand the meaning behind some types of data [2,11]. Therefore, for the A4Cloud Data Track (also called "GenomSynlig"), we developed the so-called "trace view" (see Fig. 1), presenting an overview of the data items sent to service providers, as well as the data items service providers received about the user. In addition to this "local view" of the trace view, which is graphically displaying the information that is stored locally in the Data Track about what data has been disclosed to whom, a user can also execute online access functions for exercising her data subject rights by clicking on the cloud icon next to the service provider's logo thereby switching to a "remote view" of what (disclosed or derived) data about the user are stored at the service provider side. In addition, an alternative timeline view has been developed for the A4Cloud Data Track, which lists the information about data disclosures in the Data Track records in chronological order for selected time intervals.

The latest version of the Data Track which is, as mentioned earlier, an open source and stand-alone program developed at the end of the A4Cloud project at KaU, is subject of this paper. It provides users with the visualization of data exported from the Google managing archive service. For our first version, we focused on the Google location history to be included in our archive. After successfully exporting the location data from Google and importing it to the Data Track, in addition to the trace and the timeline views, participants have a newly developed map view that allows to visualize location, activity and movement patterns as described in the location history provided by Google (see Fig. 2). Activities are data derived by Google based on the locations reported by their devices (i.e., activities are derived by Google and not by the user's device).

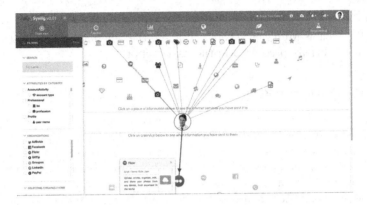

Fig. 1. Trace view of the A4Cloud Data Track

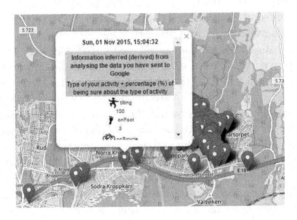

Fig. 2. Location data and activities on the map view of the stand-alone version of the Data Track

2.3   Related User Studies

User studies have been conducted for various ex-post TETs, which are mainly demonstrating the usability of graphical network-like presentations to illustrate data flows. For instance, Bier et al. present recent usability studies of the user interfaces of the PrivacyInsight tool in comparison to GenomSynlig and their different network-like data flow representations [4]. Moreover, Kane-Zabihi et al. present usability tests of an "interactive social translucence map" [13]. Other user evaluations studies or TETs using both network-like presentations and chrono-logical presentations of data disclosure events comprise user tests of previous Data Track versions (with its trace and timeline views) and a user test by Kolter et al. of a tool for visualizing transaction logs [14].

Prototypes of the trace and timeline views of the A4Cloud Data Track have been evaluated with usability tests and two focus group workshops. These user evaluations revealed that while test participants mostly valued the transparency functionality of the Data Track and could successfully use it for tracking data disclosures, many test users had however problems to understand whether data records were stored in the Data Track client on the users' side (under the users' control) or on the remote service provider's side [3,8]. The specific feature of the Data Track trace view that allows to easily switch from a local view of Data Track records to a remote view providing users with online access to the data stored at the service provider's side, might have contributed to this confusion. As previous A4Cloud Data Track user tests and usability tests conducted in the PRIME project [19] showed the user's confusion of discerning between the locally and remotely data control and access, our user study also analyzed the user's understanding of locally and user-controlled data (at the user's side) vs. remotely stored and controlled data (at the service provider's side) for the stand-alone Data Track with its new map view.

In contrast to those previous user studies of the Data Track, this paper evaluated the new stand-alone version of the Data Track with its newly added map view. This paper presents the first evaluation of the perception of a transparency tool based on exports of personal data from a service provider (Google in this case) and of its perceived value when exercising the right to receive an electronic copy of the personal data or the data portability right pursuant to the upcoming GDPR.

3   User Study and Methods

We conducted a user study with ten participants with the objective to receive insights on the users' perceptions of transparency functions and of data export and portability with the latest stand-alone version of the Data Track. Our study is primarily a qualitative study using semi-structured interviews, which are allowing to follow and explore new directions as they come up in the interview process, and a grounded theory based approach [5] to surface key themes that arise in our interviews.

Before the user study, we conducted an incremental and iterative pilot study with 16 participants. The reason to conduct the pilot user study was twofold: (1) To test, fine-tune the task and adopt the timing. (2) To tailor and manipulate the questions we ask during the study for better answering our main research questions.

Based on the feedback that we received during the pilot study, we manipulated our interview questions on the grounds that some of them were not suitable enough to answer our two main research questions. Ultimately, we also concluded to guide users during the interview through how they can download the location file from Google. In the pilot test, the participants were supposed to follow the instructions or watch a video on the Data Track to detect where on the Google they can order to export their location data. The results showed that it was really time-consuming and sometimes irritating for the users and due to the fact that we do not intend to test the usability and clarity of Google settings, we decided not to time the users but to guide them. In the following, we present the recruitment, study procedure, and demographic information of the participants.

3.1   Recruitment of Participants

We strived to get an unbiased sample of participants by recruiting arbitrary people in Karlstad city center (P1-P4, P10), via a Facebook group related to Karlstad (P5, P9) and participants of an innovation seminar in Örebro (P6-P8). Those who accepted our invitation were compensated with a 100 SEK gift card. All interviews were conducted in English in October 2016.

3.2   Study Procedure

To begin with, a study plan was written to serve as the main communication vehicle as well as a blueprint for the study. A study plan is a summary of all the containing documents needed for the user studies [21]. To avoid an active researcher (study moderator/interviewer) bias which includes mannerisms and statements made by the researcher that provide the participants with information about the researcher's preferences [17], the procedure was standardized. The leading questions were avoided in the interviews and before conducting the user study and in the recruitment advertisements, we told participants that Data Track was implemented at KaU and that we were just responsible for conducting the user study of it.

During the study, each participant received the same instructions and followed the same blueprint. The study took 30–60 min based on how much each individual participant wanted to communicate and consisted of four parts: (1) a welcome session in which we thanked them, briefly talked about what they were expected to do and we obtained informed consent from all of participants. The informed consent imparted that participants agreed to have their screen and audio recorded, alongside with their answers. Consent to the recording was not required, though all participants agreed to be recorded, (2) a pre-task questionnaire for collecting demographics, (3) a role-playing task with a fake Google account to download the location data from Google, upload the same file to the Data Track and view the location data in the map view, and (4) the semi-structured interview during which participants answered to the questions while they were still allowed to use and navigate through the tool. Two researchers, one as an interviewer (moderator) and one as a note keeper, participated in the studies.

Participants' own Google accounts were not used in the study. Instead, they were given the role of a persona to play to visualize their data. Using a persona, participants feel secure that they are not compromising their personal details when taking part in the study. Moreover, it allows full control of what each participant encounters, avouching a standard experience that can be compared between participants. The persona details in each case included a username and password of a Google account.

3.2.1 Task

After filling in the pre-task questionnaire, the participants had to conduct a task in which they export (download) the location data from Google, import (upload) it to the Data Track and view the visualization of the data and its characteristics in the map view.

Focusing on the users' perceptions of different concepts in the Data Track, the goal of defining the task was not to measure the participants' efficiency in finding how they should download the data. However, we aimed to have the location data imported to the Data Track as the starting point of discussing the interview questions, providing all participants with a common ground for enabling them to have a better insight into what downloading data from a service provider and uploading the same data to another party mean.

3.2.2 Semi-structured Interview

For learning more about the users' perceptions of transparency and of data export (via their right of access) and data portability, after the task, the participants were asked to answer different questions in semi-structured interviews, in which planned questions were asked and other questions emerged based on answers which were annotated by the note keeper (observer).

The interviews consisted of some core questions, each with the candidate follow-up questions designed to encourage participants to give more information. All interviews followed the structure listed in the study plan including but not limited to the questions below:

- How do participants understand and perceive the concept of derived and disclosed information visualized in the Data Track? What other type of information about their data are they interested in? What do they value in the Data Track and what do they suggest to improve and what are their concerns regarding using the tool?
- Who has access to their data in the Data Track and where is the data that they uploaded to the Data Track stored? Will any changes of the data in the Google account affect the uploaded data to the Data Track and the other way around ? In what circumstances would they like to download and upload their data from/to service providers? How can the Data Track help them if it provides users with the option to edit/filter data and it saves the changes? What is the preferable way for them to transfer the data between service providers (directly or via the Data Track)?

Captured screen videos were checked against notes taken in each interview. The recordings were transcribed and coded to extract participants' ideas and perceptions. Notes taken during the interviews were compared with corresponding screen recordings to reduce the observer bias and ensure the accuracy of data.

3.3 Demographic Information

Demographic information extracted from the pre-study questionnaires and summarized in Table 1 shows that six women and four men participated in our study with different age ranges. All the participants but one have Google accounts, all of them work with computers and use the Internet daily or almost every day, and all of them possess smartphones. As discussed above, we tried to get an unbiased sample by mostly inviting arbitrary people from the city center or the Facebook group for citizens of Karlstad. Nonetheless, the table shows that many of the test participants have an academic background—probably because people with a higher education are more interested to participate in a research study by Karlstad University in English and also the fact that Karlstad is a university town with a high percentage of academics and students probably contributes to this effect.

4 User Study Results

We analyzed the answers that we received during the semi-structured interviews, categorized them using the grounded theory method [5] and identified common

Table 1. Summary of participants' information

Demographic information								
ID	Age range	Gender	Educational background	Google account	Smartphone	Computer usage	Internet usage	Knowledge of computer security and privacy
P1	21–25	Female	Bachelor: Law	Yes	Yes	Almost everyday	Everyday	A bit familiar
P2	26–30	Female	Master: Psychology	Yes	Yes	Almost everyday	Everyday	A bit familiar
P3	61–65	Male	PhD: Natural sciences	No	Yes	Everyday	Almost everyday	No knowledge
P4	51–55	Male	High school	Yes	Yes	Everyday	Everyday	A bit familiar
P5	31–35	Female	High school	Yes	Yes	Everyday	Everyday	Quite familiar
P6	36–40	Male	Bachelor: Physiotherapy	Yes	Yes	Everyday	Everyday	A bit familiar
P7	46–50	Female	PhD: Business administrator	Yes	Yes	Everyday	Everyday	A bit familiar
P8	51–55	Female	Bachelor: Social sciences	Yes	Yes	Everyday	Everyday	A bit familiar
P9	46–50	Female	Bachelor: Psychology	Yes	Yes	Everyday	Everyday	A bit familiar
P10	61–65	Male	Human resource management	Yes	Yes	Everyday	Everyday	Professional

themes. In this section, we will provide the results of our user study in relation to our two main research questions.

4.1 Users' Perceptions of Transparency Functions

The results of our questions aiming to identify users' perceptions about transparency can be categorized in three main domains: (1) the users' understanding of data derived by service providers vs. explicitly or implicitly disclosed data to service providers, (2) users' attitudes about sensitivity and importance of derived data, and (3) desired transparency functions from the users' point of view.

4.1.1 Derived vs. Disclosed Data

We intended to analyze whether the users were aware of or surprised about derived data and whether they were interested in having it visualized. The exact terms used by Google for derived activities from location data displayed in the Data Track (such as "tilting" or "in vehicle") were not meaningful for the participants and most of them were not much interested in this type of derived activity data that Google reveals in the exported file. However, all of the participants expressed that they were aware that some service providers have more data about them comparing to what they disclose directly. They mostly referred to Facebook and they stated their interests in other kinds of derived data like what Facebook learns about them by analyzing the keywords and pages they search for. They were also more interested in derived data related to their long-term behavioral patterns (see Sect. 4.1.3).

We conclude that visualizing data exports using the exact wording for the derived data categories that service providers such as Google provide, may thus not always be perceived as useful and more meaningful information about this type of data may be more appropriate to be shown by TETs.

4.1.2 Sensitivity and Importance of Derived Data

Some participants expressed that they do not consider the derived activity data visualized in the Data Track as sensitive. To justify, they mentioned that they are not generally concerned about their privacy but they know that on the other hand other people do care about it. In addition, some other participants explained that it depends on different factors like what service providers can learn from analyzing the information and the combination of information and how they intend to use it. Correspondingly, P6 mentioned about activities users would like to hide and said: "**if we are on the highway and speeding in our car or if we are doing something illegal, it is really sensitive**".

Interestingly, just two of the participants said it is an important and sensitive kind of information. However, one of them mentioned she herself is not interested to know about it because too much information would only scare her.

Whether to have control or not and whether to know about the risks and benefits of derived data were the other parameters participants mentioned that contribute to the fact of importance of visualizing derived data.

It is worth mentioning that the context of derived data was location data and the kind of information that people think could be derived from. However, asking them to think of other contexts than location data, their attitudes differed from previous ones. One Participant (P2) mentioned Facebook advertisements and said: *"based on the recipe you look for, they know if you are vegan or based on your membership in different groups they know if you are depressed and it is really sensitive"* and the other (P4) expressed his concerns regarding user profiling rather than derived activities from his locations and said: *"political view is sensitive and wrong analysis could be harmful for my reputation."*

4.1.3   Transparency Functions

To clarify more about users' requirements regarding transparency features of the Data Track, we asked them about what they value in the Data Track, what are their concerns regarding using it and what they think should be improved. Moreover, to have a better insight into those transparency functions in which participants could be more interested and not to limit ourselves and our participants to the location context, we told them that they can think more generally about their most used service providers and what they would like to see visualized. In the following, we explain our observations and findings.

Values and concerns related to the Data Track. Regarding what participants value in a transparency tool like Data Track we avoided asking and reporting positive comments about whether they like the tool but we focused on the particular comments that explain how they may use such a tool. Some participants mentioned they cannot see the point of visualizing their data and they think it is not needed. Some other mentioned they prefer the visualization of the information of which they are not usually aware like behavioral patterns and statistical data about them.

Six participants expressed their concerns regarding privacy and security of their data if they want to use the tool. Also, two referred to trust and symbols making them feel less concerned. Surprisingly, one of the participants (P7) said: *"It is certified by the Google* (pointing out to the Google logo on the timeline view while navigating through the tool) *so I am not concerned. Google has a good reputation in my opinion"* and the other (P6) said: *"as it is developed at KaU I am less concerned"*. In any case, branding may play a role in lowering concerns.

What to be visualized. (1) Behavioral patterns: Most of the participants were interested in knowing more about their movement and travel patterns, usage patterns for different service providers, some statistical data about their behaviors and some information about to whom their data is sold, how it is exchanged and how they receive related advertisements. *"One does not know how much data an application really gets, it is interesting to know about it"*, said participant one (P1). P3 also mentioned about the speed and movement profile: *"by knowing the speed of movement when walking they know that I am not young. It is good for me to know my speed"*.

(2) Have more control: Three participants explained explicitly that they would like to have some functions in the Data Track to exercise more control over their data: *"Now that I am informed about the data, what can I do about it? I need to react on it"*.

(3) Knowing about benefits and usage: One participant (P8) clarified that she cannot see the point of using the tool and she needs more information about the advantages of being aware of all her disclosed data.

Some suggestions about more practical information based on the exact locations and more representative icons for location pins were also among the comments.

4.2   Users' Perceptions of Data Export and Portability

For user-side TETs like the Data Track which visualizes data exports, it is important that users comprehend the visualized data in the tool is under their control. However, as mentioned earlier, previous Data Track usability tests and related tests conducted in the PRIME project revealed the users' problems to differentiate between user and services sides and confusions about where their data are stored. So first in this section, we report on users' understanding of locally and remotely stored data and we represent the results of people's opinions about who has access to their data uploaded to the Data Track.

Furthermore, adding the new functionality for visualizing personal data exports from a service provider to the latest stand-alone version of Data Track has the objective to allow to export and visualize personal data from users' accounts. In the future, it could also help people first to visualize and then edit (in future versions) the data exports according to their requirements before sending it to other service providers while they are exercising the right of data portability. Thus we aim to learn more about people's attitudes about Data Track as an intermediary TET when they want to transfer the data from one service provider to another. Since data portability is a new concept for users and it is not offered yet by service providers, we first investigate users' perceptions about downloading their data from a service provider, uploading it to another one and whether they can consider a scenario in which they may need or use these features. Then we investigate about their preferable way when they want to transfer their data from a service provider to another. Finally, we ask about their attitudes towards Data Track as a tool with which they can visualize exports of data, change and then send the edited version to the desired service provider. The results are reported in Sect. 4.2.2.

4.2.1   Locally vs. Remotely Stored Data and Access to the Uploaded Data to the Data Track

When we asked participants about who has access to the data that they uploaded to the Data Track, we received different answers that, with participants' justifications about their statements, are summarized in Table 2. Also in Table 3 we represent participants' opinions about where the data uploaded to the Data

Table 2. Participants' attitudes about who has access to the uploaded data to the Data Track

Who has access to your uploaded (imported) data to the Data Track?				
ID	P1-P10	P2-P5-P9	P4-P7	P6-P8
Answer	Just me	Some companies - probably all the world - my phone, my account	Google	Tool developers
Justification	If hackers cannot, it is just me - I downloaded the file and gave it to Data Track	Google sells the data to others - everything online can be accessed by others - you know, big brother!	It is synchronized with Google - functioning within Google	It is developed at Kau and I uploaded my data to it

Table 3. Users' attitudes about where the data are stored

Where the uploaded data to the Data Track are stored?				
ID	P1-P2-P3-P7-P8	P6	P4	P5-P10
Answer	Somewhere on the Cloud	Hopefully in a server at Kau	On my computer	Google and my computer

Track are stored. Although some participants (P1, P10) correctly answered who has access to the data, they were confused about where the data are stored. On the contrary, P4 who recognized that the data are stored on his machine thought that Google had access to his data uploaded to the Data Track.

Data Track is running within the browser. Also, the term *upload* is usually used for transferring files from the user side to online websites. We assume both of these facts suggest people that the Data Track is a web application connecting to some servers and they usually forget about the file they download to their machines and upload to the Data Track. Also, we assume because they can upload the data which they downloaded previously from Google to the Data Track, they think the Data Track is somehow connected to Google and synchronized with it. It needs more investigations and is the subject of future works.

To further investigate about people's perceptions of locally and remotely stored data, we asked participants whether some changes in Google data would affect the visualized data in the Data Track or the other way around and we observed different answers that with participants' justifications about their statements are summarized in Tables 4 and 5.

Comparing Tables 4 and 5, it reveals that although some participants correctly recognized that to see the changes made on the Google data they should again download and upload it to Data Track, they thought that modifying the

Table 4. Users' attitudes about changes in Google data and their effects on the uploaded data to the Data Track

Does editing the Google location data affect the uploaded data to the Data Track?		
ID	P1-P2-P3-P5-P6-P9	P4-P7-P8-P10
Answer	No	Yes
Justification	I should download and upload first to see the changes, not simply refresh the page	It is synchronized with Google - It should be updated automatically - I hope so, I do not know really

Table 5. Users' attitudes about changes in uploaded data to the Data Track and their effects on Google data

Does editing the uploaded data to the Data Track affect the Google location data?		
ID	P2-P3-P5-P6-P10	P1-P4-P7-P8-P9
Answer	No	Yes
Justification	They do not work together, they are not connected - It would be a bad tool otherwise - Google does not allow, it is downloaded	If you refresh Google, it will fetch new changes - They are connected - It is a service from Google

uploaded data to the Data Track would affect the data on the Google side (P9 and P1). Moreover, although some participants correctly said that changes on the data in Data Track would not affect the Google data, the justifications about their answers were not the real reasons. One said if it removes the Google data it is a "bad software" (P3). In addition, some participants (P2, P3, P5, P6) understood that changes in the uploaded data to the Data Track or Google would not affect the other one (until we download and upload the data again to see the changes we made on Google data). However, interestingly, they could not recognize where the uploaded data to the Data Track were stored and who had access to it.

4.2.2 Users' Attitudes of Data Portability, Preferable Ways and Usefulness of Data Track

About the usefulness of download and potential upload features in service providers and ability to think of a scenario in which people may use it, we observed different opinions. Some participants explicitly said that they do not need these options because they cannot think of a scenario in which they will use it or they think the risks would outweigh benefits. Some others mentioned they think download and upload options are useful. They explained a scenario like downloading all of their Instagram pictures to have them on their machines or downloading all of their WhatsApp groups and messages to save them some-

Table 6. Participants' preferable way to transfer data from one Service Provider (SP) to another

Do you prefer to use a button directly or download the data and then upload it to a new SP?		
ID	P1-P2-P3-P4-P6-P9	P7-P8-P10	P5
Preferable way	Download and then upload	The button	I am not sure
Justification	I feel safer - I want to have control over my data - By using button, I do not know what is going on, I want to see what is transferred	less time-consuming - no need to think - easy and convenient	I remembered the Facebook login button. It transfers the data but I am not sure what Facebook sends to the others

where. Impressively, five out of ten people expressed their concerns regarding the risks in regard to security and two out of ten asked about the benefits:

"If I can see the benefits and usage of it I will think of these options" (P8) and the other said: *"I am not willing at all to download my data on my machine. It is fine on the cloud. It is too risky to have it on my machine because I am responsible for its security and if something happens it is my fault"* (P7).

We asked participants to consider a scenario in which they want to transfer their data (Facebook data including all advertisements they have clicked or the people they have searched about in Facebook) from Facebook to a new social network (because their friends moved to the new social network or according to the news the new one has better features) and tell us about their preferable way. They assumed they had two options: (1) download the data from Facebook, change/filter information and then upload it to the new website. (2) use a button on Facebook that directly sends the data to the new website. Different opinions and preferences are summarized in Table 6.

Interestingly, one of the people (P9) who preferred the button emphasized that she needs some kind of information or messages showing what is happening before she sends the data by clicking the button like the information she receives when she uses Facebook login button. The one (P5) who was not sure about her preferred option also mentioned about social login buttons and expressed her privacy concerns about what is transferred when she uses these buttons.

Finally, we asked people to consider the same scenario of transferring their Facebook data to another social network and we told them to imagine that Data Track would provide edit functionality and would be able to save the new version of data exports. Then we asked about participants' attitudes of the usefulness of Data Track in this scenario. All participants said that they can see the usefulness of the Data Track to have control over their data, change the parts they do not want to be included and it will be really helpful to adjust the data and visualize what will be transferred. However, some participants also again mentioned that they have privacy and security concerns (see Sect. 4.1.3).

5   Conclusion and Future Work

We conducted a user study with ten participants using semi-structured interviews aiming to understand the users' perceptions of data export, data portability and transparency functions in the latest stand-alone version of the Data Track. Albeit most of the participants showed rather little interest in the visualization of derived activity data revealed in the Google exported location data file, they stated their interests in other kind of derived data (e.g., by Facebook or online marketing services), like movement and travel patterns, usage patterns for different service providers, statistical data based on their behaviors and information about to whom their data are sold, how it is exchanged and how they receive related advertisements. In addition to the kind of transparency functions of their interests, some of them also stated that they would like to exercise more control over their data via this tool, e.g., they would like to have added functionality allowing them to delete or correct data (such control functions are actually offered by the previous (non stand-alone) A4Cloud Data Track version).

Analyzing users' perceptions of data export and portability, as we experienced in previous user studies, again confirmed that it is for many users confusing and difficult to differentiate between locally and remotely stored and controlled data. Several test participants were thinking that the data in the Data Track were synchronized with the data in the Google account. Several users were also concerned about the security of their data when they think of downloading the data on their own machines and being responsible for its security. Nonetheless, most participants stated that for the purpose of exercising their right to data portability, they would prefer to first export their data, inspect and filter out some information before uploading it to another service provider, and would appreciate using a tool such as the Data Track for helping them to visualize and filter data in this context. They thereby clearly would like to be in control when exercising the right of data portability over the easier option of having their personal data transmitted directly from one controller to another one.

We want to note that while we used fake location data of a persona in the first task of our user study, it will be interesting to conduct future user studies for our transparency tools with real data of test participants to analyze how they are reacting if they are confronted their own data traces. This will, however, require further careful preparation for recruiting suitable volunteers, for setting up suitable data protection and ethical procedures and for getting ethical approval by the university's ethics review board.

We are currently extending the stand-alone Data Track for allowing also to visualize data exports of other service providers like YouTube search history or Facebook data, which will let us make other types of disclosed and derived data transparent that participants in our user study showed interest in. Moreover, it will allow the users to compare what data different service providers know about them and what data the service providers have in common (a feature that the previous non-stand alone A4Cloud Data Track version already provided with its trace view).

Moreover, users should be provided with helpful instructions on how they can subsequently exercise their rights to erase or rectify data electronically by logging into the service provider's side (if these control functions are made available by the respective service provider—which is the case at least partially with Google today).

Besides, given the interest by participants to use the Data Track as a visualization and filtering tool when porting data from one service provider to another one, we intend to expand the functionality of the Data Track supporting users in all data portability steps, i.e., supporting them to export the data from one service provider, to visualize and filter data and to import the altered data set to the new service provider.

Acknowledgment. The authors gratefully acknowledge Daniel Lindegren for his contribution in conducting pilot study and John Sören Pettersson for his reviews that helped to improve the pilot study design. Furthermore, the authors also thank anonymous reviewers and participants of IFIP Summer School (2016), whose comments and suggestions greatly contributed to enhance and clarify our work.

References

1. Angulo, J., Fischer-Hübner, S., Pulls, T., Wästlund, E.: Usable transparency with the data track: a tool for visualizing data disclosures. In: Proceedings of the 33rd Annual ACM Conference Extended Abstracts on Human Factors in Computing Systems, CHI EA 2015, pp. 1803–1808, NY, USA (2015). http://doi.acm.org/10.1145/2702613.2732701
2. Becker, R.A., Eick, S.G., Wilks, A.R.: Visualizing network data. IEEE Trans. Visual. Comput. Graph. **1**(1), 16–28 (1995)
3. Bernsmed, K., Fischer-Hübner, S.: A4Cloud deliverable D.D-5.4 user interface prototypes (2015)
4. Bier, C., Kühne, K., Beyerer, J.: PrivacyInsight: the next generation privacy dashboard. In: Schiffner, S., Serna, J., Ikonomou, D., Rannenberg, K. (eds.) APF 2016. LNCS, vol. 9857, pp. 135–152. Springer, Cham (2016). doi:10.1007/978-3-319-44760-5_9
5. Charmaz, K.: Constructing Grounded Theory. Sage, Thousand Oaks (2014)
6. European Commission: Directive 95/46/EC of the European Parliament and of the Council of 24 on the protection of individuals with regard to the processing of personal data and on the free movement of such data, October 1995
7. European Commission: Regulation (EU) 2016/679 of the European Parliament and of the Council of 27 on the protection of natural persons with regard to the processing of personal data and on the free movement of such data, and repealing Directive 95/46/EC (General Data Protection Regulation), April 2016. Official Journal of the European Union, L119/1, 4 May 2016
8. Fischer-Hübner, S., Angulo, J., Karegar, F., Pulls, T.: Transparency, Privacy and Trust – Technology for Tracking and Controlling My Data Disclosures: Does This Work? In: Habib, S.M.M., Vassileva, J., Mauw, S., Mühlhäuser, M. (eds.) IFIPTM 2016. IAICT, vol. 473, pp. 3–14. Springer, Cham (2016). doi:10.1007/978-3-319-41354-9_1

9. Fischer-Hübner, S., Angulo, J., Pulls, T.: How can cloud users be supported in deciding on, tracking and controlling how their data are used? In: Hansen, M., Hoepman, J.-H., Leenes, R., Whitehouse, D. (eds.) Privacy and Identity 2013. IAICT, vol. 421, pp. 77–92. Springer, Heidelberg (2014). doi:10.1007/978-3-642-55137-6_6

10. Fischer-Hübner, S., Hedbom, H., Wästlund, E.: Trust and assurance HCI. In: Camenisch, J., Fischer-Hübner, S., Rannenberg, K. (eds.) Privacy and Identity Management for Life, pp. 245–260. Springer, Heidelberg (2011)

11. Freeman, L.C.: Visualizing social networks. J. Soc. Struct. 1(1), 4 (2000)

12. Hildebrandt, M.: Behavioural biometric profiling and transparency enhancing tools. FIDIS WP7 deliverable. http://www.fidis.net/

13. Kani-Zabihi, E., Helmhout, M.: Increasing service users' privacy awareness by introducing on-line interactive privacy features. In: Laud, P. (ed.) NordSec 2011. LNCS, vol. 7161, pp. 131–148. Springer, Heidelberg (2012). doi:10.1007/978-3-642-29615-4_10

14. Kolter, J., Netter, M., Pernul, G.: Visualizing past personal data disclosures. In: ARES 2010 International Conference on Availability, Reliability, and Security, pp. 131–139. IEEE (2010)

15. Mozilla: Lightbeam add-on for Firefox. https://addons.mozilla.org/en-US/firefox/addon/lightbeam/

16. Mun, M., Hao, S., Mishra, N., Shilton, K., Burke, J., Estrin, D., Hansen, M., Govindan, R.: Personal data vaults: a locus of control for personal data streams. In: Proceedings of the 6th International Conference, pp. 17:1–17:12. Co-NEXT 2010, NY, USA (2010). http://doi.acm.org/10.1145/1921168.1921191

17. Onwuegbuzie, A.J., Leech, N.L.: Validity and qualitative research: an oxymoron? Qual. Quant. 41(2), 233–249 (2007). http://dx.doi.org/10.1007/s11135-006-9000-3

18. Pettersson, J.S., Fischer-Hübner, S., Bergmann, M.: Outlining "Data Track": privacy-friendly data maintenance for end-users. In: Wojtkowski, W., Wojtkowski, W., Zupancic, J., Magyar, G., Knapp, G. (eds.) Advances in Information Systems Development, pp. 215–226. Springer, Heidelberg (2007)

19. Pettersson, J.S., Fischer-Hübner, S., Danielsson, N., Nilsson, J., Bergmann, M., Clauss, S., Kriegelstein, T., Krasemann, H.: Making PRIME usable. In: Proceedings of the 2005 Symposium on Usable Privacy and Security, SOUPS 2005, pp. 53–64, NY, USA (2005). http://doi.acm.org/10.1145/1073001.1073007

20. Popescu, A., Hildebrandt, M., Breuer, J., Claeys, L., Papadopoulos, S., Petkos, G., Michalareas, T., Lund, D., Heyman, R., Graaf, S., Gadeski, E., Borgne, H., deVries, K., Kastrinogiannis, T., Kousaridas, A., Padyab, A.: Increasing transparency and privacy for online social network users – USEMP value model, scoring framework and legal. In: Berendt, B., Engel, T., Ikonomou, D., Le Métayer, D., Schiffner, S. (eds.) APF 2015. LNCS, vol. 9484, pp. 38–59. Springer, Cham (2016). doi:10.1007/978-3-319-31456-3_3

21. Rubin, J., Chisnell, D.: Handbook of Usability Testing: How to Plan, Design and Conduct Effective Tests. Wiley, New York (2008)

Cloud Computing Contracts

Regulatory Issues and Cloud Service Providers' Offers: An Analysis

Shyam S. Wagle[✉]

University of Luxembourg, 6, rue R. Coudenhove-Kalergi,
Luxembourg City, Luxembourg
shyam.wagle.001@student.uni.lu

Abstract. In cloud computing, a cloud service-brokering framework mediates between cloud service users (CSUs) and cloud service providers (CSPs) to facilitate the availability of cloud services to the users according to their requirements from multi-cloud environment. The current cloud service brokering framework considers the service performance commitments of CSPs, but it is not aware of current legal/regulatory compliance status of CSPs when recommending services to the users. A cloud contract (terms of service, Service Level Agreement (SLA)) helps cloud users in their decision making to select an appropriate CSP according to their expectations. CSUs feedback and survey report show that users are still not satisfied with the current terms and conditions committed to by CSPs. They believe that the terms and conditions are unclear or unbalanced, which they sometimes are when in favour of CSPs. In this paper, we identify some major issues to be included in cloud contract to make it safe and fair to all parties involved in the agreement from the European Union (EU) data protection perspective. Another contribution of the paper is analyzing cloud contracts (their terms of service and SLAs) offered by international CSPs in respect of the standard guidelines recommended by different independent bodies to include in the cloud contracts. This information is visualized in a sorting table, called a Heat Map table, which gives a clear picture of the regulatory compliance status of CSPs in their cloud contract documents.

Keywords: Cloud contract · Legal issues · Compliance status · SLA · Provider analysis

1 Introduction

Cloud computing is a promising technology for the information technology (IT) industry that has only recently emerged. An increasing number of IT service providers are offering computational, storage, networking, and application hosting services that cover several continents. Small medium enterprises (SMEs) as well as big enterprises are attracted towards the cloud technology. Adopting

© IFIP International Federation for Information Processing 2016
Published by Springer International Publishing AG 2016. All Rights Reserved
A. Lehmann et al. (Eds.): Privacy and Identity 2016, IFIP AICT 498, pp. 182–198, 2016.
DOI: 10.1007/978-3-319-55783-0_13

cloud computing in their businesses has its pros and cons. Some institutions are attracted to cloud computing because of its easy deployment, low initial start-up cost and easily scalablility, while others are serious about the cloud adopting risks. IDC[1] has forecasted that worldwide public cloud services spending will be to double by 2019. There are many technical and legal challenges for cloud users to fully adapt cloud computing in their businesses. In such circumstances, the actual service performance status of CSPs including regulatory compliance status according to the current legal framework, can help cloud users in their decision making to choose cloud services according to their requirements. A mediator, which can facilitate among cloud users to provide cloud services according to the businesses' requirements and finds appropriate users according to the services offered by them, is called cloud service broker (CSB). Mainly, it can play following roles [10,14]:

- Discovery of SLA and law/regulation compliant services
- Monitoring run-time SLA and law/regulation compliance
- Checking of SLA and law/regulation compliance during the service on-board and at run time
- Actuation to maintain compliance.

Cloudforeurope[2] has identified the need for evaluating the performance of competing CSPs to select cloud services according to their requirements under the CloudWatchHub[3] project. The main idea is to accelerate and increase the use of cloud computing across the public and private sectors in Europe and educate SMEs how to choose the right service provider to take account of personal data protection and service level concerns as opposed to price only.

The reference document for CSBs to recommend cloud services to the users is a cloud contract document. Buyya et al. [4] have pointed out two contracting models: (1) The online agreement is a click wrap agreement where the user agrees to the terms and conditions of the CSPs in an "I agree" box or similar at the moment of service initiation. Online agreement is not subject to negotiation by cloud users. This model is the most commonly followed model by cloud providers, where by cloud users do not have any bargaining power to negotiate the standard agreement offered by CSPs. This analysis is limited to an online agreement model because all the information mentioned here are taken from CSPs' website; (2) A standard, negotiated, signature-based agreement, which generally occurs when larger companies want to move their critical data or applications to the cloud (for instance to the public cloud). In such an agreement, cloud users are free to push their terms and conditions, and requirements, in the contract document.

In summary, a CSB can play two roles in a cloud computing architecture: (1) Service matching according the requirements of the cloud users, and (2) a regulatory compliance check according to the current legal framework. Current cloud service brokering frameworks recommend cloud services to the users by considering the service performance status of the CSPs, and most of these frameworks are

---

[1] https://www.idc.com/.

[2] http://www.cloudforeurope.eu/partners.

[3] http://www.cloudwatchhub.eu.

not aware of the current legal framework. In the literature, most of the research works on the cloud service brokering are: (1) service performance service discovery and matching [13], Quality of Service (QoS) management and optimization [6], interoperability in multi-cloud architecture [5] and so on. Kousiouris et al. [12] and Casalicchio and Palmirani [7] have introduced legal compliance checking capabilities in cloud brokering but does not consider the service performance compliance in recommending cloud services to the cloud users. Wagle et al. [17,19] have proposed evaluation techniques to evaluate the performance of the CSPs. But, these papers are mainly focused on service performance analysis of cloud providers.

The current cloud service-brokering framework is not techno-legal friendly, which can be capable to check both legal and service performance compliance in a single platform. Cloud users and providers are often reluctant to take advantage of cloud computing services because they think that either the terms and conditions are unclear or are unbalanced in the favour of CSPs[4]. More often CSPs try to avoid their responsibilities, as in security and data protection for the users, to be on the safe side in terms of any legal obstacles; however, these are the current big issues in cloud computing contracts from the legal point of view. In our observation, most of the CSPs provides contractual issues under the terms of service and SLA section on their website. Our main source of information in analyzing the regulatory compliance status is: terms of service, SLA agreement, and any frequently asked questions (FAQ) available on the website of the cloud service provider.

In a survey conducted by W.K. Hon et al. [20], the authors pointed out six major terms included in standard cloud computing contracts, which cloud users are highly interested to negotiate. These are the: (1) Limitation of liability in data integrity and disaster recovery, (2) Service Level Agreement (SLA), (3) Security and privacy, (4) Vendor lock-in and exit, (5) Provider's ability to change the service features, and (6) Intellectual property rights (IPR). The survey shows that cloud users are not yet convinced with current practiced standard cloud contracts. In cloud computing, cloud contract documents are yet to be standardized and develop defined standard terminology [9]; however, some recent attempts [1] towards standardization of cloud SLA have been performed[5].

The rest of the paper is organized as follows: Sect. 2 presents the overview of the SLA assured cloud service brokering framework. Section 3 identifies data protection risks in cloud computing from a cloud contractual point of view. We briefly present terms of service and SLA commitments offered by international cloud service providers to check the regulatory compliance status of them according to the current legal framework in Sect. 4. Based on it, we point out some important points to be included in a current cloud contract to make it safe and fair for both CSPs and cloud users. An approach to checking the regulatory compliance status of CSPs has been proposed as a main contribution of the paper in Sect. 4.1. Since, in the cloud contract, most of the terms are related with

---

[4] http://ec.europa.eu/justice/contract/cloud-computing/index-en.htm.

[5] https://ec.europa.eu/digital-single-market/en/news/cloud-service-level-agreement-standardisation-guidelines.

data privacy issues, the analysis is heavily influenced by the EU data protection regime. The paper concludes with the overall concept in Sect. 5.

2 SLA Assured Cloud Service Brokering Framework

Figure 1 shows our proposed SLA assured cloud service brokering framework. The National Institute of Standards and Technology (NIST)'s cloud reference architecture [14] has defined specific roles for multiple actors in reference architectures. In the proposed SLA assured cloud service brokering framework, the cloud service broker (CSB) collects the requirements of users with their priority list of cloud services. The CSB then matches the offers of CSPs to provide services to the users according to these priority lists. The service monitoring module monitors the service performance of CSPs including regulatory compliance status of the CSPs. Wagle et al. [17,19] have addressed service verification, service performance evaluation, sorting and ranking based on service performance monitoring, service performance pattern analysis, and pattern prediction for recommending optimal sets of alternatives to the cloud users. In this paper, we mainly address

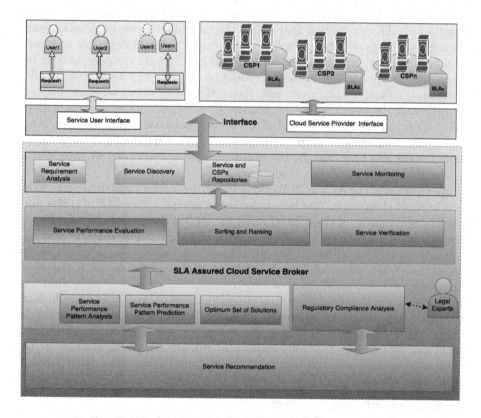

Fig. 1. SLA based brokering and service verification framework

the regulatory compliance status analysis of CSPs to recommend services to the users.

3   Safe and Fair Terms and Conditions in Cloud Computing

As the data from various cloud users is stored in a shared infrastructure environment, there exists the possibility of the accessing of confidential data by un-authorized users or media. This causes many technical issues to protect data from unwanted access as well as it creates legal issues due to the dynamic nature of service access in cloud computing. The recently enacted EU's General Data Protection Regulation (GDPR)[6] repealing the EU's Data Protection Directive 95/46/EC[7], gives fundamental rights to the data users (data subjects) with respect to their personal data while requiring "data controllers" to follow rules and restrictions with respect to their data processing operations [11]. The regulation is designed to further addressing new technological developments. Cloud users are entitled to be informed of the identity of any data controller and the purposes for which personal data are being collected or processed. According to the GDPR, data controllers should follow a main set of privacy protection principles on data protection that define the individual rights of the users and the responsibilities of data controllers that process personal data: fair and lawful processing, collection and processing only for a proper purpose; should be adequate, relevant and not excessive; should be accurate and up to date, should be retained no longer than necessary; giving the data subject access to his/her data, keeping data secure; and no transfer of personal data to a country that does not provide an adequate level of privacy and personal data protection. New penalties (including fines of up to the greater of either €100 million, or 2–5% of annual worldwide turn over) in the new regulation are intended to make CSPs serious about their regulatory compliance.

An Opinion of the Article 29 Working Party[8] has categorized data protection risks in cloud computing, into two major broad groups, (1) and (2): (1) risk due to a lack of control over the data. Under this category, lack of availability due to lack of interoperability (vendor lock-in), lack of integrity caused by the sharing of resources, lack of confidentiality in terms of law enforcement requests made directly to a CSP, lack of intervenability due to the complexities and dynamics of the outsourcing chain and data subjects' rights, and lack of isolation within the CSPs' clients are the main data protection risks, and (2) risk due to insufficient information regarding the processing operation (hence, a lack of transparency). Mainly these risks may arise from the controller not being aware of certain conditions: for example, that some form chain processing is taking place involving multiple processors and subcontractors, personal data are processed in difference

---

[6] http://ec.europa.eu/justice/data-protection/reform/index-en.htm.

[7] http://eur-lex.europa.eu/legal-content/.

[8] http://ec.europa.eu/justice/data-protection/article-29/documentation/ opinion-recommendation/files/2012/wp196-en.pdf.

geographic locations within the European Economic Area (EEA), and personal data are transferred to third countries outside the EEA.

However literature from many standardization bodies and organizations have many points to be considered in the list to make the terms and conditions in the agreement safe and fair, following some major points addressed by the Cloud Select Industry Group - Subgroup on Service Level Agreement (C-SIG-SLA)[9]. In addition, the authors in [20] considered analyzing the regulatory compliance status of CSPs through the terms of service mentioned in the contract document, which is clear and transparent to every parties involved in the agreement. All the important points mentioned in the section that follows are represented in Table 1 as criteria and sub-criteria to analyze the regulatory compliance status of the CSPs.

3.1 Liabilities

Providers try to exclude liabilities altogether or restrict liabilities as much as possible because they provide commoditized services [20]. It is also true that it is not always practical to expose the CSPs to unlimited liabilities for a small deal. Liabilities of data loss of Infrastructure as a Service (IaaS) providers, liabilities for intellectual property rights infringement of software by Software as a Service (SaaS) providers are some examples of conflicting issues mostly between users and providers [20].

3.2 Service Level Agreement

A SLA is a documented agreement between the cloud service provider and cloud user that identifies services and cloud service level objectives (SLOs). It should include minimum level objectives that CSPs can provide to the cloud users and details about what happens when the CSP has failed to provide agreed minimum level objectives. The C-SIG-SLA has defined a set of SLA standardization guidelines for CSPs and professional cloud users, while ensuring the specific needs of the cloud market and industry are taken into account. This document is specifically targeted at the European cloud market. We highlight some major points, which are important to be included in a SLA agreement:

Performance Service Level. The performance service level includes the availability of the services (uptime, percentage of successful requests, percentage of timely service provisioning requests), response time of the service, capacity parameters (number of simultaneous connections, number of simultaneous cloud service users, maximum resource capacity, service throughput) and support (support hours, support responsiveness, resolution time).

---

[9] https://ec.europa.eu/digital-single-market/en/news/cloud-service-level-agreement-standardisation-guidelines.

Security Service Level. Service reliability, authentication and authorization, cryptography, security incident management and reporting, logging and monitoring, auditing and security verification, vulnerability management and security control governance are the major points to be included in a security service level agreement. Service reliability, which is directly interconnected with the level of redundancy that a CSP can provide at the user authentication and identity assurance level, should be mentioned for authentication and authorization. How a cloud service provider handles information security incidents is of great concern to cloud service users. Incident reporting is also important in security incident management. Logging is the recording of data related to the operation and use of a cloud service. Monitoring means determining the status of one or more parameters of a cloud service. Logging and monitoring are ordinarily the responsibility of the cloud service provider.

Data Management Service Level. From the security and regulatory point of view, it is necessary to classify data, for example, the user's data, provider's data, cloud service derived data and so on. It is also necessary to include data backup, mirroring and restore, lifecycle of data and data portability with different formats and interfaces in the agreement.

Personal Data Protection Service Level. In a SLA agreement, the most important part is to define how the CSP acts as a data processor or data controller or joint controllers (notably by processing personal data for their own purposes, outside of an explicit mandate from the user). It is also necessary to describe applicable data protection codes of conduct, standards, and certifications. If personal data are processed, it is necessary to define the purposes of processing, openness and transparency of subcontractors. The document should define who is accountable for a personal data breach. Another important issue in the data management service level is a detailed list about the geographical location(s), where user data may be stored and/or processed and preferred geographical location for the storage of the user data. Last but not least, a SLA agreement must define the access request response time period within which the provider shall communicate the information necessary to allow the user to respond to access requests by the data subjects.

3.3   Provider Lock-In and Exit

Lock-in is one of the top concerns of cloud users. Most of the cloud users may not wish to be locked-in for long time with an initial contract. Users should be free to leave the service after a short, specific time. Users should be allowed to leave the service when they feel that the service is not appropriate for them or the same service is available in the market at a cheaper price from another CSP. While this is a commercial issue, the main concern is how a user's data and metadata can be recovered once the service is terminated for whatever the reason. Data formats should be easily accessible, readable and importable into other applications of other CSPs, independently. Data retention and deletion are also important issues in a cloud contract. Users should be assured about retention of their data and the complete deletion of their data after contract termination [20].

3.4 Terms and Conditions

As usual, like in other contracts there should be minimum terms, a renewal period and a notice period. Long initial terms may be one of the issues of provider lock-in. Many of the CSPs set automatic renewal provisions, which may mislead cloud users if there are not a fixed notice periods. These terms and conditions depend on types of services and types of business scale. Suspension rights must be also clearly mentioned in an agreed contract document.

3.5 Changing Service Features

CSPs should not be entitled to change terms without consent, or at least should give users notice and allow them to terminate the contract[10]. Any changes in service must not adversely affect the previous commitment. Users must be notified within a sufficient time mentioning the key changes and impact of changes.

3.6 Intellectual Property Rights

Intellectual property rights (IPR) issues arise frequently in relation to cloud processed data and, or applications. This generally happens due to the issue of who owns data in the cloud contract document not being addressed properly.

4   Analysis of Terms of Service and SLA Committed to by CSPs

In this section, we first provide the terms of service and SLA commitments of some incumbent CSPs. The main sources of information come from the terms of service, SLA document, security practices, privacy policies, the cloud documentations on getting started and other user guides, and FAQs by CSPs. We second expose some missing major items in the current cloud contracts. We third (in a following sub-section) offer two tables that explain these two sets of issues; the second table uses a simple pictorial format. What follows are the details in relation to the incumbent CSPs.

Microsoft Azure: Microsoft Azure[11] offers a specific SLA commitments in multiple services. Its SLA commitment ranges from maximum 99.9%–99.99%. It provides sector/region-wise SLA commitments to the cloud users. It offers detailed information regarding the data transfer; however, information on data

---

[10] https://www.cloudindustryforum.org/search/site/CIF3.

[11] https://azure.microsoft.com/en-us/support/legal/sla/summary/.

privacy and security issues in the terms and conditions document is not clearly detailed[12].

GMOCloud: GMO Cloud[13] offers at least 99.999% monthly uptime for all cloud services. The SLA document offered by GMO is not a service-specific commitments. It provides details of security & backup, and IPR; however, it is silent on data privacy and governing law. The terms of service place the liability on the cloud users to protect their own privacy[14]. It provides detailed information of data centre locations.

HP Cloud: The SLA offer of HP Cloud[15] ranges from at least 99.95%–100% in a specific cloud service. There is a limited information of data privacy and security in its terms of service. Detailed information of the SLA and terms of service are not easily available, as the company is not planning to expand its public cloud services further.

Amazon: Amazon provides various cloud services, however, Amazon S3[16] and Amazon EC2[17] are its most popular cloud services. It offers at least 99.9% uptime for both S3 and EC2 services. It provides a well organized contract agreement for specific services[18,19]. The contract agreement offered contains detailed information on security and data privacy, governing law and IPR.

RackSpace: Rackspace cloud[20] service provider provides a service specific SLA commitment. Monthly uptime from at least 99.9% to maximum 100% is offered in its SLA document. It guarantees the user data privacy according to applicable data protection/privacy law[21]. It also provides a detailed information on its global security policy.

Google Cloud: Google Cloud[22] offers a service specific SLA. It ranges from at least 99.9%–100% monthly uptime based on the service offer. It covers most of the important terms in its terms of service. Data processing, security terms, compliance with different regulatory frameworks, governing law and jurisdiction are all covered in the agreement[23]. The SLA monitoring issues are still not clear, however, in the commitment document. According to the document, it is possible to choose data centre according to users' preferences in different locations.

City Cloud: City Cloud[24] offers a SLA commitment of at least 100% monthly uptime in all its services, irrespective of the specific cloud services. It does not provide detailed terms of service related to security and data privacy, governing

---

[12] https://azure.microsoft.com/en-us/support/legal/services-terms-nov-2014/.

[13] https://www.gmocloud.com/common/download/catalog_iqcloud.pdf.

[14] http://us.gmocloud.com/legal/.

[15] http://www.hpcloud.com/sla/.

[16] http://aws.amazon.com/s3/sla/.

[17] http://aws.amazon.com/ec2/sla/.

[18] http://portal.aws.amazon.com/gp/aws/developer/terms-and-conditions.html.

[19] http://aws.amazon.com/agreement/.

[20] https://www.rackspace.com/information/legal/cloud/sla.

[21] https://www.rackspace.com/information/legal/cloud/tos.

[22] https://cloud.google.com/.

[23] https://cloud.google.com/terms/.

[24] https://www.citynetworkhosting.com/sla/.

law and jurisdiction. It provides the geo-locations of data centres and monitoring facility of cloud services.

Cloud Sigma: Similarly, Cloud Sigma[25] also offers at least 100% monthly uptime irrespective of a specific service. The terms of service detail liability, privacy policy, IPR, governing law and jurisdiction[26]. Information related to data centre locations is also provided. However, the terms and conditions are not clear enough as is recommended by standard cloud contract guidelines.

Elastic Host: Elastic Host[27] provides a service specific SLA offer that ranges from at least 99.95%–100%. It lacks specific details on privacy and security issues in the provided SLA agreement provided, and puts more liability on the users. The proposed agreement is specific in terms of governing law and jurisdiction.

Century Link Cloud: Century Link Cloud[28] is very specific in terms of its SLA document. It commits to 100% uptime for public/private networks and at least 99.9% for the rest of the services. It provides a privacy policy[29], data retention issues, governing law, and jurisdiction; however, it is not specific on data liability and other issues, which are necessary to make a safe and fair cloud contract. It provides data centre locations on its website.

Digital Ocean: However, Digital Ocean[30] does not provide specific SLA commitments. According to the service offers, it provides at least 99.99% monthly uptime in network, power and virtual server availability. The offered document provides information related to the liabilities, and governing law, data privacy but a detail related to physical security is still missing in the document.

GoGrid Cloud: GoGrid Cloud[31,32] provides a very specific SLA commitment for each cloud service. It also provides a regional, specific performance matrix in its SLA document. It is more specific on privacy and security issues, IPR and third party offerings, and choice of law, and jurisdiction; however, it does not take more liabilities in user's data.

UpCloud: UpCloud[33] commit to a minimum of 100% monthly uptime to all services, irrespective of the specific cloud service. The terms of service are not clear on data security and privacy, governing law, jurisdiction, and data centre locations[34].

IBM Cloud: IBM does not provide specific service SLA metrics. The terms of service of IBM is well organized, and provides the details of security descriptions, data protection, conditions of trans-boarder data flow and information regarding

---

[25] https://www.cloudsigma.com/features/.

[26] https://www.cloudsigma.com/legal-switzerland/.

[27] https://www.elastichosts.com/terms-of-service/.

[28] https://www.ctl.io/legal/sla/.

[29] https://www.ctl.io/legal/privacy/.

[30] https://www.digitalocean.com/legal/terms/.

[31] https://www.datapipe.com/gogrid/legal/sla/.

[32] https://www.datapipe.com/gogrid/legal/terms-of-service/.

[33] https://www.upcloud.com/blog/how-seriously-does-your-cloud-hosting-provider-take-redundancy/.

[34] https://www.upcloud.com/documentation/terms/.

the governing law and jurisdiction[35]. It also provides information on data centre locations.

Exoscale Cloud: Exoscale Cloud provides 95.95% availability in all its services[36]. The terms of service are well described and clear. The document is specific on data security (however, it takes less liabilities), data protection and privacy, governing law and jurisdiction, data storage and IPR.

Baremetal Cloud: It provides 99.999% availability unspecific with a cloud service. The SLA and terms of service[37] provided are not sufficient on data privacy or provider's liabilities; however, it provides an information related to physical level security and data centre locations.

Arubacloud: Aruba cloud provides at least 99.95% availability to all cloud services with the exception of 100% in power and air conditioning[38]. It provides detailed information on the processing of personal data with specific applicable law, jurisdictions and competency, but it provides the less information regarding the security issues from a technical point of view. It also provides an information related to data center locations and service monitoring details.

Softlayer Cloud: It does not provide a SLA commitment specific to particular services. In its SLA agreement document, it uses the sentence "SoftLayer will use reasonable efforts to provide a service level of 100% for the public/private network...", but it guarantees a service credit for more than two hours[39]. It is not clearly mentioned how this is provided; however, it agrees to maintain reasonable and appropriate measures related to physical security to protect user content[40]. The document is specific on data protection and privacy, governing law and jurisdictions. It also provides the geographical locations of data centres.

Vaultnetwork Cloud: The Vault network Cloud endeavours to have service(s) available for access by any party in the world 99.5% of the time[41]. The document provided does not detail security, data privacy and protection issues. It is specific on governing law and jurisdictions.

CloudCentral: It commits 99.95% uptime commitment to infrastructure services[42]. The terms and conditions[43] are clear in liabilities, governing law, and IPR, but there is not sufficient information on data privacy and physical security.

It is worthwhile to mention that cloud users still believe current contracts are not fair and remain favourable towards the CSPs. We identify here some major missing points in current cloud contracts, which can be helpful to improve the fairness and transparency of the cloud contracts. Four specific issues follow:

---

[35] https://www-03.ibm.com/software/sla/.

[36] https://www.exoscale.ch/terms/.

[37] https://www.baremetalcloud.com/legal-terms.

[38] https://www.arubacloud.com/company/general-conditions.aspx.

[39] http://static.softlayer.com/sites/default/files/sla.pdf.

[40] http://static.softlayer.com/sites/default/files/assets/page/Terms-of-Service.pdf.

[41] https://www.vaultnetworks.com/about/company-policies/terms-of-service/.

[42] https://www.cloudcentral.com.au/sla/.

[43] https://www.cloudcentral.com.au/terms-and-conditions/.

1. Lack of Liabilities and Indemnity
   Most of the providers state their entire liability according to the charge paid by the user or a maximum amount. This could be considered to limit or exclude the legal rights of the user under some laws (for instance, under EU law it is considered to be an unfair contract [8]).
2. Consent for the Collection and Processing of Personal Data for Secondary Non-Compatible Purposes
   Information that is collected from cloud users for the internal purposes of the CSPs, and gathered by them, such as billing or management of the cloud services, will belong to the CSPs [15]. However, this information should not be used for the unfair advantage. In our analysis, most of the providers do not mention theses issues in their terms of service, but some providers still use this information for other purpose without seeking the particular consent from the data subject [20].
3. Lack of Transparency
   As we already discussed, there is a lack of a standardized format and terminology of cloud contracts in cloud computing. Cloud providers prefer to include terms according to their feasibility in the proposed terms of service and SLA. Unclear, and sometimes unfair, terms of service in the cloud contract misguide the rights of cloud users in contract breaching. The lack of a clear monitoring technique in the SLA, hidden payment obligations, and automatic renewals can occur due to unclear terms of service in the cloud contract.
4. SLA agreement
   a. Lack of Service Monitoring
   The user pays as per usage in terms of cloud computing. So, service credit and other claims will be authorized according to the SLA agreement. Many of the contract terms do not mention about the methods of service monitoring. SLA monitoring has become a challenging issue, because it has been observed that all the cloud service providers may not provide services to the user according to their SLA commitments [17].
   b. Disaster Recovery
   In the most of the contract documents, how CSPs manage disaster recovery of the services is not clear. A well-managed disaster recovery plan is a very significant criterion for users who desire to select an appropriate CSP.
   c. Location of Data
   In our observation, many of the CSPs provide information related to data centre locations on their website. Cloud users can choose an appropriate location according to their requirements, but this information is not still part of the terms of service and SLA.
   d. Data portability, Data irretrievability
   Very few CSPs provide the information related to data portability and irretrievability. Cloud users should be easily able to retrieve their data if they prefer to switch to another CSP due for any reason.

Table 1. Criteria and sub-criteria for evaluating cloud services

Criteria	Sub-criteria	Short name
Liabilities	Liabilities	Li
Performance service level	Availability	Av
	Response time	Res
	Capacity	Cap
Security service level	Service reliability	Rel
	Authentication and authorization	Au
	Security incident mgmt	inc
	Reporting	Rep
	Logging	Log
	Monitoring	Mon
Data management service level	Data classification	$Dcls$
	Data backup, mirroring and restore	BMR
	Data lifecycle and portability	DLP
Personal data protection service level	Code of conduct	$Ccon$
	Purpose of specification	$Pspec$
	Openness, transparency and notice	OTN
	Accountability	Acc
	Geographical location of user data	DL
Provider lock-in and exit	Lock-in	In
	Exit	Ex
Terms and conditions	Terms and conditions	TC
Changing service features	Changing service features	CS
Intellectual property rights (IPR)	IPR	IPR

Sometimes, it is hard for most of the cloud users to follow these points, since they are not aware of the existing legal framework or they do not have sufficient legal knowledge to follow the legal framework. In the next section, we propose how a performance evaluation technique (called the Heat Map technique) can be implemented to check the regulatory compliance status of the CSPs. The Heat Map table (second of the two tables) gives complete information on the regulatory compliance status of the CSPs in a visualized form.

4.1   Pictorial Analysis of CSP's Contracts in Ordinary Values

A SLA assured service brokering framework is proposed in [18]. This framework recommends the cloud services to the user that have a verified service performance delivery against the SLA commitments of CSPs. Wagle et al. [17,19] proposed evaluation techniques to evaluate the service performance of the CSPs. These two papers are mainly focused on service performance analysis of the CSPs. In cloud computing, specifically in a public cloud scenario, regulatory compliance management is also critical issue as the cloud users outsource data processing and storage to CSPs that can be under legislation/regulation [16]. Casalicchio and Palmirani [7] have introduced a conceptual framework for legal compliance checking in cloud brokering, but the framework does not give a clear picture of the regulatory compliance status of the CSPs. Information on service performance status, including regulatory compliance status, facilitates cloud users in their decision making to choose appropriate CSPs according to their requirements. The main motivation of our paper is analyzing the regulatory compliance status of the CSPs. We assign a corresponding ordinal level according to the fair and transparent contract document that the CSPs' have committed to the users (see Table 1. We then implement a Heat Map technique [2,3,17] proposed for service performance evaluation to evaluate the regulatory compliance status of the cloud providers. Using this Heat Map technique, potential CSPs are sorted into marginal performance quantile classes to rank the CSPs with multiple performance criteria in increasing order or decreasing order [17]. Performance quantile class is associated with the colours ranging from *dark red* (worst) to *dark green* (best) for the performance heat map visualization (See the colour legend for the 7-tiles in Table 2). We have considered the major parameters described in Sect. 3 of this paper. All the information is taken from the CSPs' websites. The developed heat map table offers a graphic display, which shows to what extent CSPs are accepting regulatory compliance in their contractual documentation.

We assign 0–3 ordinary levels according to the detailed specification provided in the SLA document, terms of service and so on. If there is not any information

Table 2. Pictorial view of cloud contracts offered by International CSPs

criteria	Acc	BMR	Mon	Log	Rep	OTN	inc	Au	Rel	DL	Li	IPR	Ex	In	Res	TC	Pspec	Ccon	DLP	Dcls	Cap	Av	CS
weights	0.33	0.33	0.33	0.33	0.33	0.33	0.33	0.33	0.33	0.33	0.33	0.33	0.33	0.33	0.33	0.33	0.33	0.33	0.33	0.33	0.33	0.33	0.33
tau(*)	0.52	0.52	0.52	0.52	0.52	0.50	0.49	0.49	0.49	0.34	0.26	0.09	0.04	0.04	0.02	0.00	0.00	0.00	0.00	0.00	0.00	-0.06	-0.34
Amazon Cloud	3	3	3	3	3	3	3	3	3	3	3	2	2	1	3	3	3		NA	NA	NA	3	0
Google Cloud Storage	3	3	3	3	3	3	3	3	3	3	2	3	0	0	1	3	3	3	NA	NA	NA	3	2
Microsoft Azure	3	3	3	3	3	3	2	2	2	2	2	2	1	1	1	3	3	3	NA	NA	NA	3	1
Aruba Cloud	3	3	3	3	3	3	3	3	3	3	0	2	0	0	1	3	3	3	NA	NA	NA	3	0
IBM Cloud	2	2	2	2	2	2	3	3	3	3	2	2	0	0	1	3	3	3	NA	NA	NA	2	0
City Cloud	3	3	3	3	3	3	1	1	1	3	2	2	0	0	1	3	3	3	NA	NA	NA	3	2
Rackspace Cloud	0	0	0	0	0	0	3	3	3	0	3	3	1	1	1	3	3	3	NA	NA	NA	3	1
CenturyLinkCloud	1	1	1	1	1	1	1	1	1	3	3	1	0	0	1	3	3	3	NA	NA	NA	3	2
Gogrid Cloud	0	0	0	0	0	0	2	2	2	3	0	3	1	1	2	3	3	3	NA	NA	NA	3	3
ExoCloud	0	0	0	0	0	0	3	3	3	0	3	3	1	1	1	3	3	3	NA	NA	NA	3	3
BareMetal Cloud	0	0	0	0	0	0	3	3	3	0	1	2	0	0	1	3	3	3	NA	NA	NA	3	2
SoftLayer Cloud	0	0	0	0	0	0	2	2	2	3	1	1	1	1	1	3	3	3	NA	NA	NA	3	NA
UpCloud	0	0	0	0	0	0	1	1	1	3	2	2	1	1	1	3	3	3	NA	NA	NA	3	2
Elastic Host	0	0	0	0	0	0	2	2	2	0	1	3	0	0	1	3	3	3	NA	NA	NA	3	2
DigitalOcean Cloud	0	0	0	0	0	0	2	2	2	2	1	2	0	0	1	3	3	3	NA	NA	NA	3	2
Cloudcentral Cloud	0	0	0	0	0	0	1	1	1	0	1	3	1	1	1	3	3	3	NA	NA	NA	3	NA
Cloud Sigma	0	0	0	0	0	0	1	1	1	3	1	2	0	0	1	3	3	3	NA	NA	NA	3	2
HP Cloud	0	0	0	0	0	0	1	1	1	0	1	2	0	1	1	3	3	3	NA	NA	NA	3	2
VaultNetwork Cloud	0	0	0	0	0	0	1	1	1	0	2	1	0	0	1	3	3	3	NA	NA	NA	3	2
GMOCloud-US	0	0	0	0	0	0	0	0	0	0	0	3	1	1	1	3	3	3	NA	NA	NA	3	2

Color legend:

quantile	0.14%	0.29%	0.43%	0.57%	0.71%	0.86%	1.00%

(*) tau: Ordinal (Kendall) correlation between marginal criterion and global ranking relation.

provided, we assign 'NA' in that particular parameter. 3 - "Available, complete and included all the points", 2 - "Available, sufficient and missing some points", 1 - "Available, insufficient and missing some points", 0 - "Available, insufficient but not clear points" 'NA' - "Not Available".

We assign corresponding ordinal level according to fair and transparent contract document they have committed to the users (see Table 1). The proposed visualized table gives an idea to cloud users, cloud service brokers, and regulatory bodies of just how CSPs are aware of regulatory compliance in contractual terms in cloud computing. The first row in the Table 2 states the criteria of the evaluations. The second row represents the weight of the criteria. However, since different weights can be assigned to the evaluation according to the evaluator requirements, we have assigned an equal weight in each sub-criterion by considering that all criteria are equally important. The **tau** value represents the dominancy level of sorting (for instance 0.52 is the dominancy level in this case). However, none of the CSPs provide sufficiently complete information to make a safe and fair contract, although cloud providers *Amazon, Google Cloud Storage* and *Microsoft Azure* give more information in their contract document than other cloud providers in selected cloud providers in this regulatory compliance analysis (See Table 2). The ordinary levels and heat map tables presented in this section are only for explanatory purposes (see for example, Table 2) and should not be considered in any case as conclusive because expressing legal issues using quantitative value is not straightforward. It is worthwhile to mention here that this paper is only concerned with the transparency levels of the providers in terms of their contract document available on their website according to the current legal framework and does not check the service performance level of CSPs.

5   Concluding Remarks

A cloud contract is the most important legal binding document in cloud computing, which ensures fair and safe to all parties before delivering or receiving services. Obviously, it is not possible to cover all the terms and conditions in a cloud contract document, but any contract should nevertheless be clear enough to, and fair for all, the parties involved in the agreement. The cloud contracts currently committed to by CSPs do not seem to be sufficient as fair, safe and transparent cloud contracts. The available literature, the recommendations of different independent bodies, and an analysis of the terms of service and SLA agreements committed to by CSPs, show that cloud users are still not convinced about current cloud contracts. The heat map table presented in this paper gives the current position of CSPs according to their regulatory compliance status in their contract documents. A pictorial table of this information, committed to by the CSPs, helps cloud users in their decision making to choose an appropriate CSP according to their requirements. It also helps cloud service brokers to recommend CSPs according to users' needs. Potential future work includes an implementation of the proposed heat map technique in the SLA assured service brokering framework [18], which covers both service performance status and regulatory compliance status when recommending services to users.

Acknowledgements. I would like to thank the LAST-JD programme for financially supporting to perform this research. I am also thankful to Prof. Dr. Pascal Bouvry and Prof. Dr. Raymond Bisdorff for their valuable suggestions in preparing this paper.

References

1. Albert, E., de Boer, F., Hähnle, R., Johnsen, E.B., Laneve, C.: Engineering virtualized services. In: Proceedings of the Second Nordic Symposium on Cloud Computing &; Internet Technologies, NordiCloud 2013 (2013)
2. Bisdorff, R.: On polarizing outranking relations with large performance differences. J. Multi Criteria Decis. Anal. **20**(1–2), 3–12 (2013)
3. Bisdorff, R.: The EURO 2004 best poster award: choosing the best poster in a scientific conference. In: Bisdorff, R., Dias, L.C., Meyer, P., Mousseau, V., Pirlot, M. (eds.) Evaluation and Decision Models with Multiple Criteria. IHIS, pp. 117–165. Springer, Heidelberg (2015). doi:10.1007/978-3-662-46816-6_5
4. Buyya, R., Broberg, J., Goscinski, A.M.: Cloud Computing Principles and Paradigms. Wiley, New York (2011)
5. Buyya, R., Ranjan, R., Calheiros, R.N.: InterCloud: utility-oriented federation of cloud computing environments for scaling of application services. In: Hsu, C.-H., Yang, L.T., Park, J.H., Yeo, S.-S. (eds.) ICA3PP 2010. LNCS, vol. 6081, pp. 13–31. Springer, Heidelberg (2010). doi:10.1007/978-3-642-13119-6_2
6. Calinescu, R., Grunske, L., Kwiatkowska, M., Mirandola, R., Tamburrelli, G.: Dynamic QoS management and optimization in service-based systems. IEEE Trans. Softw. Eng. **37**(3), 387–409 (2011)
7. Casalicchio, E., Palmirani, M.: A cloud service broker with legal-rule compliance checking and quality assurance capabilities. In: 1st International Conference on Cloud Forward: From Distributed to Complete Computing, Pisa, Italy, pp. 136–150, 6–8 October 2015
8. European Commission. Unfair Contract Terms (1993)
9. Giachino, E., de Gouw, S., Laneve, C., Nobakht, B.: Statically and dynamically verifiable SLA metrics. In: Theory and Practice of Formal Methods - Essays Dedicated to Frank de Boer on the Occasion of His 60th Birthday, pp. 211–225 (2016)
10. Grozev, N., Buyya, R.: Inter-cloud architectures and application brokering: Taxonomy and survey. Soft. Pr. Exp. **44**(3), 369–390 (2014)
11. King, N.J., Raja, V.T.: Protecting the privacy and security of sensitive customer data in the cloud. CLaw Secur. Rev. **28**(3), 308–319 (2012)
12. Kousiouris, G., Vafiadis, G., Corrales, M.: A cloud provider description schema for meeting legal requirements in cloud federation scenarios. In: Douligeris, C., Polemi, N., Karantjias, A., Lamersdorf, W. (eds.) I3E 2013. IAICT, vol. 399, pp. 61–72. Springer, Heidelberg (2013). doi:10.1007/978-3-642-37437-1_6
13. Li, L., Horrocks, I.: A software framework for matchmaking based on semantic web technology. In: Proceedings of the 12th International Conference on World Wide Web, WWW 2003 (2003)
14. Liu, F., Tong, J., Mao, J., Bohn, R., Messina, J., Badger, M., Leaf, D.: NIST Cloud Computing Reference Architecture (2011)
15. Reed, C.: Information ownership in the cloud (2010)

16. Thatmann, D., Slawik, M., Zickau, S., Küpper, A.: Towards a federated cloud ecosystem: enabling managed cloud service consumption. In: Vanmechelen, K., Altmann, J., Rana, O.F. (eds.) GECON 2012. LNCS, vol. 7714, pp. 223–233. Springer, Heidelberg (2012). doi:10.1007/978-3-642-35194-5_17

17. Wagle, S.S., Guzek, M., Bouvry, P., Bisdorff, R.: An evaluation model for selecting cloud services from commercially available cloud providers. In: 2015 IEEE 7th International Conference on Cloud Computing Technology and Science (CloudCom), pp. 107–114, November 2015

18. Wagle, S.S.: SLA assured brokering (SAB) and CSP certification in cloud computing. In: 2014 IEEE/ACM 7th International Conference on Utility and Cloud Computing (UCC), pp. 1016–1017, December 2014

19. Wagle, S.S., Guzek, M., Bouvry, P.: Cloud service providers ranking based on service delivery and consumer experience. In: 4th IEEE International Conference on (CloudNet), pp. 202–205, Niagara Falls, Canada, October 2015

20. Hon, W.K., Millard, C., Walden, I.: Negotiating cloud contract: looking at clouds from both sides now. Standford Technol. Law Rev. **16**(1), 79–129 (2012)

Selected Papers (Part II) - Privacy Technologies and Frameworks

Using Differential Privacy for the Internet of Things

Carlos Rodrigo Gómez Rodríguez[✉] and Elena Gabriela Barrantes S.

Universidad de Costa Rica, Ciudad Universitaria Rodrigo Facio,
San José, Montes de Oca, Costa Rica
carlos.gomezrodriguez@ucr.ac.cr,
gabriela.barrantes@ecci.ucr.ac.cr

Abstract. In this paper we propose a hybrid privacy-protection model for the Internet of Things (IoT) with the ultimate purpose of balancing privacy restrictions and usability in data delivery services. Our model uses traditional de-identification methods (such as k-anonymity) under low-privacy requirements, but allows for the transmission of aggregate statistical results (calculated with a privacy-preserving method such as Differential Privacy) as an alternative if the privacy requirements exceed a threshold. We show a prototype implementation for this model, and present a small step-by-step example.

Keywords: Privacy negotiation · Internet of Things · Differential privacy

1 Introduction

The data collected in the context of the Internet of Things (IoT), is being incorporated in the business model of many companies, as it takes advantage of the millions of devices freely collecting and distributing data on a daily basis. CISCO states that in year 2015, 563 millions of new mobile devices and connections were added to the 7.3 billion that were already there in 2014 [1]. Data traffic reached 3.7 exabytes per month at the end of 2015, 1.6 times more than 2014, originating in 97 million of wearable devices that generated 15 petabytes of monthly traffic. It is projected that by 2020 the monthly mobile data traffic will reach 20.6 exabytes per month. All this ecosystem composed by people, smart devices, sensors, data collectors, data analyzers, predictors and applications might cause an inappropriate exposure of personal information that the user is not aware of [2]. One possibility is to allow data consumers and producers to negotiate privacy agreements in advance, and then use these agreements to try to satisfy, in the best possible way their requirements.

We are interested in the following scenario: IoT data producers (for example, residential users of smart meters) and IoT data consumers (for example, recommender or safety applications) negotiate a privacy agreement through a third trusted party (TTP), a hypothetical privacy broker. The broker will administer the aggregate full data-base of records generated by all data producers. The existence of such a third party is not a new concept [3] and it could work even on a decentralized environment [4].

A. Lehmann et al. (Eds.): Privacy and Identity 2016, IFIP AICT 498, pp. 201–211, 2016.
DOI: 10.1007/978-3-319-55783-0_14

The privacy broker will use some sort of negotiation protocol between the interested parties, and will record privacy agreements as rules between each user and each consumer. For example, producer requirements could be coded as permissions over some data attributes, and consumer requirements could be given by one or more information loss metrics. Producer requirements will always have a higher priority, given that a violation could expose sensitive data. Although there are one-to-one agreements between consumers and producers, when a consumer requests data corresponding to several producers, the calculation of a joint result that satisfies all individual producer privacy requirements is not trivial, and can cause severe information loss.

We propose a hybrid model where the broker has two privacy-preserving methods to define what to communicate to a requesting consumer: (1) a default, record-by-record descriptor method [5, 6] (also called syntactical de-identification [7]) that will be used when the satisfaction of producer requirements generates an information loss within the threshold required by the data consumer; and (2) an alternative ("statistical") method that will create a set of statistical descriptors for the original data [8]. These aggregate results are the ones that will be used to answer the consumer query if the information loss exceeds the agreed threshold. The statistical method has to be also privacy-preserving, such as Differential Privacy [9].

The motivation for the proposed model is the fact that data consumers are also an important part of the IoT ecosystem, so for cases when satisfying joint producer requirements result in a large information loss, our model could at least provide an aggregate result that might be useful to the consumer, instead of returning a useless set of records. For example, a recommender app might be able to continue functioning even in the presence of intermittent aggregate statistics instead of more granular data.

To further specify the model, we decided to use a privacy-negotiation environment such as the one proposed by Ukil et al. in [2], and take some other elements from their model. The constraints resulting from the application of negotiated parameters to a given set of data to be published provide us with a natural source of varying requirements. For our proof of concept we use k-anonymity as the syntactic de-identification method [10], and Differential Privacy (DP) [6] as the statistical privacy-preserving method. Finally, as information loss metric we use the one proposed by Iyengar in 2002 [11].

The rest of the paper is organized as follows: Sect. 2 describes the proposed model; Sect. 3 presents the proof of concept prototype; Sect. 4 describes an IoT scenario for the model; and Sect. 5 presents two examples of prototype use. Finally, in Sect. 6 there is a discussion and possibilities for future work are outlined.

2   Proposed Model

Following Ukil et al. [2], our scenario considers two actors: (1) the data producer, that is, the individual that is exposing information gathered automatically by devices like sensors; and (2) the data consumer, which requests gathered IoT data for analysis.

The actors communicate through a third party broker that stores consumer data and receives, evaluates, and answers requests for access, originating with data producers. The broker is also responsible for negotiating and reaching privacy agreements between producers and consumers. This third party must have global rules incorporating local laws and good practices. For example, the release of any personally identifiable information (PII) should be excluded from any privacy agreement by default. Furthermore, depending on the privacy-preserving release method the broker must use the settings most appropriate to defend consumer privacy. For example, the model in [2] uses the rules given in Lodha et al. [12] to define the type and degree of de-identification to be applied for the syntactic anonymization methods used.

The particular negotiation agreements between each producer and consumer could be coded as complex rules over data semantics, or be as simple as permissions given over data attributes, which is the approach used in [2]. Their rule representation is an access matrix that relates all the relevant attributes to specific data consumers using a single permission flag.

After privacy agreements have been set up, the high-level view of our model is that data consumers will query the broker for data belonging to a group of data producers. The broker will first check if the data requested could be provided under any global rules, and, if so, will query its aggregate producer database. The table resulting from this query will then be syntactically anonymized [7] (for example, with k-anonymity) using the particular rules triggered by the consumers that are part of this particular response. Once the anonymization is complete, an information loss metric would be calculated. If the data loss is within the threshold negotiated with the consumer, the anonymized table is sent. Otherwise, a set of aggregate statistical descriptors is calculated from the original resulting table using a privacy-preserving method (for example Differential Privacy), and the set of statistical descriptors is sent as response to the data consumer. This way, some useful information is still returned to the consumer.

3 Proof of Concept Prototype

As proof of concept for the model we implemented a prototype in which we use k-anonymization [10] as the syntactical model, and Differential Privacy (DP) [9] as the statistical anonymity model. In particular, for k-anonymization, we used a simple implementation locally developed, and for DP, we used PINQ, the McSherry implementation [13]. As the information loss metric we used the one proposed by Iyengar [11] because it works on generalization hierarchies.

The prototype does not currently collect data from producers and consumers, and neither executes negotiation processes. Instead, it feeds on a given dataset, a given agreement set, and reads the parameters for the global rules. Given the restrictions imposed by the McSherry implementation, the dataset is stored in a Microsoft SQL Server. The logical architecture for the prototype is shown in Fig. 1.

To represent privacy agreements between consumers and producers we use a matrix similar to the one in [2], but the semantics of the permission flag is taken as a permission to include in a syntactical result. That is, if a producer sets the flag to 0 on a specific attribute for a given consumer, that attribute for that producer could not be included in an anonymized table independently of the degree of k. The matrix is filled using a simple user interface, as the negotiation process in itself is outside the scope of this paper. Given

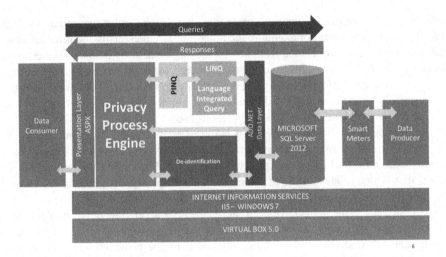

Fig. 1. Prototype logical architecture

the matrix semantic, the information loss is calculated in two phases: the first one after eliminating all records of users that were not willing to share an attribute required by the query, and the second one after applying k-anonymization to the remaining records. For the first one the information loss is calculated as the percentage of deleted records with regard to the total returned by the query. In the second phase, Iyengar's information loss is applied as if the remaining records were the original dataset. Somewhat arbitrarily, both losses are added to calculate total loss before deciding what to return to the consumer.

The global privacy rules included were: (1) The elimination of PIIs; (2) A given classification of non-PII attributes in quasi-identifiers and sensitive data; (3) A choice of k by the prototype operator for k-anonymization; (4) A choice of DP parameters by the operator (epsilon and privacy budget); and (5) A choice of information loss threshold for each consumer. Rule 1 is executed manually. For rule 2, the respective columns are marked in advance. Values for rules 3, 4, and 5 are read through several interfaces.

The interfaces were implemented in ASP.NET, using Microsoft Internet Information Services 7 on Microsoft Windows 7 Professional and running on an Oracle Virtual Box engine version 5.0.16. The whole process is encapsulated in the same ASP.NET application, using the C# class library as well and invoking PINQ 0.1.0.0 and LINQ 4.0.0.0 libraries and ADO.NET 4 to finally access the MS SQL Server 2008 R2

The process followed by our proof of concept is depicted in Fig. 2. It starts with a data consumer making a data request (1). This request generates a query, and the data resulting from the application of the query is then analyzed using the attribute access matrix, and filtering all the records that must be removed from the query as determined by the application of the privacy rules generated during the negotiation (2). After this reduction, the data loss is computed as a percentage of records lost with respect to the original query answer (3). If the data loss threshold is reached (4), a set of predefined statistical descriptors are calculated on the original query response using a DP implementation (5) and delivered to the Data Consumer as response (11). Otherwise (4), the filtered response is de-identified using – again - the applicable privacy-preserving rules (6) and the data loss (Iyengar) for this process is calculated (7) added to the loss of the first filtering process (8), and compared against the data loss threshold (9). If this integrated loss estimation reaches the threshold, the set of statistical descriptors of the original query is calculated using a DP implementation (5) and delivered to the Data Consumer as response (10).

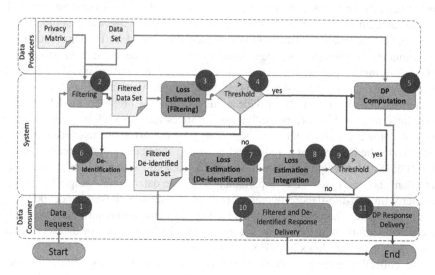

Fig. 2. Protection method selection process.

To determine the feasibility of the proposed model, we describe a possible IoT application scenario, then choose a real dataset that fits the proposed scenario, implement a prototype and show its use for a simple, and then a larger case.

4 An IoT Scenario for the Model

The composite data collected from IoT sensors and devices in different households has the potential to create unexpected (and unwanted) disclosures. For example, Greveler et al. [14], presents a case where energy consumption data transmitted to the service and application support layer, allows intrusive identification about devices located inside the households of data producers (TV set, refrigerator, toaster, oven). For example, depending on the frequency of analysis of the electricity usage profile (for instance at a 0.5 – 1 s sample rate) the data can reveal what channel a TV set in the household is displaying. Therefore, something that at first sight looks inoffensive, like taking part into an electricity consumption survey, could reveal information that the house owner might not have wanted to share. Despite the huge importance and knowledge that can be generated understanding consumption patterns for power at home, data collected from these devices can also be used as a surveillance tool.

Given the findings in [14], the scenario in which we situate the model is electricity consumption data. Each sensor sends its data to servers over the Internet, which in turn uses the data to show users their current energy consumption and estimate the monthly bill on a real-time basis. The data producer is the application that reads the sensor and sends the data it produces over the Internet. The data owner, and by extension the producer, is the user that installed the sensor: possibly the inhabitant of the house. The value for the producer of sending the data is the possibility to use the energy resources more efficiently or to get access to new technologies that could improve living. To execute calculations, the application requires permission to sense the data of all appliances in the household. Analysis of the sensed data could be used to recommend improvements to other users of the system. Furthermore, the application will need to process information gathered from different households on a particular region. The data could be very detailed and enable the profiling of people living in the house.

This paper only intends to provide evidence that the proposed model could be instantiated in a working prototype, but not yet investigate its usefulness in real environments. However, given that next step, to test the prototype, we used the collection published by the Department of Industry, Innovation and Science of Australian Government (DIIS) under the project name "Sample household electricity time of use data", that can be accessed in http://data.nsw.gov.au/data/dataset/sample-household-electricity-time-of-use-data/resource/ed7aaa03-6282-4254-9dcb-0e80bc6dc90d?
inner_span=True. The objective of DIIS for this project was to ensure that households have enough information to improve the use of electricity network. The dataset contains 10,828,120 energy readings for 808 several types of users.

The collection includes electricity use (in kwh) measured approximately every 30 min for a year using a smart meter to collect this information. It also provides basic demographic information, that could be used to infer customers. Customer demographic information includes customer ID (that allows to create a relationship between consumption and customer), address region, income range, appliances in house, people in house, and others. As mentioned before, with just the electricity consumption, it can be determined what appliances are being used in the household.

5   Examples of Model Application

The first example is presented to provide a step-by-step description of the model application. Table 1 shows a 18-record hypothetical result table (we proceed directly to the processing after the Privacy Broker has extracted the raw data corresponding to the consumer request).

Suppose we also have a previously negotiated matrix of data access for a given data consumer from each of the data providers. The matrix contains a column for each quasi-identifier (QI), and a value of 0 or 1 indicating whether the user is willing to share the QI in a release or not. The matrix is shown in Table 2.

Table 1. Example result table.

Cust. Id	County	Sex	Age	Reading Value	Outlet
1	101	M	47	393	TV
2	101	F	42	423	TV
3	101	F	55	231	TV
4	101	M	49	554	TV
5	103	M	31	334	TV
6	102	M	42	676	TV
7	103	F	29	445	TV
8	101	F	25	332	TV
9	102	M	43	553	TV
10	103	M	44	445	TV
11	103	F	29	765	TV
12	102	F	57	432	TV
13	101	F	47	113	TV
14	101	M	31	455	TV
15	103	M	57	321	TV
16	102	M	33	334	TV
17	103	F	34	654	TV
18	103	F	54	442	TV

Table 2. Example privacy matrix

Customer Id	County	Sex	Age
1	1	1	1
2	1	1	1
3	1	0	1
4	0	1	0
5	1	1	1
6	1	1	0
7	1	1	1
8	0	0	0
9	1	1	1
10	1	1	1
11	1	1	1
12	1	0	0
13	0	0	1
14	1	1	1
15	1	1	0
16	1	1	1
17	1	1	1
18	1	0	0

The resulting table has to be filtered against the preset values from the privacy matrix shown in Table 2. In this case, a total of 8 records must be removed from the result table, since those data producers will not allow to show information for at least one of the requested columns. The records that must be removed are shown with a shadow on them.

The first information loss calculation is just the number of removed records divided by the total number of records that should be considered. For this particular case the loss for the first pass is 0.444. For a 0.5 threshold, the de-identification process has to proceed.

To provide k = 2 k-anonymity the quasi-identifiers were categorized as follows: County: 100 to 101, and 102 to 103; Sex: * (suppressed); Age (years): less than 32, 32 to less than 40, 40 to less than 48, 48 to less than 56, 56 to less than 64, and 64 and more. Any combination of these quasi-identifiers ranges provides 2 or more records, accomplishing the $k = 2$ requirement. The information loss metric was calculated for this as 0.44. Table 3 shows the 2-anonymized data.

Table 3. Result of filtering the data in Table 1 given the restrictions in Table 2. Using k = 2 k-anonymity. ID is an identifier value, QI are quasi-identifiers.

ID	QI	QI	QI	DATA	DATA
Customer Id	County	Sex	Age	Reading_Value	Outlet
*	[100,101]	*	[40–48[	393	TV
*	[100,101]	*	[40–48[	423	TV
*	[100,101]	*	[0–32[	334	TV
*	[102,103]	*	[0–32[	445	TV
*	[102,103]	*	[40–48[	553	TV
*	[102,103]	*	[40–48[	445	TV
*	[102,103]	*	[0–32[	765	TV
*	[100,101]	*	[0–32[	455	TV
*	[102,103]	*	[32–40[	334	TV
*	[102,103]	*	[32–40[	654	TV

Adding both information loss metrics, it results in a value of 0.95, exceeding the preset threshold of 0.5. So in this particular case, the privacy selection process had to deliver DP aggregated functions to the data consumer. For the purpose of showing the noise induced by DP, six consecutive answers are shown in Table 4.

Table 4. Results from DP computation for 6 identical requests performed by the data consumer. Data Request = Information from all records that County equals {101, 102,103} and Outlet = 'TV'

•	Request Nbr	1	2	3	4	5	6	Actual data
•	Record count	16.00	20.00	15.00	16.00	19.00	15.00	**18.00**
Age	Percentile 25	28.00	26.00	33.00	30.00	26.00	27.00	**31.00**
	Percentile 50	43.50	42.50	41.50	47.50	43.50	37.50	**42.50**
	Percentile 75	48.25	53.25	50.25	48.25	50.25	45.25	**50.25**
Reading Value	Percentile 25	330.50	331.50	335.50	330.50	335.50	332.50	**333.50**
	Percentile 50	437.00	436.00	435.00	439.00	435.00	438.00	**333.50**
	Percentile 75	554.25	552.25	551.25	554.25	556.25	551.25	**333.50**
•	Sum	7,794.00	7,545.00	7,068.00	6,945.00	6,481.00	5,787.00	**7,902.00**

As it could be seen, instead of delivering a nearly useless de-identified dataset to the consumer, a set of statistical descriptors was provided, partially preserving utility for a hypothetical consumer application.

For the second example, we chose to use the energy readings for the retail/domestic users of the DIIS database (a total of 222 users and 8,908,454 registers), with the attributes Customer Identification, Region Name, Reading Time, Appliance Name, and Reading Value. An example record is (10036802, CANTERBURY, 2013-11-14

03:37:59, TV, 202.242). The DIIS dataset information is published in CSV format, and the data was imported to a Microsoft SQL Server for the prototype.

Attribute Customer Identification is a direct identifier, so it is not included in the negotiation, and it is automatically suppressed from any result. Attributes Reading Time and Reading Value are assumed to be the sensitive values, and Region Name and Appliance Name are the ones taken to be the quasi-identifiers and therefore included in the negotiation.

As an approximation to the negotiation values reflected by the matrix, we used the classification of privacy concern given by Humphrey Taylor based on a telephone survey by Harris Poll, conducted on a USA nationwide cross section of 1,010 adults [15]. Taylor concludes that 26% of respondents were "privacy fundamentalists", 10% were "privacy unconcerned", and 64% were "privacy pragmatists". Based on this classification, around 26% of the 222 users (58) were randomly assigned with a negative decision on the sharing of both quasi-identifiers, around 10% of the users had a positive sharing decision on both quasi-identifiers (22), and the remaining approximately 64% of the population (142 users) were assigned random decision values for the quasi-identifiers (all positive, one of them positive, both negative).

For the test, we assumed a data consumer query for the electrical readings of 22 users (10%) randomly chosen users in the week between the 8 and 15 of February of 2014. The privacy matrix of each of those users revealed 8 users with a do-not-share preference, 4 asserting a use-everything preference, and 10 users that allowed access to one attribute but not the other. In this test the filtering interprets the matrix as "do not communicate anything from users with both attributes hidden", so we remove all the records belonging to the do-not-share users which correspond to 12,863 out of a total of 23,610 readings for this query. Therefore, the first-step total data loss was slightly over 35%, which is still within the preset threshold. Afterwards, a k = 60 anonymization was performed, and the loss metric (LM) was calculated as 0.118. Combining this with the first-step, the combined loss is still below 50% so we communicate the anonymized results to the data consumer.

6   Discussion and Future Work

We have proposed a hybrid model to deliver data with privacy protections to consumers, and presented a particular implementation just to test its feasibility. Both the model and the prototype provide us with a flexibility in the semantic of the negotiation, the application of either semantic or statistical anonymization.

Taking into account the high volume of data generated by IoT, and that this data could have traces of private information that producers are not aware of, it is important to provide privacy protection. Privacy negotiation might provide usable methods of accomplishing this goal. To satisfy not only data producer but also data consumer requirements, in this paper DP is added to the negotiation model to be able to provide some utility in constrained settings, without sacrificing privacy. An implementation of this design was shown.

Extending DP implementations like PINQ could help to adhere this privacy protection layers to different contexts. So far, PINQ has few aggregated computations (count, sum, average, statistic order and median), and even when DP seems to have increased its application in different scenarios recently, Microsoft left behind new implementations for PINQ, and even when current version 0.1 is fully functional, it lacks of many other functions to provide even more utility to the data consumers. It was last released back in 2009, but it is still downloadable from the Microsoft official web site and it is supported in Windows 10, their latest operating system.

It would be very valuable if the attribute two-dimensional matrix, could be improved to a multidimensional matrix that can represent not only data fields and consumers with binary resolutions, but also consider time, purpose of queries, data age, etc. Also, settings could be more than just 1's and 0's, but adding different levels, for instance, k values (k-anonymity parameter) and/or epsilon and privacy budget (DP parameters) values.

There are many complexities involved in the application of hybrid models. It is not known, for example, if–in the long run- the intermittent application of each would lead to unintended disclosures. This is a well-known problem for any hybrid model, and needs to be studied in this case.

A less theoretical, but equally important issue is to be able to establish if the data that a statistical model returns to the data consumer would be useful at all, that is, would reduce the negative impact of this privacy protection. Acceptance from reasonable data consumers is important for the dissemination of these models.

On a different level, for the test case we made many assumptions, so it is necessary to experimentally explore what would be the effect of different queries on the threshold. For example, what percentage of the time the prototype returns a k-anonymized dataset instead of a DP summary. This requires a careful tuning of the k and the threshold to reflect more realistic values.

Acknowledgements. This work was partially supported by the Programa de Posgrado en Computación e Informática (PCI), the Escuela de Ciencias de la Computación e Informática (ECCI), the Centro de Investigaciones en Tecnologías de la Información y Comunicación (CITIC), and the Sistema de Estudios de Posgrado (SEP) all at the Universidad de Costa Rica (UCR), the Ministerio de Ciencia, Tecnología y Telecomunicaciones (MICITT), and by the Consejo Nacional para Investigaciones Científicas y Tecnológicas (CONICIT) of the Government of Costa Rica.

References

1. Cisco: Cisco Visual Networking Index: Global Mobile Data Traffic Forecast Update, 2015 – 2020. White Paper, Cisco (2016)
2. Ukil, A., Bandyopadhyay, S., Joseph, J., Banahatti, V., Lodha S.: Negotiation-based privacy preservation scheme in internet of things platform. In: Proceedings of the First International Conference on Security of Internet of Things, pp. 75–84. ACM, New York (2012)
3. Yusuf, S.: Survey of Publish Subscribe Communication System. Technical report, Department of Computer Science, Kent State University (2004)

4. Zyskind, G., Nathan, O., Pentland A.: Decentralizing privacy: using blockchain to protect personal data. In: Binnig C., Dageville, B. (eds.) Proceedings of the 2015 IEEE Security and Privacy Workshops (SPW 2015), pp 180-184. IEEE Computer Society, Washington, DC (2015)
5. Cormode, G., Srivastava, D.: Anonymized data. In: Proceedings of the 2009 ACM SIGMOD International Conference on Management of Data (SIGMOD 2009), pp. 1015–1018. ACM, New York (2009)
6. Angiuli, O., Blitzstein, J., Waldo, J.: How to de-identify your data. Queue 13(8), 1–20 (2015)
7. Clifton, C., Tassa, T.: On syntactic anonymity and differential privacy. Trans. Data Priv. 6(2), 161–183 (2013)
8. Dinur, I., Nissim, K.: Revealing information while preserving privacy. In: Proceedings of the Twenty-Second ACM SIGMOD-SIGACT-SIGART Symposium on Principles of Database Systems (PODS 2003), pp. 202–210. ACM, New York (2003)
9. Dwork, C.: Differential privacy. In: Bugliesi, M., Preneel, B., Sassone, V., Wegener, I. (eds.) ICALP 2006. LNCS, vol. 4052, pp. 1–12. Springer, Heidelberg (2006). doi: 10.1007/11787006_1
10. Sweeney, L.: k-anonymity: A Model for Protecting Privacy. Int. J. Uncertainty Fuzziness Knowl. Based Syst., 10(5), 557–570 (2002)
11. Iyengar, V.: Transforming data to satisfy privacy constraints. In: Proceedings of the Eighth ACM SIGKDD International Conference on Knowledge Discovery and Data Mining (KDD 2002), pp. 279–288. ACM, New York (2002)
12. Lodha, S., Thomas, D.: Probabilistic anonymity. In: Bonchi, F., Ferrari, E., Malin, B., Saygin, Y. (eds.) PInKDD 2007. LNCS, vol. 4890, pp. 56–79. Springer, Heidelberg (2008). doi: 10.1007/978-3-540-78478-4_4
13. McSherry, F.: Privacy integrated queries: an extensible platform for privacy-preserving data analysis. In: Proceedings of the 2009 ACM SIGMOD International Conference on Management of Data, pp. 19–30. ACM, New York (2009)
14. Greveler, U., Glösekötterz, P., Justusy, B., Loehr, D.: Multimedia content identification through smart meter power usage profiles. In: Proceedings of the International Conference on Information and Knowledge Engineering (IKE), pp. 1–8. The Steering Committee of The World Congress in Computer Science, Computer Engineering and Applied Computing (WorldComp) (2012)
15. Taylor, H.: Most people are "privacy pragmatists" who, while concerned about privacy, will sometimes trade it off for other benefits. Harris Poll. 17, 1–6 (2003)

Implicit Bias in Predictive Data Profiling Within Recruitments

Anders Persson[✉]

Division of Visual Information and Interaction, Department of Information Technology,
Uppsala University, Uppsala, Sweden
anders.persson@it.uu.se

Abstract. Recruiters today are often using some kind of tool with data mining and profiling, as an initial screening for successful candidates. Their objective is often to become more objective and get away from human limitation, such as implicit biases versus underprivileged groups of people. In this explorative analysis there have been three potential problems identified, regarding the practice of using these predictive computer tools for hiring. First, that they might miss the best candidates, as the employed algorithms are tuned with limited and outdated data. Second, is the risk of directly or indirectly discriminate candidates, or, third, failure to give equal opportunities for all individuals. The problems are not new to us, and from this theoretical analysis and from other similar work; it seems that algorithms and predictive data mining tools have similar kinds of implicit biases as humans. Our human limitations, then, does not seem to be limited to us humans.

Keywords: Data mining · Social exclusion · Discrimination · Implicit bias · Recruitment · Big Data · People Analytics · Machine-learning

1 Introduction

How can a company looking for a specific person for a specific role find the most likely candidate to succeed among thousands of applicants? This is a problem facing many recruiters that are either headhunting, or have a job advertisement for popular positions, with often 500–1000 applicants applying for a single job.

To meet this challenge, recruiters within many firms and organizations use profiling to screen applicants for the most promising candidates. Typically it is used as an initial big cut, where some candidates later will be interviewed and evaluated in more detail. Today, this initial big cut of candidates is often made "automatically", by an algorithm, with the selection based on a set of values. This is a technological feat that simplifies the life of a recruiter tremendously, and really can be seen as a necessary advancement to meet the conditions of hundreds and thousands of applicants for single positions, in today's job market.

What companies' uses are more specifically is data mining: machine learning with algorithms and statistical learning. This if often referred to as using "Big Data", or "People Analytics"; i.e. using large datasets to identify parameters that represents the

A. Lehmann et al. (Eds.): Privacy and Identity 2016, IFIP AICT 498, pp. 212–230, 2016.
DOI: 10.1007/978-3-319-55783-0_15

best candidates for various positions. The motivation for companies is often the claim to become more *objective* in their assessment [1, 2]. They can also be claimed to want to become more *certain* in their decision making for hiring. But what consequences does this reliance on technology have on the process of selecting and discarding applicants?

Let us start by taking a step back; if there are no other means at the recruiters and managers disposal to make judgements, they will have to rely on their *intuition*. Field-expert's intuition can very well be very good and accurate for making estimations within their specific area of expertise, but they will nevertheless be estimations based on subjective value assessment, and at times faulty. There is also the problem of *discrimination*, even without conscious intent. Today this is controlled by equal opportunities law; it is illegal to (explicitly) discriminate based on categories such as skin color, ethnicity, gender and age (and to some extent avoid also implicit discrimination). Yet, even with such countermeasures in place, discrimination seems to remain. As Pager and Shepherd exemplifies: "today discrimination is less readily identifiable, posing problems for social scientific conceptualization and measurement" [3]. This is often explained as the unconscious phenomenon of implicit bias.

1.1 Implicit Bias and Predictive Machines

More generally, implicit bias is often referred to as unconscious associations. This is what could lead to so-called *stereotype threats*; to attribute certain abilities and predicted behavior to generalized categories of people. For example, several studies have examined how different individuals judge a written application, as a resume or CV [4, 5]. The only independent variable in the studies has been the name of the applicant; either native or foreign sounding, alternatively a name associated to a minority group. In USA as well as in Sweden, an applicant with a native name is much more likely to be called to an interview, than one with a foreign name, even if their resumes were identical, and their merits therefore should have been identical.

There is a similar effect for hiring women to management positions. An illuminating example of the effect of how implicit bias could work is the following:

"There is good news and bad news about actual gender-related managerial differences. The good news is that some do exist. The bad news is that they are overused as the basis for sexual stereotyping" [6].

This might be a controversial finding, that there seemed to be a difference between female and male performance related to management positions. However, the authors also note that the difference is overused in recruitment. This is very much what can be seen happening when over-categorizing. While there might be a difference in performance, the difference is neither black and white, nor clear-cut. Yet it continues to affect diversity, and remains as an obstacle for diversity and equality.

I will exemplify this further with a more concrete example (see Subsect. 3.5 about predictive brains), but let us first get back to the machines and algorithms that try to predict the likely performance of applicants for a job position. Barocas and Selbst [2] argue that an analysis and an algorithm are never better than the dataset on which they are based; if the dataset is biased, so will the result be. Data sets are, just as in empirical science, historical data, which may themselves be laden with implicit biases of a discriminatory nature. Thus, even if there is no explicit rule or class inferences made in the algorithm to look for sensitive categories, the result from the algorithm may still be (implicitly) biased.

One example of this is in plain view; our language and our use of lexical words. Within our semantic use of words, implicit association tests (IAT) show how we, for example, associate the word "dangerous" more to "black", rather than "white" (mainly in a context of US). This can feel troublesome, if you discover an implicit bias in yourself, and there are several IAT's on the web that anyone can use to investigate their own implicit biases. When it comes to machine learning and algorithms, a standard use is keyword-associations, and pure statistical learning. What Caliskan-Islam et al. [7] show is that when running IAT's on algorithms such as these, they show similar kind of implicit biases as humans do. It makes sense, if you accept Barocas and Selbst [2] message that an analysis is never better than the data set, and if there are (historical) biases embedded, as there seems to be in language, the results of this kind of machine-learning algorithms will also be biased.

But, discrimination is punishable by law, you might object, and has been for quite a while in most western countries. However, as you may already have realized from the section above, the use of algorithms is technically quite complicated, and their effects are not at all transparent. Therefore, there are currently holes in the available laws, allowing some types of biased machine-based profiling, for example of applicants and employees. I will discuss if better laws could solve this, such as those that are under way in EU (see Subsect. 4.2), and I will also discuss solutions involving "better" algorithms and machine learning techniques (see Subsect. 4.1).

Solution with human thinking. My main claim in this paper, however, is that it is necessary to look deeper on the human side of the equation. Behind all the use of algorithms and computers, there is at least at some stage, a human considering a selection of applicants, or making a decision. Another approach could be to try to stimulate better thinking, with the use of assistive technological tools, and I will make an initial exploration if lessons from methodology of science can be used. As mentioned above, when using machines and data, there is often a perception that you gain certainty and objectivity; cold hard facts, if you like, that are mined from the ground like minerals [8]. Science, however, would hold that what you need is *uncertainty* and *doubt*, and to always be open minded to question, critique, and try to falsify what you think is true. Empirical conclusions in science are, in other words, never facts set in stone, but always changing and open to new interpretations and new explanations.

1.2 Methodology and Disposition

There is an inherent problem in this sphere of investigation: companies using Big Data and data profiling. Namely that currently there are insufficient laws to force them to disclose their processes, or algorithms. As Frank Pasquele names it, we currently very much live in "The Black Box Society" [9], where we do not know what algorithms and technologies are affecting us. In lack of empirical data concerning the effects on society, what are left are either journalistic endeavors trying to peek into those black boxes, or theoretical works, looking at the mechanism of the algorithms that we at least to some extent know to be at work in the background.

The latter is my approach in this paper, and in Sect. 2 I start by looking into the mechanisms within machine learning and data profiling. This is continued with an analysis of potential problem, in Sect. 3, and a continued discussion follows in Sect. 4, in which I also propose different solutions and remedies to tackle the problems at hand. The methodological limitation of limited empirical data in this sphere is addressed more in the ending sections.

2   Organizations Using Big Data

The term *Big Data* is fairly new, but the phenomenon behind it is not necessarily as new. Broadly speaking, it concerns the acquisition of useable, meaningful data, out of larger data set, with the emphasis of the scale of the data set, or multiple data sets. This can also be called *data mining,* and they remain closely related [8]. Another term that is ubiquitous within the domain is *machine learning*, which focuses on using algorithms that "learn" to identify patterns for classification, from training data. Data Profiling is a more specific term within data management, and is defined as: "a specific kind of data analysis used to discover and characterize important features of the data sets. Profiling provides a picture of the data structure, content, rules and relationships, by applying statistical methodologies to return a set of standard characteristics about data" [10].

In other words, what you get and can use from data mining and profiling is much like data from empirical, statistical research. What the different fields also have in common is that they mainly look for patterns in the data/training set; in much the same manner as a speculative scientist could do to generate hypotheses from empirical data.

The usage of big data and data mining is widespread. According to a survey in North America in 2014, 73% of companies stated they had invested, or planned to, invest in Big Data analytic tools [11]. Larger employers today are, almost, forced into using some kind of Internet-based management systems for handling job applications, either themselves or through an external agency. In such systems, they typically use Applicant Tracking Systems (ATS), to electronically manage information [12]. From this, it is a small to also rank applicants, and typically present only the select few applicants that are deemed to be the best fit, for recruiters and managers. The rest are, in other words, disregarded and never considered by anyone but the machine and the ranking system. Below I give a glimpse into the kind of parameters that can be used in ranking systems like these, with an example of Xerox looking for customer service personnel.

2.1   Example of Xerox Using Data Profiling

Xerox is a global business services company with over 130,000 employees within various technological fields, as well as organizational development. An important element in their business model is customer service support. To manage their human-resources within this field they have implemented big data analyses. One explicit performance value that they look for in a candidate is *longevity* within the company, as in how long a person stays within the employer [13]. The motivation is often that longevity of workers builds organization-specific knowledge over time, and it is important that this stays within the company. As an analytic tool they have been using Evolv, currently part of a larger platform called Cornerstone OnDemand [14].

Xerox state that they put applicants through a series of tests to predict how they would perform within customer service [13]. This is later followed up in regards to performance measures, such as longevity. Evolv claim to have "500 million points of employment data on over 3 million employees" (see Christl and Spiekerman [15] for a more detailed overview of software used in hiring today). Part of the tests are surveys regarding attitudes towards work, such as how long they are willing to travel/commute to work, and how much overtime per week they would be willing to work. Additional information is also gathered from CV's.

Four measures were correlated with longevity: (1) Willingness to work 1–3 h overtime per week, 15 times more likely, (2) Applicants with bachelor's degrees stay 5% longer, and those with technical diplomas stay 26% longer, than those with high school diplomas, (3) Those that have had a customer service job where they have had to use empathy, rather than just taking orders, and, finally, (4) living closer to job, or having reliable transportation [13].

It is also claimed that their ideal customer worker is someone that (1) scores well at typing tests, to be better at taking in background documentation on clients, (2) is creative, and (3) uses social media (but not too much). It is unclear how this data is correlated to performance [13].

The result here is a profile, with a set of variables and parameters (a pattern), which human-resource management use as a predictor of performance and how well an applicant fits for the position considered. In other words, someone that lives further away from the working place, only has a high school diploma, and does not use social media very much or at all; ends up with a low predictor and is likely to be cut at an early stage in the hiring process.

Some also propose using data mining profiles together with expert systems, to help make the selection of applicant [16]. This could be done with more or less automation, either by giving suggestions to a recruiter (a suggestion the recruiter is probably likely to follow), or by the system itself making initial selections. As mentioned above with ATS's, this process of profiling was previously more manual, and is today highly automated.

No example has been found of recruiters using content data extracted from social media to include in a job profile predictor. However, a study in Sweden showed that at least half of the interviewed recruiters in big and middle-sized organizations did scan applicant social media profiles themselves, at some point before hiring [17]. In the survey they stated they looked for risk behaviors, where the applicant shared the organization's values, and things that might damage a company's reputation. It would not be a difficult step to include data from publicly, obtainable, social media profiles of applicants, and make a keywords-association analysis to (try to) capture potential risk behavior.

This gets us into an even more intricate sphere of privacy and the use of personal data, and it will expand the ways in which a person can be unfairly disregarded and discriminated. However, it may be enough to look at the data that an applicant has to include in a resume, as I will argue for in this paper.

On the face of it, when it comes to unfairness, social exclusion and discrimination, it is important to look for diversity, and if you like, uniqueness. This term is also used in data profiling, which I will consider next.

2.2 Uniqueness in Data Profiling

An important concept with data profiling is *uniqueness*. Technically understood, one value for a parameter, or a set of values for a set of parameters, has maximum uniqueness when there are no other sets of values like it. Non-uniqueness is achieved when two or more sets of values are all the same, which is the strongest kind of pattern and correlation.

Translated to a dataset of applicants and their level of academic degree, it would mean that maximum uniqueness is achieved when every candidate has a different level. On the other hand, if, for example, a test of programming skills is included in the dataset, maximum uniqueness would be when every individual has a different test score. This might become a bit more complicated when you have numbers with decimals, and in general higher uniqueness when there are a greater number of possible values. The principle, however, remains the same: that minimal uniqueness will be acquired when (groups of) individuals are (nearly) identical.

Taking the same dataset and looking at a relation between variables of programming skills, as a performance measure, and academic degree, *minimal uniqueness* is achieved if all individuals with high programming skills also are at a *certain level of degree*. This would make these easy to identify; just by looking at their academic degree it would be possible to tell something about their programming skills. On the other hand, if programming skills and academic degree are *not well correlated* but varies greatly, with good and bad programmer within all degrees, then *uniqueness is high*.

What does this mean for a recruiter who is looking at applicants and wants to find the best fit, given the motivation that you want to be as certain as possible? On one hand, you would like to be able to make the clearest distinction between, for example, a high and low performer. That you would get by having low uniqueness: if all low performers have a high school diploma, and all high performers have a bachelor's degree, the inference is easy to make, solely by looking at academic achievement. On the other hand, having high uniqueness will give you a much more narrow set of candidates that may be the *best fit*, and be able to disregard a larger portion of applicants. The latter likely depends on having a profile with a specialized pattern of skills and parameters.

3 Analysis of Potential Problems

Using profiles to cut a large portion of applicants might be seen as an efficient way of siphoning out the candidates less likely to perform well, and consequently a mere "fair and square" competition between applicants. Overall, employers and companies should be able to perform better, with more people in the right positions. Companies like Xerox also report results going upwards after using data profiling for hiring [13].

I will start by analyzing some potential problems in the use of data profiling as described above. Initially, there might be a problem of effectiveness, and long-term performance, and I will use the conceptualization of local optimums. Secondly, and thirdly, I will get to the problems that are of more concern in this paper; regarding discrimination and unfairness. Further on in this section I will look at some initial technological remedies to the problems, with re-profiling, which seem to deepen the problems at hand.

3.1 Local Optimums and Stagnation

An ongoing research question within product development concerns innovation and success in different economic contexts. To shed light on this matter, some have applied an evolutionary perspective, and something called a fitness landscape [18]. This is related to the theory of evolution, in the sense that you make an analogy to which "ideas" will survive and progress, and will have the best fitness for a specific environment. Within this concept you can also make a difference between local and global maximums, and this related to what machine learning call optimums as I will henceforth use. To explain it further; an organism, with certain attributes at its disposal (a certain genotype), adapting to a certain environment, is theorized to sooner or later end up on a local peak (performance) optimization, for that specific environment and context.

Related to humans and organizations, this could mean that given a certain type of workforce you will end up at a certain level of performance. Within your own workforce you should with a large enough dataset also be able to observe different peaks. This could probably be done in larger organizations with (big) data analyses, or large collections of data points as in the program Evolv and Cornerstone (see Subsect. 2.1). You would then typically want to identify where the peak performances are, and spread *the type of abilities* that those people have to other positions in the same occupation. To put it differently; you would like to have the profile of peak performers in all relevant positions, given the current conditions.

However, when changing to a different environment, the same set of optimized abilities may not be as effective or competitive, compared to other sets of abilities. The same thing happens in the natural environment with highly specialized organism. If you change their environment, they might not be able to adapt, and dies out. The data that is used to make job profiles, like all data in empirical research; it is historical data. They do not really say anything about the future, and they only say what worked well in that historical context/environment.

This could be problematic, given that the global market, influenced by people and societies all around the globe, can involve quickly changing conditions for success. This is a problem for any use of profiling, of course, not just data mined. I will discuss a potential solution with re-profiling below (Sect. 3.4), and get back to this problem in Sect. 4.

3.2 Problem with Discrimination

The most ethically relevant problem is probably that of discrimination in the selection process. As mentioned in the introduction, discrimination is controlled by legislation in most countries, and is usually defined as: "the treatment of a person or particular group of people differently, in a way that is worse than the way people are usually treated" [19]. Expressed in a different way, it is about judging people based on things like social group categories, rather than individual merit. Most commonly this is an issue about features such as: (1) gender, (2) ethnical background, and (3) sexual orientation.

It is important to note that discrimination can be direct and based on discriminatory categories, such as those mentioned. It can also be indirect; a selection based on non-discriminatory categories, which, however, are strongly correlated to the discriminatory ones.

There are, for example, reports of companies scanning employee's health records, to predict those likely to get on sick-leave, or those that might be pregnant [20]. Why this is possible, and not an offence, currently, is highlighted in discussing solution with law and regulation (see Subsect. 4.2).

3.3 Unfairness and Loss of Opportunities

A more general problem and much related to discrimination, is simply *unfairness* in the selection process, and a *loss of opportunity* for those who deviate from (outliers) the resulting profile. That is, this is the individuals that differ from the norm of the (predicted) most likely high performers, but who in reality still is just as likely to perform at the same level. This is likely to occur, given the premise that measures for the applicants have statistical normal distributions. To use the example of Xerox (see Subsect. 2.1), it is unlikely that *all* applicants with high school diplomas would perform worse than *all* the applicants with a bachelor's degree.

This is to some extent related to uniqueness in data profiling. Given that if the more informative measures related to performance will have lower uniqueness, they will also be less forgiving towards outliers. Those outliers could be seen as losing an opportunity, and this loss could be an ethical problem of *social exclusion*.

It is important to note, though, that we would probably not perceive it as unfair if other candidates in fact had stronger merits, but it would be perceived as unfair if you are excluded based on something not directly associated as a merit for the position. Xerox was, for example, looking for people with mid-range social media use, for a position in customer service. Using social media is not, at least, directly related to the task that they are expected to do, but apparently it might be indirectly related to a performance measure. It could possibly exclude applicants solely based on not using social media, or not using it enough. Given that people are adapting to the demands of the job markets they want to get into, it might mean that people will have to conform their private life, as well.

3.4   Reprofiling for Quality of Data

One approach to remedy some of the problems just mentioned might be to simply seek better quality of the data. It could be claimed that the problems of local optimums could be avoided if the profiles were continuously updated to reflect what kind of workers are needed at a specific moment in time. Even more so, if the quality of the (meaningful) data extracted from the big data set is good enough, and detailed enough, it should be possible to pick out those individual outliers who nevertheless are performing at a high level.

This does not seem to be an unreasonable claim, but it might be problematic in practice. As I will show further down, the process of applying a profile might reduce all the outliers. I will also relate to this process to intuition and implicit bias in the next subsection.

Data quality is first and foremost an issue when it comes to, so to speak, living data sets that change over time (such as what correlates with performance within a certain organization on renewed global markets). To remedy this, most data sets can benefit from what is called *reprofiling;* a new analysis of the dataset to see if statistical patterns and relations have changed [10].

However, a risk, as far as I can analyze it, is that rather than including outliers it might exclude them further. Let us say that we mine out a profile P1, with features such as those that Xerox are looking for in customer service personal. You then choose people based on profile P1 to be added to the workforce for the specific occupation, and then re-profile on this new population with the new selection of individuals added, yielding a profile P2.

If nothing significant has changed in regards to what measures are correlated to high performance between P1 and P2, the added employees will have reinforced the pattern, which statistically will become "stronger", as in, having less deviations from means, and lower p-values. This will most likely mean that P2 would be even less forgiving to outliers, unless your data analysis is detailed enough. Big organizations like Xerox with abundant resources at their hand might be able to make the profiles detailed enough, but would probably be difficult for others.

Revisiting Local Optimums. So, what does this then mean for the problem of ending up on low local peaks of performance in changing market-environment? If profiles P1, or P2, have had any impact on the workforce, you would after some time have few outliers to rely on. With fewer outliers it will be more difficult to find the pattern for peaks of performance in a new environment. The workers who would be better suited for this new environment might simply not be left in the company.

On the face of it, then, reprofiling might not be enough to solve the problem of local optimums. I would like to note three premises for this effect to be relevant: (1) profiling and reprofiling is made on a closed group, as in not including a larger part of a specific market environment, (2) that using profile P1 actually makes the pattern P2 have lower p-values, and stronger correlations with performance measures, and (3) that the analysis is not focusing on specific, high performing outliers, but rather use the profile for generalized big cuts of applicants, like Xerox seems to use it (see Subsect. 2.1). Otherwise the theorized effect would not be there.

3.5 Human Intuition and Our Predictive Mind

As already has been touched upon in the introduction, the problem with profiling and reprofiling might not be too different from what we initially wanted to get away from; the human, intuitive way of reasoning and categorizing. The data could be biased, implicitly towards certain categorizations. What I want to propose here is that profiling and trying to predict future high performance might be even more directly related to human cognition.

An explanatory theory within neuroscience that has gained momentum lately propose that the brain essentially should be seen as a hypothesis-testing mechanism, that performs a kind of statistical analysis within the neurons [21]. From this perspective, the main goal is for the brain to be able to predict what will happen, before it happens. Within the connections between the neurons there is both a forward progressive movement; receiving input from nerve-endings, for example our eyes, to be processed in succession in the neural cortex. But there is also a backward progression, where signals are constantly being sent backwards, from higher-cognitive areas of the brain, towards lower. This has previously been explained as a kind of feedback-loop, but lately the backward progression has been given more emphasis and use to explained human cognition the other way around.

Rather than starting blank and use input to create a model of the surroundings, the human brain starts with a working model of the world that is projected backwards within our connective network; and ultimately onto the world around us. The signal input functions as an error-correction function to adjust our working model of the world, where it is needed in order to explain what is happening in a specific moment. Accordingly, no corrections of our model will be made, as long the model can explain what is going on around us.

Studies also show that the kinds of categorizations we do to learn about the world are very much like statistical analyses. We more or less make a *mirrored casual structure of the world* in our brain, based on what we have experienced [21].

All this can be related to something called *confirmation bias*, which means that humans have a tendency to direct attention, unconsciously, towards aspects which confirm our prior beliefs. In relation to the theory of our predictive mind, this would mean that in a backward loop we project a working model of the surroundings, and the attention is drawn towards that which confirms this model to be true. In a sense then, our prior beliefs and categorizations made from experience, determines what kind of information we will look for when facing a new situation; that which confirm what we already know, or believe that we know. Only when there are too much obvious errors, we start to look for a different explanation, and correct the working model. It is then also important to note that often there is insufficient feedback to correct our model when it comes to valuation of people, or groups of people, that we encounter. In the absence of sufficient errors, the working model will be reinforced; as functional to predict the outcome.

In some sense this can be related to profiling and reprofiling. After making a categorization, like for a profile, it will direct attention only to the feature you know they are related to. Even when attempting to reassess that knowledge, as in if you re-profile a population that has been modified by the previous profile, it is likely that you will end up looking at the same features. These features have then also become statistically stronger, as was hypothesized in the previous subsection and that will further reinforce your prior belief. A risk with human intuition is that prior beliefs dominates, controls your attention, and determines your future beliefs; the same risk can be found with reprofiling in data mining.

Revisiting implicit bias. What seems to happen with the described function of our predictive mind is essentially what is happening with implicit biases; namely an attempt for the brain to predict future outcomes based on previous experience and working models. As already mentioned, recruiters seem to try to predict performance of applicant, solely by looking at their names (see Subsect. 1.1, [4]). Implicitly, we seem to have working models with rough estimations, based on categorizations of people.

The delicate problem of this can perhaps be emphasized more clearly with an example of gender difference in math-skill. SAT-results in USA from 2013 show that male students performed better; an average of 531 (SD = 121) for male students, versus 499 (SD = 114) for female students (p < .001) [22]. However, given the standard deviations, and normal distribution around the mean, 38% of female participants outscored 50% of the male participants (this is illustrated in Fig. 1).

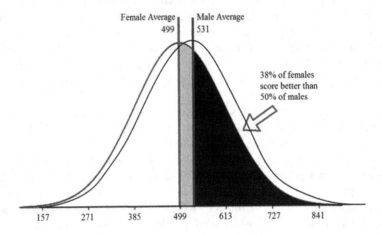

Fig. 1. Division of SAT math-test scores of 2013 in US [22]. Even if there is a significant difference in average score between genders (p < .001), 38% female student will still outperform the average male participant, statistically. This is represented by the black part of the graph.

Faced with one male and one female in front of us, and the task of selecting one we deem most likely be best in math; then the difference in score is not very informative. There is almost 40% chances to be wrong if choosing the one associated to the group with the highest mean. That is not very good odds, considering that 50% is pure chance. Despite this, most people will feel confidence in their intuition in cases like this, and gender based stereotyping and over-categorization will therefore remain. If this is anything like implicit biases it will also be difficult to get direct feedback on this implicit bias to adjust our belief, to at least not be as certain in our categorization.

This is ultimately a limitation of statistical significance measures, that even if you have as strong of a significance as you basically can get ($p < .001$), you end up with a "meaningless" knowledge. This has, of course, also been recognized by others, and a way to counter that limitation is to look for *statistical power,* or *importance;* more specifically to include a measure of effect size [23–25].

Analyzing effect size, the gender difference shown in the SAT math-test can be concluded to represent only about 3% of the difference attributed to gender, and the other 97% attributed to other factors (Choen's d = .37, effect size r-squared = .03) [22]. This would be another way, a statistical way, to say something about how informative a significant difference is, as in the situation of choosing between two applicants of different gender based on average SAT-math score.

Revisiting the customer service profile. Making an analogy between the example of SAT-math score above, and the profile measures from Xerox, it may be significantly more likely that applicants that live closer to work will on average perform better, and stay longer at the company. However, some applicants living further away might be just as likely to perform well at the job. Nonetheless, if all other parameters are the same, the one who live further away will likely not be presented to the managers that hire the new customer service personnel.

4 Possible Solutions

What I have argued for so far are potential risks for using data profiling when hiring. I have also tried to show that these are not necessarily any new risks, but can be seen in any use of profiles. It even seems to relate to the way our human intuition categorizes from experience; we try to predict future outcomes just like algorithms.

There may be different ways to try to attack the problems highlighted in the previous section; i.e. local optimums and stagnation, discrimination and unfairness. I will recapitulate some previously discussed approaches, mainly; (1) create better and more accurate algorithms and technology, and (2) introduce more extensive laws and regulations. I will add to the discussion a third approach: (3) promote better thinking for the individuals who, at some stage or another, still will be involved in the decision and selection of applicants. They are not intended to be mutually exclusive measures; on the contrary, all could contribute and be equally as important for a sustainable solution.

4.1 Solving It with Technology and Better Algorithms

An initial concept to consider is that of overfitting in machine learning. It is a term related to "fitting a model" to a training set of data, as in trying to explain the dataset, its relations, and its values. In overfitting, the statistical model has included irrelevant features, random error, or just noise, rather than only valid relationships and correlations. Consider the SAT scores discussed above; adding an analysis of effect size reduced the importance of the significant result of gender difference. You could do the same analysis of statistical power, such as looking at effect size, on a model in machine learning. What you can do after that is something called "pruning", which means, analogically, to cut off the branches of the decision tree that lack predictive power (like gender difference in the above case), which will improve the overall predictive power of the model (or pattern).

There is reason to be a bit skeptical whether this is a solution that will be implemented in practice. In psychology research, a standing advice for 25 years has been to include analyses such as effect size. Sedlemeir and Gigerenzer [24] could conclude that only 2 out of 64 experiments even mentioned power and effect size, and instead solely relied on statistical significance. Another meta-analysis concludes that statistical power has not improved significantly in the 60 years since the concept was introduced [25]. Thus, it is likely even more difficult to get employers and companies in the job market to use measures of statistical power instead of relying on (simple) significantly correlated relationships.

Including Diversity. Another way of solving the problem of discrimination could perhaps be to directly include diversity. Potentially this could also solve problems of stagnating at local maximums. If conditions in the environment change, a diversity of skills in the workforce would make a company more likely to be able to adapt. But is diversity enough to remain innovative and adaptive? Some research seems to suggest just that, where one study finds a correlation between occupational diversity and likelihood of innovative research [26], and another study finds that openness to cultural diversity was correlated with the likelihood for a company's continued economic performance, which was interpreted as being able to renew itself and to innovate [27].

Whether it would be a solution against discrimination might depend on in what categories, and how, you create diversity. However, you could at least try to account for actual differences, rather than overgeneralize. For example, let's say we have a specific task to find someone solely based on math skill. Related to the example of gender differences in SAT-math score in Subsect. 3.4, implementing diversity could be to, at least, have result distributions similar to the test scores. In other words, you would want to see about 38% female and 62% male candidates, instead of over-generalizing to only look for male applicants. Just any man will not be the most likely best mathematician.

The same thing, then, could be applied to the relation between academic degree and customer service workers within Xerox (see Subsect. 2.1). Without having specific numbers or distributions available, but based on the assumption that these will follow normal distributions, you would want to, at least, see a similar spread and diversity in the applicants that you accept. Those with bachelor's degree will be more in numbers, but not exclusively.

This could also be a possible way to open up for equal opportunities for people that are just as likely to perform well within a certain occupation, that otherwise would not have gotten the chance. In a very direct way the purpose can be said to be to not limit uniqueness too much in your data as well as with individuals, when including diversity.

If this is the case, that diversity is wanted, you could ask yourself why profiling at all. Why data profiling at all, if it is good to have a diverse workforce instead of one with certain, highlighted, high performing features? To some extent it might be a question of balancing between long-term and short-term goals. On one hand, the data probably doesn't lie, and if a company *adopts* the profile they get from current data, the company would probably perform well in the near future. On the other hand, it might become difficult to *adapt* to changing conditions, and will not perform as well long-term.

Including anonymity. Another technical solution to unfairness in selection processes could perhaps be to make applicants anonymous. This is an often proposed remedy for discrimination; to anonymize resumes [28]. Technically, it could for example be to use k-anonymity [29]; that a person is anonymized with k-other people. It could mean that applicants are anonymized with all the other (k-amount) applicants for the position; as in, removing all personally identifiable data, like names and address. It remains a problem that smart algorithms can correlate impersonal data to other databases, and still figure out who is who, but this remains a separate problem.

Anonymizing could then be a solution to unfairness, to not include categorizes of people that are laden with pre-conceptions in the evaluation and prediction of future performance. However, it seems less of a solution for some of the problems discussed so far in this paper. Like the use of academic degree, and other data that inevitably must the included in a resume and CV.

This can be discussed further; what should be considered as merits for a position? Basic qualifications should be met, of course, but should it always be in terms of an academic degree for example? Working with telephone marketing, or customer support, may have a performance measure related to academic degree, but is it really necessary? This is a bigger discussion that does not fit within the limited space for this paper. More importantly, discussed below is the use of laws that effectively could function as anonymization if the use of personal data is prohibited.

4.2 Solving It by Law

The skepticism mentioned above, regarding wether companies would really implement certain solutions, could perhaps simply be regulated by law. Currently, laws are not proficient to hinder (potentially) harmful profiling. Barocas and Selbst [2], for example, examines anti-discrimination laws in the US, and conclude there is limited support if there is no (conscious) intent involved. The "Equal Employment Opportunity Commission Uniform Guidelines", as well, does not seem to be able to hinder such analyses. Rather they seem to explicitly allow the necessity for predicting future outcomes of recruitment and employment; very much what profiling on the surface is doing [2].

Crawford [30] also notes that Big Data systems seem to have similar problems as many governmental administration systems have; like the lack of notification for affected individuals. The proposed solution is to, at least, notify an individual potentially affected to "predictive privacy harms" [30]. And if they do not agree with the use of their personal data, individuals should be able to retract it; also from the predictive algorithms that does not affect them personally.

In just a couple of years, 2018, EU will incorporate a new set of rules; the "General Data Protection Regulation" (GDPR). In it, there is a specific section (Article 22) for decision-making of individuals, including profiling. Data processing is defined as profiling when "it involves (a) automated processing of personal data; and (b) using that personal data to evaluate certain personal aspects relating to a natural person" [31]. In other words, it does not have to be yourself that the usage of your personal data affects. This would often be the case in the examples used in this paper, with personal data from previous applicant and employees that is applied on new applicants. Personal data is defined as any data that relates to a person's private, professional or public life; like a name, photo, posts on social networks, or your computer IP address.

This seems to be quite extensive, and my analysis will not go into detail of how effective they will be put into practice. I will merely note that there is an exception clause if you give consent to its use. You are still able to retract it afterwards, but on the face of it, there seems to be an opt-out implementation; as in, only those that actively opt to restrict their use of personal data, like in a consent form, will hinder the use. It is not likely a majority of people will opt-out of this kind of use, and there for there will probably still be much data to be data mined. The transparency of when you have been affected by an algorithm-based decision, is not straight forward; unless, perhaps, if you do not also adopt the notification principles as Crawford [30] proposed above.

4.3 Promoting Better Thinking

The last approach would be to more explicitly look at the human side of the decision process. Will regulations and technical opportunities be enough to guide human behavior, towards fair and non-discriminatory behavior? Laws and technology can create restrictions and constraints for what kind of behavior is likely to be performed, but if profiling in an unrestricted fashion remains profitable, it is likely many will find a way through the blockades, so to speak. It would demand further analysis if it would be enough to change recruiter's and manager's behavior, and at this point I will merely remain skeptical. This skepticism can neatly bring us to the main argument in this section.

What recruiters and managers often seek when hiring, is support in their decision; they want to be more *certain* of their choice [1, 2, 16]. Similarly the brain wants to be more certain of the future, predicting what comes next. As was touched upon in the previous section, the way our brain functions in this regard may also lead us a bit astray at times, leading to implicit biases and negatively value laden pre-conceptions. What might be needed, then, is a bit more *uncertainty,* and a motivation for this can be found in the methodology of how *good science* is performed.

A key conception in modern empirical science is to *not* try to confirm what you believe to be true, but to falsify it. This relates very much to our confirmation biases and our tendency to look for that which confirms our prior beliefs and current working model in our brain (see Subsect. 3.5 for details). What the methodology of science does is, instead, to critique and to doubt, and try to disprove what we believe to be true. As

Kothari puts it: "All progress is born of inquiry. Doubt is often better than overconfidence, for it leads to inquiry, and inquiry leads to invention" [32]. A similar message is delivered by Nobel Prize awarded physicist Richard Feynman:

> "We have found it of paramount importance that in order to progress we must recognize our ignorance and leave room for doubt. Scientific knowledge is a body of statements of varying degrees of certainty — some most unsure, some nearly sure, but none *absolutely* certain" [33].

So, rather than certainty, what you would like for scientifically more sound knowledge, is a promotion of *uncertainty*; or varied degrees of certainty and uncertainty, based on empirical data and arguments. What a scientific approach to data mining for applicant prediction could mean is that you as a recruiter should actively try to disprove your own hypothesis regarding who you believe is the best candidate for the position.

5   Conclusions

The main purpose of this paper is to present an initial, explorative investigation of ethical aspects within recruitment and hiring using Big Data and data profiling. It is found that the use of data mining in companies is often motivated as an attempt to increase objectivity in regards to performance predictions. As far as has been analyzed here, there seems to be some potential problems that companies risk running into. The first is to end up on low peaks of local maximums and therefore miss out on achieving long-term performance gains and resilience against changing conditions. The second is a concern for discrimination when using data mining algorithm. The third and final, and perhaps a sometimes forgotten focus, is a concern for loss of equal opportunities and unfairness for applicants in a selection process.

The problems discussed here are not new, in two ways. First of all, the problem of biases in data mining and data sets is well known, and even more specifically, implicit bias has been shown to exist in the use of data mining [2, 7]. Secondly, problems with discrimination and (human) biases are well known and studied, and as I propose in this paper, these phenomena seem to be related in more intricate ways than perhaps often considered. Once again relating to the prediction-error theory of our mind (see Subsect. 3.5), data mining and profiling is an attempt to predict the future, in a similar way as the brain is trying to predict the immediate surrounding and what will come next. An inherent limitation in data mining and the ability to predict the future is that it is based on historical data. Similarly, the brain's predictions are based on historical experiences, and the brain can also be understood to do a kind of statistical analysis, leading to estimations and generalizations. This makes the brain prone to faulty predictions and discriminatory categorizations of people, and similar effects can be seen in statistical methods of data mining.

To continue on that analogy, it could be seen as if (big) data profiling, purely by its statistical method, can have implicit biases. Alternatively, it can reinforce the idea that humans through the perception of the world are (imperfect) statistical machines.

In this paper I have briefly touched upon some previously discussed ways to remedy these limitations in data mining and machine learning; through technological means (see Subsect. 4.1), or by laws and regulations (see Subsect. 4.2). A third option proposed here is to look at the quality of the human thinker and decision maker, and more precisely what could be the remedy in the scenarios of discussed with recruiters and managers. If it is better knowledge in our predictions we want, the proposition is to look at scientific methodology (see Subsect. 4.3). In that case, rather than looking for objectivity and certainty in decisions and selections of applicants, we should look for uncertainty, and doubt, and try to falsify our initial judgements of applicants ability to perform well.

How this openness to uncertainty, and a varied degree of certainty, is not either so clear. These are abilities that can relate to critical thinking skills, and how this is taught and improved is still an open problem without a clear answer. Even if we are able to define such a skill-set, and how to promote them using the predictive data-mining tools recruiters can use, it is an inherent difficulty why this would ever be implemented by companies doing the hiring. In the environment of big companies using Big Data, a common understanding often heard is that "all you need is correlations", with no need to go beyond that understanding (Roger Clarke in lecture at IFIP 2016, Aug 21st). As has been shown in this paper, using only significance and p-values as statistical mean, you might end up with limited knowledge, and at times knowledge that breeds implicit biases (see Subsect. 3.5).

To conclude; what might be needed to promote a more conscious use of predictive tools, then, is a mix of technology and laws that is grounded in an understanding of how human decision-making and prediction-making is made.

5.1   Further Investigations

As was mentioned in the methodological Subsect. 1.2, there are currently some obstacles in doing research in the field of recruitment using data mining algorithms. Presently, companies and agencies do not have to disclose what algorithms they use, and how it affects populations [9]. This paper remains mostly theoretical. To get more insight into the effects on individuals and society, researchers would need access to more information about what kind of algorithms are in use, and also data from populations (applicants) it is applied on.

Some of the things argued for in this paper could be simulated and tested. For example, the effect argued for with reprofiling; that statistical patterns would become more significant and with lower p-value, and consequently result in less deviation from means for individual features. Another effect to expect if lots of data points are added is that p-value will be low.

Finally, the discussion on what constitutes discrimination and unfairness would serve to be expanded. What counts as merits? When is it ok to use predictive measurements? Should they never be allowed? If they are statistical estimations and generalizations, they would inevitably lead to excluding some individuals. Should profiling be allowed if the statistical measure is good enough, and what constitutes good enough? These are some questions that do not seem to have clear and immediate answers.

Acknowledgements. I would like thank my supervisors Mikael Laaksoharju and Iordanis Kavathatzopoulos of Uppsala University, for extensive feedback and conceptual contributions.

References

1. Chien, C.-F., Chen, L.-F.: Data mining to improve personnel selection and enhance human capital: a case study in high-technology industry. Expert Syst. Appl. **34**, 280–290 (2008)
2. Barocas, S., Selbst, A.D.: Big data's disparate impact. Calif. Law Rev. **104**, 671–732 (2014)
3. Pager, D., Shepherd, H.: The Sociology of discrimination: racial discrimination in employment, housing, credit, and consumer markets. Ann. Rev. Sociol. **34**, 181–209 (2008)
4. Bertrand, M., Mullainathan, S.: Are Emily and Greg more employable than Lakisha and Jamal? A field experiment on labor market discrimination. Am. Econ. Rev. **94**, 991–1013 (2004)
5. Jost, J.T., Rudman, L.A., Blair, I.V., Carney, D.R., Dasgupta, N., Glaser, J., Hardin, C.D.: The existence of implicit bias is beyond reasonable doubt: a refutation of ideological and methodological objections and executive summary of ten studies that no manager should ignore. Res. Organ. Behav. **29**, 39–69 (2009)
6. Sexton, D.L., Bowman-Upton, N.: Female and male entrepreneurs: psychological characteristics and their role in gender. J. Bus. Ventur. **5**, 29 (1990)
7. Caliskan-Islam, A., Bryson, J.J., Narayanan, A.: Semantics derived automatically from language corpora necessarily contain human biases. ArXiv Prepr. ArXiv160807187 (2016)
8. Portmess, L., Tower, S.: Data barns, ambient intelligence and cloud computing: the tacit epistemology and linguistic representation of Big Data. Ethics Inf. Technol. **17**, 1–9 (2015)
9. Pasquale, F.: The Black Box Society: The Secret Algorithms That Control Money and Information. Harvard University Press, Cambridge (2015)
10. Sebastian-Coleman, L.: Measuring Data Quality for Ongoing Improvement: A Data Quality Assessment Framework. Elsevier Science, Burlington (2013)
11. Gartner Survey Reveals That 73 Percent of Organizations Have Invested or Plan to Invest in Big Data in the Next Two Years. http://www.gartner.com/newsroom/id/2848718
12. Rosenblat, A., Kneese, T., et al.: Networked Employment Discrimination. Open Soc. Found. Future Work Comm. Res. Pap. (2014)
13. Morse, T.: Big data can take the guesswork out of the hiring process (2016). http://qz.com/146000/big-data-can-take-the-guesswork-out-of-the-hiring-process-2/
14. Evolv I Cornerstone OnDemand. https://www.cornerstoneondemand.com/evolv
15. Christl, W., Spiekerman, S.: Networks of Control: A Report on Corporate Surveillance, Digital Tracking, Big Data & Privacy. Facultas Verlags- und Buchhandels AG, Wien (2016)
16. Mehrabad, S.M., Brojeny, F.M.: The development of an expert system for effective selection and appointment of the jobs applicants in human resource management. Comput. Ind. Eng. **53**, 306–312 (2007)
17. Backman, C., Hedenus, A.: Will your Facebook profile get you hired? Employers use of information seeking online during the recruitment process. Presented at the 6th Biannual Surveillance and Society Conference, Barcelona, Spain, 24 April 2014
18. Kwasnicki, W., Kwasnicka, H.: Market, innovation, competition: an evolutionary model of industrial dynamics. J. Econ. Behav. Organ. **19**, 343–368 (1992)
19. discrimination Meaning in the Cambridge English Dictionary. http://dictionary.cambridge.org/dictionary/english/discrimination
20. Wilkinson, J.: Companies secretly tracking employees' health and lives in big data. http://www.dailymail.co.uk/news/article-3456691/How-companies-secretly-tracking-employees-health-private-lives-big-data-save-money-lead-big-problems.html
21. Hohwy, J.: The Predictive Mind. OUP Oxford, Oxford (2013)

22. Cummins, D.: Why the Gender Difference on SAT Math Doesn't Matter (2014). https://www.psychologytoday.com/blog/good-thinking/201403/why-the-gender-difference-sat-math-doesnt-matter
23. Kelley, K., Preacher, K.J.: On effect size. Psychol. Methods. **17**, 137–152 (2012)
24. Sedlmeier, P., Gigerenzer, G.: Do studies of statistical power have an effect on the power of studies? Psychol. Bull. **105**, 309 (1989)
25. Smaldino, P.E., McElreath, R.: The natural selection of bad science. R. Soc. Open Sci. **3**, 160384 (2016)
26. Söllner, R.: Human capital diversity and product innovation: a micro-level analysis. Jena Econ. Res. Pap. **27**, 1–33 (2010)
27. Østergaard, C.R., Timmermans, B., Kristinsson, K.: Does a different view create something new? The effect of employee diversity on innovation. Res. Policy **40**, 500–509 (2011)
28. Hutchison, K., Jenkins, F.: Women in Philosophy: What Needs to Change? Oxford University Press, Oxford (2013)
29. LeFevre, K., DeWitt, D.J., Ramakrishnan, R.: Incognito: efficient full-domain k-anonymity. In: Proceedings of the 2005 ACM SIGMOD International Conference on Management of Data, pp. 49–60. ACM (2005)
30. Crawford, K., Schultz, J.: Big data and due process: toward a framework to redress predictive privacy harms. BCL Rev. **55**, 93 (2014)
31. Heimas, R.: Top 10 operational impacts of the GDPR: Part 5 - Profiling (2016). https://iapp.org/news/a/top-10-operational-impacts-of-the-gdpr-part-5-profiling/
32. Kothari, C.R.: Research Methodology: Methods & Techniques. New Age International (P) Ltd., New Delhi (2004)
33. Feynman, R.P., Robbins, J.: The Pleasure of Finding Things Out: The Best Short Works of Richard P. Feynman. Perseus Books, Cambridge (1999)

A Survey of Security Analysis in Federated Identity Management

Sean Simpson and Thomas Groß[✉]

Newcastle University, Newcastle upon Tyne, UK
thomas.gross@newcastle.ac.uk

Abstract. We conduct a systematic survey of security analysis in Federated Identity Management (FIM). We use a categorisation system based off the Malicious and Accidental Fault Tolerance framework (MAFTIA) to categorise security incidents in FIM. When security incidents are categorised, we can paint a picture of the landscape of problems that have been studied in FIM. We outline the security incidents that are happening across FIM protocols and present solutions to those security incidents as proposed by others.

Keywords: FIM · Survey · Dependability · MAFTIA · Microsoft Passport · OAuth · OpenID · Facebook Connect · SAML · Liberty Alliance

1 Introduction

Federated Identity Management (FIM) aims to alleviate the problem of a user having to remember too many credentials by allowing the user to sign into multiple Service Providers (SP) using the same credentials which are provided by an Identity Provider (IdP). Typically in FIM, the user will attempt to access a SP which will then redirect the user to authenticate with the IdP which will vouch for the user, communicating with the SP to say that the user is who they say they are. FIM solutions are seeing increasing use and numerous attacks on protocols used in FIM have been found, which is motivation to do a survey in the area.

Protocols in FIM have been analysed by others in an attempt to find security problems. The issue is that there is a lot of different information on the analysis of security protocols in FIM that remains uncompiled. Our goal is to create a survey paper for security analysis in FIM. We review existing peer reviewed academic publications that perform security analysis on FIM protocols to establish a common ground and collect knowledge. In addition, we want to create a unified way of looking at security incidents in FIM and offer a framework to do that. We do this to provide insight on attacks that are seen on multiple protocol suites and state the solutions to security incidents as provided by the authors of the surveyed papers.

© IFIP International Federation for Information Processing 2016
Published by Springer International Publishing AG 2016. All Rights Reserved
A. Lehmann et al. (Eds.): Privacy and Identity 2016, IFIP AICT 498, pp. 231–247, 2016.
DOI: 10.1007/978-3-319-55783-0_16

2   Related Work

Delft & Oostdijk presented a paper which collects the security issues that exist in OpenID [5]. There is an additional need to examine security issues across FIM which is what we aim to do. There have been attempts to survey FIM in general. For instance, Ghazizadeh et al. [2] survey issues within OAuth, OpenID and SAML. The FIM standards surveyed is somewhat limited because Liberty Alliance and WS-Federation are not considered. In addition, analysis on FIM implementations—such as Microsoft Passport—are not considered in the survey which also provide information on security issues in FIM.

3   Method

3.1   Aim

RQ1: Understanding the Security Landscape in FIM. What is the landscape of the security analysis in FIM? We investigate to what extent FIM vulnerabilities, attacks and intrusions can be modelled systematically in a fault-tolerance formalization to understand security issues in FIM. What areas in this landscape might be missing research attention?

RQ2: Common Attack Classes. Which attack classes are prevalent across protocol suites? Do these attack classes apply to protocol specifications or implementations? Which papers go a step further and find a flaw in the specification and test it on implementations.

RQ3: Solutions/Mitigations. What solutions have been proposed to mitigate attack classes?

3.2   Search Methodology

We have done a systematic literature review based on the foundations described by Kitchenham [4]. We used two search engines to perform the literature search: Scopus and Google Scholar. Figure 1 contains the overall search term, in the Scopus format.

We observed a number of key words being used and used synonyms. We based the protocols searched off of surveys done in the area of FIM protocols [6]. We needed a logically equivalent search in Google Scholar. Below is a part of the resulting search term. We executed the search term with the "search by relevance" radio option selected and the "where the words appear anywhere in the article" radio button selected. *Protocol* as can be seen in the template search below is substituted with the twelve FIM protocol terms that can be seen in the Scopus search (Fig. 2).

3.3   Inclusion and Exclusion

Inclusion. We included papers returned from the search based on the following criteria:

TITLE–ABS–KEY((Analysis OR Evaluation OR Examine OR Proof OR
    Attack OR Intrusion OR Vulnerability OR Risk) AND
Security AND Identity AND
(OAuth OR OpenID OR ''Liberty Alliance'' OR SAML OR ''Security
    Assertion Markup Language'' OR WS–Federation OR ''
    Microsoft Passport'' OR (Passport AND Protocol) OR
    Cardspace OR ''Facebook Connect'' OR ''Google Accounts''
    OR Shibboleth)) AND
(LIMIT–TO(SUBJAREA, ''COMP''))

Fig. 1. Overall search term used in Scopus, modulo plural forms.

Protocol Security Identity Analysis OR Evaluation OR Examine
    OR Proof OR Attack OR Intrusion OR Vulnerability OR Risk

Fig. 2. Overall search term in Google Scholar, modulo plural forms.

– Be in the subject area of computer science.
– Reference FIM protocols.
– Be published as part of a peer-reviewed venue (i.e., workshop, conference or journal).
– Be unique: some papers are published somewhere, and then a very similar version of that paper can appear from the same authors at other venues.

Exclusion. After the inclusion phase, we excluded papers based on the following criteria:

– We exclude secondary sources (hence, constrain the SLR to original research).
– We exclude papers that do not offer a combination of vulnerabilities and anticipated exploits thereof. Claiming a vulnerability is not sufficient.
– We exclude hypothetical analyses, which modify a standardized FIM protocol to conduct a "what-if" analysis. We want to collect security incidents for real FIM systems and not for proposed extensions which may or may not be acted upon.
– We exclude security incidents that are put forward for FIM in general. The security incident has to be specific to a certain FIM protocol. The reason for this is to ensure that we get a representation of security incidents possible on real FIM systems.

3.4   Data Collection

After the inclusion/exclusion refinement we have a sample of 31 papers. From those papers, we manually code parts that describe security incidents and weaknesses (e.g., vulnerabilities or attacks). These observations are classified using our categorisation system described in Sect. 3.6.

3.5   Malicious and Accidental Fault Tolerance (MAFTIA)

We categorised security incidents based on Malicious and Accidental Fault Tolerance (MAFTIA) principles [3]. MAFTIA is built upon the foundation of dependability [1]. The dependability area is concerned with understanding what happens when a system fails in order to apply fault tolerance to avoid a failure. While dependability focuses on accidental failures, MAFTIA adapts the founding notions of dependability for use in understanding how systems fail under the influence of a malicious adversary. We use the notions founded by the dependability community to understand and thereby categorise security incidents in FIM. We introduce a number of key terms from MAFTIA which we use to build our categorisation system.

Definition 1. Adversary *Malicious person or organizations at the origin of attacks.*

Vulnerability *A fault that is created during the development or operation of the system that if exploited causes an intrusion.*

Attack *A malicious interaction fault that attempts to exploit a vulnerability. Can be thought of as an intrusion attempt.*

Intrusion *An adversary-introduced fault. An intrusion is created as the product from an attack successfully exploiting a vulnerability by an adversary.*

Failure *When the system is adjudged to not be offering correct service.*

3.6   Our Categorisation System

While MAFTIA terms help us understand a security incident, they are too low level to be used for categorisation. In addition, there are some additional aspects to a security incident in FIM that are desirable to capture which are not considered by the MAFTIA framework. We therefore introduce our categorisation system for use in categorising security incidents in FIM. The categorisation system has six dimensions *Vulnerability, Attack Class, CIA Failure, Target Protocol, Incident Type,* and *Solution Presented.* The term *Vulnerability* has already been defined in Sect. 3.5. We will go on to define what the rest of these terms mean.

Definition 2. Attack Class *A collection of attacks, intrusions and resultant errors in a system that form casual chains from vulnerabilities to a security failure if the errors are not dealt with.*

Considering a casual MAFTIA fault-error-failure tree for vulnerabilities, attacks, intrusions, errors and ultimately security failures, the attack class contains the trunk of the tree. An attack class is an abstraction of the adversary attack which attempts to exploit a vulnerability—therefore it is separate from the vulnerability—and all of the resulting intrusion states and further attacks (which sometimes can be trivial, like entering a user password) that produce errors in a system—up until the point at which a failure occurs. The purpose of the attack class is to capture the essence of what an adversary does and abstract away from the unimportant details. The unimportant details being the order of attack events, intrusions and errors occur in and slight variations in what errors, intrusions and errors actually occur. There is always a critical attack event which the attack class derives it's handle from and the surrounding details can vary. It is often the case that certain vulnerabilities lead to certain attack classes (i.e., Weak DNS leading to DNS Poisoning) but that is not always the case (i.e., a replay attack class can be caused by unencrypted communications or from a lack of binding)—which is why we distinguish between the vulnerability and attack class.

Definition 3. Confidentiality, Integrity, Availability (CIA) Failure *We view a system to have failed when the confidentiality, integrity or availability of a service is violated for a user.*

In essence we translate what a failure would mean in a FIM system. We want to know how a user is affected by a security incident in order to discern the impact of intrusions. Also of note is that an account can be compromised by a security incident, in this case, the confidentiality, integrity and availability of the service can all be affected.

We also consider the target FIM protocol, the incident type—was the security incident found at the protocol level, the implementation level, or found at the protocol level and tested on the implementation—and whether a solution was proposed—sometimes that solution is implemented before the publishing of the paper and this will be stated when it happens. The introduced terms have evolved to capture six different dimensions in a surveyed security incident: What is the weakness in the system (*Vulnerability*)? What does the adversary do to attack the system (*Attack Class*)?) How does the security incident affect the user (*CIA Failure*)? What FIM protocol is the subject of the attack (*Target Protocol*)? Is the incident due to an implementation or design flaw (*Incident Type*)? Was a solution put forward by the author (*Solution Presented*)? We use all of these terms to describe surveyed security incidents in FIM in subsequent sections.

3.7   Limitations of Survey

We performed a systematic literature review on Scopus and Google Scholar. The limitations of this is that we might miss things. We are aware of one notable paper which did not appear from our search in Microsoft Passport by Kormann and Rubin [7]. We included this paper in the survey as an exception. This is the only paper we made this exception for and the reason we did this for this one paper is because we consider it a cornerstone in analysis of FIM systems. A number of other security analysis papers cite the paper by Kormann and Rubin and it was the first paper, to the best of our knowledge, to bring security issues in FIM to light.

We do not attempt to discern the quality of the reviewed papers. This introduces the fact that security incidents, which some may deem to be trivial, are represented in the survey. In addition, we cannot guarantee that every security incident is correct because if we begin to use our judgement to discriminate what we perceive as incorrect results we risk compromising the survey.

4   Surveyed Papers

In this section we briefly outline the landscape of what we have seen, sorted by targeted FIM protocols that we have considered in the survey in order to address RQ1. We can see if attack classes are occurring at the protocol or implementation level which relates to RQ2. Some solutions proposed by the authors are also presented which relates to RQ3. The various protocols considered can have a number of different versions—to keep the survey into the protocols simple, we ignore this complication.

4.1   Microsoft

We are considering the papers that are concerned with the numerous attempts made by Microsoft to implement the concept of FIM (Passport .NET, Microsoft Accounts and Cardspace). We found four papers in this category [7–10] and all four papers proposed security incidents effective at the protocol level but did not test them on implementations. Three papers [7,9,10] reported on the vulnerability of weak DNS being exploited by a DNS poisoning attack class which would force an unknowing user onto a malicious domain that is supposed to look familiar to them, in order to trick the user into logging on. The adversary will steal these credentials since the adversary owns the malicious domain and will then compromise the account of the user—leading to a myriad of CIA problems. Alrodhan & Mitchell proposed a solution, which is the uptake of DNSSEC [9].

Two of these papers point out a bogus merchant attack class capitalising on the FIM no trust infrastructure vulnerability (there is no safe infrastructure list, meaning a user does not know who to trust) which would lead to compromised user accounts [7,10].

Alrodhan & Mitchell [9] brings up the possibility of a malicious provider—which is a provider that wants to track the actions of a user—exploiting the centralised infrastructure vulnerability that FIM suffers from (IdP at the center of FIM system being able to track user actions). The malicious provider in control of the IdP will observe the SPs a user visits and build a profile. No solution was proposed by the author for this security incident. Kormann & Rubin also state that the centralised infrastructure vulnerability can lead to a Denial of Service (DDoS) attack.

4.2   OAuth

The papers that we found to have security incidents in this category [11–17] widely report on a Cross-Site-Request-Forgery (CSRF) attack that capitalises on a weak SP vulnerability. The OAuth specification outlines things the SP must do to resist CSRF attacks, which some SPs do not do. In fact, five of the seven OAuth papers analysed reported this vulnerability [11,13–16] on the implementations of OAuth. It was found that these security incidents were possible because of the implementations of the protocol themselves rather than fundamental problems with the OAuth protocol. All five papers suggested solutions to be implemented by the relevant providers—such as proposals to attempt to bind authorisation requests to browsers—and Ferry et al. [13] reported that the CSRF attack had been addressed immediately upon the report.

Two papers [12,17] both point out the same security incident, which is the idea that a weak user credential vulnerability can be exploited by a brute force attack. Alotaibi & Mahmmod suggested a solution to this attack, which was to implement a biometric authentication system [12].

Sun & Beznosov pointed out a large number of security incidents for OAuth [11], which included the already mentioned CSRF incident. Additional vulnerability-attack class relationships that are pointed out by this paper: Unencrypted communications (HTTP being used) leading to message modification (can tailor a message from an existing base message), automatic authorisation (if the user has granted a privilege it is automatically granted again) leading to Cross-Site-Scripting (XSS), a lack of binding (vulnerability where a sent message is not sufficiently tied to the sender) allowing a message to be modified with a public URL which is used to authenticate a user, a lack of binding vulnerability leading to session swapping (an honest user is logged in to an adversary account—potentially divulging confidential information). All of the security incidents relating to these vulnerability-attack class relationships were possible at the implementation level.

4.3 OpenID

The first notable thing about the surveyed OpenID papers [17–26] is how the message formatting (a parameter or part of the message is not signed properly—common in OpenID) vulnerability is exploited by the message modification (possible because the message is not protected properly) attack class for the purposes of compromising a user account. For instance, an adversary could modify parameters such as Openid.ext1.value.email as shown by Wang et al. [37]. Oh & Jin [18] exploit this and note an issue with the protocol specification that allows for this security incident to take place and tests it on a real implementation—but no solution is offered. Sovis et al. [19] only goes as far to note the possibility of the attack at the protocol level without appearing to test it on a real system. Sun et al. [21] formally analyses the specification to find flaws and then exploits those flaws on real implementations to make the incident type tested—in addition, a solution is suggested for this security incident which is to further cryptographically protect the message.

Another notable vulnerability-attack class combination is observed. The no-trust-infrastructure being exploited by a bogus merchant to compromise user accounts—three papers put forward this idea [20,22,23] on the protocol level. Feld & Pohlmann [20] put forward an identity card solution to counter the bogus merchant. Abbas et al. [22] proposes a challenge-response scheme based on public key cryptography. Hsu et al. [23] leverages mobile phones to provide a physical token.

Mainka et al. [26] pointed out two security incidents at the implementation level which compromised user accounts. The first exploited a lack of binding by launching a MITM attack and had a suggested solution. The second incident (described as three incidents, but can be broadly boiled down) involves a lack of binding vulnerability which can be exploited by a message modification attack.

Two papers listed a large number of attacks too numerous to list here. Krolo et al. [24] puts forward five security incidents at the protocol level with suggested solutions and one affected the availability of the service while the others compromised user accounts. Li & Mitchell [25] introduces seven security incidents at the implementation level with suggested solutions and two incidents affected user confidentiality and the other five resulted in a compromised user account.

Sun et al. [21] also provides two more security incidents that were tested on real implementations: a lack of binding leading to a replay attack and a vulnerable SP leading to a CSRF attack—recommendations for the SP to follow were suggested to counter these attack classes.

4.4   SAML

Out of the five SAML analysis papers we found [27–31], three show how a lack of binding can be exploited by a MITM attack class to compromise a user account. Armando et al. [27] pointed out the discovered incident at the protocol level and that that by the time the paper is published Google implemented a fix. Groß [28] described a protocol level incident—which also exploited a weak DNS vulnerability with a DNS poisoning attack class to progress to the MITM attack which a solution was presented for. Mainka et al. [31] shows that when the adversary has access to a valid access token several MITM style scenarios are possible that were fixed upon publication.

Two more security incidents are introduced by Groß [28] at the protocol level: an unencrypted message vulnerability is stated to be exploitable by a message modification attack class which sniffs the message and then modifies a part of it to send to a SP which will compromise the account of a user; and a lack of binding vulnerability exploitable by a replay attack to compromise a user account. A countermeasure to the replay attack class was proposed to check the IP address of the sender. A countermeasure was also proposed for the message modification attack class, it is suggested that the referrer tag is dropped by browsers.

Mayer et al. [30] put forward two unique security incidents. The first exploits a vulnerable IdP and is referred to as an ACS Spoofing attack class which is similar to a bogus merchant attack class but the bogus merchant in the ACS Spoofing variant steals the user credentials and logs into many SPs—rather than requiring the user to manually enter credentials. A vulnerable IdP is exploited again by a UI redressing attack class, which involves tricking a user into clicking a malicious web element through a transparent web element. Both of these incidents were said to be because of poor implementations and compromise the user account. The paper also reviews several countermeasures.

4.5   Liberty Alliance

We found two papers describing security incidents in Liberty Alliance [32,33]. Pfitzmann & Waidner [32] exploits the vulnerability lack of binding by launching a MITM attack of which the aim is to compromise the user account. The security incident was shown to be possible on the protocol level but was not tested on real implementations. A fix was implemented before the paper was published because Liberty Alliance acknowledged the issue and acted quickly although it was not stated which solution of the list of possible solutions outlined in the paper Liberty Alliance chose.

Ahmad et al. [33] outlined that a centralised infrastructure can be exploited by a malicious provider who wants to breach user confidentiality. The incident was proposed at the protocol level and no solution was presented.

4.6   Facebook Connect

We are considering the papers that claim to find security incidents [35–37] for Facebook's FIM protocol—Facebook Connect. Two papers that we found to have security incidents in this category [35,36] were found to have the unencrypted communications vulnerability. The unencrypted communications vulnerability was exploited by two different attack classes: the replay attack class [35] and communications sniffing (being able to read a message, but not being able to modify it or replay it) attack class [36]. The replay attack class was proposed as possible on the protocol level but the communications sniffing attack class was tested in practice. Miculan & Caterina [35], suggests a solution where a Diffie-Hellman key exchange is added to the protocol. Urueña et al. [36] suggests forcing HTTPS.

A centralised infrastructure vulnerability pointed out by Urueña et al. [36] was exploited by a malicious provider attack class which would affect the confidentiality of the user. The attack class was proposed at the protocol level and no solution suggested.

Wang et al. [37] states a message formatting vulnerability which can be exploited by a message modification attack class which aims to compromise the account of the user. The attack class was tested in practice, reported to Facebook, who fixed the issue before the publishing of the paper. This same kind of security incident was also found to be possible on Google Accounts.

4.7   Google Accounts

There were two papers [27,37] with security incidents in Google Accounts but we discuss these in the SAML and Facebook section.

4.8   Shibboleth

Chadwick [38] points out that Shibboleth can be exploited by a bogus merchant attack class with the aim of compromising a user account. The author

Table 1. Coded Vulnerabilities & Attack Classes in FIM

(a) Coded Vulnerabilities

Vulnerabilities
Unencrypted Communications
Centralised Infrastructure
Lack of Binding
No Trust Infrastructure
Weak DNS
Vulnerable SP
Vulnerable IdP
Automatic Authorisation
Message Formatting
Automatic Authorisation
Weak User Credentials

(b) Coded Attacks

Attacks
Replay Attack
Communications Sniffing
Malicious Provider
MITM
Message Modification
Bogus Merchant
Brute Force
XSS
Session Swapping
DNS Poisoning
DDoS
CSRF
ACS Spoofing
UI Redressing

notes that this is because there is no trusted infrastructure list for Shibboleth (unlike Microsoft Cardspace, which the author advocates). The security incident is stated at the protocol level and no solution is presented.

5   Results

5.1   Vulnerabilities and Attack Classes in FIM

We found 11 unique vulnerabilities and 14 unique attack classes from our survey which can be seen in Table 1. We consider attacks and vulnerabilities the main raw output from our categorisation system. Where it might not be clear what a vulnerability or attack class is, we define them in their first appearance in Sect. 4.

5.2   Cross-Protocol Issues

This answers RQ2. We identify 14 different cross protocol issues (cf. Table 2). We identify a cross-protocol issue when the same vulnerability, is exploited by the same attack class and creates the same CIA failure across at least one additional protocol.

5.3   The Numbers

Sample Size: When we conducted our SLR search of security analysis of FIM protocols initially we included **145 papers**. We excluded papers that did not

Table 2. Cross-protocol issues in FIM

ID	Vulnerability	Attack Class	CIA Failure	Affected Protocols
1	Message Format	Message Modification	Compromised Account	Facebook, Google, OpenID
2	Centralised Infrastructure	Malicious Provider	Confidentiality	Facebook, Liberty, Microsoft, OpenID
3	Unencrypted Communication	Replay	Compromised Account	Facebook, Microsoft
4	Weak User Credentials	Brute Force	Compromised Account	OpenID, OAuth
5	Unencrypted Communications	Message Modification	Compromised Account	OAuth, OpenID, SAML
6	No trust infrastructure	Bogus Merchant	Compromised Account	Microsoft, OpenID, Shibboleth
7	Vulnerable SP	CSRF	Compromised Account	OpenID, OAuth, SAML
8	Lack of Binding	MITM	Compromised Account	Liberty, SAML
9	Lack of Binding	Replay	Compromised Account	OpenID, SAML
10	Weak DNS	DNS poisoning	Compromised Account	Microsoft, SAML
11	Unencrypted Communications	Communications Sniffing	Confidentiality	Facebook, OpenID
12	Lack of Binding	Session Swapping	Confidentiality	OAuth, OpenID
13	Vulnerable SP, Automatic Authorisation	XSS	Compromised Account	OAuth, OpenID
14	Lack of Binding	Message Modification	Compromised Account	OAuth, OpenID, SAML

present security incidents until we had **31** papers left and **60** security incidents were found from the papers.

CIA: The proportion of security incidents which had a CIA failure listed as "Compromised Account" was **83.3%**. Confidentiality breaches accounted for **13.3%** and availability denials **13.3%**.

Solution Offered: Of the incidents proposed by authors, **16.6%** of those authors provided evidence that the protocol was fixed before the paper was even published. **66.6%** of authors at least suggested a solution while **16.6%** offered no solution.

6   Discussion

6.1   The Landscape of Security Analysis of FIM

We discuss this to address RQ1. In the majority of security incidents we survey, the "Compromised Account" was the most common CIA failure. This also happens to be the CIA failure with the most impact, seeing as an adversary can potentially compromise any CIA property from a compromised user account. In addition, we do not observe many security incidents that exploit solely integrity or availability (without first compromising an account).

We have seen a fair balance between security incidents at the protocol, implementation, and tested (where a protocol flaw is found and then tested on real implementations) level. It is important to continue to evaluate both Protocols and the implementations in FIM because one can not succeed without the other.

Some protocols have received more attention from analysts than others (such as OpenID, OAuth) and we can therefore paint a clear history of the security issues for those protocols. Other protocols have not received such wide spread attention, especially WS-Federation which our survey did not turn up a security analysis that presented a security incident. There is work in the area, such as work done by Groß [28] that demonstrates the protocol is secure under certain assumptions, but work investigating the flaws in WS-Federation seems to be missing. Other low attendance protocols are Shibboleth and Google Accounts. Are these low-attention protocols more secure or are researchers turning a blind eye to them for one reason or another i.e., perception of less people using these protocols?

A positive story is that the majority of security analysis are not only pointing out vulnerabilities and attack classes which can be used to exploit those vulnerabilities, solutions are attached also with only **16.6%** of authors not claiming a solution.

6.2   Cross-Protocol Issues

We discuss this to further answer RQ2. There were 14 security incidents we found that were cross protocol. Of these 14, some were not surprising as they capitalise on well known FIM weaknesses. Cross-protocol incident **2**, happens across FIM protocols because if an IdP is malicious, they can easily track a user. Cross-protocol incident **4** is also not a surprising find, it is well known that user credentials suffer from low entropy and in addition user credentials will generally be more valuable for an IdP in a FIM system because of the potential to more deeply compromise a single user. In a FIM system, the burden of authenticating a user is merely shifted to the IdP and so the cross-protocol incident **6**, which involves a bogus merchant attack class, is still a menace.

In fact, it could be argued that it's made worse because of the interconnected nature of FIM systems. In a similar vein, **10** involves a DNS poisoning attack which is also arguably more effective on a FIM system. All of the aforementioned cross-protocol issues are not surprising to be found to be happening cross-protocol.

Liberty Alliance is built on SAML and we can also see that the same security issue **8** has been reported for both of these protocols. OpenID and OAuth also have this relationship and the same issue is also reported in **13**.

What is surprising is that vulnerabilities such as "unencrypted communications" are not just seen on one protocol but across Facebook and Microsoft as can be seen by this cross-protocol issue **3**. It is worrying that such large ubiquitous organisations harbour these sorts of vulnerabilities. Cross-protocol issue **11** is also observed on Facebook and in this case confidential information is sent without protection and can therefore be intercepted and used by an adversary.

One creative issue is issue **12** where an adversary gets a user to sign into the attacker's account. The attacker hopes that the user will divulge confidential information because the user thinks they are safely using their own account. This highlights the importance of an in-depth security analysis because without it, unexpected issues like this would likely be overlooked.

Another worrying sign is brought to light by **7**, where vulnerable SPs have been exploited by CSRF attack classes on OAuth, OpenID and SAML. What we observed is that even though the protocol itself is thought of as secure, a bad implementation can create risks for users. This is worrying because not only is OAuth, OpenID and SAML ubiquitous on the web, but a single bad implementation could spell trouble for a user as shown by the numerous papers presented by our survey that demonstrate the CSRF attack class on real implementations.

6.3   Solutions/Mitigations

We concentrate on the solutions for dealing with the vulnerabilities and attack classes shown to occur cross protocol in order to address RQ3. This is in no way a survey of how these attack classes can be mitigated, we simply use a solution provided in the already surveyed literature.

Cross-Protocol issue 1: The basis of this attack class lies in the fact that the OpenID message (which is used in Facebook and Google implementations) can be modified by an adversary. Sun et al. [21] present a Diffie-Hellman key exchange to mitigate the attack class. The IdP also has to sign an assertion for the Diffie-Hellman key exchange to be secure.

Cross-Protocol issue 2: The malicious provider profiling a user is difficult to stop so most of the papers do not present a solution for it. There is one exception, Feld & Pohlmann [20] reference a German identity card called nPA where a person attests to another person who they are using biometrics.

Cross-Protocol issue 3: The solution to the replay attack as put by Miculan & Caterina [35] is to ensure SSL/TLS is used.

Cross-Protocol issue 4: Alotaibi & Ausif Mahmmod [12] state that biometrics can be used as a solution to weak user credentials.

Cross-Protocol issue 5: Messages can be modified if they are not properly protected. Sovis et al. [19] suggest ensuring all relevant message parameters are protected by a MAC code.

Cross-Protocol issue 6: According to Feld & Pohlmann [20], the German based identity card nPA can address bogus merchants by introducing a higher level of authentication.

Cross-Protocol issue 7: Sun et al. [21] suggest binding requests to the session taking place by hashing a secret together with a session id and appending that token into a hidden field in the login form as a solution to CSRF.

Cross-Protocol issue 8: When access tokens are not explicit to single SPs a MITM attack class can be launched. Pfitzmann & Waidner [6] propose (amongst other methods) a way of binding the token to the SP it is intended for.

Cross-Protocol issue 9: Groß [28] suggests binding the IP address to a request to stop Replay attacks.

Cross-Protocol issue 10: Alrodhan & Mitchell [9] point out that the widespread use of DNSSEC could mitigate the difficult to address DNS Poisoning attack.

Cross-Protocol issue 11: Manuel Urueña et al. [36] suggest disabling the HTTP referrer tag which is known to leak information.

Cross-Protocol issue 12: Lie & Mitchell [25] suggest adding a state value to bind a message in order to mitigate Session Swapping.

Cross-Protocol issue 13: We have observed that an XSS attack which results in an account being compromised requires two vulnerabilities: a Vulnerable SP and Automatic Authorisation. Sun et al. [11] state that inputs should be properly sanitized in order to prevent an injection.

Cross-Protocol issue 14: Sun et al. [11] note that SPs do not actually check some credentials which allow an attacker to engineer fake credentials, so the SP checking those credentials is a mitigation to the problem.

7 Conclusion

We put forward three research questions RQ1–RQ3 and these have been answered. We emphasise the contribution of providing a landscape of security incidents (RQ1) and common attack classes across protocols (RQ2). These contributions together provide overall insight into security issues in FIM on the whole but also particular issues that are affecting different FIM systems.

References

1. Avizienis, A., Laprie, J.-C., Randell, B., et al.: Fundamental concepts of dependability. Computing Science, University of Newcastle upon Tyne (2001)
2. Ghazizadeh, E., Zamani, M., Pashang, A., et al.: A survey on security issues of federated identity in the cloud computing. In: 2012 IEEE 4th International Conference on Cloud Computing technology and Science (CloudCom 2012), pp. 532–565. IEEE (2012)
3. Powell, D., Stroud, R., et al.: Conceptual model and architecture of maftia. Technical report Series, University of Newcastle Upon Tyne Computing Science (2003)
4. Kitchenham, B.: Procedures for performing systematic reviews. Keele University (2004)
5. Delft, B., Oostdijk, M.: A security analysis of OpenID. In: Leeuw, E., Fischer-Hübner, S., Fritsch, L. (eds.) IDMAN 2010. IAICT, vol. 343, pp. 73–84. Springer, Heidelberg (2010). doi:10.1007/978-3-642-17303-5_6
6. Pfitzmann, B., Waidner, M.: Federated identity-management protocols. In: Christianson, B., Crispo, B., Malcolm, J.A., Roe, M. (eds.) Security Protocols 2003. LNCS, vol. 3364, pp. 153–174. Springer, Heidelberg (2005). doi:10.1007/11542322_20
7. Kormann, D.P., Rubin, A.D.: Risks of the passport single signon protocol. Comput. Netw. 33, 51–58 (2000). Elsevier
8. Oppliger, R.: Microsoft.net passport and identity management. Inf. Secur. Tech. Rep. 9, 26–34 (2004). Elsevier
9. Alrodhan, W., Mitchell, C.: Improving the security of cardspace. EURASIP J. Inf. Secur. 1 (2009). Springer
10. Gajek, S., Schwenk, J., Steiner, M., Xuan, C.: Risks of the CardSpace protocol. In: Samarati, P., Yung, M., Martinelli, F., Ardagna, C.A. (eds.) ISC 2009. LNCS, vol. 5735, pp. 278–293. Springer, Heidelberg (2009). doi:10.1007/978-3-642-04474-8_23
11. Sun, S.-T., Beznosov, K.: The devil is in the (implementation) details: an empirical analysis of OAuth SSO systems. In: Proceedings of the 2012 ACM Conference on Computer and Communications Security, pp. 378–390. Springer (2012)
12. Alotaibi, A., Mahmmod, A.: Enhancing OAuth services security by an authentication service with face recognition. In: Systems, Applications and Technology Conference (LISAT), pp. 1–6. IEEE (2015)
13. Ferry, E., Raw, J.O., Curran, K.: Security evaluation of the OAuth 2.0 framework. Inf. Comput. Secur. 23, 73–101 (2015). Emerald Group Publishing Limited
14. Li, W., Mitchell, C.J.: Security issues in OAuth 2.0 SSO implementations. In: Chow, S.S.M., Camenisch, J., Hui, L.C.K., Yiu, S.M. (eds.) ISC 2014. LNCS, vol. 8783, pp. 529–541. Springer, Cham (2014). doi:10.1007/978-3-319-13257-0_34
15. Shernan, E., Carter, H., Tian, D., Traynor, P., Butler, K.: More guidelines than rules: CSRF vulnerabilities from noncompliant OAuth 2.0 implementations. In: Almgren, M., Gulisano, V., Maggi, F. (eds.) DIMVA 2015. LNCS, vol. 9148, pp. 239–260. Springer, Cham (2015). doi:10.1007/978-3-319-20550-2_13
16. Yang, R., Li, G., Lau, W., et al.: Model-based security testing: an empirical study on OAuth 2.0 implementations. In: Proceedings of the 11th ACM on Asia Conference on Computer and Communications Security, pp. 651–662. ACM (2016)
17. Grzonkowski, S., Corcoran, P.M., Coughlin, T.: Security analysis of authentication protocols for next-generation mobile and CE cloud services. In: 2011 IEEE International Conference on Consumer Electronics-Berlin (ICCE-Berlin), pp. 83–87. IEEE (2011)

18. Oh, H.-K., Jin, S.-H.: The security limitations of sso in openid. In: Advanced Communication Technology, pp. 1608–1611. IEEE (2008)
19. Sovis, P., Kohlar, F., Schwenk, J.: Security analysis of OpenID, pp. 329–340. Sicherheit (2010)
20. Feld, S., Pohlmann, N.: Security analysis of OpenID, followed by a reference implementation of an nPA-based OpenID provider. In: Pohlmann, N., Reimer, H., Schneider, W. (eds.) ISSE 2010 Securing Electronic Business Processes, pp. 13–25. Springer, Heidelberg (2011)
21. Sun, S.-T., Hawkey, K., Beznosov, K.: Systematically breaking and fixing OpenID security: formal analysis, semi-automated empirical evaluation, and practical countermeasures. Comput. Secur. **31**, 465–483 (2012). Elsevier
22. Abbas, H., Qaemi, M.M., Kahn, F.A., et al.: Systematically breaking and fixing OpenID security: formal analysis, semi-automated empirical evaluation, and practical countermeasures. Secur. Commun. Netw. (2014). Wiley Online Library
23. Hsu, F., Chen, H., Machiraju, S.: WebCallerID: leveraging cellular networks for web authentication. J. Comput. Secur. **19**, 869–893 (2011). IOS Press
24. Krolo, J., Marin, Š., Siniša, S.: Security of web level user identity management. In: 32nd International Convention MIPRO 2009 (2009)
25. Li, W., Mitchell, C.J.: Analysing the security of Google's implementation of OpenID connect. arXiv preprint arXiv:1508.01707 (2015)
26. Mainka, C., Mladenov, V., Schwenk, J.: Do not trust me: using malicious IdPs for analyzing and attacking single sign-on. In: 2016 IEEE European Symposium on Security and Privacy (EuroS&P), pp. 321–336. IEEE (2016)
27. Armando, A., Carbone, R., Compagna, L., Cuellar, J., Tobarra, L.: Formal analysis of SAML 2.0 web browser single sign-on: breaking the SAML-based single sign-on for google apps. In: Proceedings of the 6th ACM Workshop on Formal Methods in Security Engineering, pp. 1–10. ACM (2008)
28. Groß, T.: Security analysis of the SAML single sign-on browser/artifact profile. In: Computer Security Applications Conference, pp. 298–307. IEEE (2003)
29. Kumar, A.: A lightweight formal approach for analyzing security of web protocols. In: Stavrou, A., Bos, H., Portokalidis, G. (eds.) RAID 2014. LNCS, vol. 8688, pp. 192–211. Springer, Cham (2014). doi:10.1007/978-3-319-11379-1_10
30. Mayer, A., Niemietz, M., Mladenov, V., et al.: Guardians of the clouds: when identity providers fail. In: Proceedings of the 6th edition of the ACM Workshop on Cloud Computing Security, pp. 105–116. ACM (2014)
31. Mainka, C., Mladenov, V., Feldmann, F., et al.: Your software at my service: security analysis of saas single sign-on solutions in the cloud. In: Proceedings of the 6th Edition of the ACM Workshop on Cloud Computing Security, pp. 93–104. ACM (2014)
32. Pfitzmann, B., Waidner, M.: Analysis of liberty single-sign-on with enabled clients. In: IEEE Internet Computing, pp. 38–44. IEEE (2003)
33. Ahmad, Z., Ab Manan, J.-L., Sulaiman, S.: Trusted computing based open environment user authentication model. In: 2010 3rd International Conference on Advanced Computer Theory and Engineering (ICACTE), pp. V6–487. IEEE (2010)
34. Groß, T., Pfitzmann, B., Sadeghi, A.-R.: Browser model for security analysis of browser-based protocols. In: Vimercati, S.C., Syverson, P., Gollmann, D. (eds.) ESORICS 2005. LNCS, vol. 3679, pp. 489–508. Springer, Heidelberg (2005). doi:10.1007/11555827_28
35. Miculan, M., Caterina, U.: Formal analysis of Facebook Connect single sign-on authentication protocol. In: SOFSEM, pp. 22–28 (2009)

36. Urueña, M., Muñoz, A., Larrabeiti, D.: Formal analysis of Facebook Connect single sign-on authentication protocol. In: Multimedia Tools and Applications, pp. 159–176. Springer (2014)

37. Wang, R., Chen, S., Wang, X.F.: Signing me onto your accounts through facebook and google: a traffic-guided security study of commercially deployed single-sign-on web services. In: 2012 IEEE Symposium on Security and Privacy, pp. 365–379 (2012)

38. Chadwick, D.W.: Federated identity management. In: Aldini, A., Barthe, G., Gorrieri, R. (eds.) FOSAD 2007-2009. LNCS, vol. 5705, pp. 96–120. Springer, Heidelberg (2009). doi:10.1007/978-3-642-03829-7_3

Evaluating Users' Affect States:
Towards a Study on Privacy Concerns

Uchechi Nwadike[1], Thomas Groß[1(✉)], and Kovila P.L. Coopamootoo[2]

[1] Newcastle University, Newcastle upon Tyne, UK
thomas.gross@newcastle.ac.uk
[2] University of Derby, Derby, UK

Abstract. Research in psychology suggests that affect influences decision making. Consequently, we ask the question how affect states such
as happiness and fear impact a user's privacy concerns. To investigate
this question, we need to prepare the ground in validating methods to
induce and measure emotions. While most empirical privacy research is
based on self-report questionnaires [20], such an experiment design—and
the field at large—will benefit from psycho-physiological tools that offer
immediate measurements of the user's state [11]. To bridge this gap,
this study constructs an experiment design that induces emotions and
tightly controls this manipulation. Furthermore, it offers a pretest that
compares self-report and psycho-physiological tools for measuring users'
affect states. We administer validated video affect stimuli in a within-
subject trial, in which participants were exposed to both happy and sad
stimuli in random order, after setting a neutral baseline state. The results
indicate, first, that participants' affect states were successfully manipulated using stimuli films. Second, a systematic comparison between the
tools indicates their strengths and weaknesses in sensitivity and tightness
of confidence intervals, hence lays the foundations for future experiment
design. Finally, we contribute an experiment design to investigate the
impact of affect state on privacy decision making, which draws on the
lessons learned from the experiment.

Keywords: Privacy concerns · Affect states · PANAS-X · Facereader ·
Emotion recognition · Psycho-physiological

1 Introduction

Users' concern over the safety of their personal details has been a long-standing
issue in privacy research. To evaluate users' privacy concerns, the methodologies offered have been based on self-report and give a subjective account of
users' privacy concerns. These were mostly questionnaires ranging from Westin's
Privacy Segmentation Index [13] that group individuals in broad categorizations

K.P.L. Coopamootoo—Mainly contributed while being at Newcastle University.

of privacy fundamentalists, pragmatists or unconcerned to those more focused on online privacy such as the Internet Users' Information Privacy Concerns [16].

First, Preibusch [20] observed that evaluation of these measurement instruments and the methodology at large has been "fragmented and ad-hoc." We take this as a call to action to invest in the validation of tools for privacy research, especially those suitable to support evidence-based contributions. Second, users' privacy concern, intention and subsequent behavior, at the time of evaluation, is under the influence of their current internal states. We believe that eliciting affect states would provide an important dimension that impacts privacy concerns. We therefore set out to investigate the influence of users' affect states on privacy concerns.

We report on a pretest which evaluates users' affect states when exposed to standardized video stimuli for happiness and sadness. We investigate two face-geometry-based affect analysis tools (Facereader and Emotion Recognition) and evaluate their properties systematically as components for future experiments. We validate these instruments against the Positive and Negative Affect Schedule (PANAS-X) [30], a well-vetted self-report questionnaire.

Contribution. Our pre-test findings indicated that the two psycho-physiological tools accurately measured the users' affect states. Our findings not only provide a valuable systematic comparison of the measurement tools, but also techniques for inducing and measuring affect states, beneficial for other researchers. We also provide re-usable building blocks that can be plugged into further research. In addition, to the best to our knowledge, this is the first study employing affect inducing and psycho-physiological tools in usable privacy research.

Outline. The paper is organized as follows: first, we provide background information on privacy and emotion; then present our research model and hypotheses. Next we report on the pretest experiment conducted and the results obtained. Subsequently we present the structured abstract for the main experiment. We conclude the paper by discussing the implications and limitations of our work.

2 Background

In this section, we begin with the issues associated with privacy definition, its multidimensional characteristics, then review existing literature on privacy concerns, and affect states with their measurement methods. Subsequently we describe the use of stimuli from affective psychology to induce emotions, and use of affect measurement as manipulation checks. In conclusion, we report on existing measurement instruments for privacy concerns.

2.1 Information Privacy

Nissenbaum [17] proposed that privacy is a contextual concept that occurs in different spheres of life: legal, medical, information technology to mention a few. This has led scholars to propose different definitions: starting from "the right of an individual to be left alone" [29] to "the claim of individuals, groups, or institutions to determine for themselves when, how, and to what extent information about them is communicated to others" [31] amongst other privacy definitions.

Privacy Definition. Burgoon et al., Clarke, and DeCew [4–6] are known for their multidimensional definitions of privacy. For the purpose of this paper we adopt the definition by Smith et al. [24] as stated in Li [14], information privacy refers "to the ability of individuals to personally control information about themselves." Information privacy enables individuals or groups or organizations to protect themselves against actual or perceived intrusions on the information about them [6,31]. The possible occurrence of privacy intrusions can trigger a sense of panic or anxiety in users. This causes them to express their concerns over maintaining adequate access protection to their personal details.

Privacy Concerns. Privacy concerns can be described as "concerns about possible loss of privacy as a result of information disclosure to an online business" [32]. Scholars rely on the users' expression of their privacy concerns to measure the privacy levels and classify users" [31]. Given the multidimensional properties of privacy, it is not a surprise that different survey tools have been developed for measuring privacy concerns. Some of the survey tools which adopted the use of a multidimensional approach in measuring privacy have been considered as validated and reliable. These include Concerns for Information Privacy (CFIP), Internet Users Information Privacy Concerns (IUIPC) [16,24]. These are widely used as the standard surveys for privacy concerns.

Measuring Privacy Concerns. The development and use of differing scales have not been without issues. In his overview of the existing survey instruments used in measuring privacy concerns, Preibusch pointed out that "approaches to measure privacy concerns are fragmented and often ad-hoc, at the detriment of reliable results" [20]. The survey results derived from these tools rely on users' feedback, memories, and rated perception of subjective factors considered to affect privacy concerns, [12].

2.2 Emotion and Affect

In this section, first we present the definition of emotion, affect, and highlight their differences. We highlight the differing views on the relationship between emotion and behavior, followed by a brief overview on the effect of emotion on behaviors, concerns, decision making.

We adopt Baumeister et al's description of emotion as "a conscious feeling state" [2]. It is stimulated either by actual events that happen to the individual ("actions") or anticipated events that are yet to occur ("outcomes").

Emotion has been classified based on the duration of the feeling state [23]. Affect has been described as the "faint whisper of emotion" [23]. Affect is said to have more impact on behavior than emotion [2,18]. Hence in this paper, we use the term affect state to describe the state of feelings experienced by the participants. This is because the stimuli films can trigger a type of quick reaction within the individual.

The sole use of surveys as the main measurement tool of a multidimensional concept like privacy is inadequate. This is in line with the findings by Paine et al., which point out that "the concept of privacy is highly complex, therefore it is unlikely that surveys can accurately reflect respondents' true concerns" [19]. We suggest the use of a complimentary set of survey and psycho-physiological tools such as facial and emotion recognition devices. We believe users' privacy concerns, are associated with non verbal expressions, which are unconscious, facially expressed and fleeting in nature [8]. They cannot be captured by survey tools, hence the need for psycho-physiological tools. Hall et al. [12] noted "psycho-physiological measures are particularly sensitive to the fleeting and non-conscious nature of emotional experience." In this report we discuss the use of Facereader and Microsoft Emotion Recognition in the studies presented in this paper.

The literature review we conducted, revealed the contrasting views on the causative relationship between emotion and behavior. Loewenstein et al. [15] suggests that "the idea that emotions exert a direct and powerful influence on behavior receives ample support in the psychological literature on emotions." In a similar vein, Frijda [9] had suggested that "emotion arouses behavior and drives it forth." On the other hand, Baumeister et al. [2] suggest opposing views. In their review of the direct causation theory, they argue that "if a given emotion does not consistently cause same specific behavior, then again the influence of emotion on behavior can hardly be considered as direct." Rather they suggested that behavior is indirectly influenced by anticipated emotional outcomes.

2.3 Theory and Research Model

The Theory of Planned Behavior (TPB) states that attitude, subjective norms and preconceived behavioral control have a direct influence on behavioral intention which in turn influences actual behavior. However scholars have argued that a subjective norm is "inadequate and rarely predicts behavioral intentions" as stated in Armitage et al. [1]. Researchers have also highlighted the inefficacy of the TPB to influence or predict behaviors especially in the health field, this can be extended to privacy research based on the observed privacy paradox [25].

We present our research model in Fig. 1. We investigate the influence of stimuli films, S, on users' affect states, and consequently investigate the influence of affect states on their privacy concerns. We recognize that confounding factors, $F_{1...n}$ such as user's consumption of alcohol and recreational drugs could have

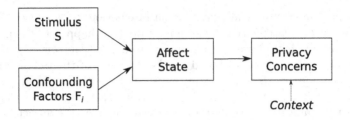

Fig. 1. Research model for the experiment.

an influence on the affect state. To test our research model, we first explore the influence of stimuli films on users affect states by carrying out a pilot study or pretest as it is referred to in this paper. We build on the outcomes of the pretest and present the design of an upcoming main experiment in Sect. 4.

3   Pretest

Affective psychology predicts that stimuli from films impact human affective states [22]. We designed a pretest study to assess and validate the manipulation from such stimuli and their measurement.

RQ1: Manipulation Method. How do standardized stimuli films (for *happiness* and *sadness*) influence the user's affect state?

$H_{1,0}$: There is no change in users' happy and sad affect states under induced happy and sad stimuli films.

$H_{1,1}$: Users' happy and sad affect states are impacted by induced standardized happy and sad stimuli films.

RQ2: Measurement Tools. We make a systematic comparison between the manipulation test in the validated PANAS-X questionnaire and the psychophysiological measurement tools. What are the tools' sensitivity, confidence intervals, their strengths and weaknesses? For the operationalization of the hypotheses, we define *sensitivity* as the effect size (in difference between means) between measuring the affect state of a participant exposed to a happy stimulus versus the affect state of the same participant exposed to a sad stimulus. We refer to the 95% confidence interval on the effect size.

$H_{2,0}$: There is no difference in the sensitivity and confidence intervals on happiness and sadness measurements of the tools PANAS-X, Facereader and Emotion Recognition.

$H_{2,1}$: The tools PANAS-X, Facereader and Emotion Recognition differ in either sensitivity or confidence interval when measuring happiness or sadness affect states.

3.1   Method

Participants were exposed to video stimuli to induce diametrical emotions in a within-subject design. They received a happiness as well as a sadness stimulus in random order. The observed affect was measured with PANAS-X [30], Noldus FaceReader and Microsoft Emotion Recognition and compared across conditions.

Participants. $N = 9$ students from Computing Science Department of Newcastle University, of whom six males and three females, participated in the study. The participants' age range was from 23 to 30 years, ($M = 26.43$, $SD = 2.23$).

Operationalization. We induced the independent variable (IV) *affect* with three levels: (a) neutral baseline, (b) happy, and (c) sad.

We checked this manipulation with a self-report questionnaire, a 60-item PANAS-X [30] (joviality and sadness) with a designated time horizon "at this moment."

We measured the Dependent Variable(DV) affect (happiness and sadness) on a scale of $[0, \ldots, 1]$ with the psycho-physiological measurement tools (a) Facereader (FR) [3,7], (b) Emotion Recognition (ER). During the stimulus exposure, a video of the participant's face is recorded. The video is inputed into FR; a still image of the face is taken at the end of the corresponding stimulus and inputed into ER.

Procedure. The pretest proceeded in the following steps, where Fig. 2 illustrates the main experiment design:

(a) a demographics questionnaire,
(b) Neutral state.
   – Induction of a neutral baseline affect state,
   – Measurement of manipulation check (PANAS-X), ER and FR.
(c) Affect State 1: Either *happy* or *sad*, determined by random assignment.
   – Show video stimulus to induce affect.
   – Measurement of manipulation check (PANAS-X), ER and FR.
(d) Affect State 2: Complement of Affect State 1.
   – Show video stimulus to induce affect.
   – Measurement of manipulation check (PANAS-X), ER and FR.
(e) a debriefing survey, which checks for the participants feedback regarding the affect state experienced.

Inducing and Measuring Affect State. We adopted the induction of happy and sad from standardized stimuli defined in Gross et al. [10] For the induction of happiness, and sadness affect states, we used the restaurant scene from the movie *When Harry meets Sally* and the dying scene from the movie *The Champ* as stimuli films. Participants were exposed to both stimuli films clips in a within-subject experiment. Whether they received the happy or the sad film first was

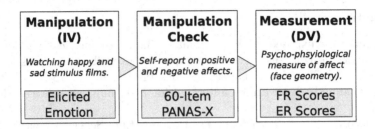

Fig. 2. Experiment design template for the pretest.

determined by random block assignment. After the neutral state and after each film participants filled a full 60-item PANAS-X questionnaire, with a designated time horizon of "at this moment."

During the neutral state and during watching each film, the faces of the participants were filmed with a high-resolution video camera. The video feeds constituted the inputs for the Facereader, which computed affect scores based on changes in face geometry. At the end of the stimulus exposure, a still image is taken from the video feed, which serves as input to Emotion Recognition. Both Facereader and Emotion Recognition compute scores on the scale $[0, \ldots, 1]$ for the variables anger, contempt, disgust, fear, happiness, neutral state, sadness and surprise. Only *happiness* and *sadness* were considered for further analysis.

3.2   Results

Figure 3 contains an overview of the results, in which we have normalized PANAS-X to the interval $[0, \ldots, 1]$ to put all tools on the same scale. All inferential statistics are computed with two-tailed tests and at an alpha level of .05. We report asymptotic significance values.

Assumptions. We tested the the normality of the measurements from PANAS-X, ER and FR towards the eligibility of parametric statistics. The Shapiro-Wilk test was statistically significant for PANAS-X Sadness, all Emotion Recognition and Facereader measurements (all $p < .001$). The PANAS-X Joviality results were borderline, $W = 0.92$, $p = .087$. Consequently we are not entitled to use parametric tests and opt for a two-tailed Wilcoxon signed-rank test.

Manipulation Check: PANAS-X. A self report-based manipulation check was carried out. We used the 60-item full PANAS- X questionnaire [30] as manipulation check on the induced affect state, following the methodology endorsed by Rottenberg et al. [21]. Of the different variables PANAS-X provides, we focused on *sadness* and *joviality* as equivalent of happiness.

There is a statistically significant difference between both videos stimuli for both measurements on joviality and sadness measurements. We offer a comparison of PANAS-X results for both stimuli in Table 1a. Consequently, we reject

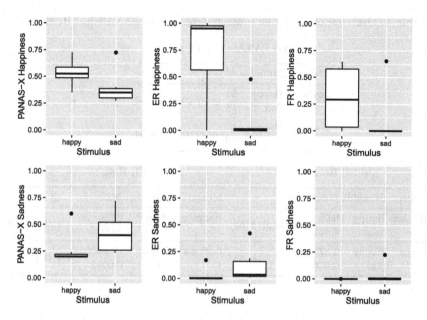

Fig. 3. Comparative boxplots for happiness and sadness measurements, with stimuli "happy" and "sad" on the x-axes. The y-axes are normalized to $[0, \ldots, 1]$.

the null hypothesis $H_{1,0}$ and accept that the video stimuli have a measurable impact.

Emotion Recognition. We observed with the measurements of the Emotion Recognition tool that there are statistically significant differences between the stimulus conditions, for happiness measurements as well as sadness measurements. Table 1b contains an overview of the ER results. This informs RQ2 that ER is a suitable measurement tool for affect comparisons with small samples.

Facereader. The Facereader measurements across video stimuli were neither statistically significant for the happiness nor for the sadness measurements. Table 1c contains an overview of the FR results. This informs RQ2 in that Facereader-based measurements do not have sufficient power to differentiate between these emotions at the small sample size of the pretest.

3.3 Comparison of Measurement Tools

One of the key outcomes of the pretest is a systematic comparison of the measurement tools (PANAS-X, FR and ER) while ascertaining the overall effectiveness of the induction of emotions with standardized video stimuli.

Table 1. Overview of results for measurement devices PANAS-X, FR, and ER.

(a) PANAS-X Results.

Measure	Stimulus	Mdn	Z	p	r
Joviality	Happy	21	−2.207	.027	.59
	Sad	14			
Sadness	Happy	5	−2.023	.043	.54
	Sad	10			

(b) ER Results.

Measure	Stimulus	Mdn	Z	p	r
Happiness	Happy	0.95	−2.366	.018	.63
	Sad	0.011			
Sadness	Happy	2.37	−2.366	.018	.63
	Sad	0.038			

(c) FR Results.

Measure	Stimulus	Mdn	Z	p	r
Happiness	Happy	0.29	−1.483	.14	.37
	Sad	0.0008			
Sadness	Happy	< 0.00001	−1.483	.14	.37
	Sad	0.0002			

Qualitative. We first made qualitative observations based on the boxplot comparison in Fig. 3. We are aware that we had one participant who entered the experiment in a morose state, which shows as an out-lier throughout the measurements. We observe that PANAS-X provides a clear distinction between happiness and sadness stimuli in both measurements. As one can expect from a standardized and validated measurement instrument for affect, PANAS-X can be considered a sound benchmark.

Emotion Recognition (ER) offers a precise recognition of happiness. While it was able to distinguish the stimuli on the sadness measurement, as well, this difference was less pronounced.

Facereader (FR) recognized happiness in face of a participant exposed to a happy stimulus, however, FR does not use the full scale, reporting a $Mdn \sim .3$. The result of the FR sadness measurement is striking in that it only uses $< .025$ of the scale $[0, \ldots, 1]$. At the same time, the interquartile range is closely bracketed.

Meta Analysis. We compared the standardized mean differences for measuring either happiness or sadness across happy or sad stimuli. Figure 4 summarizes the outcome of this comparison in a meta-analysis forest plot. The meta-analysis was computed with the R package metafor [27].

Let us consider the left-hand-side Fig. 4a, which contains measurements of happiness with the three tools in question. For each measurement tool, we computed the mean difference between the happy video stimulus and the sad video stimulus, standardized over the joint standard deviation of the respective tool's measurements.

For happiness scores, we see that all tools measure positive difference (i.e., a higher mean happiness in the case of the happy video vs. the case of the sad video).

We observe that FR has the smallest mean difference, which can be interpreted as being least sensitive to measuring happiness differences. We observe further that ER shows the greatest mean difference, however is also impacted by the greatest confidence interval. The line "FE Model" below the three measurement tools offers a combined fixed-effect model of all three measurements, which informs us how our strongly happiness induced by the given videos registers in our measurement apparatus. This model is weighted by the standard deviations of the respective tools. Finally, we expect to measure happiness with a standardized mean difference of about 1 SD, which is a large effect.

The right-hand-side Fig. 4b compares the results for sadness measurements. All tools measure a negative difference (i.e., a lower mean sadness in case of the happy video vs. the case of the sad video). We notice that PANAS-X even though observing the greatest mean difference also comes with the greatest confidence interval. Again, FR reports a lower mean difference than ER. Overall, the combined fixed-effect model shows a standardized mean difference of -0.72, also a large effect.

In conclusion, we observe that all three measurement tools have picked up happiness and sadness as expected from the video stimuli. Consequently, we know that the video stimuli work for inducing the emotions happiness and sadness, resulting in a medium to large effect size depending on the measurement device. This answers RQ1 and gives evidence to reject the null hypothesis $H_{1,0}$. FR as well as ER worked as psycho-physiological measurement tools picking up the participant's emotional state without the interference of a self-report questionnaire. ER obtained the largest effect sizes for the case of measuring happiness as well as sadness. FR obtained the lowest effect size of the field, especially in the case of measuring sadness. From these observations, we can answer RQ2 in terms of qualitative differences sensitivity and confidence intervals. However, these differences are not statistically significant, by which we will retain the null hypothesis $H_{2,0}$.

3.4   Discussion

We answer the research questions as follows: For RQ1, we observe that the standardized video stimuli [21] can indeed be employed to induce affects. Our manipulation check with PANAS-X shows large effect sizes in the differences between video stimuli conditions. Consequently, we can use video stimuli to establish experiment conditions for true experiments in privacy and identity management, such as the main experiment we design in Sect. 4. We thereby recommend to replicate existing manipulation apparatuses from affective psychology.

For RQ2, we observe that the different measurement tools at our disposal differ in sensitivity and confidence intervals even if the evaluation did not turn out to yield statistical significance. While the psycho-physiological measurements (ER and FR) both worked by and large, we observed weaknesses of FR in the measurement of sadness. In addition, the meta and power analyses will need to inform future experiment designs. In particular, FR had the least power to

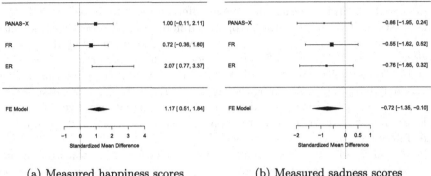

(a) Measured happiness scores   (b) Measured sadness scores

Fig. 4. Meta-Analysis forest plot of measurement tools across induced emotions. The position of the square dot determines the effect size, the diameter of the dot shows the weight, the whiskers the 95% confidence interval on it.

distinguish between happiness and sadness conditions, which directly translates to a higher required sample size.

The three measurement devices exhibit strengths and weaknesses which need to be taken into account in experiment design. PANAS-X has been validated and used frequently in psychology research. However, it is a self-report questionnaire, which takes about 10 min to fill in for the full 60-item version. Consequently, we need to expect that emotional stimuli are wearing off over the time the questionnaire is answered. Even if the time horizon is set to "at this moment," the outcomes will not be as immediate as with psycho-physiological measurements. ER works on still images and can thereby be used to measure momentary affect of the user. However, then the decision which time instant to use for the measurement becomes crucial. FR operates on video streams and comes with the capability to track affects over time. This, however, comes at a cost of less sensitivity to distinguish between conditions.

4 Main Experiment

We took on board a comment from the IFIP workshop, which highlighted the necessity to assess user's privacy behavioral intentions whilst measuring privacy concerns. The reason given was privacy concerns questionnaires seem to be based on subjective norms, which are long term and not easily influenced. This was confirmed by a pretest we conducted on privacy concerns surveys and has led to the inclusion of a survey on behavioral intentions. The selected questionnaires are same as those used by Yang and Wang [33]. A structured abstract of the upcoming experiment is presented in the next section.

RQ3 Impact of Affect on Privacy Concern. The upcoming experiment will investigate to what extent an affect state causes differences in privacy concern. The research hypotheses being tested are:

$H_{3,0}$: There is no difference in privacy concern scores between cases with induced happiness and induced fear.

$H_{3,1}$: Privacy concern scores differ between cases of induced happiness and induced fear.

In particular, we hypothesize as a refinement of $H_{3,1}$ that users exhibit higher scores on privacy concerns when they feel fear than when they feel happiness. However, with $H_{3,1}$ we retain the capacity to evaluate two-tailed tests.

4.1 Method

A sample of $N = 60$ participants will be exposed to standardized video stimuli [10, 22] to induce emotions (*happiness* and *fear*) in a within-subjects design. The participants will receive the video stimuli in random order. Privacy concern and behavioral intention scores will be measured and compared across video conditions.

Operationalization. We will induce the independent variable (IV) *affect* with three levels: (a) neutral baseline, (b) happy, and (c) fearful.

We will check this manipulation against self-report and psycho-physiological measurement tools: (a) 15-item PANAS-X [30] (joviality and fear) with a designated time horizon "at this moment." (b) FR (happiness and fear), (c) ER (happiness and fear). For the manipulation check, a video of the participant's face will be recorded during the stimulus exposure. The video stream will serve as input for FR, a still image of the said face-recording will be taken at the end of the corresponding stimulus and used as input for ER. There will be a time of three minutes allocated to fill in the PANAS-X after the stimulus exposure.

We will measure the DV, the user's behavioral intent on privacy concerns, using the same self-report questionnaires used by Yang and Wang [33], because they have been rigorously tested and found reliable [26].

Participants. The sample size of $N = 60$ will be chosen following an a priori power analysis, informed by the pretest in Sect. 3. As one constraint, we have seen a minimum sample size of $N' = 39$ for a within-subject experiment using the Wilcoxon signed-rank test to reach 95% power across the board. We will therefore choose a larger sample size, because we are preparing for the use of a two-tailed test and are expecting a smaller effect size in the impact of affect on privacy concerns. With $N = 60$ we can expect a sensitivity of .49, a medium effect size.

Procedure. The main experiment is designed to enable a comparison of the influence of affect states on privacy concerns and privacy behavioral intentions. The study will be spread over two days; the first day will entail the participants carrying out the first three steps, i.e. (a)–(c). On the second day, the participants

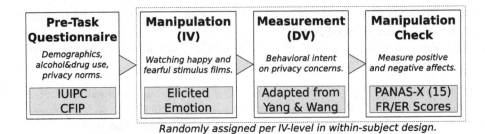

Fig. 5. Design for the main experiment.

will first be induced to a neutral state and then complete steps (d) and (e). The reason for this is to minimize the carryover effects of the video stimuli and effect of "questionnaire fatigue."

The procedure consists of the following steps, where Fig. 5 illustrates the key elements of the experiment design:

(a) Completion of pre-task questionnaire on demographics, alcohol/recreational drug use, IUIPC and CFIP surveys.
(b) Neutral state.
  – Induction of a neutral baseline affect state,
  – DV questionnaires on privacy behavioral intentions,
  – Manipulation check with PANAS-X, ER and FR.
(c) Affect State 1: Either *happy* or *fearful*, determined by random assignment.
  – Show video stimulus to induce affect.
  – DV questionnaire on privacy behavioral intentions,
  – Manipulation check with PANAS-X, ER and FR.
(d) Affect State 2: Complement of Affect State 1.
  – Show video stimulus to induce affect.
  – DV questionnaire on privacy behavioral intentions,
  – Manipulation check with PANAS-X, ER and FR.
(e) a debriefing questionnaire, used to check for missed or misreported information, subjective thoughts during study session.

The analysis compares the DV privacy concern measurements across the main levels of the IV (happy and fearful), using a two-tailed matched-pairs Wilcoxon signed rank test.

Depending on the properties of the sample (e.g., normality, homogeneity of variances) further analysis of the impact of the IV on privacy concern as target variable is possible with Univariate Analysis of Variances (ANOVA/GLM) or Linear Regression.

5   Conclusion

While Wakefield [28], and Nyshadham and Castano [18] have explored the relationship between affect, information disclosure and online privacy concerns, we employ induced emotions and psycho-physiological tools in our empirical study of users' affect states. To the best of our knowledge, there is currently, no such endeavor in usable privacy research.

Our pretest results provide empirical evidence that the specific stimuli films used had significant influence on users' happiness and sadness. The pretest showed a successful manipulation of users' affect states. The pretest results also indicate that ER, FR, and PANAS-X can measure users' happiness and sadness, where ER is more sensitive in particular small sample sizes due to its large effect size.

Our pretest has therefore systematically evaluated and validated the tools for the upcoming main experiment. It further yields a detailed analysis of effect sizes and power of different psycho-physiological measurement tools that are of independent interest for usable privacy research. Other researchers can glean insights from the pretest results, use the tools employed here as validated components to induce or measure affects. Furthermore, with the design for the main experiment, we offer a template for true experiments that induce affect, control the manipulation tightly and then measure the impact on privacy concerns. The reported effect sizes and power calculations can form the basis for rigorous design for future experiments.

References

1. Armitage, C.J., Conner, M.: Efficacy of the theory of planned behaviour: a meta-analytic review. Br. J. Soc. Psychol. **40**(4), 471–499 (2001)
2. Baumeister, R.F., Vohs, K.D., DeWall, C.N., Zhang, L.: How emotion shapes behavior: feedback, anticipation, and reflection, rather than direct causation. Pers. Soc. Psychol. Rev. **11**(2), 167–203 (2007)
3. Brodny, G., Kołakowska, A., Landowska, A., Szwoch, M., Szwoch, W., Wróbel, M.R.: Comparison of selected off-the-shelf solutions for emotion recognition based on facial expressions. In: 2016 9th International Conference on Human System Interactions (HSI), pp. 397–404. IEEE (2016)
4. Burgoon, J.K., Parrott, R., Le Poire, B.A., Kelley, D.L., Walther, J.B., Perry, D.: Maintaining and restoring privacy through communication in different types of relationships. J. Soc. Pers. Relat. **6**(2), 131–158 (1989)
5. Clarke, R.: What's privacy. In: Australian Law Reform Commission Workshop, vol. 28 (2006)
6. DeCew, J.W.: In Pursuit of Privacy: Law, Ethics, and the Rise of Technology. Cornell University Press, Ithaca (1997)
7. Den Uyl, M., Van Kuilenburg, H.: The faceReader: online facial expression recognition. Proc. Measuring Behav. **30**, 589–590 (2005)
8. Ekman, P.: An argument for basic emotions. Cogn. Emot. **6**(3–4), 169–200 (1992)
9. Frijda, N.H.: The emotions: Studies in emotion and social interaction. Cambridge University Press, Cambridge (1986)
10. Gross, J.J., Levenson, R.W.: Emotion elicitation using films. Cogn. Emot. **9**(1), 87–108 (1995)
11. Haapalainen, E., Kim, S., Forlizzi, J.F., Dey, A.K.: Psycho-physiological measures for assessing cognitive load. In: Proceedings of the 12th ACM International Conference on Ubiquitous Computing, pp. 301–310. ACM (2010)

12. Hall, R.H., Lockwood, N.S., Sheng, H.: Psychophysiological assessment tools for evaluation of learning technologies. In: Yamamoto, S. (ed.) HIMI 2013. LNCS, vol. 8018, pp. 33–42. Springer, Heidelberg (2013). doi:10.1007/978-3-642-39226-9_5

13. Kumaraguru, P., Cranor, L.: Privacy indexes: a survey of westin's studies. Technical report, CMU-ISRI Technical Report (2005)

14. Li, Y.: Empirical studies on online information privacy concerns: literature review and an integrative framework. Commun. Assoc. Inform. Syst. **28**(1), 453–496 (2011)

15. Loewenstein, G.F., Weber, E.U., Hsee, C.K., Welch, N.: Risk as feelings. Psychol. Bull. **127**(2), 267–286 (2001)

16. Malhotra, N.K., Kim, S.S., Agarwal, J.: Internet users' information privacy concerns (IUIPC): the construct, the scale, and a causal model. Inf. Syst. Res. **15**(4), 336–355 (2004)

17. Nissenbaum, H.: Privacy in Context: Technology, Policy, and the Integrity of Social Life. Stanford University Press, Stanford (2009)

18. Nyshadham, E.A., Castano, D.: Affect and online privacy concerns. SSRN 2051044 (2012)

19. Paine, C., Reips, U.D., Stieger, S., Joinson, A., Buchanan, T.: Internet users' perceptions of 'privacy concerns' and 'privacy actions'. Int. J. Hum. Comput. Stud. **65**(6), 526–536 (2007)

20. Preibusch, S.: Guide to measuring privacy concern: review of survey and observational instruments. Int. J. Hum. Comput. Stud. **71**(12), 1133–1143 (2013)

21. Ray, R.D.: Emotion elicitation using films. In: Handbook of Emotion Elicitation and Assessment, pp. 9–28 (2007)

22. Schaefer, A., Nils, F., Sanchez, X., Philippot, P.: Assessing the effectiveness of a large database of emotion-eliciting films: a new tool for emotion researchers. Cogn. Emot. **24**(7), 1153–1172 (2010)

23. Slovic, P., Peters, E., Finucane, M.L., MacGregor, D.G.: Affect, risk, and decision making. Health Psychol. **24**(4S), S35–S40 (2005)

24. Smith, H.J., Milberg, S.J., Burke, S.J.: Information privacy: measuring individuals' concerns about organizational practices. MIS Q. **20**(2), 167–196 (1996)

25. Sniehotta, F.F., Presseau, J., Araújo-Soares, V.: Time to retire the theory of planned behaviour. Health Psychol. Rev. **8**(1), 1–7 (2014)

26. Stewart, K.A., Segars, A.H.: An empirical examination of the concern for information privacy instrument. Inf. Syst. Res. **13**(1), 36–49 (2002)

27. Viechtbauer, W., et al.: Conducting meta-analyses in R with the metafor package. J. Stat. Softw. **36**(3), 1–48 (2010)

28. Wakefield, R.: The influence of user affect in online information disclosure. J. Strateg. Inf. Syst. **22**(2), 157–174 (2013)

29. Warren, S.D., Brandeis, L.D.: The right to privacy. Harvard Law Rev. **4**(5), 193–220 (1890)

30. Watson, D., Clark, L.A.: The PANAS-X: Manual for the positive and negative affect schedule - expanded form. Technical report, University of Iowa, Department of Psychology (1999)

31. Westin, A.F.: Privacy and freedom. Wash. Lee Law Rev. **25**(1), 166 (1968)

32. Xu, H., Dinev, T., Smith, H.J., Hart, P.: Examining the formation of individual's privacy concerns: toward an integrative view. In: ICIS 2008 Proceedings, p. 6 (2008)

33. Yang, S., Wang, K.: The influence of information sensitivity compensation on privacy concern and behavioral intention. ACM SIGMIS Database **40**(1), 38–51 (2009)

Privacy Salience: Taxonomies and Research Opportunities

Meredydd Williams[✉], Jason R.C. Nurse, and Sadie Creese

Department of Computer Science, University of Oxford, Oxford, UK
meredydd.williams@cs.ox.ac.uk

Abstract. Privacy is a well-understood concept in the physical world, with us all desiring some escape from the public gaze. However, while individuals might recognise locking doors as protecting privacy, they have difficulty practising equivalent actions online. Privacy salience considers the tangibility of this important principle; one which is often obscured in digital environments. Through extensively surveying a range of studies, we construct the first taxonomies of privacy salience. After coding articles and identifying commonalities, we categorise works by their methodologies, platforms and underlying themes. While web browsing appears to be frequently analysed, the Internet-of-Things has received little attention. Through our use of category tuples and frequency matrices, we then explore those research opportunities which might have been overlooked. These include studies of targeted advertising and its affect on salience in social networks. It is through refining our understanding of this important topic that we can better highlight the subject of privacy.

Keywords: Privacy salience · Privacy awareness · Taxonomy · IoT

1 Introduction

Privacy is a well-understood concept in the physical world. We all need some respite from the public gaze to enjoy our lives; indeed, it is essential to natural human development [10]. However, whereas individuals might consider a locked door as protecting one's privacy, they have difficulty practising equivalent actions online [16]. This can create a number of risks as users might be unaware of the digital dangers they face. Combining the definition of 'salience' [38] with informational privacy [15], we define 'privacy salience' as whether *"informational privacy is prominent in a person's awareness or their memory of past experience"*. This differs slightly from 'privacy awareness', which we take to reflect long-term awareness of privacy, such as that which can be improved through educational campaigns. Risk in cyberspace is often intangible [27] and research [2] suggests reduced salience can lead to unwise decisions. Some [52] have claimed this intangibility could even contribute to the 'Privacy Paradox' [8], the disparity between what individuals claim about privacy and how they act. As technology

© IFIP International Federation for Information Processing 2016
Published by Springer International Publishing AG 2016. All Rights Reserved
A. Lehmann et al. (Eds.): Privacy and Identity 2016, IFIP AICT 498, pp. 263–278, 2016.
DOI: 10.1007/978-3-319-55783-0_18

permeates our society and we begin to live our lives 'online', privacy salience gains critical importance.

Previous research has considered the topic from a number of angles. For example, John et al. [28] conducted several field experiments: two seeking to highlight privacy and one looking to hide the issue. They found that when privacy concerns were primed, participants were less likely to disclose their data. In contrast, Tsai et al. [47] modified search engine interfaces to promote privacy-respecting results. Their analysis of 15,000 queries found that their alterations encouraged prudent selections. Adjerid et al. [3] studied how the provision of privacy information could influence user actions. They discovered that a delay of only 15 s between notice and decision could lead to less-private behaviour. Although previous studies concern a range of platforms and themes, the field has seen little systemisation of knowledge. Neither an extensive literature review nor a taxonomy have yet been produced: instruments which can both structure existing work and highlight future opportunities. Such developments are crucial to ensure that new studies do not overlook the varied findings of past research.

Therefore, we develop three extensive taxonomies of privacy salience literature, classifying studies by the themes they concern, the methodologies they apply and the platforms on which they are based. We select these factors as we believe they best encapsulate the content of the articles. Through a data-driven process of inductive coding [46], we formulate categories ranging from social networks to smartphones, privacy seals to permissions. We classify our surveyed articles within these groups and discuss the literature most relevant to each section. We move on to investigate those category combinations, whether (*Methodology, Platform*), (*Methodology, Theme*) or (*Platform, Theme*), which are both feasible and underexplored. Our frequency matrices, populated by this series of category tuples, enable identification of both popular research areas and potential lacunas. For example, while privacy documents were often studied during web browsing, salience is rarely explored in the Internet-of-Things (IoT). This is of concern as unfamiliar devices could potentially mask the topic of privacy. We conclude by recommending both future work and potential extensions to our taxonomies.

The remainder of our paper is structured as follows. Section 2 discusses our methodology, including literature selection, exclusion criteria, coding processes and taxonomy construction. Section 3 then explores our three taxonomies in detail, highlighting relevant previous literature. In Sect. 4 we present our distribution matrices and identify opportunities for future research. Finally, we conclude the paper in Sect. 5 and reflect on possible extensions to this work.

2   Methodology

We first outline our definitions, before describing our processes to select and exclude existing work. We continue by discussing our inductive coding processes [46] and how our privacy salience taxonomies were constructed.

2.1 Definitions

To ensure our taxonomies are representative of the literature, we should precisely define our terms. The Oxford English Dictionary defines salience to be "*[t]he quality or fact of being more prominent in a person's awareness or in his memory of past experience*" [38]. As privacy can be a nebulous topic, we scope our definition to encompass informational privacy. Clarke [15] described this concept as "*the interest an individual has in controlling, or at least significantly influencing, the handling of data about themselves*". Therefore, to reiterate, we define privacy salience as whether "*informational privacy is prominent in a person's awareness or their memory of past experience*". This differs slightly from 'privacy awareness', which we take to reflect long-term awareness of privacy, such as that which can be improved through educational campaigns.

We also explicitly specify what we consider to be a taxonomy. The Oxford English Dictionary [39] defines a taxonomy as a "*particular system of classification*", and in this work we classify privacy salience research. De Hoog [22] explains how construction consists of three parts: ordering, representation and nomenclature. In terms of ordering, categories should be arranged in a certain order and this order expressed through "*character correlation*". For representation, the elements should be "*maximally simple*" and atomic in character. Finally, the categories should be named formally to ensure the structure is usable. We incorporated these key principles into the development of our taxonomies.

2.2 Literature Selection

We first surveyed existing research to identify those works which concerned privacy salience. We did not explicitly constrain ourselves to particular disciplines, as we sought to explore the topic from multiple angles. Accordingly, we conducted our literature search on a wide range of databases from a variety of fields. These consisted of Google Scholar, Scopus, Web of Science, SpringerLink, JSTOR and Mendeley (general); IEEE Xplore, ACM Digital Library, CiteSeerX and DBLP Computer Science (computer science, Human-Computer Interaction (HCI) and cyber security); ScienceDirect (sciences); the Social Science Research Network (SSRN) (social sciences) and HeinOnline (law). These databases index those fields from which privacy salience research frequently originates, such as HCI and psychology. With engines such as Google Scholar searching broader academia and SSRN considering the social sciences, we retrieved work from a wide range of disciplines. Since we frequently located the same articles in multiple search results, we are confident the literature was well surveyed.

We also used a variety of search terms to ensure all works considering privacy salience were identified. We began with the synonymous terms '*privacy salience*' and '*privacy saliency*', in addition to '*privacy tangibility*' due to its similar definition. Being cognisant that the '*privacy salience*' term only gained popularity in the late 2000s, we also searched for '*privacy awareness*'. Frequently salience was not mentioned in articles, even though studies considered the effects of highlighting policies and notices. For this reason, we also used 'privacy poli-cies', 'privacy seals', 'privacy notices', 'privacy warnings', 'privacy indicators' and 'privacy nudges'. By expanding our list of phrases, we successfully identified articles which might have been otherwise overlooked.

To further survey this topic, we undertook literature snowballing through the references and citations of identified works. This was performed in the systematic method of Wohlin [53], with extensive backwards and forwards snowballing fol-lowing our database search. This collection was then manually-filtered to verify that selected works concerned the topic. This ensured that we did not sacrifice quantity for quality by expanding our search terms. Although terms can never be fully exhaustive, our broad selection concerns topics frequently associated with privacy salience. Since many search results were sorted by both relevance and citation count, it is unlikely we overlooked articles of significance.

2.3   Exclusion Criteria

To complement our search term expansion, we strengthened our exclusion cri-teria. Firstly, we only analysed articles in the English language to ensure works could be judged fairly. Secondly, we verified whether our search results actually concerned privacy salience, of which a majority did not. This is simply an arte-fact of database searches, where works can refer to 'privacy' or 'salience' but not both in combination. Furthermore, through our use of associated terms such as 'privacy policies', we retrieved many articles which considered these documents but not their effect on salience. These works were filtered out at this stage.

Thirdly, we excluded papers which directly duplicated research. For example, two articles by Hughes-Roberts [24,25] concerned the development of the same social networking interface. In these cases, we included the most recent paper as would be more likely to possess additional findings. For a similar reason, when multiple databases returned different versions of a work, we selected the most recent instance. Finally, as a means of ensuring our research was of a high quality, we excluded articles which were not peer-reviewed. Although this approach might have reduced the breadth of our survey, it is important that taxonomies are constructed on credible works.

2.4   Coding Process

Inductive reasoning can be beneficial when conducting research which has not been previously attempted. Since we are the first to either survey privacy salience or construct taxonomies on the topic, inductive coding appeared most appro-priate. We conformed to the popular approach of Thomas [46] which consists of data cleaning, text analysis, category creation, overlapping coding and category refinement. We defined our coding units physically [44], based on the natural boundaries of each article. We began coding by ensuring all text was legible, accessible and downloaded in a persistent format. We then analysed the docu-ments to familiarise ourselves with the main topics.

After studying our articles on multiple occasions, we created initial groups based on their main concepts. As inductive coding progressed, we recognised that our categories clustered around methodologies, platforms and themes. We believe these factors best encapsulate the paper content, since they concern the research technique, the target of research and the research topic. Methodologies can influence how an issue is approached: while literature reviews reflect on an issue, field experiments conduct empirical studies. Although article frequency does not directly indicate which techniques are most fruitful, it acts as a useful proxy. While certain methodologies might be more appropriate for privacy salience research than others, we still expect a general trend between frequency of use and utility. We define platform as the domain on which salience is analysed, with instances ranging from social networks [45] to smartphones [40]. As privacy is inherently contextual, findings on one platform might differ from those on others. Although each article concerns privacy salience, the topic is explored through a range of themes. For example, while some researchers study the effect of privacy policies [48], others analyse the influence of framing [29].

It was at this stage we decided to develop three distinct taxonomies rather than a combined chart. While our factors each offered interesting insights, they differed excessively for a single structure. Although we considered a taxonomy with methodology, platform and theme top-level categories, this introduced unnecessary complexity. By developing three separate taxonomies and classifying our works, we can identify those combinations which might be underexplored.

Thomas' fourth coding procedure [46] accepts that texts can be coded into multiple categories, or indeed no categories at all. This is useful in the case of themes, as a study might concern a number of topics. For example, Yang et al. [54] investigated the influence of both privacy policies and trust seals, and their work should not be excluded from either group. As articles predominantly used one methodology and one platform, these factors support single categories. Finally, we refined our groups to ensure clarity and consistency. For example, although one work might analyse social media disclosures [25] and another might study Facebook behaviour [45], both concern social networks. This was crucial for de Hoog's taxonomy 'ordering' principle [22], as we ensured similar elements were grouped consistently.

2.5   Taxonomy Completion

We continued our construction processes in compliance with the 'representation' and 'nomenclature' principles [22]. Where categories contained otherwise differing elements, further subdivisions were made. For example, although policies and seals both highlight privacy, their approaches are far from identical. We next created representative names for our categories, complying with the 'nomenclature' principle [22]. Naming was undertaken iteratively, refining definitions as categories evolved. Titles aimed to encapsulate commonalities in a group; for example, privacy policies and notices could both be considered types of privacy document.

Table 1. Literature distribution

Privacy Salience Literature					
Relevant and Included					73
Methodology		Platform		Theme	
Field Experiments	35	Web	23	Interfaces	28
Tool Development	26	Social Networks	18	Framing	27
Literature Reviews	8	General	16	Documents	23
Lab Experiments	4	Smartphones	10	Controls	14
		Internet-of-Things	4	Design	13
		Software	2	Social	9
				Marketing	5

3 Privacy Salience Taxonomies

We begin by outlining category metrics before discussing our three taxonomies in detail. Through our database search and snowballing process, we received over 1000 potential results. After manual filtering, we found only 76 articles actually concerned privacy salience, with the other works just matching on search terms. This list was further reduced to 73 papers based on our aforementioned exclusion criteria. While our search dates were not constrained, our selected literature ranged from 1977 to June 2016. Research was conducted through a range of methodologies, with Field Experiments and Tool Development appearing most prevalent. In terms of platform, the Web was found to be most popular, with Social Networks also frequently explored. Interfaces were the most commonly-identified theme, followed by Framing and privacy Documents. Table 1 below presents our categories and the quantitative distribution of works. As articles could concern multiple topics, this is reflected in our larger theme totals.

3.1 Methodology Taxonomy

As shown below in Fig. 1, we subdivided methodologies into four approaches: Literature Reviews, Lab Experiments, Field Experiments and Tool Development. Methodologies were identified by comparing research techniques with standard definitions. Although a minority of articles possessed multiple approaches, we classified based on the predominant methodology. For example, when an application is created and then evaluated through a field study, it would be categorised within the Tool Development group [33]. Although we considered supporting multiple methodologies, this approach would have introduced complexity not warranted by our literature.

   Literature Reviews study an existing body of work to derive novel findings. For example, Aguirre et al. [4] drew on prior research to discuss how firms can best manage consumer relationships. They found that although service personalisation offers benefits, it can increase the salience of privacy risk. Cichy and

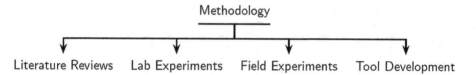

Fig. 1. Methodology taxonomy

Salge [14] also analysed previous work, studying 35 years of privacy discourse in The New York Times. Through considering social norms and topic salience, they found perceptions to be susceptible to myopia and manipulation.

Lab Experiments are empirical studies conducted in well-controlled environments. For example, a 24-person study was used to evaluate three privacy-enhancing extensions [43]. The researchers found that although the plug-ins highlighted data collection, concerns were mitigated by the applications themselves. Vemou et al. [49] established social network accounts to analyse profile registration and privacy policies. After exploring third-party access and audience management, they concluded that simplified settings might improve salience.

Field Experiments are undertaken in realistic environments, benefiting from greater ecological validity than lab studies. To explore the effects of framing, 280 participants were tasked to create a social networking profile [3]. It was found that when privacy notices were followed by time delays, data disclosure increased. John et al. [28] conducted three user studies, with the former increasing privacy salience and the latter two disguising the topic. They saw that even when risks are low, people refuse to disclose when their concerns are primed.

Tool Development concerns research which develops interfaces or applications to increase privacy salience. For example, PrivAware was a social networking tool which highlighted information loss [9]. The system could infer personal details with 60% accuracy and gave recommendations for friend deletion. Lipford et al. [35] developed an 'audience view', allowing users to observe their profiles as others do. After adding this tab to the Facebook interface, they found individuals better-understood the consequences of their actions.

3.2 Platform Taxonomy

Platforms were defined based on the domain in which privacy salience research was undertaken. As presented below in Fig. 2, we distinguished between six categories: General, Web, Social Networks, Mobile, Software and Internet-of-Things. We found the General class to be beneficial, as several works [1, 18, 29] consider salience without reference to a particular platform. As Social Networks are distinctive portals which may be accessed via either web browsers or smartphones, we deemed these to define a separate category.

General works study privacy salience without direct consideration of a specific environment. For example, Acquisti [1] discussed the importance of 'nudging' for realigning user behaviour. He emphasised the benefits of soft paternalism, but did not constrain privacy concepts to a particular domain. In a 1979

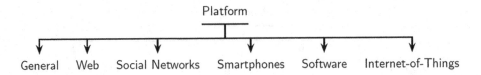

Fig. 2. Platform taxonomy

study, Reamer [41] analysed whether guarantees of confidentiality paradoxically reduced disclosure. He found survey participants which were assured anonymity were less likely to respond, suggesting salience had an effect.

The **Web** category concerns works which study privacy salience during web browsing. Tsai et al. [47] found that privacy indicators on search engines can encourage prudent behaviour. Through their use of the Privacy Finder tool, they found sites were more popular if annotated as privacy-respecting. Plug-ins can also analyse online behaviour, such as the Privacy Fox browser extension [6]. This application both translated policies into short notices and highlighted website practices which might cause concern.

Since **Social Networks** support the interaction of online individuals, they are of great interest to privacy researchers. During a 6-week trial, Facebook users were nudged to remember their post audiences [51]. By illustrating the potential consequences of their actions, unintended disclosures were reduced. Bonneau and Preibusch [11] evaluated 45 sites in a comprehensive analysis of social network protections. They saw that since data disclosure can be reduced by salient privacy, this influences interface design.

The **Smartphones** category concerns those works which study mobile phones and their apps. For example, the AppOps tool was used to highlight the data shared between smartphone applications [5]. When the consequences of lax privacy were illustrated, over half the participants changed their permissions. Balebako et al. [7] explored the timing of privacy notices through an Android field experiment. They found salience was increased more by in-app dialogs than those shown before installation.

The **Software** section concerns works which analyse desktop applications, rather than online portals or mobile apps. In a similar manner to Balebako et al. [7], a 222-person study explored how notice timing affects user behaviour [21]. The researchers found that risky installations were reduced by summarising license agreements. Bravo-Lillo et al. [12] modified user interfaces to highlight security and privacy threats. In their study of dialog messages, they discovered salient warnings could reduce dangerous installations.

The **Internet-of-Things** category concerns the privacy analyses of smart devices. For example, it was proposed that RFID privacy salience could be increased by personal privacy assistants [32]. This gadget would process tag data and display risks on a mobile interface. Gisch et al. [19] developed the Privacy Badge, an awareness tool specifically designed for small devices. Their data loss visualisations were evaluated through a user study, which found their application to be usable and informative.

3.3 Theme Taxonomy

Themes refer to the range of topics considered in the privacy salience literature. We identified 17 themes through inductive coding, ranging from Nudging [1] to Adverts [50] to privacy Settings [45]. Through our process of taxonomy construction, these classes were grouped under 7 top-level categories. This structure is presented below in Fig. 3. This design both highlights theme commonalities and assists the lacuna identification discussed in Sect. 4. While we considered limiting works to a single theme, such an approach would underrepresent the secondary topics found in articles. Recognising that the vast majority of papers did concern several topics, we decided each work could support multiple themes.

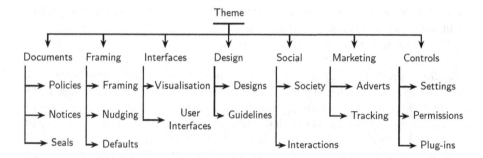

Fig. 3. Theme taxonomy

Documents refer to a range of privacy statements, such as policies, notices and seals. In one study, documents were presented which either concerned tech company protections or their negative activities [37]. The authors found disclosure decreased even when they highlighted positive behaviour, suggesting privacy salience influenced action. Hui et al. [26] analysed how privacy statements and TRUSTe seals affect user behaviour. They discovered that seals had little impact, suggesting increased salience does not always translate into action.

Framing relates to the way in which information or choices are presented. For example, two online surveys explored whether default responses affect privacy decisions [29]. When choices were made opt-in, the researchers found that agreement increased by 30%. Joinson et al. [30] discovered that 'prefer not to say' options were used more frequently when privacy was salient. After priming the topic through a privacy questionnaire, they also found that sensitive questions were commonly avoided.

The **Interfaces** category refers to both visualisations and user interface developments. Kani-Zabihi and Helmhout [31] discussed online interactive privacy features; tools designed to support user decision-making. They described an enquiry system which helps individuals discuss their privacy concerns with service providers. In another study, graphical warnings were evaluated on mobile interfaces [13]. The researchers discovered that after their dialogs were presented, 70% of the participants claimed they would change their permissions.

Design guidelines can inform the development of technologies which make privacy salient. One article [34] presented five pitfalls for privacy design, including obscuring information flow and inhibiting existing practice. The authors explained how *"users can make informed use of a system only when they understand the scope of its privacy implications"*. Schaub et al. [42] outlined requirements and best practices for privacy notice design. They went on to discuss how dialog messages could be challenged by Internet-of-Things interfaces.

Privacy is a **Social** construct and therefore many studies concern user interactions. For example, eight Facebook users were interviewed on the topic of online friendship [23]. The researchers discovered that unwise disclosures often originated from a lack of privacy salience. Ziegeldorf et al. [55] observed that comparisons are a natural behaviour, with individuals evaluating their actions against those of their peers. Their nudging system aimed to incentivise privacy by highlighting the behaviour of others.

With **Marketing** frequently raising privacy concerns, this category concerns adverts and tracking. A study of 447 users analysed how smartphone ad awareness affects privacy perceptions [50]. Individuals were found to make better privacy decisions when informed of data use procedures. Goldfarb and Tucker [20] also analysed marketing, studying how relevance and obtrusiveness influence purchasing intent. They discovered that while ads are effective when either salient or targeted, combined approaches trigger privacy concerns.

Controls refer to the permissions and configurations which affect user privacy. 444 students were surveyed to gauge the popularity of 'friends-only' Facebook settings [45]. Although respondents were not aware of their exposure, privacy discussions were found to increase salience. Malandrino et al. [36] analysed data leakage through a browser plug-in. By highlighting the information collected by third-party services, they increased the salience of privacy violations.

4 Research Gaps and Opportunities

By highlighting those areas not frequently explored, we sought to identify potential research opportunities. We first considered the prevalence of our methodologies, platforms and themes. Although our surveyed works concern a wide variety of themes, we constrained our analyses to the top-level categories. While this simplification sacrificed a degree of depth, it assisted the identification of sparse research areas.

We next considered all possible 2-tuples for (*Methodology, Platform*), (*Methodology, Theme*) and (*Platform, Theme*) combinations. Again, use of all 17 low-level themes would have introduced significant complexity to this process. Furthermore, as the vast majority of combinations would not have been previously explored, we would have no direction in selecting future opportunities. While we considered the use of triples, this approach challenges tabular visualisation (as explained shortly). By analysing our 2-tuples individually, we could identify combinations with greater flexibility.

Through analysing the tuple frequency in our literature, we populated the entries in three matrices. Figure 4 presents (*Methodology, Platform*) works, Fig. 5

concerns (*Methodology, Theme*) and Fig. 6 relates to (*Platform, Theme*) combinations. As we supported one methodology and platform per paper (due to the predominance of this distribution), the first matrix was simple to complete. Since articles could concern several themes, each work could conform to multiple (*Methodology, Theme*) and (*Platform, Theme*) tuples. While this could skew the frequency of non-theme categories, it assisted the identification of less-populated research areas.

By comparing the frequency of matrix entries, we discerned which combinations are most popular. For example, Web Field Experiments were prevalent (14 instances), as were Tools with privacy Interfaces (17). Privacy Documents were commonly analysed during Web browsing (12), reflecting the research interest in policies and seals. Finally, these tuple frequencies were colour-coded based on their magnitude. This assisted identification of those areas least investigated in existing work. Although many combinations have been infrequently explored, we continue by exploring those sparse intersections with the greatest viability. A low frequency alone does not imply an opportunity, as some combinations are less feasible than others. However, whereas Social interactions might not be best analysed through Lab Experiments, several combinations do appear viable.

4.1   Research Opportunities

Through inspection of our frequency matrices, we observed three main areas with feasible opportunities. This is not to say that other alternatives are not

	General	Software	Web	Social Networks	Smartphones	Internet-of-Things
Literature Reviews	8	0	0	0	0	0
Lab Experiments	0	0	2	2	0	0
Field Experiments	8	2	14	6	4	1
Tool Development	0	0	7	10	6	3

Fig. 4. (*Methodology, Platform*) frequency matrix

	Documents	Framing	Interfaces	Design	Social	Market	Controls
Literature Reviews	1	1	1	6	1	1	0
Lab Experiments	2	0	1	1	1	1	2
Field Experiments	14	18	9	4	4	2	3
Tool Development	6	8	17	2	3	1	9

Fig. 5. (*Methodology, Theme*) frequency matrix

	Documents	Framing	Interfaces	Design	Social	Market	Controls
General	2	8	1	6	2	1	0
Software	1	0	2	1	0	0	0
Web	12	7	8	3	1	3	3
Social Networks	5	5	8	1	5	0	7
Smartphones	2	6	6	0	1	1	3
Internet-of-Things	1	1	3	2	0	0	1

Fig. 6. (*Platform, Theme*) frequency matrix

valuable, such as much-needed Literature Reviews and Software studies, but the below topics appear of particular interest.

Due to the novelty of the platform, the Internet-of-Things (IoT) appears underexplored. As presented in Fig. 4, few Lab or Field Experiments have analysed IoT salience. Although privacy risks can obscured by our current technologies, unfamiliar devices might exacerbate this issue. Researchers could use controlled lab studies to investigate how much data is leaked by novel products. This could be complemented by field experiments exploring how these tools are actually used. We could analyse how salient privacy is in smart home environments; locations which are personal and increasingly popular. Figure 6 suggests that while Social Network Controls are frequently studied, several platforms do not receive similar attention. IoT settings might be unfamiliar, hidden or challenging to adjust, resulting in unintentional data disclosure. Future work could explore whether privacy salience can enhanced by simplifying these interfaces.

Figure 5, the (*Methodology, Theme*) matrix, suggests that while Tool Developments are popular, principles of their Design are rarely considered. While guidelines have been constructed for Privacy Enhancing Technologies (PETs) [17], the topic of salience has not been approached. Social network modifications [25] and smartphone interfaces [5] have successfully highlighted privacy, resulting in improved user behaviour. For these achievements to be replicated generally, researchers should develop design principles for what could be considered 'Salience-Enhancing Technologies'.

Much of the web is supported by affiliate networks and targeted advertising. This has led many individuals to decry the increasingly-personalised nature of online ads. Despite this fact, Fig. 6 suggests that few have explored the relationship between Marketing and privacy salience. Companies face the challenge of advertising their services without priming concerns. Future research could study whether online portals can respect user privacy while delivering targeted advertising. Alternatively, with the increasing popularity of ad-blocking software, researchers could explore how salience is affected when adverts are removed. It is of particular surprise these Marketing studies have not analysed Social Networks, especially considering Facebook's advertising strength. Researchers could investigate how privacy concerns are suppressed and suggest approaches for highlighting these ads.

5   Conclusions

In this work we have considered at length the important topic of privacy salience. We begun by surveying a wide range of existing literature before identifying common themes and topics. Through iteratively refining these categories we developed the first taxonomies on privacy salience. We structured these divisions on methodologies, platforms and themes; factors which encapsulate the content of existing research. By classifying prior work within these taxonomies, we systematise the knowledge in the literature. We proceeded by analysing category frequency and which factor combinations are most popular. We found that field studies of the web were prevalent, as were tools with privacy interfaces.

Finally, through exploring our colour-coded matrices, we identified opportunities for future research. These include IoT field experiments and investigations of online marketing. We also recommend further analyses of privacy settings, whether in ubiquitous environments or desktop computers.

While we believe our taxonomies support the study of privacy salience, we accept several limitations to our work. A minority of articles possessed multiple methodologies or studied a variety of platforms. Due to the sparsity of these instances, we constrained our analyses in the interest of simplicity. An expanded future work would reflect the diversity inherent in many privacy studies. While we chose methodologies, platforms and themes to structure our taxonomies, we accept that there are several alternatives. We could have divided research by discipline as a means of highlighting interesting fields. Although this was considered, we felt it would be challenging to divide disciplines in an objective fashion. Alternatively, we could have categorised articles based on the metrics they analysed. For example, while many works studied disclosure [28,41], others explored settings alteration [5,13]. In future analyses, metrics could be incorporated to consider how salience can be best investigated.

While our research presents an initial analysis, we envisage many instances of future work. As a means of validating our taxonomies, we could invite privacy experts to categorise the literature. In this approach, we would solicit a panel to analyse and classify each of our surveyed works. Through exploring their range of classifications, we could refine the consistency of our structures. Although research has been conducted in a range of platforms, there have been few comparative studies. Whereas privacy might be salient on a familiar web browser, the topic could be obscured by smartphone interfaces. Through conducting user studies on multiple platforms, we could explore how contexts affect privacy concerns. Finally, metrics should be studied to enable us to deconstruct the concept of privacy salience. While disclosure might relate to notions of confidentiality, privacy settings might be concerned with user control. As novel technologies proliferate, we believe privacy salience will only become increasingly important.

References

1. Acquisti, A.: Nudging privacy: the behavioral economics of personal information. IEEE Secur. Priv. **7**(6), 82–85 (2009)
2. Adjerid, I., Acquisti, A., Loewenstein, G.: Framing and the malleability of privacy choices. In: Proceedings of the 13th Workshop on the Economics of Information Security (2014)
3. Adjerid, I., Acquisti, A., Brandimarte, L., Loewenstein, G.: Sleights of privacy: framing, disclosures, and the limits of transparency. In: Proceedings of the Ninth Symposium on Usable Privacy and Security (2013)
4. Aguirre, E., Roggeveen, A., Grewal, D., Wetzels, M.: The personalization-privacy paradox: implications for new media. J. Consum. Mark. **33**(2), 98–110 (2016)
5. Almuhimedi, H., Schaub, F., Sadeh, N., Adjerid, I., Acquisti, A., Gluck, J., Cranor, L.F., Agarwal, Y.: Your location has been shared 5,398 times!: a field study on mobile app privacy nudging. In: Proceedings of the 33rd Annual ACM Conference on Human Factors in Computing Systems, pp. 787–796 (2015)

6. Arshad, F.: Privacy fox - a JavaScript-based P3P agent for mozilla firefox. Priv. Policy Law Technol. **17**, 801–810 (2004)

7. Balebako, R., Schaub, F., Adjerid, I., Acquisti, A., Cranor, L.: The impact of timing on the salience of smartphone app privacy notices. In: Proceedings of the 5th Annual ACM CCS Workshop on Security and Privacy in Smartphones and Mobile Devices, pp. 63–74 (2015)

8. Barnes, S.: A privacy paradox: social networking in the United States. First Monday, **11**(9) (2006). http://firstmonday.org/ojs/index.php/fm/article/view/1394

9. Becker, J., Chen, H.: Measuring privacy risk in online social networks. In: Proceedings of the 2009 Web 2.0 Security and Privacy Workshop (2009)

10. Berscheid, E.: Privacy: a hidden variable in experimental social psychology. J. Soc. Issues **33**(3), 85–101 (1977)

11. Bonneau, J., Preibusch, S.: The privacy jungle: on the market for data protection in social networks. In: Moore, T., Pym, D., Loannidis, C. (eds.) Economics of Information Security and Privacy, pp. 121–167. Springer, Heidelberg (2010)

12. Bravo-Lillo, C., Komanduri, S., Cranor, L., Reeder, R., Sleeper, M., Downs, J., Schechter, S.: Your attention please: designing security-decision UIs to make genuine risks harder to ignore. In: Proceedings of the Ninth Symposium on Usable Privacy and Security (2013)

13. Christin, D., Michalak, M., Hollick, M.: Raising user awareness about privacy threats in participatory sensing applications through graphical warnings. In: Proceedings of International Conference on Advances in Mobile Computing & Multimedia, pp. 445–455 (2013)

14. Cichy, P., Salge, T.: The evolution of privacy norms: mapping 35 years of technology-related privacy discourse, 1980–2014. In: 2015 International Conference on Information Systems (2015)

15. Clarke, R.: Introduction to dataveillance and information privacy, and definitions of terms. Technical report (1999). http://www.qatar.cmu.edu/iliano/courses/10F-CMU-CS349/slides/privacy.pdf

16. Creese, S., Lamberts, K.: Can cognitive science help us make information risk more tangible online? In: Proceedings of the WebSci 2009 (2009)

17. Federrath, H. (ed.): Designing Privacy Enhancing Technologies. LNCS, vol. 2009. Springer, Heidelberg (2001)

18. Frey, J.: An experiment with a confidentiality reminder in a telephone survey. Public Opin. Q. **50**(2), 267–269 (1986)

19. Gisch, M., De Luca, A., Blanchebarbe, M.: The privacy badge: a privacy-awareness user interface for small devices. In: Proceedings of the 4th International Conference on Mobile Technology, Applications, and Systems, pp. 583–586 (2007)

20. Goldfarb, A., Tucker, C.: Online display advertising: targeting and obtrusiveness. Mark. Sci. **30**(3), 389–404 (2011)

21. Good, N., Grossklags, J., Mulligan, D., Konstan, J.: Noticing notice: a large-scale experiment on the timing of software license agreements. In: Proceedings of the SIGCHI Conference on Human Factors in Computing Systems, pp. 607–616 (2007)

22. de Hoog, G.: Methodology of taxonomy. Taxon **30**(4), 779–783 (1981)

23. Houghton, D., Joinson, A.: Privacy, social network sites, and social relations. J. Technol. Hum. Serv. **28**(1–2), 74–94 (2010)

24. Hughes-Roberts, T., Kani-Zabihi, E.: On-line privacy behavior: using user interfaces for salient factors. J. Comput. Commun. **2**(4), 220 (2014)

25. Hughes-Roberts, T.: Reminding users of their privacy at the point of interaction: the effect of privacy salience on disclosure behaviour. In: Tryfonas, T., Askoxylakis, I. (eds.) HAS 2015. LNCS, vol. 9190, pp. 347–356. Springer, Cham (2015). doi:10. 1007/978-3-319-20376-8_31

26. Hui, K., Teo, H., Lee, S.: The value of privacy assurance: an exploratory field experiment. MIS Q. **31**(1), 19–33 (2007)

27. Jackson, J., Allum, N., Gaskell, G.: Perceptions of Risk in Cyberspace. Edward Elgar, Cheltenham (2005)

28. John, L., Acquisti, A., Loewenstein, G.: The best of strangers: context dependent willingness to divulge personal information. In: The Best of Strangers. Pittsburgh, Carnegie Mellon-University (2009)

29. Johnson, E., Bellman, S., Lohse, G.: Defaults, framing and privacy: why opting in-opting out. Mark. Lett. **13**(1), 5–15 (2002)

30. Joinson, A., Paine, C., Buchanan, T., Reips, U.: Measuring self-disclosure online: blurring and non-response to sensitive items in web-based surveys. Comput. Hum. Behav. **24**(5), 2158–2171 (2008)

31. Kani-Zabihi, E., Helmhout, M.: Increasing service users' privacy awareness by introducing on-line interactive privacy features. In: Laud, P. (ed.) NordSec 2011. LNCS, vol. 7161, pp. 131–148. Springer, Heidelberg (2012). doi:10.1007/ 978-3-642-29615-4_10

32. Konomi, S.: Personal privacy assistants for RFID users. In: Proceedings of the International Workshop Series on RFID, pp. 1–6 (2004)

33. LaRose, R., Rifon, N.: Promoting i-safety: effects of privacy warnings and privacy seals on risk assessment and online privacy behavior. J. Consum. Aff. **41**(1), 127–149 (2007)

34. Lederer, S., Hong, J., Dey, A., Landay, J.: Personal privacy through understanding and action: five pitfalls for designers. Pers. Ubiquit. Comput. **8**(6), 440–454 (2004)

35. Lipford, H., Besmer, A., Watson, J.: Understanding privacy settings in Facebook with an audience view. In: Proceedings of the First Conference on Usability, Psychology, and Security, pp. 1–8 (2008)

36. Malandrino, D., Petta, A., Scarano, V., Serra, L., Spinelli, R., Krishnamurthy, B.: Privacy awareness about information leakage: who knows what about me?. In: Proceedings of the 12th ACM Workshop on Privacy in the Electronic Society, pp. 279–284 (2013)

37. Marreiros, H., Tonin, M., Vlassopoulos, M., Schraefel, M.: 'Now that you mention it': A survey experiment on information, salience and online privacy. In: CESifo Working Paper, Ludwig Maximilian University of Munich (2016)

38. Oxford English Dictionary: Salience (2016). http://www.oed.com/view/Entry/ 170000

39. Oxford English Dictionary: Taxonomy (2016). http://www.oed.com/view/Entry/ 198305

40. Rajivan, P., Camp, J.: Influence of privacy attitude and privacy cue framing on android app choices. In: Twelfth Symposium on Usable Privacy and Security (2016)

41. Reamer, F.: Protecting research subjects and unintended consequences: the effect of guarantees of confidentiality. Public Opinion Q. **43**(4), 497–506 (1979)

42. Schaub, F., Balebako, R., Durity, A., Cranor, L.F.: A design space for effective privacy notices. In: Proceedings of the Eleventh Symposium On Usable Privacy and Security, pp. 1–17 (2015)

43. Schaub, F., Marella, A., Kalvani, P., Ur, B., Pan, C., Forney, E., Cranor, L.: Watching them watching me: Browser extensions' impact on user privacy awareness and concern. In: NDSS Workshop on Usable Security (2016)

44. Stemler, S.: An overview of content analysis. Pract. Assess. Res. Eval. **7**(17), 137–146 (2001)
45. Stutzman, F., Kramer-Duffield, J.: Friends only: examining a privacy-enhancing behavior in Facebook. In: Proceedings of the SIGCHI Conference on Human Factors in Computing Systems, pp. 1553–1562 (2010)
46. Thomas, D.: A general inductive approach for analyzing qualitative evaluation data. Am. J. Eval. **27**(2), 237–246 (2006)
47. Tsai, J., Egelman, S., Cranor, L., Acquisti, A.: The impact of privacy indicators on search engine browsing patterns. In: Proceedings of the Fifth Symposium on Usable Privacy and Security (2009)
48. Vail, M., Earp, J., Antón, A.: An empirical study of consumer perceptions and comprehension of web site privacy policies. IEEE Trans. Eng. Manage. **55**(3), 442–454 (2008)
49. Vemou, K., Karyda, M., Kokolakis, S.: Directions for raising privacy awareness in SNS platforms. In: Proceedings of the 18th Panhellenic Conference on Informatics, pp. 1–6 (2014)
50. Wang, N., Zhang, B., Liu, B., Jin, H.: Investigating effects of control and ads awareness on android users' privacy behaviors and perceptions. In: Proceedings of the 17th International Conference on Human-Computer Interaction with Mobile Devices and Services, pp. 373–382 (2015)
51. Wang, Y., Leon, P.G., Acquisti, A., Cranor, L.F., Forget, A., Sadeh, N.: A field trial of privacy nudges for Facebook. In: Proceedings of the 32nd Annual ACM Conference on Human Factors in Computing Systems, pp. 2367–2376 (2014)
52. Williams, M., Nurse, J.R.C., Creese, S.: The perfect storm: the privacy paradox and the Internet-of-Things. In: Workshop on Challenges in Information Security and Privacy Management at the 11th International Conference on Availability Reliability and Security (ARES) (2016)
53. Wohlin, C.: Guidelines for snowballing in systematic literature studies and a replication in software engineering. In: Proceedings of the 18th International Conference on Evaluation and Assessment in Software Engineering, pp. 38–48 (2014)
54. Yang, R., Ng, Y., Vishwanath, A.: Do social media privacy policies matter? Evaluating the effects of familiarity and privacy seals on cognitive processing. In: Proceedings of the 48th Hawaii International Conference on System Sciences, pp. 3463–3472 (2015)
55. Ziegeldorf, J.H., Henze, M., Hummen, R., Wehrle, K.: Comparison-based privacy: nudging privacy in social media (position paper). In: Garcia-Alfaro, J., Navarro-Arribas, G., Aldini, A., Martinelli, F., Suri, N. (eds.) DPM/QASA -2015. LNCS, vol. 9481, pp. 226–234. Springer, Cham (2016). doi:10.1007/978-3-319-29883-2_15

Author Index

Printed in the United States
By Bookmasters